Indigenous Peoples' Cultural Heritage: Rights, Debates and Challenges

Indigenous Peoples' Cultural Heritage: Rights, Debates and Challenges

Edited by

Alexandra Xanthaki, Sanna Valkonen, Leena Heinämäki and Piia Nuorgam

MINISTRY FOR FOREIGN AFFAIRS OF FINLAND

BRILL
NIJHOFF

LEIDEN | BOSTON

Typeface for the Latin, Greek, and Cyrillic scripts: "Brill". See and download: brill.com/brill-typeface.

ISBN 978-90-04-34218-7 (hardback)
ISBN 978-90-04-34219-4 (e-book)

This book is printed on acid-free paper and produced in a sustainable manner.

Contents

Introduction

This edited collection derived from our need to learn more about the cultural heritage of Indigenous Peoples. Indigenous rights to heritage have not been at the centre of academic scholarship until quite recently. The UN Expert Mechanism on the Rights of Indigenous Peoples decided in 2015 to embark on a study on this theme. The University of Lapland organised with the help of the Office of the High Commissioner for Human Rights a conference on this topic. During the conference it became clear that important information on Indigenous cultural heritage has remained rather unexplored or has not been adequately linked with specific actors (p.ex. WIPO) or specific issues (p.ex. free, prior and informed consent). Indigenous leaders talked about the misappropriation of their cultural heritage and explained the importance that disrespect of their cultural heritage has had on their identity, well-being and development. Experts in humanities and social sciences explained the intricacies of indigenous cultural heritage. Human rights scholars talked about the inability of current international law to fully address the injustices towards indigenous communities. International organisations' representatives discussed new positive developments. The conference became a meeting of complimentary ideas by researchers, activists and civil society, a real and genuine discussion about the challenges ahead.

Such wealth of experiences, materials, ideas and knowledge had to be disseminated. It became clear that more work needs to be done on this topic, more stones to be uncovered, and more discussion to be had. Multi-disciplinary work is especially important in this field. Ideas and knowledge have remained to a large part compartmentalised to the detriment of imaginative ways forward. The need to break down borders of disciplines and backgrounds is reflected in the multidisciplinary editorial team. We are aware that this collection of essays does not cover all the themes related to the topic. Yet, we feel that it is a solid step towards more interaction of ideas and perspectives, led by Indigenous voices.

We would like to thank the University of Lapland for the conference which started this discussion. We would also like to thank the Unit for Human Rights Policy of the Ministry for Foreign Affairs of Finland for the funding we received. Also thanks to the Minority and Indigenous Unit of the Office of the High Commissioner for Human Rights for their encouragement and support. Many thanks to Lindy Melman for her support and patience and to Jules Guldenmund for his excellent editing. Finally, many thanks to all Indigenous individuals who allowed us an insight into their concerns and aspirations regarding the protection and development of their cultural heritage.

The Editors

International Instruments on Cultural Heritage: Tales of Fragmentation

Alexandra Xanthaki

On 30 September 2016, the UN Human Rights Council adopted Resolution A/HRC/33/L.21 on 'Cultural rights and the protection of cultural heritage'. This development highlights the attention that cultural heritage is currently attracting at the international level. The resolution notes the detrimental impact that the loss of cultural heritage has for the enjoyment of cultural rights and calls for action. The resolution does not once refer to sub-national groups. Yet, in calling for international co-operation in restoring 'the stolen, looted or trafficked cultural property to its countries of origin' (para. 4), it puts the issue of cultural heritage firmly within the human rights agenda of the United Nations. This was not the case until rather recently.

The recent attention that cultural heritage has attracted by the international human rights law system is of course very welcoming. Talking in specific about tangible heritage, Roger O'Keefe notes: 'The framing of the conservation of tangible cultural heritage as a human right reminds us that we seek to preserve and protect such heritage not for its own sake but as an indispensable element of human flourishing'.[1] Indeed, the cultural heritage of individuals as well as of sub-national groups is essential for the protection and development of their identity. Unfortunately, in far too many parts of the world, cultural heritage is under threat. Indigenous art is widely misappropriated and indigenous traditional knowledge is ignored or used without the consent of the groups. Historical injustices, such as the brutal removal of indigenous children from their families have cut their bond of indigenous peoples with their heritage, especially the intangible parts. The unruly development of projects by transnational corporations continuously disregard indigenous spiritual sites and indigenous communities of their natural heritage. Also, tourism, often encouraged by the state as an important means of resources, lacks the necessary cultural sensitivity and commodifies important indigenous sites. And who can ignore the destruction of cultural artefacts as a means of retaliation in situations of ethnic conflict; and the stealing of such artefacts from indigenous

---

1 R. O'Keefe, 'Tangible cultural heritage and international human rights law' in L.V. Prott, R. Redmint-Cooper and S. Urice (eds.), *Realising Cultural Heritage Law, Festschrift for Patrick O'Keefe* (Institute of Art and Law, 2013), 87 at 95.

Xanthaki, Valkonen et al. (eds.), *Indigenous Peoples' Cultural Heritage: Rights, Debates and Challenges.*
 ISBN 978-90-04-34218-7. PP. 1-19

lands. There is an urgent need to protect the cultural heritage of individuals and groups; and such protection cannot take place without the involvement and implementation of a strong human rights system.

For a long time, heritage was seen as falling outside the domain of human rights and more into UNESCO's domain. It is still widely seen as a matter of concern for the states, rather than any sub-national group. Similarly, a 'right to cultural heritage' as such was not included in any human rights instrument. Recently, there has been recognition of 'the right to access to cultural heritage' and 'the right to enjoying the benefits of cultural heritage'. The Faro Convention (2011), for example, recognizes the right of everyone 'to benefit from cultural heritage'. The UN Independent Expert in the Field of Cultural Rights referred for the first time in 2011 to a right to cultural heritage. 'Considering access to and enjoyment of cultural heritage as a human right', she noted, 'is a necessary and complementary approach to the preservation/safeguard of cultural heritage.'[2] In a similar way, *indigenous* cultural heritage was not on the radar of international bodies.

One reason why cultural heritage was not explicitly discussed within the context of human rights was that it was part of cultural rights. But then again, cultural rights were a neglected area of international law until very recently. Several United Nations bodies have been pivotal in clarifying the scope of cultural rights in general, which has had a direct impact on a better understanding of indigenous cultural rights. Notable is *General Comment 25 (50)* of the Human Rights Committee which refers to the broad nature of indigenous culture; it observes that 'culture manifests itself in various forms' and mentions indigenous traditional activities such as fishing or hunting and the right to live in reserves protected by law. The jurisprudence of the UN Human Rights Committee also made a difference with the *Kitok* and *Lubicon Lake Band* cases reaffirming an understanding of indigenous culture consistent with the indigenous views. The *International Convention on the Elimination of All Forms of Racial Discrimination* has also used the rather generic prohibition of discrimination in religion, cultural rights, education and participation in cultural activities to promote indigenous cultural rights. Apart from the frequent references to indigenous cultural rights in its Concluding Observations, the Committee has issued *General Recommendation XXIII (51)* that calls for the recognition and respect of indigenous distinct cultures, histories, languages and ways of life as an enrichment of the State's cultural identity. The Committee on Economic, Social and Cultural Rights has in 2009 discussed in depth the meaning of cul-

2 United Nations, Report of the Independent Expert in the field of Cultural Rights, Farida Shaheed, UN Doc A/HRC/17/38 of 21 March 2011, para. 2.

ture. In 2012, the United Nations turned its attention to indigenous languages and cultures and published a report on this topic by the UN Expert Mechanism on the Rights of Indigenous peoples (EMRIP). In 2016, EMRIP published a report on indigenous cultural heritage. This volume is based on submissions and discussions that took place in a conference in Rovaniemi, co-organised by the University of Lapland and the Office of the High Commissioner for Human Rights.

PART A: THE MEANING OF CULTURAL HERITAGE

From Cultural Property to Cultural Heritage

Indigenous rights scholars have welcomed the attention on cultural heritage. The term 'cultural heritage' has been seen as a good substitute of the term 'cultural property' which prevailed in earlier documents of international law. 'Cultural property' was associated with the understanding of culture as capital and ownership. The (1954) UNESCO *Convention for the Protection of Cultural Property in the event of Armed Conflict* defines cultural property as: 'irrespective of origin or ownership... movable or immovable property of great importance to the cultural heritage of every people'. The restrictiveness of this definition is maintained in the (1999) *Second Protocol* to the Convention, even though its preamble emphasises that rules in this area should reflect developments in international law.[3] The (1970) UNESCO *Convention on the Means of Prohibiting and Preventing the Illicit Import, Export, and Transfer of Ownership of Cultural Property* is more detailed: cultural property is defined as 'property which, on religious or secular grounds, is specifically designated by each State as being of importance for archaeology, prehistory, history, literature, art or science'. The Convention also includes a very detailed account of objects of cultural property. The (1972) UNESCO *Convention Concerning the Protection of the World Cultural and Natural Heritage* is the exception to these early instruments, as it refers to cultural heritage, instead of cultural property.

Indigenous perceptions of culture are quite alien to the concept of culture as capital and the link of culture with ownership. Indigenous peoples have always viewed culture as part of the community:

---

3 See para. 4 of the Preamble and article 1.b. of the (1999) *Second Protocol to the Hague Convention of the 1954 for the Protection of Cultural Property in the Event of Armed Conflict* (1999) 38 *International Legal Materials* 769-782 at 769.

> No person 'owns' or holds as 'property' living things. Our Mother Earth and our plant and animal relatives are respected sovereign living beings with rights of their own in addition to playing an essential role in our survival.[4]

For them, culture signifies the continuous relationship between human beings, animals, plants and places with which culture is connected. In this relationship, economic rights have no place. Indigenous peoples have noted:

> culture as 'property' (therefore commodities to be exploited freely and bought and sold at will) has resulted to disharmony between human beings and the natural world, as well as the current environmental crisis threatening all life. This concept is totally incompatible with a traditional Indigenous world view.[5]

Even since the early 90s, the United Nations Special Rapporteur on Indigenous Cultural and Intellectual Property has urged the use of the term 'indigenous cultural heritage', rather than 'cultural property'. She has defined 'cultural heritage' as:

> everything that belongs to the distinct identity of a people and is therefore theirs to share, if they wish, with other peoples. It includes all of those things which international law regards as the creative production of human thought and craftsmanship, such as songs, stories, scientific knowledge and artworks. It also includes inheritances from the past and from nature, such as human remains, the natural features of the landscape, and naturally-occurring species of plants and animals with which a people has long been connected.[6]

During the elaboration of the UN *Declaration on the Rights of Indigenous Peoples*, a similar change of terminology was initiated by the UN Secretariat: it was

---

4 See International Indian Treaty Council (IITC), IITC Discussion Paper on Biological Diversity and Biological Ethics, 30 August 1996, p. 5 (on file with author).

5 See International Indian Treaty Council (IITC), IITC Discussion Paper on Biological Diversity and Biological Ethics, 30 August 1996, p. 5 (on file with author).

6 Working paper on the question of the ownership and control of the cultural property of indigenous peoples prepared by E.-I. Daes, UN Doc. E/CN.4/Sub.2/1991/34, para. 6.

suggested that the term cultural, intellectual, religious and spiritual 'property' be replaced by the term 'heritage'.[7]

'Cultural heritage' is also the term used in the Faro Convention, adopted in 2005 and put into force in 2009. The convention is very clear about the value of heritage. The Preamble emphasises 'the value and potential of cultural heritage' as 'a resource for sustainable development and quality of life in a constantly evolving society'. Article 1d also links cultural heritage to the 'construction of a peaceful and democratic society' and 'cultural diversity'.[8] The Convention defines cultural heritage as 'a group of resources inherited from the past which people identify, independently of ownership, as a reflection and expression of their constantly evolving values, beliefs, knowledge and traditions. It includes all aspects of the environment resulting from the interaction between people and places through time'.

Although the term 'cultural heritage' is gaining quite a momentum in international human rights fora, including a 2015 UN Study on indigenous cultural heritage, a 2016 UN Study on the right to cultural heritage and the HRC Resolution A/HRC/33/L.21 mentioned above, academic scholarship is not united in promoting the concept. Some writers have even been negative about the use of this term. For example, McCrone has suggested that the start of the heritage concept is placed at the post-Fordist economic climate of the US and argues that heritage 'has its roots in the reconstructing of the world economy – a process which began in the 1970s'.[9] Hence, McCrone links the concept of cultural heritage to the marketplace. Harvey responds that irrespective of when its protection started, heritage 'is a product of wider social, cultural, political and economic transitions'.[10]

7 See Technical review of the United Nations draft declaration on the rights of indigenous peoples, E/CN.4/Sub.2/1994/2, para. 16.

8 Council of Europe Framework Convention on the Value of Cultural Heritage for Society (2005).

9 D. McCrone, A. Morris and R. Kiely, *Scotland – The Brand. The Making of Scottish Heritage*, Edinburgh: Polygon, 1995, p. 2.

10 D. Harvey, 'Heritage Pasts and Presents, Temporality, meaning and the scope of heritage studies' (2001) 7(4) *International Journal of Heritage Studies* 319-338 at 324.

Cultural Heritage and Culture

Certainly, cultural heritage is a vague concept.[11] Larkham warns us that heritage seems to be 'all things to all people',[12] while Johnson and Thomas maintain that heritage is 'virtually anything by which some kind of link, however tenuous or false, may be forged with the past'.[13] In her seminal article, Blake noted already in 2000 the problems of defining cultural heritage for lawyers. In particular, the distinction between culture and cultural heritage is not clear at all.[14] Is this distinction based on time? Is it based on the nature of the elements to be protected?

'Past'

The time element is one widely identified as an important criterion that distinguishes culture to cultural heritage. If indeed cultural heritage is 'everything that is considered to be worthy of preserving in culture and that one wants to leave to subsequent generations',[15] then what is culture? And if culture is not what deserves to be preserved, then why does international law protect culture? Maybe culture should not be protected but cultural heritage should? Or is it that culture has some meaning in the present, whereas cultural heritage has more meaning in the past? Yet, this distinction does not seem very precise either. Konsa, like Harvey, notes that 'heritage is far from a fixed or objectively defined phenomenon'.[16] But, if cultural heritage is not a fixed concept, it is then a concept that relates to the present too. Thus, the distinction between culture and cultural heritage on the basis of time crumbles.

Maybe cultural heritage is different to culture because the former signifies the artefacts that need to be protected for future generations. Although this was the understanding some decades ago, the inclusion of intangible and natural elements into the meaning of cultural heritage as protected in inter-

---

11 B. Graham, P. Howard, 'Introduction: Heritage and Identity' in B. Graham, P. Howard (eds.), *The Ashgate Research Companion to Heritage and Identity* (Aldershot, Burlington: Ashgate, 2008), 1-15.

12 P.J. Larkham 'heritage as planned and conserved' in D.T. Herbert (ed.), *Heritage, Tourism and Society* (London: Mansel, 1995), 85.

13 P. Johnson and B. Thomas, 'Heritage as Business' in D.T. Herbert (ed.), *Heritage, Tourism and Society* (London: Mansell, 1995) 170.

14 J. Blake, 'On defining the Cultural Heritage; 49 (2000) *International and Comparative Law Quarterly* 61 at 68.

15 K. Konsa, 'Heritage as a socio-cultural construct: problems of definition' 12 (2013) *Baltic Journal of Art History* 125 at 126.

16 K. Konsa, 'Heritage as a socio-cultural construct: problems of definition' 12 (2013) *Baltic Journal of Art History* 125 at 125.

national law makes this distinction blurred. Since the early 2000s, intangible heritage has rightly become an accepted part of cultural heritage. The 2003 UNESCO *Convention for the Safeguarding of the Intangible Cultural Heritage* has played an important role in this.[17] Even though this is a positive development, the maintenance of such heritage must be subject to the evolution of the contemporary societal processes'.[18] In other words, illiberal practices cannot be preserved in the name of cultural heritage.

Choice

In addition to the lack of clarity on what is included in 'cultural heritage', critics also put forward the choice that is involved in the elements that will be viewed as cultural heritage. 'The political aspect of the decision as to what is to be preserved for future generations'.[19] Charlesworth notes that 'the definition of 'culture' is a highly political and contentious one – who defines 'culture', and who benefits from it?'[20]

It is true that usually these choices are being left to the elites of each section of the population, either the elites of the community itself or of the elite in the state structure. Very often, it is the 'experts' who decide what needs to be preserved and what not, at times without even consulting and getting the agreement of the community. Hortloff warns us against the recent emphasis on preservation and conservation of cultural heritage. He notes that 'destruction and loss are not the opposite of heritage but part of its very substance'.[21] According to him, 'it is not the acts of vandals and iconoclasts that are challenging sustainable notions of heritage, but the inability of both academic and political observers to understand and theorize what heritage does, and what is done to it, within the different realities that together make up our one world.'[22] He joins other scholars warning against preserving just for the sake of preservation. The preserved item becomes heritage not because the group thought it needed preserving but because it so happened that it was preserved. In any case, it has to be recognised that such process, benign as it may be, relates to

17 J. Blake, 'Seven Years of Implementing UNESCO's 2003 Intangible Heritage Convention – Honeymoon Period or the "Seven-Year Itch"?' (2014) 21 *International Journal of Cultural Property*, 291-304.

18 K. Konsa, 125.

19 J. Blake, *International and Comparative Law Quarterly*, at 69.

20 H. Charlesworth, 'Cultural Diversity in International Law' in *Human Rights, Faith and Culture*, pp. 35-45 at 35.

21 C. Hortloff, 'Can less be more? Heritage in the age of terrorism' 5 (2006) *Public Archaeology*, 101-109.

22 C. Hortloff, Public Heritage at 108.

the formation of identity, but also relates to power and authority. In this sense, it maintains the centres of power and the powerlessness of the peripheries. It maintains the exclusion of the vulnerable communities from deciding on their heritage as well as the exclusion of the vulnerable individuals within the communities that have no say in the formation of cultural heritage. Seen in this light, the protection of cultural heritage does not lead to the protection of the individual's identity but to the maintenance of inequality and exclusion.

PART B: COHERENCE

1 Fragmentation of 'Cultural Heritage' Research

It becomes obvious from the discussion above that although international lawyers have been pushing rather uncritically for the adoption of the term 'cultural heritage' in international human rights and in particular on indigenous rights, scholars in humanities have been problematizing about the concept. Indeed, international law debates on the rights of indigenous peoples to their heritage are to a large degree focused in legal interpretations of relevant provisions with little discussion of the consequences of such rights for global art and artists. At the same time, the discourse of cultural heritage in the humanities has tended to over-emphasise the authority of knowledge, which is not followed anymore by recent standards in international human rights law, that prioritize indigenous communities over experts. Clearly, the various disciplines have not been 'listening' to one another, nor have they been bouncing ideas off each other. A closer look within the various disciplines, namely international human rights, humanities, ethnography and history, reveals considerable variations in the understanding, the evaluation and the priorities on cultural heritage.

Indeed, one can sense the limited interaction of disciplines in this respect: International law has focused on the fragmentation that exists among its different parts, but the multi-disciplinary fragmentation in the study of specific areas, such as cultural heritage, needs also to be addressed.[23] One can clearly see the downsides of such fragmentation: responses of international law to the challenges posed currently in cultural heritage cannot be comprehensive unless they consider the politics and history of cultural heritage and acknowl-

23 However, look at A. Jakubowski, 'A constitutionalised legal order – exploring the role of the World Heritage Convention (1972)' in A. Jakubowski and K. Wierczyńska (eds.), *Fragmentation vs the Constitutionalisation of International Law* (London: Routledge, 2016), p. 182 at 187.

edge the tensions between archaeological knowledge and community claims. International lawyers can only reach an accurate interpretation of the existing law and suggest helpful ways forward, if they take into account the possible downsides of every such suggestion.

In all this discussion, indigenous peoples have been mere observers for a long time, while experts from various disciplines have been deciding on their behalf how to protect their heritage. Their participation in interpreting and exposing their heritage has been minimal, even though as Jody Joy (2004) has explained, 'historic objects are not innately meaningful but become meaningful only when they are socially constituted in a particular way'.[24] Yet, recently one can see evidence of a change. Indigenous peoples are taking initiatives to be in control of their heritage. For example, Lanauze, Forbes and Solomon have recorded the struggle of Moriori, an indigenous group living in Rekoku (the Moriori name for Chatham Islands) to retain and control their heritage.[25] After centuries of having items of their cultural heritage stolen from their island, the Moriori have created 'a comprehensive cultural database that involves re-recording archaeological evidence in a way that combines elder knowledge and experience, oral traditions and recollections of past land use and events'.[26] Also important are community-level strategies for protecting indigenous heritage, such as ethical guidelines and cultural protocols.[27] These initiatives are a realisation of the indigenous right to self-determination and are in sync with the current approaches of the humanities as well as the current standards of international law on indigenous rights.

---

24 C. Hortloff, 'Can less be more? Heritage in the age of terrorism' (2006) 5 *Public Archaeology* 101-109 at 103.

25 T. Lanauze, S. Forbes and M. Solomon, 'A practical approach to traditional knowledge and indigenous heritage management: A case study of Moriori heritage management practice' in S, Subramanian and B. Pisupati (eds.), *Traditional knowledge in Policy and Practice* (United Nations University Press, 2010), p. 327.

26 Ibid., 330.

27 K. Barrister, 'Non-Legal instruments for the protection of intangible cultural heritage: Key roles for ethical code and community protocols' in C. Bell and R. Paterson (eds.), *Protection of First Nations Cultural Heritage, Laws, Policy and Reform* (University of British Columbia, 2009) p. 278.

2 Fragmentation of International Law Relevant to Indigenous Cultural Heritage

Fragmentation specifically within international law also affects indigenous rights to their cultural heritage. Fragmentation in international law has been defined as 'the profound systemic rupture in the structure of international law, reflected in the lack of well-developed and established hierarchies or other techniques to deal with normative conflicts and tensions between general international law norms and its specialized regimes, as well as between those regimes *inter se*.'[28] It has been widely argued that the expansion of international law 'has created problems of harmony between its different branches, institutions and norm-systems'.[29] Such developments have led to a lack of coherence of the various regulatory contexts in international law, which prevent the formation and application of shared principles and interpretations across international law.[30] This compartmentalization and specialization is very obvious in the study of indigenous cultural heritage with detrimental effects to a coherent development of the law.

International Human Rights Law

There are three main international law systems related to indigenous cultural heritage. The most recent one is the international human rights law system. The level of protection evolved quite considerably in the last few years. Paramount in this system is the UN *Declaration on the Rights of Indigenous Peoples* as a tool that clarifies how general human rights standards apply on indigenous cultural heritage. Article 31 UNDRIP explicitly recognises the right of indigenous peoples to 'maintain, control, protect and develop their cultural heritage, traditional knowledge and traditional cultural expressions, as well as the manifestations of their sciences, technologies and cultures.' The article specifically includes the following in the manifestations of cultural heritage, knowledge and expressions to be protected: 'human and genetic resources, seeds, medicines, knowledge of the properties of fauna and flora, oral traditions, lit-

---

28 A. Jakubowski and K. Wierczyńska (eds.), *Fragmentation vs the Constitutionalisation of International Law* (London: Routledge, 2016), p. 1.

29 Study Group of the International Law Commission, 'Fragmentation of International Law: Difficulties Arising from the Diversification and Expansion of International Law', Report Finalized by M. Koskenniemi, UN Doc. A/CN.4/L.682.

30 A. Jakubowski and K. Wierczyńska, above, p. 2, also citing M.A. Young (ed.), *Regime Interaction in International Law Facing Fragmentation* (CUP 2012); N. Krisch, *Beyond Constitutionalism. The Pluralist Structure of Postnational Law* (OUP 2010).

eratures, designs, sports and traditional games and visual and performing arts.' One can see that the text does not make a clear distinction between tangible, intangible and natural heritage, a positive element and different to the approach of the older UNESCO documents on cultural heritage. Rights related to cultural heritage are also recognised in several other parts of the Declaration. Article 11 UNDRIP recognises the intangible aspects of cultural heritage: indigenous peoples have the right to 'practice and revitalize their cultural traditions and customs', which includes 'past, present and future manifestations of their cultures'. The text also includes tangible elements: 'archaeological and historical sites, artefacts, designs, ceremonies, technologies and visual and performing arts and literature.' Article 12 follows the same pattern: it protects the right of indigenous peoples 'to manifest, practise, develop and teach their spiritual and religious traditions, customs and ceremonies; the right to maintain, protect, and have access in privacy to their religious and cultural sites; the right to the use and control of their ceremonial objects; and the right to the repatriation of their human remains'. Interesting is the recognition of the right to access in privacy to sacred sites, as will be discussed below. Article 13 recognises indigenous rights to histories, languages, oral traditions, philosophies, writing systems and literatures, and to designate and retain their own names for communities, places and persons.

The above-mentioned provisions in UNDRIP do not create new law. They interpret existing binding human rights treaties. They interpret how article 15 of the *International Covenant on Economic, Social and Cultural Rights* (ICESCR)[31] and article 27 ICCPR apply to indigenous peoples' cultural heritage.[32] The content of UNDRIP on indigenous cultural heritage is also an expression of cross-fertilisation of ideas and standards among the various bodies of international human rights law. The provisions reflect comments made by international human rights bodies and feed back as the basis to comments by United Nations bodies. For example, CERD has recently asked questions on the effect of relocation on indigenous cultural heritage,[33] whereas the Human Rights Committee had talked about protection of sites of religious or cultural

31 United Nations International Covenant on Economic, Social and Cultural Rights, adopted and opened for signature, ratification and accession by General Assembly resolution 2200A (XXI) of 16 December 1966, entry into force 3 January 1976, http://www.ohchr.org/EN/ProfessionalInterest/Pages/CESCR.aspx.

32 A. Xanthaki, 'Indigenous Rights to Culture' in M. Weller and J. Hofmann (eds.), *Commentary on the UN Declaration on the Rights of Indigenous Peoples* (Oxford University Press, 2017), (forthcoming).

33 UN Doc. CERD/C/LAO/CO/15, para. 18.

significance.[34] In its concluding observations for New Zealand, the Committee has used language very similar to the UNDRIP. The Committee recognised 'Māori's right to conserve, promote and develop their own culture, language and cultural heritage, traditional knowledge and traditional cultural expressions, and the manifestations of their sciences and cultures.'[35] The HR Committee's comments in its concluding observations followed discussions on indigenous cultural rights in the case-law, including *Apirana Mahuika et al. v. New Zealand,*[36] *Ominayak v. Canada, Lansman et al. v. Finland* in 1994[37] and 1996,[38] *Francis Hopu and Tepoaitu Bessert v. France,*[39] *Lovelace v. Canada*[40] *and Kitok v. Sweden.*[41] These comments of the Human Rights Committee have been important in convincing the States of the validity of the UNDRIP related to cultural rights. Cross-fertilisation has also been possible between the universal human rights system and the Inter-American system of human rights. Even as far back as 1993, the Inter-American Court took into account the customary marriage practices of the Saramacan people.[42] In 2004, the Court found in the *Massacre of Plan de Sánchez* case that the deaths of the women and elderly, who were traditionally the oral transmitters of the Mayan Achí culture, interrupted the passage of cultural knowledge to future generations and the militarization and repression after the massacre resulted in the indigenous peoples' loss of faith in their traditions.[43] The prohibition of the indigenous group to practice their traditional burial ceremonies because of their relocation was deemed a violation of their rights,[44] which Guatemala accepted as a violation of 'the freedom to manifest their religious, spiritual, and cultural beliefs'.[45] In the *Bámaca Velásquez* case, the court also noted that the funeral ceremonies of the Mam ethnic group were 'something that is traditional in the indigenous

34 For example UN A/55/40, para. 510 regarding Australia.

35 UN International Committee on Economic, Social and Cultural Rights, Concluding observations on the fifth periodic report of New Zealand, UN Doc. E/C12/NZL/CO/3 (2012) para. 26.

36 A/56/40, Volume I, Annex X, A (Communication No. l 547/1993).

37 CCPR/C/52/D/511/1992, Case No. 511/1992.

38 CCPR/C/58/D/671/1995, Case No. 671/1995.

39 CCPR/C/60/D/549/1993/Rev.1, Communication No. 549/1993.

40 A/36/40, Annex 7(G) (1998).

41 A/43/40, Annex 7(G) (1988).

42 *Aloeboetoe et al. v Suriname* (*Reparations*) IACtHR Series C 15 (1993); 1-2 IHRR 208 (1993).

43 *Plan de Sánchez Massacre v. Guatemala* (Reparations) IACtHR Series C 116 (2004).

44 *Plan de Sánchez Massacre v. Guatemala* (Merits), IACtHR Series C 105 (2004), para. 42(30).

45 Ibid., para. 36(4).

culture',[46] whereas in the *Case of Moiwana Community v. Suriname* the Court ordered Suriname to take all measures 'to recover promptly the remains of the Moiwana community members killed' by the national army in 1886.[47] Therefore, in fulfilling indigenous peoples' cultural rights, states are now under the obligation to act in positive and precise ways in order to recover the remains of indigenous members.

UNESCO Law

Unfortunately, the human rights standards are not reflected in the UNESCO conventions. Even though Article 5 of the *Universal Declaration on Cultural Diversity* (2001) noted that the flourishing of cultural diversity requires 'the full implementation of cultural rights as defined in Article 27 of the *Universal Declaration of Human Rights* and in Articles 13 and 15 of the *International Covenant on Economic, Social and Cultural Rights*', the link between the *Convention on the Diversity of Cultural Expressions* and human rights is too generic and vague.[48]

One of the main challenges is that UNESCO documents still frame cultural heritage in a binary way, either belonging to the state or to the individual. So, for example, the (1970) UNESCO *Convention on the Means of Prohibiting and Preventing the Illicit Import, Export, and Transfer of Ownership of Cultural Property* protects:

> (a) Cultural property created by the individual or collective genius of nationals of the State concerned, and cultural property of importance to the State concerned created within the territory of that State by foreign nationals or stateless persons resident within such territory; (b) cultural property found within the national territory.

All these earlier provisions have to be interpreted in the light of UNDRIP. The Convention for the Safeguarding of the Intangible Cultural Heritage (2003) does ensure respect for the intangible cultural heritage of groups; individuals are almost an exception to the protection of the convention.[49] Also, ac-

46 *Bámaca Velásquez v. Guatemala* (Reparations), IACtHR Series C 91 (2002), para. 82.

47 *Case of Moiwana Community v. Suriname* (Preliminary Objections, Merits, Reparations and Costs), IACHR, Judgment of 15 June 2005, Series C No 124, para. 208.

48 Y. Donders, 'Cultural Rights and the Convention on the Diversity of Cultural Expressions, Included or Ignored?' in T. Kono and S. van Uytsel (eds.), *The UNESCO Convention on the Diversity of Cultural Expressions* (Intersentia, 2012), p. 165 at 177 onwards.

49 A. Meijknecht, 'The Convention on the Diversity of Cultural Expressions, What is its Added Value for Minorities and Indigenous Peoples' in T. Kono and S. van Uytsel (eds.),

cording to article 11 of the convention, each State Party shall '(b) identify and define the various elements of the intangible cultural heritage present in its territory, with the participation of communities, groups, and relevant non-governmental organisations.'[50] Nevertheless, currently communities continue to have very little input in identifying the elements constituting cultural heritage. For example, it is the state party to the *World Heritage Convention* (WHC) that nominates potential heritage sites.[51] In this respect, States rely heavily on the state narratives, rather the indigenous narratives about specific elements. So, often, indigenous peoples have to satisfy the entities that have been undermining their cultural heritage that it is worthy enough to be nominated for international protection. Also, in other cases, the indigenous heritage is being pushed to be presented and perceived as part of national heritage. In addition, indigenous peoples have had minimum input in the conservation, exhibition and protection discussions relating to their own cultural heritage. Hence, although States can acquire UNESCO protection and recognition for the indigenous sites and elements that exist within their territories, yet they do not have any obligation from UNESCO to recognise and protect the link between the indigenous heritage and the community. The WHC convention does recognise the States' 'duty of ensuring the identification, protection, conservation, presentation and transmission to future generations of the cultural and natural heritage' (Art. 4), but recognises no right of any group to such heritage. In other words, there is no strong link between the UNESCO protection, which goes mainly towards the state according to state requests and understandings, and the human rights obligations that such States have towards the actual owners of the cultural heritage, i.e. indigenous peoples. This has to change and relevant UNESCO documents need to be interpreted in the light of UNDRIP.

For example, the 1995 UNDROIT *Convention on Stolen or Illegally Exported Objects*, created to compliment the 1970 Convention, does recognise the heritage of tribal and indigenous communities living in a Contracting State. Although the 1995 Convention puts the State where such heritage comes from in charge of such claims against another state and is of no use for heritage taken

---

The UNESCO Convention on the Diversity of Cultural Expressions (Intersentia, 2012), p. 201 at 214.

50 Article 11 of the Convention for the Safeguarding of the Intangible Cultural Heritage (2003).

51 R. Coombe and J. Turcotte, 'Indigenous cultural heritage in development and trade: perspectives from the dynamics of cultural heritage law and policy' in C.B. Graber, K. Kuprecht and J.C. Lai (eds.), *International Trade in Indigenous Cultural heritage: Legal and policy issues* (Edward Elgar, 2012), 272-305.

by the state without the consent of the indigenous community, nevertheless it explicitly proclaims that the missing object 'will be returned' to the tribal or indigenous community to which it belongs. Provisions like this have to take a more central stage within UNESCO and have to be implemented.

There are also other areas where the compartmentalisation of the UNESCO protection of cultural heritage and the human rights protection to indigenous cultural heritage differ. One such area is the distinction in UNESCO documents between tangible and intangible culture, something that is alien to indigenous peoples and is avoided in the UNDRIP. Notable is the (2003) UNESCO *Convention for the Safeguarding of Intangible Cultural Heritage*, a convention adopted while the UNDRIP was at the end of its elaboration and several discussions were taking place in the UN on indigenous cultural heritage. In contrast, the WHC has been trying to incorporate cultural and natural elements in heritage. This is a big step forward and although there are still issues in the degree to which natural heritage is identified and protected, it is a positive development.

Another such area where fragmentation is obvious and detrimental to indigenous cultural heritage is the UNESCO concept of 'objects of outstanding value', which goes against the trend of associating heritage to everyday life but which also raises further issues about the entity that makes such judgments (and it is usually not the indigenous community who is the owner of such heritage). The (1972) Convention specifically protects objects of outstanding or monumental value, and thus excludes large parts of indigenous cultural heritage. Even the (1972) UNESCO *Convention Concerning the Protection of the World Cultural and Natural Heritage* which uses cultural heritage, defines cultural heritage as 'individual artistic works, artefacts and handicrafts; objects of religious significance; music, folklore and design; archaeology and human remains; sacred and historical sites'. So, for example, it is debatable whether human skeletons could be included in the 'products of archaeological excavations and discoveries'. Also doubtful is the inclusion of oral history in the Convention; arguably, it can be protected as part of 'sound, photographic and cinematographic archives'. More generally, both the 1972 UNESCO Convention and the 1970 UNESCO Convention make no reference to spiritual or religious criteria that might apply in identifying areas of cultural heritage, although these are the main criteria for indigenous heritage. These omissions by the Convention leave many cultural objects open to the possibility of uncontrollable use and abuse. An illustrative example is unauthorised filmings of indigenous religious ceremonies and secret recordings of songs and rituals: the Convention protects photographs, films and sound recordings that have a historical value (hence the use of the term 'archive'), but it is arguable whether indigenous peoples have any protection against all unauthorised filmings and recordings.

Intellectual Property Rights

In addition, the human rights standards on indigenous cultural heritage have not yet penetrated the international regime on intellectual property rights. The *Convention on Biological Diversity* (CBD), enforced in 1993, and the TRIPs agreement, enforced in 1995, take a very different approach to the human rights system outlined above, as they encourage the commercialisation of cultural heritage and traditional knowledge. Even though the CBD was the first convention that recognised the value of traditional knowledge, it also promoted the wider application of cultural heritage and traditional knowledge and made indigenous IP rights subject to national law. CBD, article 8j, reads

> Subject to national legislation, respect, preserve and maintain knowledge, innovations and practices of indigenous and local communities embodying traditional lifestyles relevant for the conservation and sustainable use of biological diversity and promote their wider application with the approval and involvement of the holders of such knowledge, innovations and practices and encourage the equitable sharing of the benefits arising from the utilization of such knowledge innovations and practices

Article 8j attracted invested commercial interests. Further, the TRIPs Agreement promoted a universal scheme that broadened the scope of intellectual property commercially understood that includes cultural heritage such as genetic resources, plant varieties and pharmaceuticals.[52]

Essentially the Intellectual Property Rights system views intellectual property rights, including indigenous peoples' cultural heritage rights, as individual rights and focuses on the financial benefits resulting from protecting such individual interests.[53] WIPO has so far encouraged the commercialisation of heritage, has promoted the individualistic understanding of heritage, and has adopted a way of looking at cultural heritage which is alien and detrimental to indigenous peoples.[54] This system clearly collides with the human rights standards recognised on indigenous cultural heritage. Unfortunately, the IP system has a much clearer enforcement mechanism than the human rights system. The conflict between the intellectual property system and the human rights

52 Helfer 2004, Dutfield 2003.

53 J. Morijn, 'The place of cultural rights in the WTO system' in F. Francioni and M. Scheinin (eds.), *Cultural Human Rights* (Leiden: Martinus Nijhoff, 2007), p. 285.

54 R. Fan, 'Evolution of indigenous peoples' rights and indigenous knowledge debate' in C. Lennox and D. Short (eds.), *Handbook of Indigenous Peoples Rights* (Routledge, 2016) p. 237.

standards has been identified by the then Sub-Commission on the Promotion and Protection of Human Rights even since 2000. In its resolution 2000/7, the Sub-Commission identified that the IPR system violates the right of everyone to enjoy the benefits of scientific progress, the right to food, to health and to self-determination. In 2001, the UN Committee on Economic, Social and Cultural Rights specifically recognised the conflict and noted that all parties are required to observe the human-rights based approach that 'focuses particularly on the needs of the most disadvantaged and marginalised individuals and communities' including indigenous peoples.[55] The Committee, but also subsequently the UN Special Rapporteur in the field of cultural rights, called upon all member states, UN organs and specialised agencies as well as international organisations to take effective measures to implement article 15 ICESCR. WIPO has not formally adopted the UNDRIP, which represents an interpretative tool of article 15 on the right to culture specifically for indigenous peoples. However, they are in the process of elaborating three draft treaties on genetic resources, traditional knowledge and folklore and traditional cultural expressions. These treaties, if adopted, will have a deep impact on bringing together the human rights standards on indigenous cultural heritage and IP rights.

3 Fragmentation within Human Rights Law

A third place where one can talk about fragmentation is within the international human rights law system, where traditional liberals emphasise the importance of individual rights to cultural expression, whereas scholars working on indigenous rights emphasise the importance of collective rights related to heritage. A major underpinning in the rights of artists is the protection of their right to seek inspiration from anywhere as well as the protection of the final product as one belonging to them. McRobie talks about the 'symbiotic relationship' between the author and the society/societies'[56] and notes that literature may 'occup[y] a peculiar position of both belonging to a particular group, and belonging to humanity as a whole'.[57] A lot of artists would say the same for other expressions. Article 15 of the *International Covenant on Economic, Social and Cultural Rights* protects the right of everyone to enjoy the benefits of scientific progress and its applications and to benefit from the moral and material interests resulting from scientific production. In the 1950 *Agreement*

55 UN CESCR 2006, para. 8.

56 H.K. McRobie, *Literary Freedom, A Cultural Right to Literature* (zero books, 2011), p. 50.

57 Ibid., 51.

on the Importance of Educational, Scientific and Cultural Materials (*the Florence Agreement*), the Contracting States undertook 'that they will as far as possible 'contribute their common efforts to promote by every means the free circulation of educational, scientific and cultural material, and abolish or reduce any restrictions to that free circulation…'.[58] Yet, both these rights are at times in contrast with indigenous cultural heritage which does not have one creator, neither does it allow access to every single aspect of it.

The right to the common heritage of mankind is also one that is in conflict with the indigenous claims for respect to their specific hidden/sacred heritage. There is this widespread understanding that protecting the common heritage of mankind is way beyond any individual right or even group right. This does not sit well with indigenous claims for respect of their hidden/secret cultural sites. For example, in the Finnish side of Saamiland, there are documented sacred sites, with specific rules about who should approach the sites and how. There are sites used by the whole community, common and shared sacrificing places of multiple households or more personal sites that belonged to the families and individuals.[59] Yet, for some, complete control of indigenous peoples over their artefacts will result in a renewed tribalism and a further alienation of indigenous peoples from the mainstream as lack of access will mean lack of understanding and respect of non-indigenous populations towards the indigenous knowledge system and cultural heritage. Therefore, several authors have defended the need for openness, which exhibitions of indigenous heritage in international museums allegedly encourage. In contrast, Macmillan condemns the insistence of museums to keep indigenous artefacts in the name of the right to the common culture of mankind as 'a kind of appropriation of cultural heritage through a discourse that claims their heritage as the patrimony of humankind – some sort of global patrimony'.[60]

Certainly, such claims, claims of individual artists for the protection of their rights, claims of indigenous peoples and claims for access to the common heritage of mankind have to be developed consistently and coherently; and discussed together rather than in parallel ways. Blake rightly notes that 'much

---

58 A. Vrdoljak, 'Self-Determination and Cultural Rights' in F. Francioni and M. Scheinin (eds.), *Cultural Human Rights* (Leiden: Martinus Nijhoff, 2008), 41.

59 A. Xanthaki, L. Heinämäki, A.-M. Magga, 'Indigenous Peoples' Customary Rights and Sacred Sites of Sámi' in L. Heinämäki and T. Herrmann (eds.), *Sacred Artic: Experiencing and Protecting Sacred Sites of Sámi and other Arctic Indigenous Peoples* (Springer, 2017), 65-82.

60 F. Macmillan, 'The Protection of Cultural Heritage: Common Heritage of Humankind, National Cultural "Patrimony" or Private Property?' (2013) 64(3) *Northern Ireland Legal Quarterly* 351.

work is also needed to understand better the content and nature of these rights and the need to consider several distinct areas of international law if we wish to resolve these questions'.[61]

Conclusions

This chapter argues that the current recognition of indigenous cultural heritage must penetrate all areas of international law. Therefore, UNESCO documents must be interpreted in line with the provisions of the UN Declaration on the Rights of Indigenous Peoples. WIPO instruments must find a way to be in sync with the standards on indigenous cultural heritage as recently developed. It is imperative that the standards of the UN Declaration on the Rights of Indigenous Peoples are recognised and implemented by international law bodies. This will ensure a coherent development of the law but also, and most importantly, the effective protection of indigenous peoples and their cultural heritage.

This chapter also argues that the debate on indigenous cultural heritage needs to break the existing fragmentation in order to encourage looking at issues holistically. Discussions on the role of the elites, both state and community ones, in deciding which parts of the indigenous past are cultural heritage; and on the limited role of indigenous women and youth in the decision-making; as well as on the effects of complete control of communities over their heritage can only be welcome. The methodologies of the humanities on the concept, history and politics of cultural heritage are invaluable in adding context and depth when balancing conflicting rights and interests, but all discussions need to support and follow the indigenous viewpoints and voices on the issues.

61 J. Blake, *Exploring cultural rights and cultural diversity* (Institute of Art and the Law, 2014) 99-100.

Indigenous Peoples, Human Rights, and Cultural Heritage: Towards a Right to Cultural Integrity

Jérémie Gilbert

Introduction

In recent years, indigenous peoples' human rights have greatly evolved at the international level. This has notably included the adoption of the United Nations Declaration on the Rights of Indigenous Peoples (UNDRIP) in 2007, but also a very robust jurisprudence emerging from international human rights monitoring bodies and regional human rights institutions. The protection of cultural heritage constitutes an important aspect of such developments. Across the globe, indigenous peoples' representatives have made it clear that the protection and recognition of their cultural heritage is an essential element of their survival as distinct peoples. The word often attached to cultural heritage for indigenous peoples is 'holistic' as cultural heritage encompasses traditional practices in a broad sense, including for example language, art, music, dance, song, but also sacred sites, traditional territories, the use of natural resources, including bio-cultural heritage and traditional food production systems such as rotational farming, shifting cultivation, pastoralism, artisanal fisheries and other forms of access to natural sources.[1] Many indigenous peoples have thus highlighted how their cultural heritage needs to be apprehended in a holistic and inter-generational manner based on common material and spiritual values influenced by their environment.

For many indigenous peoples, the challenge has been to make their holistic approach to cultural heritage fitting within the international legal regime governing cultural heritage. Under international law, a multitude of legal regimes exist to protect cultural heritage. This notably includes the protection of 'intangible', 'tangible', 'natural' heritage, but also the division between intellectual, immaterial, and material protection of the cultural heritage.[2] This

1 See: Study by the Expert Mechanism on the Rights of Indigenous Peoples, 'Promotion and protection of the rights of indigenous peoples with respect to their cultural heritage', UN Doc. A/HRC/EMRIP/2015/2 (2015).

2 See: C. Forrest, *International Law and the Protection of Cultural Heritage* (Routledge, 2010); J. Blake, 'On Defining the Cultural Heritage', 49 (1) International and Comparative Law Quarterly 61-85 (2000); L. Lixinski, *Intangible Cultural Heritage in International Law* (Ox-

Xanthaki, Valkonen et al. (eds.), *Indigenous Peoples' Cultural Heritage: Rights, Debates and Challenges.*
 ISBN 978-90-04-34218-7. PP. 20-38.

overall complex legal regime, which is based on a cross-competency between several international organisations, often leads to a fragmentation between a multitude of legal frameworks, which ultimately do not adequately embody the holistic cultural heritage of indigenous peoples.[3] The system notably fails to recognise that, for indigenous peoples, cultural heritage is holistic and encompasses their spiritual, economic, and social connections to their lands and territories.

The present chapter proposes to examine to what extent human rights law could offer a comprehensive and holistic approach to the protection of the cultural heritage of indigenous peoples, notably in avoiding the clusters between 'intangible', 'tangible', 'natural' and intellectual heritage that is developed under international law. It explores how the nascent development of the 'right to cultural integrity' could support such comprehensive approach to cultural heritage. The right to cultural integrity, which has been put forward by several human rights institutions and advocates,[4] could support a much more holistic approach to the protection of cultural heritage as it is based on the recognition that cultural heritage includes indigenous peoples' rights to culture, religion, health, development and natural resources. While references to a right to cultural integrity have increasingly been used by international and regional human rights bodies as well as civil society actors and academic circles, there is nonetheless a lack of analysis on the content and legal grounding of such a right to cultural integrity. This chapter aims at analysing the emergence of such a right and its relevance to the protection of indigenous peoples' cultural heritage.

---

ford University Press, 2013); St. Disko and H. Tugendhat (eds.), *Indigenous Peoples and the World Heritage Convention* (IWGIA and Forest Peoples Programme, Nov. 2014).

3 See: Study by the Expert Mechanism on the Rights of Indigenous Peoples, 'Promotion and Protection of the Rights of Indigenous Peoples with Respect to Their Cultural Heritage', UN Doc. A/HRC/EMRIP/2015/2 (2015); and A. Xanthaki, 'Culture' in J. Hohmann and M. Weller (eds.), *The UN Declaration on the Rights of Indigenous Peoples: A Commentary* (OUP, forthcoming).

4 See: J. Anaya, *Indigenous Peoples in International Law* (OU, 2004), pp. 134-141; F MacKay, 'Universal Rights or a Universe unto Itself – Indigenous Peoples' Human Rights and the World Bank's Draft Operational Policy 4.10 on Indigenous Peoples', 17 Am. U. Int'l L. Rev. 527 (2001-2002); J. Anaya, 'International Human Rights and Indigenous Peoples: The Move toward the Multicultural State', 21 Ariz. J. Int'l & Comp. L. 13 (2004); Asia Pacific Forum of National Human Rights Institutions and the Office of the United Nations High Commissioner for Human Rights, The United Nations Declaration on the Rights of Indigenous Peoples: A Manual for National Human Rights Institutions (United Nations, August 2013); and see references in section 2 below.

To undertake such analysis, the chapter will first examine how the right to cultural integrity could place itself within the overall human rights-based approach to cultural heritage (section 1). Based on such overview, it will then examine how the right to cultural integrity has been developed within the jurisprudence of regional human rights institutions (section 2). The chapter will then examine how the right to cultural integrity also finds echoes in the legal framework regarding protection of indigenous peoples against genocide, and notably how the debates which have surrounded the issue of cultural genocide have included a reference to the protection the cultural integrity of indigenous peoples (section 3). Finally, it will focus on the protection of cultural practices developed under human rights law and how such protection includes the integrity of indigenous cultural heritage (section 4).

1 Cultural Heritage, Cultural Rights and Indigenous Peoples: An Overview

The aim of this short section is not to offer a comprehensive review of all the human rights norms that are relevant for the protection of indigenous peoples' cultural heritage, but to provide a short overview of the main legal avenues available for indigenous peoples when it comes to cultural heritage protection.[5] As demonstrated by the study undertaken by the UN Expert Mechanism on the Rights of Indigenous Peoples (EMRIP) in 2015 on cultural heritage, human rights law addresses cultural heritage under various instruments.[6] While cultural heritage is not directly mentioned in the core human rights treaties, cultural rights form an important and overarching right proclaimed in most human rights instruments. A number of provisions in international human rights instruments constitute the legal basis for a right of access to and enjoyment of cultural heritage.[7] This notably includes the Universal Declaration of Human Rights (art. 27), the International Covenant on Economic, Social

5 For a comprehensive analysis on human rights law, indigenous peoples and cultural heritage, see chapter XX in this book; and M. Langfield, W. Logan, and M. Nic Craith (eds.), *Cultural Diversity, Heritage and Human Rights: Intersections in Theory and Practice* (Routledge, 2009).

6 Study by the Expert Mechanism on the Rights of Indigenous Peoples, 'Promotion and Protection of the Rights of Indigenous Peoples with Respect to Their Cultural Heritage', UN Doc. A/HRC/EMRIP/2015/2 (2015).

7 See: Report of the independent expert in the field of cultural rights, Farida Shaheed, UN Doc. A/HRC/17/38 (2011).

and Cultural Rights (art. 15), the International Covenant on Civil and Political Rights (art. 27), and the Convention on the Rights of the Child (art. 29). All these provisions focusing on cultural rights have been interpreted to support indigenous peoples' cultural heritage.

Moreover, the more specific instruments dedicated to indigenous peoples' rights also put a strong emphasis on cultural rights and cultural heritage. Several articles of the UNDRIP are directly relevant to the cultural heritage of indigenous peoples, including protection of the tangible heritage, traditions and customs of indigenous peoples (art. 11); the spiritual and religious traditions and customs of indigenous cultures (art. 12); their intangible heritage (art. 13); their right to uphold the dignity and diversity of their cultures and languages in relation to education and public information (arts. 14 and 15). The Declaration upholds the rights of indigenous peoples to develop their own culture and customs; to the use and control of their ceremonial objects; not to be subjected to destruction of their culture or to discrimination on the ground of their culture; and to redress mechanisms for action that deprives them of their cultural values.

The International Labour Organization Indigenous and Tribal Peoples Convention (No. 169) contains several provisions relating to the cultural heritage of indigenous peoples. Governments are notably required to respect and safeguard the cultural and traditional values of indigenous peoples and (art. 13) and their use and management of the land and natural resources (arts. 14 and 15), and to ensure that the traditional activities of indigenous peoples are strengthened and promoted (art. 23). It is also worth noting that the right of peoples to self-determination, proclaimed in the International Covenants and the UNDRIP, protects the right of peoples to freely pursue their cultural development and to dispose of their natural wealth and resources, which has a clear link with cultural heritage.

Overall, all these norms and instruments support different aspects of indigenous peoples' cultural rights that are relevant to their cultural heritage. This includes the right to take part in cultural life, the right to enjoy one's own culture, and the right to maintain, control, protect and develop their cultural heritage. As summarised in a document produced by the Office of the High Commissioner on Human Rights, indigenous cultural rights include the following rights:

- The right to maintain and strengthen their distinct cultural institutions;
- The right to belong to an indigenous community or nation in accordance with the customs of the community or nation concerned;

- The right to practice, revitalize and transmit their cultural traditions and customs;
- The right to control their education systems and institutions providing education in their own languages;
- The right to promote, develop and maintain their institutional structures, customs, spirituality, traditions and juridical systems;
- The right to maintain, control and develop their cultural heritage and traditional knowledge;
- The right not to be subjected to forced assimilation or destruction of their culture.[8]

Taken as a whole, human rights law offers a wide-ranging approach to cultural rights for indigenous peoples addressing many aspects of cultural heritage.

However, one may wonder if this complex layer of various instruments and norms does not in itself represent an overly convoluted and segregated approach to cultural heritage. Indeed, for indigenous peoples, claiming the protection of their cultural heritage involves using several aspects of human rights law, which are not always interrelated and connected to cultural heritage. For example, for indigenous peoples claiming the protection of their cultural heritage might involve invoking their right to freedom of religion, their right to land and natural resources, their right to development, their right to food, and their cultural rights. All these rights form part of their cultural heritage but are scattered across the human rights legal framework. There is no right in itself that is capturing the holistic approach necessary to protect cultural heritage. Whilst the UNDRIP does contain a specific article dedicated to cultural heritage, in general any claim to cultural heritage has to be based on a series of different norms that are disseminated across various instruments. From that perspective, the proposal to focus on a right to cultural integrity might offer a more holistic and comprehensive approach to cultural heritage.

As noted earlier, we have recently witnessed the emergence of what has been labelled as a 'right to cultural integrity' for indigenous peoples.[9] While the right to cultural integrity does not appear in any of the international hu-

---

8 The United Nations Declaration on the Rights of Indigenous Peoples: A Manual for National Human Rights Institutions (Asia Pacific Forum of National Human Rights Institutions and the Office of the United Nations High Commissioner for Human Rights, August 2013), p. 13.

9 See report from the former UN Special Rapporteur on Indigenous Peoples' Rights stating: '[t]his duty is a corollary of a myriad of universally accepted human rights, including the right to cultural integrity, the right to equality and the right to property (…).' Report of

man rights treaties, it refers to a bundle of different human rights such as rights to culture, subsistence, livelihood, religion and heritage.[10] The Inter-American Commission on Human Rights (IACHR) refers to a 'collective right to cultural integrity' encompassing many different essential elements of indigenous peoples cultural heritage.[11] As such it offers a promising way to adopt a much more holistic approach to cultural heritage by including cultural rights, the right to freedom of religion, the right to health, and the right to development under the same umbrella.

Legally speaking, references to the need to respect the integrity of indigenous peoples are made in article 8 (2) of the UNDRIP which prohibits any action 'which has the aim or effect of depriving them of their integrity as distinct peoples, or of their cultural values or ethnic identities.' Likewise, Article 2 of the ILO Convention 169 states: 'Governments shall have the responsibility for developing, with the participation of the peoples concerned, coordinated and systematic action to protect the rights of these peoples and to guarantee respect for their integrity.' The Committee on Economic, Social and Cultural Rights has also alluded to the need to protect the cultural integrity of indigenous peoples. For example, in its 2014 concluding observations regarding the situation in Guatemala, the committee has urged the government to ensure that measures are put in place to 'preserve the cultural integrity' of indigenous peoples in the context of exploration and exploitation of mining resources and hydrocarbons located on indigenous territories.[12] Both former and present Special Rapporteurs on the Rights of Indigenous Peoples have often made specific references to the need to protect the cultural integrity of indigenous peoples.[13] The Special Rapporteur on the right to food has also mentioned the need to respect the cultural integrity of indigenous peoples in his 2012 report

the Special Rapporteur on the situation of human rights and fundamental freedoms of indigenous people, James Anaya. UN Doc. A/HRC/12/34, July 15, 2009, para. 41.

10 See: J. Gilbert, 'Custodians of the land: Indigenous peoples, human rights and cultural integrity', in W. Logan, M. Nic Craith, M. Langfield (eds.), *Cultural Diversity, Heritage and Human Rights Intersections in Theory and Practice* (Routledge, 2009).

11 IACHR, 'Indigenous and Tribal Peoples' Rights over Their Ancestral Lands and Natural Resources: Norms and Jurisprudence of the Inter-American Human Rights System' (2009) OEA/Ser.L/V/II. Doc. 56/09 at para. 57; see also paras. 205-6, and n. 647.

12 See: Concluding Observations: Guatemala, UN Doc. E/C.12/GTM/CO/3, at para. 7.

13 See for examples: Report of the Special Rapporteur of the Human Rights Council on the rights of indigenous peoples, Victoria Tauli-Corpuz, UN Doc. A/69/267 (2014), paras. 16, 18 and 29; Report of the Special Rapporteur on the situation of human rights and fundamental freedoms of indigenous people, S. James Anaya, UN Doc. A/HRC/9/9 (2008), para. 22; Report by the Special Rapporteur on the situation of human rights and fundamental free-

which followed his visit to Canada.[14] It is also worth noting that one of the main objectives of the Second Decade of the World's Indigenous Peoples is to promote the full and effective participation of indigenous peoples in 'decisions which directly or indirectly affect their cultural integrity.'[15] Nonetheless, it is mainly within the jurisprudence of the regional human rights institutions that such concept of cultural integrity is the most strongly reflected upon, and has been emerging.

2 Regional Human Rights Institutions and Cultural Integrity

Regional human rights institutions, and notably the African Commission on Human and Peoples' Rights (ACHPR) and the Inter-American Court of Human Rights (IACtHR) have made several references to the indigenous peoples' right to cultural integrity. The Inter-American Court has notably emphasized that the close relationship between indigenous peoples and their lands must be recognized and understood as the fundamental base of their culture, spiritual life, *integrity*, economic survival and cultural preservation.[16] Based on such a holistic approach to indigenous peoples' relationship with their lands and territories, the Court has often made references to the need to protect the cultural integrity of indigenous peoples.[17] For example, in a case against Suriname, an indigenous community had specifically made the claim that the government had violated their right to cultural integrity. The Court received the argument highlighting that 'in order for the culture to preserve its very identity and integrity, [indigenous peoples]… must maintain a fluid and multidimensional relationship with their ancestral lands.'[18] The Court clearly implied the importance of considering the integrity of indigenous peoples' cultures, which includes a

doms of indigenous people, James Anaya, Situation of indigenous peoples in Australia, UN Doc. A/HRC/15/37/Add.4 (2010), paras. 4, 13, 16, 28, 44, 65, 72.

14 Special Rapporteur on the Right to Food, Visit to Canada, UN Doc. A/HRC/22/50/Add.1, 25 December 2012, para. 62.

15 Second International Decade of the World's Indigenous People, UN Doc. A/RES/59/174; and Report of the Secretary-General, Mid-term Assessment, UN Doc. A/65/166.

16 I/A Court H.R, Yakye Axa Indigenous Community v. Paraguay, judgement of 17 June 2005 (Series C, No. 125) para. 51.

17 See: I/A Court H.R., Case of the Yakye Axa Indigenous Community v. Paraguay (Merits, Reparations and Costs) Judgment of June 17, 2005. Series C No. 125, paras. 147 and 203; Kuna Indigenous People of Madungandí and the Emberá Indigenous People of Bayano v. Panama, Ser. C No. 284, para. 143.

18 I/A Court H.R, Moiwana Village Case, at paras. 101, 102-3.

strong connection with their lands, territories, and their natural resources. The Inter-American Commission has also often referred to the need to protect and respect the 'socio-cultural integrity' of indigenous peoples.[19] For example, the Commission has noted that: 'extractive concessions in indigenous territories, in having the potential of causing ecological damage, endanger the economic interests, survival, and cultural integrity of the indigenous communities and their members (...).'[20] Overall, both the Inter-American Court and Commission have made several references to the need to protect the integrity of indigenous peoples' cultures, highlighting how this concept of integrity is relevant in ensuring a holistic approach to indigenous peoples' rights.

One the clearest judicial expressions of the right to cultural integrity and its content comes from the 2010 decision of the African Commission on Human and Peoples' Rights in the Endorois case against Kenya.[21] In this case, the Endorois, an indigenous pastoralist community, claimed that access to their ancestral territory 'in addition to securing subsistence and livelihood, is seen as sacred, being inextricably linked to the *cultural integrity* of the community and its traditional way of life.'[22] As highlighted in their pleadings, access to their traditional lands relates to 'health, livelihood, religion and culture', as they 'are all intimately connected with their traditional land, as grazing lands, sacred religious sites and plants used for traditional medicine are all situated around the shores of Lake Bogoria.'[23] Lake Bogoria, which has been inscribed to the World Heritage List,[24] is part of the traditional territory of the Endorois and constitutes an essential element of their cultural heritage. They argued that by removing them from their land, and not allowing access to this important

19 IACHR, Third Report on the Human Rights Situation in Colombia. Doc. OEA/Ser.L/V/II.102, Doc. 9 rev. 1, 26 February 1999, Chapter IX, para. 37. IACHR, Report on the Situation of Human Rights in Brazil, Doc. OEA/Ser.L/V/II.97, Doc. 29 rev. 1, September 29, 1997, para. 47.

20 IACHR, 'Indigenous and Tribal Peoples' Rights over Their Ancestral Lands and Natural Resources: Norms and Jurisprudence of the Inter-American Human Rights System' (2009) OEA/Ser.L/V/II. Doc. 56/09 at para. 206.

21 African Commission on Human and Peoples' Rights, Centre for Minority Rights Development (Kenya) and Minority Rights Group International on behalf of Endorois Welfare Council v. Kenya, Communication 276/2003 (2010).

22 Ibid., para. 16, emphasis added.

23 Ibid., para. 16.

24 On this issue, see: African Commission on Human and Peoples' Rights, Resolution on the Protection of Indigenous Peoples' Rights in the Context of the World Heritage Convention and the Designation of Lake Bogoria as a World Heritage site, November 2011 in Banjul, The Gambia.

site, the government had violated their fundamental right to cultural integrity. There is no specific provision in the African Charter on Human and Peoples' Rights referring to a 'right to cultural integrity'. Instead the Endorois claimed that their removal meant a violation of their right to practice their own religion (Article 8), their right to culture (Article 17) and their right to access natural resources (Article 21). They nonetheless put forward the argument that all these rights were to be regarded as part of their right to cultural integrity.

The Endorois argued that the decision to remove them from their traditional territories was directly affecting their right to religious freedom. Access to Lake Bogoria plays an important role in the spiritual tradition of the Endorois, as it is a place of an annual ritual and at the centre of other important places of worship for the community. The Endorois contended that their dispossession amounted to a violation of Article 8 of the African Charter which states: 'Freedom of conscience, the profession and free practice of religion shall be guaranteed. No one may, subject to law and order, be submitted to measures restricting the exercise of these freedoms.' They claimed that their spiritual beliefs and ceremonial practices attached to the land constitute a religion. They highlighted that an indigenous group whose spiritual belief is intimately tied to the land requires special protection that should fall under the protection of freedom to practice a religion. By not allowing them to access their ancestral spiritual sites, the Government had violated their right to practice their religion.

The African Commission did recognise that the concerned territory was a significant spiritual place for the community on the basis that the Endorois regularly hold religious ceremonies at several spiritual sites situated around Lake Bogoria, and that their ancestors are buried near the Lake. The Commission acknowledged that 'religion is often linked to land, cultural beliefs and practices, and that freedom to worship and engage in such ceremonial acts is at the centre of the freedom of religion.'[25] Taking into consideration the Human Rights Committee's General Comments on religion,[26] as well as its own jurisprudence,[27] the Commission accepted that the Endorois' spiritual beliefs and ceremonial practices constitute a religion under the African Charter. The African Commission found that the restriction imposed on the Endorois to

25 Ibid., para. 166.

26 Human Rights Committee, General Comment 22, Article 18 (Forty-eighth session, 1993), Compilation of General Comments and General Recommendations Adopted by Human Rights Treaty Bodies, U.N. Doc. HRI\ GEN\1\ Rev.1 (1994).

27 See *Free Legal Assistance Group v. Zaire, African Commission on Human and Peoples Rights*, Comm. No. 25/89, 47/90, 56/91, 100/93 (1995).

practice their religion was a significant restriction to their freedom of religion that was not justified by any significant public security interest or other justification. The Commission concluded that Kenya had violated Article 8 of the African Charter since their forced eviction from their ancestral land 'interfered with the Endorois' right to religious freedom and removed them from the sacred grounds essential to the practice of their religion, and rendered it virtually impossible for the Community to maintain religious practices central to their culture and religion.'[28] This recognition that access to a territory is part of the freedom to practice their religion for indigenous peoples is an important statement at the international level, since little jurisprudence exists on such a correlation.[29]

The spiritual attachment to their territory was only one part of the Endorois' claim that their displacement was violating their right to cultural integrity. The second focus was on cultural rights. The community contended that their eviction from their ancestral lands was a violation of their right to enjoy their own culture, protected under the African Charter in Article 17 (2) which states: 'Every individual may freely, take part in the cultural life of his community.' They argued that 'Article 17 extends to the protection of indigenous cultures and ways of life' and that by encroaching on their land rights, the government had committed a violation of their cultural rights.[30] The issue was to define whether access to a territory could be regarded as part of the cultural life of the community. The Commission found that the Government had violated the Endorois' right to take part in the cultural life of their community, and highlighted that in general States have an obligation to ensure that the access of indigenous communities to their traditional territories is protected under Article 17 of the African Charter as constituting cultural rights. The Commission concluded that the Government had 'denied the community access to an integrated system of beliefs, values, norms, mores, traditions and artefacts closely linked to access to the Lake.'[31] This broader approach to cultural rights

28 Ibid., para. 173.

29 For references, see: J. Briones, 'We Want to Believe Too: The IRFA and Indigenous Peoples' Right to Freedom of Religion'; 8 U. C. Davis J. Int'l L. & Pol'y 0 (2002); N.I. Goduka and J.E. Kunnie (eds.), *Indigenous Peoples' Wisdom and Power: Affirming Our Knowledge Through Narratives* (Ashgate, 2006); J.L. Cox, *From Primitive to Indigenous: The Academic Study of Indigenous Religions* (Ashgate, 2007); P.P. Arnold and A. Grodzins Gold (eds.), *Sacred Landscapes and Cultural Politics: Planting a Tree* (Ashgate, 2001).

30 Endorois Decision, supra note 21, para. 115.

31 Ibid., para. 250.

integrates the indigenous peoples' claim that cultural rights are part of their way of life, which includes access to land central to their own culture.

Another important aspect of the Endorois decision was the connection between cultural rights and access to natural resources. One of the arguments put forward by the community was that by restricting the access to their natural resources, the government was not respecting the cultural heritage of the Endorois, which includes the use of these resources. The land around Lake Bogoria is a fertile soil and rich in salt licks providing great support to the cattle, which represent an important aspect of the pastoralist way of life of the community. The lack of access to these specific lands, the water and the salt licks resulted in serious loss of cattle for the Endorois. Beyond the economic aspect of the restriction, one of the arguments put forward by the community was that this infringement was disrupting their pastoralist way of life, an important element of their cultural heritage, and therefore encroaching on their right to cultural integrity. In the view of the Commission, this restriction constituted a violation of the community's cultural rights since 'by forcing the community to live on semi-arid lands without access to medicinal salt licks and other vital resources for the health of their livestock, the Respondent State have [*sic*] created a major threat to the Endorois pastoralist way of life.'[32] For the African Commission, this constituted a violation of Article 21 of the African Charter which states that 'all peoples shall freely dispose of their wealth and natural resources.' In finding a violation of Article 21, the Commission did acknowledge that the right to freely dispose of natural resources is of crucial importance to indigenous peoples and their way of life.[33] On this issue, the decision is based on the rationale that access to natural resources is a fundamental aspect of cultural heritage of the concerned indigenous community. While not directly mentioning cultural heritage, the Commission made a clear link between indigenous peoples' rights to use natural resources found on their ancestral territories and their cultural way of life. From this perspective it represents an important connection between a traditional way of using natural resources (in this case salt licks) and the cultural heritage of a community. The vehicle used by the Commission to make such connection between natural resources and cultural heritage was the reference to the right to cultural integrity of the community.

32 Endorois Decision, supra note 21, para. 251.

33 On the correlation between cultural rights and access to natural resources, see also: *Social and Economic Rights Action Center and the Center for Economic, and Social Rights/Nigeria*, Communication No. 155/96.

This decision of the African Commission clearly supports the recognition of a 'right to cultural integrity' for indigenous peoples. It shows how the different rights that are relevant to indigenous peoples' cultural heritage, in this case religion, culture and natural resources should be considered under the same umbrella of cultural integrity rather than divided and clustered into different rights. This decision embraced the evolution towards the affirmation of a right to cultural integrity, developing its own approach to the meaning and content of such a right. The decision indicates that the right to cultural integrity is now to be considered part of the Commission's jurisprudence based on freedom of religion (Article 8), right to culture (Article 17), and access to natural resources (Article 21). This marks an important evolution towards a holistic approach to the recognition of indigenous peoples' cultural heritage. The right to cultural integrity fully integrates the holistic approach that indigenous peoples have with their cultural heritage, which is rooted in their spiritual, cultural, economic and social norms, and which is central to the integrity and survival of their culture.

3 From Cultural Genocide to Cultural Integrity

Another important aspect of the development of a right to cultural integrity, relates to the debates that took place around the issue of cultural genocide. Many indigenous peoples have highlighted that their cultural heritage is essential for their survival as a people, indeed physical survival is connected to their cultural survival as distinct people. The importance of protecting indigenous peoples against the threat of cultural annihilation was at the heart of one of the debates that dominated the 22-year long process that finally led to the adoption of the UNDRIP. An important debate focused on the inclusion of cultural genocide within the text of the Declaration.[34]

Cultural genocide broadly refers to 'the extermination of a culture that does not involve physical extermination of its people.'[35] Cultural genocide is based on the idea that a group can be destroyed by targeted attacks on its capacity

34 See: S. Mako, 'Cultural Genocide and Key International Instruments: Framing the Indigenous Experience', 19 International Journal on Minority and Group Rights (2012) 175-194; and J. Gilbert, 'Perspectives on Cultural Genocide: From Criminal Law to Cultural Diversity', in M. de Guzman and D. Amann (eds.), *Arcs of Global Justice; Essays in Honor of William A. Schabas* (Oxford University Press, 2016).

35 K. Jonassohn and F. Chalk, 'A Typology of Genocide and some Implications for the Human Rights Agenda' in I. Wallimann, M.N. Dobkowski, R.L. Rubenstein (eds), *Genocide*

to preserve and transmit its own specific culture which would then disappear. The destruction of indigenous peoples' cultures can take many forms, including forced relocation, removal of children from their communities, invasion of their lands, aggressive assimilationist policies, or restriction to access to their traditional means of livelihoods. The need to protect indigenous peoples against cultural attacks against them did represent an important aspect of the drafting of the UNDRIP. The proposal was to include a strong protection against cultural genocide, with notably the aim of preserving the cultural integrity of indigenous peoples. In an earlier draft of the Declaration submitted in 1994 to the former Commission on Human Rights, a specific article was dedicated to the crime of cultural genocide stating:

> Indigenous peoples have the collective and individual right not to be subjected to ethnocide and cultural genocide, including prevention of and redress for any action which has the aim or effect of depriving them of their integrity as distinct peoples, or of their cultural values or ethnic identities (...).[36]

During the drafting process, several indigenous representatives had notably highlighted that their removal from their traditional territories and the loss of access to their cultural heritage often amounted to cultural genocide, as the practice of dispossession, forced relocation or population transfer amounted to the destruction of their community.[37] However, the reference to cultural genocide led to serious debates when it reached States' representatives. Some of the member States, including the United States, Norway, New Zealand and Canada, called for the use of an alternative language noting that cultural genocide was not defined under international law.[38] This debate went back to earlier discussions during the drafting of the Convention on the Prevention and Punishment of the Crime of Genocide in 1948, when cultural genocide was

---

and the Modern Age: Etiology and case studies of Mass Death (Syracuse University Press, 1987), p. 11.

36 UN Doc. E/CN.4/Sub.2/1994/56, UN Draft Declaration on the Rights of Indigenous Peoples, Article 7.

37 See: UN Doc. E/CN.4/2002/98, p. 18.

38 United Nations High Commissioner for Human Rights, Indigenous Issues: Report of the Working Group Established in Accordance with Commission on Human Rights Resolution 1995/32 , UN Doc. E/CN.4/2003/92, 2003.

rejected from the text of the convention.[39] Ultimately, the draft article on cultural genocide was removed from the text.[40]

Instead, the adopted text affirms that indigenous peoples have 'the right not to be subjected to forced assimilation or destruction of their culture.' Article 7(2) asserts that 'indigenous peoples have the collective right to live in freedom, peace and security as distinct peoples and shall not be subjected to any act of genocide or any other act of violence, including forcibly removing children of the group to another group.' But cultural genocide as such was rejected. Despite the rejection of cultural genocide, the Declaration still makes reference to cultural attacks against indigenous peoples, since Article 8 states: 'indigenous peoples and individuals have the right not to be subjected to forced assimilation or destruction of their culture.' Getting into more details, the text adds that States shall provide effective mechanisms for prevention of, and redress for: 'any action which has the aim or effect of depriving them of their *integrity* as distinct peoples, or of their cultural values or ethnic identities (...).'[41] This reference to integrity as distinct peoples puts the emphasis on the need to ensure the survival of indigenous peoples, not only physically but also as cultural entities. It is significant as, despite the rejection of cultural genocide from the text of the Declaration, it does put the emphasis on the need to consider all attacks against indigenous peoples, and not only physical, which have the effect of touching on the integrity of their cultural structures and heritage. As noted by Vrdoljak, in providing a clear statement against assimilation and cultural destruction, this article straddles 'the divide between the international crime of genocide and positive human rights related to culture and cultural heritage.'[42]

39 See: W. Schabas, *Genocide in International Law* (Cambridge University Press, 2nd ed., 2009).

40 See: J.M. Hohmann, 'The UNDRIP and the Rights of Indigenous Peoples to Existence, Cultural Integrity and Identity, and Non-Assimilation', in *Oxford Commentaries on International Law – A Commentary on the United Nations Declaration on the Rights of Indigenous Peoples* (OUP, Forthcoming 2016).

41 UNDRIP, article 8 (2), emphasis added.

42 A. Vrdoljak, 'Reparations for Cultural Loss', in F. Lenzerini (ed.), *Reparations for Indigenous Peoples: International & Comparative Perspectives* (Oxford University Press, 2008), p. 209.

4 Cultural Integrity and Traditional Cultural Practices

As noted earlier, an important avenue of protection for the cultural heritage of indigenous peoples comes under the minority rights approach to cultural practices developed under article 27 of the International Covenant on Civil and Political Rights (ICCPR). This article provides for the right of members of minorities to enjoy their own culture, practice their own religion and use their own language. This article has been interpreted to be particularly protecting the traditional way of life of indigenous peoples. The connection between cultural rights and indigenous peoples constitutes one of the strong features of the Human Rights Committee's (HRC) interpretation of article 27 of the ICCPR. In an often-quoted general comment on article 27 the HRC stated:

> With regard to the exercise of the cultural rights protected under article 27, the Committee observes that culture manifests itself in many forms, including a particular way of life associated with the use of land resources, especially in the case of indigenous peoples. That right may include such traditional activities as fishing or hunting and the right to live in reserves protected by law.[43]

The strong connection between cultural rights, and notably cultural practices from indigenous peoples, has been reiterated in several concluding observations and individual communications of the Committee.[44] There have been many individual complaints throughout the 1990s, and some of these individual decisions such as Ominayak v Canada,[45] Lansman v Finland,[46] and Lovelace v Canada[47] have become key elements of the international jurisprudence and doctrine regarding the connection between cultural rights and a traditional way of life. Under this approach, any traditional activity that is forming an essential element of indigenous peoples' culture should be protected. The main approach of the Committee has been to ensure the right of indigenous peoples

43 Human Rights Committee, General Comment 23, Article 27 (Fiftieth session, 1994), Compilation of General Comments and General Recommendations Adopted by Human Rights Treaty Bodies, UN Doc. HRI/GEN/1/Rev.1 at 38 (1994), para. 7.

44 See: Indigenous Peoples and United Nations Human Rights Treaty Bodies: A Compilation of Treaty Body Jurisprudence Volume (Forest Peoples Programme).

45 UN Doc. CCPR/C/60/D/549/1993/Rev. 1, Communication No. 549/1993.

46 UN Doc. CCPR/C/52/D/511/1992, Case No 511/1992.

47 A/36/40, Annex 7(G) (1998).

to maintain and practice traditional activities which form part of their cultural heritage.

One of the difficulties for the HRC was to determine the meaning of 'an activity forming an essential element of indigenous peoples' culture'. Two main issues have been raised before the Committee regarding the meaning of a traditional activity. The first relates to defining whether activities that have an economical aspect could qualify as cultural practices. For example in a case relating reindeer herding by the Sami populations in Sweden, one of the arguments developed by the government was that reindeer herding was more an economic, rather than a purely cultural activity. On this point the HRC concluded that: 'the regulation of an economic activity is normally a matter for the State alone. However, where that activity is an essential element in the culture of an ethnic community, its application to an individual may fall under article 27 of the Covenant.'[48] This was later confirmed in other cases in which the HRC re-affirmed that economic activities may come within the ambit of article 27, if they are an essential element of the culture of an indigenous community, including for example fishing, herding, and hunting.

The other issue that was raised before the Committee relates to the definition of the meaning of a 'traditional' activity. Indeed, some of the States have raised the fact that some of the activities undertaken by indigenous peoples were not 'traditional' anymore as they were using modern technology. For example, this was raised regarding the use of skidoos and helicopters by reindeer herders, or nets for fishing. On this issue, in a case concerning Sami communities in Finland, the HRC highlighted: 'that the authors may have adapted their methods of reindeer herding over the years and practice it with the help of modern technology does not prevent them from invoking article 27 of the Covenant.'[49] Likewise, in a case concerning fisheries in New Zealand, the HRC re-affirmed 'that article 27 does not only protect traditional means of livelihood of minorities, but allows also for adaptation of those means to the modern way of life and ensuing technology.'[50] In adopting such an approach the Committee highlighted that the notion of culture, as protected under article 27, is not static; while it does protect traditional cultural practices, these practices may have nevertheless evolved over the centuries. Importantly, avoiding the danger

48 Ivan Kitok v. Sweden, Communication No. 197/1985, CCPR/C/33/D/197/1985 (1988), para. 9.2.

49 Länsman et al. v. Finland, Communication No. 511/1992, U.N. Doc. CCPR/C/52/D/511/1992 (1994), para. 9.3.

50 Apirana Mahuika et al. v. New Zealand, Communication No. 547/1993, UN Doc. CCPR/C/70/D/547/1993 (2000), para. 9.4

of adopting a very rigid, or 'frozen' approach to the meaning of cultural activities, the committee has consistently been highlighting that indigenous peoples who adapt their methods of traditional activities over the years and practice it with the help of modern technology are not prevented from invoking international covenant protections.[51] As described by the Australian Aboriginal and Torres Strait Islanders Social Justice Commissioner: '[T]he right to enjoy a culture is not 'frozen' at some point in time when culture was supposedly 'pure' or 'traditional'. The enjoyment of culture should not be falsely restricted as a result of anachronistic notions of the 'authenticity' of the culture.'[52]

In adopting a 'non-frozen' approach to cultural practices, the HRC has touched on the debate relating to the 'authenticity' of a cultural practice. The notion of 'authenticity' is a term often used in cultural heritage studies, but also by museum curators or the tourism industry.[53] It refers to the idea of an 'authentic' culture rather than a 'modern' form of culture, meaning a culture which has not been affected or 'contaminated' by the outside and modern world.[54] Hence authenticity is quite a rigid approach to culture as it evaluates a culture from a static perspective. In rejecting such an approach based on 'authenticity' of cultural practices, the HRC has instead highlighted that the integrity of indigenous peoples' practices should be respected. As such, human rights law has clearly balanced towards an approach favouring the integrity of indigenous peoples' cultural practices rather than putting too much emphasis on so-called authenticity. This approach is extremely important as it highlights that human rights law is able to support traditional activities as part of cultural heritage in a modern sense, an approach respecting the integrity of indigenous peoples' cultural heritage. Protecting indigenous peoples' cultural heritage has to be intertemporal, not fixed in the past, but allowing contemporary expression of cultural practices to be recognised as such. This not only rejects a traditional approach which was often focusing too much on protecting the material and immaterial heritage of the past,[55] it also supports the claim made by many indigenous advocates to the right to re-vitalize their cultural heritage.

---

51 Ilmari Lansman et al. v. Finland. CCPR/C/52/D/511/1992 (1994) at [9.3].

52 Report of the Aboriginal and Torres Strait Islanders Social Justice Commissioner to the Attorney General, Aboriginal and Torres Strait Islander Social Justice Commissioner, Native Title Report 2000.

53 See: A J McIntosh, R C Prentice, 'Affirming authenticity: Consuming cultural heritage', 26(3) Annals of tourism research 589-612 (1999); R. Handler, 'Authenticity', 2(1) Anthropology today 2-4 (1986).

54 See: E. Cohen, 'Authenticity and commoditization in tourism' 15.3. Annals of tourism research 371-386 (1988).

55 L. Smith, *Uses of Heritage* (London: Routledge 2006), p. 17.

Conclusion

The legal framework protecting cultural heritage for indigenous peoples is fragmented into a multitude of different approaches, making the holistic approach to cultural heritage for indigenous peoples difficult to apprehend. The right to cultural integrity captures such a holistic approach by being a composite right which incorporates all the different norms that are relevant to protect indigenous peoples' cultural heritage. As stated earlier, although this right is not strictly speaking integrated into international human rights norms, in recent years it has been used as a legal concept encapsulating all the different aspects that are essential to indigenous peoples' cultural rights. The affirmation of the right to cultural integrity involves the recognition that culture for indigenous peoples is much more than the traditional expression of culture, as it also embraces the social and spiritual values embedded in their territorial connections. As demonstrated by the African Commission's decision in the Endorois case, the right to cultural integrity formally recognises the connection between access to ancestral territories and freedom of religion, cultural rights, and the right to access natural resources. The Inter-American Court and Commission have both put the emphasis on the need for States to recognise and protect indigenous peoples' cultural integrity, highlighting the importance to embrace a comprehensive and holistic approach to indigenous peoples' cultural rights. In terms of law making, the American Declaration on the Rights of Indigenous Peoples adopted in 2016 includes a specific article on the right to cultural integrity. It states: 'Indigenous peoples have the right to their own cultural identity and integrity and to their cultural heritage, both tangible and intangible, including historic and ancestral heritage; and to the protection, preservation, maintenance, and development of that cultural heritage for their collective continuity and that of their members and so as to transmit that heritage to future generations.'[56] This article connecting cultural integrity and cultural heritage makes an important contribution towards the firm establishment of a holistic approach to cultural heritage protection. It is true that such developments towards the affirmation of a right to cultural integrity are mainly emerging from regional human rights institutions, but when it comes to indigenous peoples' rights, regional institutions, and notably the Inter-American Commission and Court, have often paved the way for further development of international law. Moreover, as highlighted in this chapter, the

56 Organization of American States (OAS), American Declaration on the Rights of Indigenous Peoples, adopted at the third plenary session, held on June 15, 2016, AG/RES. 2888 (XLVI-O/16), Article XXIII.

notion of integrity and the need to ensure indigenous peoples' rights to both their physical and cultural integrity is also integrated in the UNDRIP. Likewise, the comprehensive approach of the HRC to indigenous peoples' cultural rights relies on the important notion of respecting the integrity of indigenous peoples' culture rather than focusing on its so-called authenticity. All these markers are indicating the slow maturing of a right to cultural integrity, which would support a much more cohesive and holistic approach to cultural heritage. The emergence of the concept of a right to cultural integrity supports a new normative approach to cultural heritage by offering a holistic approach to the meaning and content of cultural rights, notably relying on the spiritual, tangible, intangible, and natural aspects of cultural heritage. It is innovative in the sense that it supports a holistic approach to cultural heritage, something that is still missing in the international legal architecture.

Indigenous Cultural Heritage in the Implementation of UNESCO's World Heritage Convention: Opportunities, Obstacles and Challenges

Stefan Disko

Introduction

A substantial part of the 2015 study by the UN Expert Mechanism on the Rights of Indigenous Peoples ('EMRIP') on the promotion and protection of the rights of indigenous peoples with respect to their cultural heritage[1] is dedicated to a discussion of UNESCO's 1972 Convention Concerning the Protection of the World Cultural and Natural Heritage ('World Heritage Convention', or 'the Convention'). The study also contains several important recommendations on World Heritage, aimed at ensuring that the implementation of the Convention is consistent with the UN Declaration on the Rights of Indigenous Peoples ('UNDRIP') and that the protection of World Heritage sites 'does not undermine indigenous peoples' relationship with their traditional lands, territories and resources, their livelihoods and their rights to protect, exercise and develop their cultural heritage and expressions'.[2] Related recommendations of EMRIP are contained in its 2011 Study on indigenous peoples and the right to participate in decision-making,[3] and a 2012 proposal adopted on the occasion of the Convention's 40th anniversary.[4] The other two UN mechanisms with specific mandates concerning indigenous peoples, the Permanent Forum on Indigenous Issues ('UNPFII') and the Special Rapporteur on the Rights of Indigenous Peoples, have also issued a number of recommendations on World Heritage in recent years.[5]

---

1 UN Doc A/HRC/30/53.

2 Ibid, annex, para. 27.

3 UN Doc A/HRC/18/42, annex, para. 38.

4 EMRIP, Report on its fifth session (2011) UN Doc A/HRC/21/52, 7 (Proposal 9).

5 See, e.g., UNPFII, Report on the tenth session (2011) UN Doc E/2011/43, paras. 40-42; UNPFII, Report on the twelfth session (2013) UN Doc. E/2013/43, para. 23; Report of the Special Rapporteur on the rights of indigenous peoples, James Anaya (2012) UN Doc

Xanthaki, Valkonen et al. (eds.), *Indigenous Peoples' Cultural Heritage: Rights, Debates and Challenges.*

The reason for the growing attention paid by the three UN mechanisms to the World Heritage Convention are the repeated concerns raised by indigenous peoples about violations of their rights in the implementation of the Convention and a lack of regard for their cultural heritage, livelihoods and values in the nomination and protection of World Heritage sites. Considering the increasingly large number of World Heritage sites that are fully or partially located within the traditional territories of indigenous peoples,[6] the importance and urgency of this matter is evident.

The engagement of the three mechanisms with the World Heritage Convention is all the more important given that the Convention is not only the most widely known and ratified, but also the most influential international standard-setting instrument in the field of heritage. Although its application is limited to a relatively narrow range of heritage, namely immovable, tangible heritage of 'outstanding universal value' (i.e. World Heritage sites), it has shaped current understandings of heritage and contemporary practices of heritage management to a greater extent than any other international instrument. A main reason for this can be seen in the Convention's claim to the universality of the values it seeks to protect.[7] Because of this claim, it has been necessary for the World Heritage Committee ('WHC', or 'the Committee'), the Convention's governing body,[8] to constantly adapt and redefine the notion of 'heritage' under the Convention, in order to accommodate different peoples' understandings and values and protect the Convention's credibility as an instrument

A/67/301, paras. 33-42; Letter of the Special Rapporteur, James Anaya, to the World Heritage Committee (18 November 2013) OTH 10/2013, UN Doc A/HRC/25/74, 127.

6 Establishing an exact number of the indigenous sites is difficult. The author estimates that there are around a hundred such sites. Additionally, a large number of indigenous sites are included on States Parties' tentative lists of potential World Heritage sites in their territories. See <http://whc.unesco.org/en/list> and <http://whc.unesco.org/en/tentativelists>.

7 As proclaimed in articles 1 and 2 defining the scope of the Convention, but also in several other places including the Preamble.

8 The WHC is an intergovernmental body consisting of 21 States Parties to the Convention. Established 'within' UNESCO according to the Convention (art 8.1), the WHC is assisted by UNESCO's World Heritage Centre, which functions as its secretariat. The WHC also has three official advisory bodies, all of whom are mentioned in the Convention text (arts 8, 13, 14): the International Union for Conservation of Nature (IUCN), the International Council on Monuments and Sites (ICOMOS), and the International Centre for the Study of the Preservation and Restoration of Cultural Property (ICCROM). On the roles of the Advisory Bodies, see Operational Guidelines for the Implementation of the World Heritage Convention (2015) Doc WHC.15/01, paras. 30-37.

equally representative of all the peoples and cultures of the world. This process 'has had a profound effect on global practices of heritage management… and on contemporary definitions of heritage', as Rodney Harrison notes.[9]

Some of the strongest criticism over the years of the concept of heritage embodied in the Convention has come from indigenous peoples and has related to its separation of natural and cultural heritage and its focus on tangible aspects at the expense of intangible aspects. As emphasized in EMRIP's study on cultural heritage, 'for indigenous peoples, cultural heritage is holistic and encompasses their spiritual, economic and social connections to their lands and territories'.[10] Therefore, '[h]eritage policies, programmes and activities affecting indigenous peoples should be based on full recognition of the inseparability of natural and cultural heritage, and the deep-seated interconnectedness of intangible cultural heritage and tangible cultural and natural heritage.'[11] The criticism voiced by indigenous peoples has significantly contributed to some important developments in the implementation of the notion of 'cultural heritage' under the Convention.[12] However, as will be discussed in more detail below, these developments have not been adequate for ensuring that indigenous cultural values are consistently and adequately taken into account in the designation and management of World Heritage sites, and have therefore not been effective in resolving indigenous peoples' concerns.

Nevertheless, the World Heritage Convention can be, and in some cases has undoubtedly been, an important tool for the promotion and protection of the rights of indigenous peoples with respect to their cultural heritage. World Heritage sites can help indigenous peoples protect their lands, territories and resources, and the associated cultural heritage, from development pressures such as extractive industry activities or threats posed by major infrastructure projects. Also, the international attention and oversight resulting from World

9 R Harrison, *Heritage: Critical Approaches* (Routledge 2013) 116.

10 Study on cultural heritage (n 1) para. 24. Accordingly, there is 'strong recognition within international human rights law and jurisprudence that cultural rights for indigenous peoples entail rights to land and natural resources, and that there is an obligation to protect the cultural heritage of indigenous peoples through recognition of their rights to own, control and manage their ancestral territories'. J Gilbert, 'Indigenous Peoples' Heritage and Human Rights' in S Disko and H Tugendhat (eds), *World Heritage Sites and Indigenous Peoples' Rights* (IWGIA 2014) 55, 58.

11 Study on cultural heritage (n 1), annex, para. 6. Similarly, E-I Daes, 'Study on the protection of the cultural and intellectual property of indigenous peoples' (1993) UN Doc E/CN.4/Sub.2/1993/28, paras. 31, 164.

12 See Harrison (n 9) 118-39; K Whitby-Last, 'Article 1: Cultural Landscapes' in F Francioni (ed), *The 1972 World Heritage Convention: A Commentary* (OUP 2008) 51, 59.

Heritage listing can potentially be used to encourage improved indigenous participation in decision-making processes, enhanced benefit-sharing, or redress for past violations of indigenous rights.[13] Moreover, due to its prominence and influence the World Heritage Convention has the potential to play an important role in promoting respect for indigenous rights in heritage sites and conservation practice more generally. As noted by the IUCN[14] World Conservation Congress, the Convention 'can and has played a leadership role in setting standards for protected areas as a whole and… World Heritage sites with their high visibility and public scrutiny have the potential to act as "flagships" for good governance in protected areas'.[15]

It is clear, however, that the Convention's potential to contribute to the promotion of respect for indigenous rights is largely not being realized. On the contrary, the protection of World Heritage has in many cases aggravated or consolidated indigenous peoples' loss of control over their lands and resources, led to restrictions on traditional land-use practices, and undermined their livelihoods. In many World Heritage sites, indigenous peoples are primarily considered as threats, or potential threats, to conservation objectives. For the Convention to play a consistently positive role for indigenous peoples, several serious shortcomings in its implementation need to be rectified. These shortcomings include, among other things, the differentiation between natural and cultural heritage in World Heritage sites incorporating indigenous peoples' territories; a highly problematic application of the concept of 'outstanding universal value' ('OUV'); and a lack of regulations and appropriate mechanisms to ensure the meaningful participation of indigenous peoples in Convention processes affecting them.

---

13 See, e.g., WHC Decisions 39 COM 7B.5 (2015), para. 5 (Lake Bogoria National Reserve, Kenya); 37 COM 7B.30 (2013), para. 8b (Talamanca Range-La Amistad Reserves/National Park, Costa Rica/Panama); 35 COM 7B.34 (2011), para. 4d (Manu National Park, Peru); 33 COM 7B.9 (2009), para. 7 (Ngorongoro Conservation Area, Tanzania); 35 COM 12E (2011), paras. 15e, 15f (generally).

14 The International Union for Conservation of Nature (IUCN) is the world's oldest and largest global environmental network, with more than 1,300 government and non-governmental member organizations. Its highest decision-making body is its members' assembly, the quadrennial 'World Conservation Congress'. IUCN functions as the WHC's official advisory body on natural heritage (see n 8).

15 IUCN World Conservation Congress, 'Implementation of the United Nations Declaration on the Rights of Indigenous Peoples in the context of the UNESCO World Heritage Convention' Res. 5.047 (Jeju 2012) preamble.

Problematic Separation of Natural and Cultural Heritage

The World Heritage Convention is remarkable in that it establishes a common regime for the protection of natural and cultural heritage, and is widely celebrated for its 'unprecedented recognition of the close link between culture and nature'.[16] In fact, UNESCO considers this the most significant feature of the Convention:

> The most significant feature of the 1972 World Heritage Convention is that it links together in a single document the concepts of nature conservation and the preservation of cultural properties. The Convention recognizes the way in which people interact with nature, and the fundamental need to preserve the balance between the two.[17]

These ideas are also reflected in the official emblem of the Convention (Figure 1), which symbolizes the interdependence of cultural and natural heritage. While the central square is meant to represent the results of human skill and inspiration, the circle represents nature, 'the two being intimately linked'.[18] The emblem was adopted by the WHC in 1978 and is supposed to 'symbolize for future generations the principles embodied in the Convention' and 'conve[y] the essential objectives of the Convention'.[19]

FIGURE 1 *World Heritage Emblem*

However, the experiences of many indigenous peoples with World Heritage sites established in their territories stand in sharp contrast to these ideas and objectives and throw into question the ways in which the Convention is being implemented. Despite its recognition of the interdependence of cultural and natural heritage, the WHC maintains a separation between 'cultural' and 'natural' World Heritage sites which is highly problematic in the context of many sites, and in particular those within indigenous peoples' territories.

16 F Francioni, 'Introduction' in Francioni (n 12) 3, 5.

17 UNESCO, 'The World Heritage Convention' <http://whc.unesco.org/en/convention> accessed 21 April 2015.

18 UNESCO, Report on the second session of the WHC (Washington D.C., 1978) CC-78/CONF.010/10 Rev, para. 51.

19 Ibid, para. 53. Also see Operational Guidelines 2015 (n 8) para. 258.

The vast majority of World Heritage sites in indigenous peoples' territories are listed as natural sites, without any recognition of associated indigenous heritage values in the justification for inscription and in contrast to indigenous peoples' holistic view of their heritage. This lack of respect for indigenous peoples' own values attached to their lands, territories and resources not only raises serious questions regarding the validity of the meanings attributed to the respective sites by UNESCO, but can also have significant adverse effects on the livelihoods, living cultural heritage and well-being of the indigenous peoples concerned. Indigenous peoples have therefore repeatedly pointed to the need for concerted action by the WHC to ensure that due recognition and attention is given to indigenous values in the nomination, declaration and management of World Heritage sites.[20]

The Concept of Heritage in the Convention

The underlying reason for the WHC's differentiation between cultural and natural World Heritage sites lies in the text of the World Heritage Convention itself, more concretely, the definition of heritage contained in the Convention. The Convention establishes a rigid distinction between cultural and natural heritage by defining them separately, in Articles 1 and 2 respectively. Thus, 'the architecture of the Convention perpetuates the dichotomy between cultural and natural heritage', as Kathryn Whitby-Last notes.[21]

In accordance with Article 11(2) of the Convention, the World Heritage List is comprised of sites that fall within the definitions of Articles 1 or 2 and which the WHC 'considers as having outstanding universal value in terms of such criteria as it shall have established'. One of the first tasks completed by the WHC, at its first session in 1977, was the adoption of two separate sets of criteria for the determination of OUV: six criteria related to cultural heritage (i-vi) and four criteria related to natural heritage (i-iv).[22] On this basis, the Committee maintains its distinction between cultural and natural World Heritage sites, the classification of a given site depending on the criteria under which it is inscribed on the World Heritage List or nominated for inscription. Although there is a possibility for sites to be listed as 'mixed' cultural and natural heritage sites, this can only happen when they satisfy both cultural and natural criteria

20 See, e.g., the 2000/2001 proposal by indigenous peoples that a 'World Heritage Indigenous Peoples Council of Experts (WHIPCOE)' be established as a consultative body to the Committee. UNESCO, Report on the Proposed WHIPCOE (2001) WHC-2001/CONF.205/WEB.3.

21 Whitby-Last (n 12) 59.

22 UNESCO, Report on the first session of the WHC (Paris, 1977) CC-77/CONF.001/9.

of OUV.[23] The number of mixed sites on the World Heritage List is therefore very small – as of the writing of this chapter, only 32 out of 1,031 World Heritage sites were listed as mixed sites. In any case, inscription as a mixed site does not necessarily reflect a recognition of a symbiosis or interplay between cultural and natural values; the recognized cultural and natural attributes may have only tangential links and may not readily coincide in spatial terms.[24]

It is important to note, however, that the separation between culture and nature in the Convention's definition of heritage is not absolute. Most significantly, the definition of cultural heritage in Article 1 includes a reference to 'combined works of nature and man... which are of outstanding universal value from the historical, aesthetic, ethnological or anthropological point of view'. As will be further discussed below, this provision provides an important basis for the recognition of interrelationships between culture and nature in the context of *cultural* (or mixed) World Heritage sites.

Efforts to Bridge the Divide

There have been various attempts by the WHC to bridge the divide between nature and culture and enable a recognition of nature-culture interlinkages in the implementation of the Convention. Most significantly, in 1977, when the Committee adopted the initial criteria for the determination of OUV, it included a reference to 'man's interaction with his natural environment' into the criteria for natural sites (natural criterion ii), as well as a reference to 'exceptional combinations of natural and cultural elements' (natural criterion iii).[25] These references were invoked in the context of the nomination and inscription of some of the indigenous sites listed as natural World Heritage sites in

23 Operational Guidelines 2015 (n 8) para. 46. When nominations of mixed sites are evaluated, the cultural and natural values are assessed separately, 'almost as if one would be looking at two different nominations'. L Leitão and T Badman, 'Opportunities for Integration of Cultural and Natural Heritage Perspectives under the World Heritage Convention: Towards Connected Practice' in K Taylor, A St Clair and NJ Mitchell (eds), *Conserving Cultural Landscapes: Challenges and New Directions* (Routledge 2015) 75, 82.

24 UNESCO, 'Reflections on processes for mixed nominations' (2014) WHC-14/38.COM/9B, para. 20. Moreover, 'management [of cultural and natural values] may be undertaken separately and through distinct agencies and it is not unusual to find separate management plans in place'. PB Larsen and G Wijesuriya, 'Nature-culture interlinkages in World Heritage: Bridging the gap' (2015) 75 *World Heritage* 4, 10.

25 See Operational Guidelines for the Implementation of the World Heritage Convention (1977) CC-77/CONF.001/8 Rev, 4.

the 1980s, such as Uluṟu-Kata Tjuṯa National Park (Australia) or Manu National Park (Peru).[26]

In 1992, the WHC made some modifications to the cultural criteria to accommodate the listing of 'cultural landscapes'.[27] In addition, a document containing guidance on definitions and categories of cultural landscapes was annexed to the Operational Guidelines for the Implementation of the World Heritage Convention ('Operational Guidelines', or 'the Guidelines').[28] This document clarifies that 'cultural landscapes... represent the "combined works of nature and of man" designated in Article 1 of the *Convention*' and distinguishes between three categories of cultural landscapes: designed, organically evolved and associative cultural landscapes.[29] Inscription of the latter on the World Heritage List is 'justifiable by virtue of the powerful religious, artistic or cultural associations of the natural element rather than material cultural evidence, which may be insignificant or even absent'. The inclusion of the category of associative cultural landscapes is noteworthy as it represents an important move towards the recognition of intangible values in the context of the World Heritage Convention. It has facilitated a better recognition of the cultural and spiritual values indigenous peoples attach to their lands and territories in some World Heritage sites, such as Tongariro National Park (New Zealand), Uluṟu-Kata Tjuṯa National Park and, more recently, Pimachiowin Aki (Canada).[30]

The introduction of the cultural landscapes concept had some serious drawbacks, however. Ironically, it has in some ways contributed to deepening the divide between culture and nature in the implementation of the Convention. First, it can be argued that the concept of cultural landscapes 'actually continues to reinforce this dualism [of culture and nature] through its maintenance

26 For details, see R Layton and S Titchen, 'Uluru: An Outstanding Australian Aboriginal Cultural Landscape' in B von Droste, H Plachter and M Rössler (eds), *Cultural Landscapes of Universal Value – Components of a Global Strategy* (Gustav Fischer 1995) 174, 176; D Rodriguez and C Feather, 'A Refuge for People and Biodiversity: The Case of Manu National Park, South-East Peru' in Disko and Tugendhat (n 10) 459, 467.

27 C Cameron and M Rössler, *Many Voices, One Vision: The Early Years of the World Heritage Convention* (Ashgate 2013) 67-68; Leitão and Badman (n 23) 78.

28 The Operational Guidelines were initially issued in 1977 and are periodically revised by the WHC to reflect new concepts, knowledge or experiences. All historic versions of the Guidelines are available at <http://whc.unesco.org/en/guidelines>. The current version was adopted in July 2015 (Doc WHC.15/01).

29 Operational Guidelines 2015, annex 3.

30 A revised proposal was considered by the Committee in 2016 but decision was deferred after Ontario's Pikangikum First Nation withdrew its support. In January 2017, another proposal for recognition of a smaller area as World heritage Site was submitted.

of the separation of "cultural" and "natural" landscapes – in other words, the "really natural" landscapes are separated from the "cultural" ones', as Harrison notes.[31] This conclusion is supported by the fact that cultural landscapes are treated as cultural sites and inscribed on the World Heritage List under cultural criteria only. Second, and more significantly, concurrent with the introduction of the cultural landscapes category, the WHC deleted the references to 'man's interaction with his natural environment' and 'exceptional combinations of natural and cultural elements' from the text of the natural criteria, based on the consideration that these phrases were inconsistent with the legal definition of natural heritage in Article 2 of the Convention.[32]

These deletions have made it even more difficult, if not impossible, to acknowledge indigenous peoples' relationship with their lands, territories and resources when defining the OUV of natural World Heritage sites[33] and may well have contributed to a denial and curtailment of indigenous peoples' rights to their lands and resources in the designation and management of some natural World Heritage sites. As Robert Layton and Sarah Titchen remarked in 1995:

> We deplore the deletion of references to human agency from the natural heritage criteria. The deletions appear to revive the outmoded concept of wilderness areas purified of human action… We fear that in promoting the idea of wholly natural landscapes, UNESCO may inadvertently deny the continuing traditional use of the natural resources contained within World Heritage properties by indigenous peoples and unwittingly collude in the displacement of indigenous peoples from areas included in the World Heritage List.[34]

---

31 Harrison (n 9) 206. Similarly, Whitby-Last (n 12) 61.

32 Whitby-Last (n 12) 57.

33 It should be noted that in the context of mixed sites, the WHC has recently sometimes referred to cultural and spiritual aspects, human interaction with nature and local people's traditional way of life in the justifications for natural criteria. See the OUV Statements for the Ecosystem and Relict Cultural Landscape of Lopé-Okanda (Gabon), Ancient Maya City and Protected Tropical Forests of Calakmul (Mexico), and Trang An Landscape Complex (Viet Nam). An interesting approach is used in the 2015 revised nomination of Pimachiowin Aki (also a mixed site), where the justification for natural criteria mentions sustainable hunting and trapping by Anishinaabeg as part of ecologically essential predator-prey interactions. <http://www.pimachiowinaki.org/sites/default/files/docs/Pim_Aki_Dossier_2015_tk301_LR%20Jun%209.pdf> accessed 15 October 2015. One case of a natural site inscribed after 1992 where spiritual aspects are mentioned in the justification for criteria is Mount Kenya National Park/Natural Forest (Kenya).

34 Layton and Titchen (n 26) 179-80.

In the late 1990s, the continued lack of recognition of the links between culture and nature and interactions between people and the environment in many World Heritage sites, especially natural sites, was a central focus of the discussions at two important UNESCO expert meetings held at the Parc national de la Vanoise, France (1996) and in Amsterdam (1998).[35] One of the recommendations that came out of these meetings was to reinsert the reference to 'human interaction with the environment' into natural criterion ii,[36] but this recommendation was subsequently discarded by the WHC due to strong opposition from its advisory body on natural heritage, IUCN, who insisted that this was 'essentially a "natural" criterion'.[37] A proposal to add a reference to 'exceptional... spiritual importance' to natural criterion iii[38] was also not accepted. The Committee did accept a suggestion of the Vanoise meeting, however, to add a provision to the Operational Guidelines recognizing that:

> ... no area is totally pristine and that all natural areas are in a dynamic state, and to some extent involve contact with people. Human activities, including those of traditional societies and local communities, often occur in natural areas. These activities may be consistent with the Outstanding Universal Value of the area where they are ecologically sustainable.[39]

Additionally, the WHC took up a recommendation of the two expert meetings to merge the six cultural and four natural criteria into a unified set of ten criteria (i-x), 'to better reflect... the nature/culture continuum'.[40] This was little more than a renumbering procedure though, as it did not entail any real

---

35 UNESCO, 'Report of the expert Meeting on Evaluation of general principles and criteria for nominations of natural World Heritage sites (Parc national de la Vanoise, France, 22-24 March 1996)' (1996) WHC-96/CONF.202/INF.9; 'Report of the World Heritage Global Strategy Natural and Cultural Heritage Expert Meeting, 25-29 March 1998, Theatre Institute, Amsterdam, The Netherlands' (1998) WHC-98/CONF.203/INF.7.

36 Amsterdam report (n 35) 11-13.

37 UNESCO, 'Revision of the Operational Guidelines for the Implementation of the World Heritage Convention' (1999) WHC-99/CONF.204/10, annex I, annex III; 'Report of the International Expert Meeting on the Revision of the Operational Guidelines for the Implementation of the World Heritage Convention (Canterbury, UK, 10-14 April 2000)' (2000) WHC-2000/CONF.204/INF.10, 20-21. There are signs that IUCN may be reconsidering this position. See Leitão and Badman (n 23) 88.

38 Amsterdam report (n 35) 13; Doc WHC-99/CONF.204/10 (n 37) annex III.

39 Operational Guidelines 2015, para. 90. Compare the Vanoise report (n 35) 3.

40 WHC Decision 6 EXT.COM 5.1 (2003) annex, para. 3.2.a); UNESCO, Report on the twenty-third session of the WHC (Marrakesh, 1999) WHC-99/CONF.209/22, 39.

integration among the criteria. The Committee maintained the distinction between cultural and natural criteria and continues to differentiate between 'cultural' and 'natural' World Heritage sites depending on the criteria under which a site is nominated or inscribed.[41] Sites nominated under criteria i-vi are considered cultural sites and evaluated by ICOMOS,[42] whereas sites nominated under criteria vii-x are considered natural sites and evaluated by IUCN. Therefore, '[d]espite the unified set of criteria, the World Heritage system continues to operate as if nothing has changed', as Christina Cameron notes.[43]

The WHC's Advisory Bodies on cultural heritage, ICOMOS and ICCROM,[44] already remarked in 1999 that:

> the amalgamation of the 10 criteria in one consolidated list falls short of the potential which exists to fuse consideration of cultural and natural values within individual criteria. While adoption of such an approach would radically alter the evaluative framework used by the Committee

---

41 The WHC therefore did not follow the 'consolidated view' of its three Advisory Bodies that the criteria should be merged 'into a single list of ten criteria… with a consequential focus on areas inscribed as "World Heritage sites", rather than as World Heritage cultural and/or natural sites'. Amsterdam report (n 35) 4. IUCN also stated that it 'consider[ed] the four categories of World Heritage (natural, cultural, mixed and cultural landscape) as confusing and undermining the uniqueness of the *Convention*'. Ibid. Similarly, Vanoise report (n 35) para. 2(d).

42 The International Council on Monuments and Sites (ICOMOS) is an international non-governmental organisation and expert network dedicated to the conservation of monuments, building complexes and sites. Its main focus and expertise lies in the conservation of architectural and archaeological heritage. ICOMOS is one of the three formal advisory bodies to the WHC (see n 8). In this capacity, ICOMOS is responsible for the evaluation of all cultural sites nominated for World Heritage listing (including cultural landscapes, which are evaluated by ICOMOS in consultation with IUCN). The main purpose of these evaluations is to make recommendations to the WHC on whether nominated sites meet the standard of OUV. Nominations of mixed sites are evaluated jointly by ICOMOS and IUCN. Operational Guidelines 2015, para. 146.

43 C Cameron, 'Entre chien et loup: World Heritage Cultural Landscapes on the Fortieth Anniversary of the World Heritage Convention' in Taylor, St Clair and Mitchell (n 23) 61, 70.

44 The International Centre for the Study of the Preservation and Restoration of Cultural Property (ICCROM) is an international intergovernmental organization created in 1959 at the proposal of UNESCO's General Conference. Dedicated to the conservation of cultural heritage worldwide, it has today 132 Member States (as of 2015). As an official advisory body to the WHC (compare n 8), it assists the WHC in monitoring the state of conservation of cultural World Heritage sites, training for cultural heritage and capacity-building. Operational Guidelines 2015, para. 33.

> since its beginnings, it is nevertheless a logical outcome of a commitment to bring together treatment of cultural and natural heritage within the Committee's work.[45]

In 2013, the inadequacy of the existing criteria for recognizing nature-culture interlinkages again became a focus of the deliberations of the WHC due to difficulties encountered in the context of the nomination of Pimachiowin Aki as a mixed site, a collaborative effort of five First Nations and two Canadian provincial governments. In its evaluation of the nomination, ICOMOS criticized that:

> the recognition of both cultural and natural aspects in one property still needs in effect two nominations, one for cultural criteria and one for natural criteria, each of which is evaluated separately and each of which can be accepted without reference to the other. Although cultural and natural criteria have been merged, their use has not. Currently there is no way for properties to demonstrate within the current wording of the criteria, either that cultural systems are necessary to sustain the outstanding value of nature in a property, or that nature is imbued with cultural value in a property to a degree that is exceptional.[46]

Recognizing that the Pimachiowin Aki nomination had raised 'fundamental questions in terms of how the indissoluble bonds that exist in some places between culture and nature can be recognized on the World Heritage List', the WHC at its 37th session in Phnom Penh requested the World Heritage Centre and the Advisory Bodies to prepare a joint report containing 'options for changes to the criteria and/or to the Advisory Body evaluation process to address this issue'.[47] However, the respective report and the ensuing discussion remained exclusively focused on mixed site nominations, i.e. nominations of sites where natural as well as cultural elements are thought to be of OUV. A discussion on changes to the criteria did not occur because IUCN and ICOMOS submitted that there was 'no evidence that the wording of the criteria created difficulties for the evaluation of mixed sites', saying that the problems were

45 Doc WHC-99/CONF.204/10 (n 37) annex II, para. 1.

46 ICOMOS, 'Evaluations of Nominations of Cultural and Mixed Properties' (2013) WHC-13/37.COM/INF.8B1, 45.

47 WHC Decision 37 COM 8B.19 (2013).

rather due to shortcomings in the evaluation process, in particular a lack of shared decision-making between the Advisory Bodies.[48]

Therefore, the problem remains that an appropriate recognition of indigenous peoples' relationship with the environment, and interconnections between nature and culture, is only possible in cultural sites or mixed sites, when at least some aspects of the indigenous culture are assessed to be of OUV in their own right. However, due to the questionable ways in which the concept of OUV is interpreted and applied, and the frequent exclusion of indigenous peoples from the processes by which the OUV of sites is determined, this is not a realistic possibility in the context of many sites. In natural sites, which account for the majority of indigenous sites inscribed on the World Heritage List, cultural values do not form part of the OUV, preventing a proper recognition of indigenous values.

Problematic Application of the Concept of 'Outstanding Universal Value'

The concept of OUV is of central importance in the implementation of the World Heritage Convention, its purpose being the establishment of 'an effective system of collective protection of the cultural and natural heritage of outstanding universal value'.[49] The determination by the WHC that a site is of OUV is the main prerequisite for its inscription on the World Heritage List and after inscription the focus of conservation strategies and site management must be on the protection of those aspects that have been recognized as part of its OUV. According to the Operational Guidelines, the Statement of OUV adopted by the WHC at the time of listing provides 'the basis for the future protection and management of the property', and each World Heritage site should have 'an appropriate management plan or other documented management system which must specify how the Outstanding Universal Value of a property should

48 See UNESCO, 'Progress report on the reflection on processes for mixed nominations' (2015) WHC-15/39.COM/9B, paras. 4-6. Also see Doc WHC-14/38.COM/9B (n 24). Despite the special relevance of this issue for indigenous peoples, there was no opportunity for them to participate in this discussion, although the Special Rapporteur James Anaya had emphasized 'the importance of consulting with indigenous peoples throughout the entirety of such a review process in order to address indigenous peoples' rights, interests and concerns'. Letter to the WHC (n 5).

49 World Heritage Convention, preamble.

be preserved'.[50] Protection and management of World Heritage sites 'should ensure that their Outstanding Universal Value... [is] sustained or enhanced over time'.[51] Moreover, States must ensure that human use within World Heritage sites 'does not impact adversely on the Outstanding Universal Value'.[52]

From this it is obvious that the question which values are recognized as part of a site's OUV, and which ones are not, can have major ramifications for indigenous peoples living within or near a World Heritage site, and the protection of their rights. OUV affects management priorities and frameworks, and if the recognized OUV of a site does not reflect or coincide with the values attached to the site by indigenous peoples, this can lead to restrictions and prohibitions on their traditional land use activities and thus have significant consequences for their lives, livelihoods, cultures and well-being.

Considering these potentially significant implications, questions arise as to how the concept of OUV is defined, and under what circumstances indigenous peoples' interpretations may be reflected and their cultural and spiritual values and traditional practices recognized, if the indigenous peoples so desire. Closely related questions are by whom and through what processes the OUV of World Heritage sites is determined, and what mechanisms and possibilities exist for indigenous peoples to effectively participate in these processes and decisions.

Defining and Determining Outstanding Universal Value

Despite the fundamental importance of the concept of 'Outstanding Universal Value' for the implementation of the World Heritage Convention, no explicit definition of the term is contained in the Convention. It is clear from the Convention's *travaux préparatoires* that the concept was introduced into the text of the Convention 'to limit its application to the protection of a select list of the most important cultural and natural heritage places in the world';[53] however, the drafters of the Convention deliberately left the definition of OUV to the

---

50 Operational Guidelines 2015, paras. 108, 155.

51 Ibid, para. 96.

52 Ibid, para. 119.

53 S Titchen, 'On the construction of "outstanding universal value": Some comments on the implementation of the 1972 UNESCO World Heritage Convention' (1996) 1 Conservation and Management of Archaeological Sites 235, 236-37. The Operational Guidelines 2015 state that the Convention is 'not intended to ensure the protection of all properties of great interest, importance or value, but only for a select list of the most outstanding of these from an international viewpoint' (para. 52).

WHC.[54] Therefore, the concrete meaning of the concept is largely shaped by the practice of the WHC, as reflected in the Operational Guidelines and in particular the criteria for the determination of OUV. Since these have undergone several significant changes over the years and may continue to be revised in the future, it can be seen as 'an evolving concept'.[55] The ability to change and modify the criteria 'accommodates the mutability of the concept of heritage value or significance'[56] and provides some flexibility in the types of sites that can be included in the World Heritage List.

Since 2005, the Operational Guidelines contain a paragraph defining OUV as 'cultural and/or natural significance which is so exceptional as to transcend national boundaries and to be of common importance for present and future generations of all humanity.'[57] More important in practice, however, are the ten criteria for the assessment of OUV, at least one of which a site must meet to be included on the World Heritage List. The criteria that are most often used to recognize living cultural values of indigenous peoples (criteria iii, v and vi) require sites to 'bear a unique or at least exceptional testimony to a cultural tradition or to a civilization which is living or which has disappeared' (criterion iii), 'be an outstanding example of a traditional human settlement, land-use, or sea-use which is representative of a culture (or cultures), or human interaction with the environment…' (criterion v), or to 'be directly or tangibly associated with events or living traditions, with ideas, or with beliefs, with artistic and literary works of outstanding universal significance' (criterion vi).[58] Additionally, to be deemed of OUV, sites must meet the conditions of integrity[59] and/or

---

54 See arts 11(2) and 11(5) of the Convention, according to which the WHC shall define the criteria by which the OUV of World Heritage sites will be identified.

55 C Forrest, International Law and the Protection of Cultural Heritage (Routledge 2010) 233.

56 Titchen (n 53) 236-37.

57 Operational Guidelines 2015, para. 49.

58 Ibid, para. 77.

59 Operational Guidelines 2015, para. 78. Integrity is a 'measure of the wholeness and intactness of the natural or cultural heritage and its attributes'. Ibid, para. 88. For details on the conditions of integrity, see ibid, paras. 87-95.

authenticity[60] (the latter only in the case of cultural properties), and have an adequate protection and management system to ensure their safeguarding.[61]

A key factor in defining the OUV of individual World Heritage sites is the process by which sites are inscribed on the World Heritage List. While the final decision whether to inscribe a site or not rests with the WHC, sites can only be listed following a formal nomination by the State Party in whose territory they are located.[62] The nomination documents submitted by the States Parties are 'the primary basis on which the Committee considers the inscription of the properties on the World Heritage List'.[63] They must include a 'proposed Statement of Outstanding Universal Value… mak[ing] clear why the property is considered to merit inscription on the World Heritage List' and 'indicate the World Heritage criteria… under which the property is proposed, together with a clearly stated argument for the use of each criterion'.[64] States Parties are encouraged to involve indigenous peoples, local communities and other stakeholders in preparing the nominations. However, as will be discussed in more detail below, this is not a mandatory requirement.[65]

Once submitted, nominations are evaluated by the WHC's Advisory Bodies IUCN and/or ICOMOS, who present their views to the Committee on whether the nominated site meets the criteria under which inscription is proposed by the State Party, and on whether the site should be listed or not. The Advisory Bodies can also recommend that the State Party be asked to re-nominate the site under different criteria. If the Advisory Bodies recommend an inscription, they present an updated draft of the OUV Statement to the Committee. On this basis, the Committee then makes an independent decision whether or not

60 Ibid, para. 78. The demand to pass the test of authenticity can be understood as the requirement to be genuine, i.e., 'the nominated resource should be truly what it is claimed to be'. J Jokilehto and J King, 'Authenticity and Integrity' <http://whc.unesco.org/en/events/443> accessed 22 November 2015. For details on the conditions of authenticity, see Operational Guidelines 2015, paras. 79-86 and annex 4 (Nara Document on Authenticity).

61 Operational Guidelines 2015, para. 78. For details on this requirement, see ibid, paras. 96-119. Note that the Guidelines since 1999 explicitly acknowledge that traditional protection and management can be adequate to ensure the safeguarding of both cultural and natural World Heritage sites (para. 97).

62 According to art 3 of the Convention, '[i]t is for each State Party to this Convention to identify and delineate the different properties situated on its territory' that may fall under the protection regime of the Convention. Moreover, art 11(3) stipulates that '[t]he inclusion of a property in the World Heritage List requires the consent of the State concerned'.

63 Operational Guidelines 2015, para. 120.

64 Ibid, para. 132(3).

65 Ibid, para. 123.

to inscribe the site, and under which criteria.[66] Formerly the Committee occasionally inscribed sites under different criteria than those proposed by the State Party;[67] however, under the current Guidelines the application of new criteria requires a resubmission of the nomination and the consent of the State Party.

It follows from the above that indigenous values will only be recognized as part of a World Heritage site's OUV with the consent of the State Party concerned. It is the States that decide which sites in their territories are proposed for listing, which elements, attributes and values are highlighted in the nomination documents, and under which criteria inscription is proposed. Additionally, for indigenous cultural values to be recognized, the WHC must conclude – taking into account the expert advice provided by IUCN and ICOMOS – that they are significant enough in their own right to fulfill the World Heritage criteria, including the requirements of integrity and authenticity.

'Universal' Values Versus Indigenous Values

There are a number of World Heritage sites that were listed in recognition of indigenous peoples' cultural heritage and whose OUV is therefore, fully or in part, based on indigenous heritage. (To what extent the OUV reflects indigenous peoples' own understandings of that heritage is a separate question.) Many of these sites are marked by the presence of historic material evidence of indigenous culture such as rock art (e.g. Kakadu National Park, Tsodilo), architectural features (Taos Pueblo, Machu Picchu), or monumental artifacts (SGang Gwaay, Rapa Nui). This is a reflection of the fact that the World Heritage Convention was inspired by a 'European-inspired monumentalist vision of cultural heritage which isolated its physical dimensions from its-non-physical ones'[68] and favored – at least initially – the inscription of built and archaeological heritage. However, in the 1990s two important decisions of the WHC led to an expanded notion of cultural heritage in the implementation of the Convention and thus facilitated the listing of other kinds of indigenous heritage: the introduction of the cultural landscapes category in 1992, and the

66 The WHC is obviously not bound to follow the recommendations of IUCN and ICOMOS. In recent years, there has been an increasing trend toward divergence between the Committee decisions and the recommendations of its Advisory Bodies. See L Meskell, 'UNESCO's World Heritage Convention at 40: Challenging the Economic and Political Order of International Heritage Conservation' (2013) 54(4) *Current Anthropology* 483, 486.

67 See, e.g., J Jokilehto, *What is OUV? Defining the Outstanding Universal Value of Cultural World Heritage Properties* (ICOMOS 2008) 79-89.

68 A Yusuf, 'Article 1 – Definition of Cultural Heritage' in Francioni (n 12) 23, 29.

adoption of the 'Global Strategy for a Balanced, Representative and Credible World Heritage List' in 1994. These developments have resulted in a stronger emphasis on living culture and intangible heritage, and have aided the recognition of indigenous peoples' spiritual and physical relationships with their lands, territories and resources when the OUV of cultural (or mixed) World Heritage sites is defined.[69] They have for instance enabled the recognition of Māori cultural and spiritual values associated with Tongariro National Park, Anangu values related to Uluru-Kata Tjuta National Park, Nama pastoralism in the Richtersveld Cultural and Botanical Landscape (South Africa) and Saami reindeer herding in the Laponian Area (Sweden).[70]

However, the fact remains that in the vast majority of World Heritage sites traditionally owned, inhabited or used by indigenous peoples, the OUV does not encompass indigenous cultural values, and in many cases the OUV Statements adopted by the WHC do not even mention the existence of the indigenous peoples. What is more, in some OUV Statements the indigenous peoples are identified as current or potential threats to the OUV.[71] The OUV of those sites therefore not only does not coincide with the indigenous heritage values, but conflicts with them in significant ways and may even be harmful to their protection. As noted by EMRIP:

> The establishment of World Heritage sites, or other forms of protected areas can have a negative impact on indigenous peoples because, often, their ancestral rights over their lands and territories are not respected or protected. In many nature-protected areas, including areas inscribed on the World Heritage List, narrow restrictions are imposed on traditional

69 See ibid, 31-37; and Harrison (n 9) 114-39.

70 The case of the Laponian Area shows that the recognition of indigenous cultural values as part of a site's OUV not only ensures a continued consideration of those values in conservation strategies, but can also greatly assist indigenous peoples in their efforts to gain a greater role in local decision-making processes and site management. See C Green, 'Manging Laponia: A World Heritage Site as Arena for Sami Ethno-Politics in Sweden' (2009) 47 *Uppsala Studies in Cultural Anthropology*.

71 See e.g. the OUV Statement for the Ngorongoro Conservation Area, WHC Decision 34 COM 8B.13 (2010) para. 4. There are also some cases where indigenous peoples have been 'physically removed from protected areas as a way of justifying inscription of an area on the World Heritage list as a place of natural importance devoid of what is perceived as the negative impact of local inhabitants'. S Titchen, 'Indigenous peoples and cultural and natural World Heritage sites' (Panel presentation, New York, 15 May 2002) <http://www.dialoguebetweennations.com/n2n/pfii/english/SarahTitchen.htm> accessed 22 September 2015.

> practices and activities, such as hunting, gathering, farming or animal husbandry, in violation of the cultural and subsistence rights of indigenous peoples. To be included on the World Heritage List, sites must be of "outstanding universal value", a concept which can lead to management frameworks that prioritize the protection of those heritage aspects at the expense of the land rights of indigenous peoples. As a result, the protection of world heritage can undermine indigenous peoples' relationship with their traditional lands, territories and resources, as well as their livelihoods and cultural heritage, especially in sites where the natural values are deemed to be of outstanding universal value but the cultural values of indigenous peoples are not taken into account.[72]

The reasons for the common lack of recognition of indigenous peoples' values, perspectives and cultural heritage when the OUV of sites is defined are diverse. In most cases, the indigenous values are already ignored in the nominations submitted by States. The main reason often lies in the fact that the relevant States Parties have no political or economic interest to include indigenous heritage in their nominations, and the indigenous peoples concerned have no legal standing or voice at the domestic level that would ensure their meaningful involvement in the preparation of the nominations. Some government agencies and conservation organizations involved in the preparation of nominations may also be opposed to a recognition of indigenous values as this could enhance the role of indigenous peoples in site management and reduce their own authority. At the same time, recognition of only the natural values of a site may provide a convenient means to justify the imposition of restrictions on indigenous peoples' livelihoods and further deprive them of rights to lands and resources.[73]

But even if States have the best intentions, there are significant practical and financial reasons why they may choose to disregard indigenous values in preparing nominations. In particular, they may prefer to nominate nature-pro-

---

72 Study on cultural heritage (n 1) para. 55.

73 See e.g. the case of Lake Bogoria National Reserve where the Kenyan Government appears to be using the World Heritage status as a pretext for not restituting the land to the Endorois people as required by the landmark 2009 decision of the African Commission on Human and Peoples' Rights in the 'Endorois' case (Communication 276/2003). Endorois Welfare Council, Statement at the 39th session of the WHC (Bonn, 2015) <http://whc.unesco.org/en/sessions/39com/records> (File: Jul 1, 2015 – 9:30 AM, at 1:41:16) accessed 15 October 2015. Also see K Sing'Oei, 'Ignoring Indigenous Peoples' Rights: The Case of Lake Bogoria's Designation as a UNESCO World Heritage Site' in Disko and Tugendhat (n 10) 163, 171.

tected areas as natural rather than mixed sites because mixed nominations are considered too complex.[74] It is in many ways easier to gain recognition as a natural site than as a mixed site, because natural and cultural values are evaluated separately (by IUCN and ICOMOS respectively) and a successful nomination as a mixed site normally requires a positive assessment of both Advisory Bodies. While a State's decision not to nominate a site for its indigenous values may of course be based on a realistic assessment that such an effort would likely not be successful under the existing regulations and criteria, there can be no doubt that many natural World Heritage sites hold indigenous values that would have fulfilled the cultural criteria at the time of inscription. A noteworthy example is the Sangha Trinational (Cameroon/Central African Republic/Congo), which was nominated and subsequently inscribed under natural criteria alone although the WHC and IUCN had explicitly encouraged a mixed nomination due to the evident significance of the 'rich indigenous cultural heritage of the area'.[75] In the case of the Okapi Wildlife Reserve, a natural site in Congo, the WHC at the time of inscription in 1996 noted 'the importance of the pygmy population living at the site and the interaction between traditional people and nature' and encouraged the State Party to 'consider nomination also under cultural criteria in the future',[76] however, until today the site has not been renominated.

Conversely, there are also several sites that were inscribed only for their natural or archaeological values by the WHC although they had also been nominated for their indigenous heritage values. A case in point is Purnululu National Park (Australia), listed as a natural site in 2003 after having been proposed as a mixed site and living Aboriginal cultural landscape. The reason for this was that ICOMOS, while agreeing that Purnululu possesses outstanding cultural values, raised several questions concerning the integrity, authenticity and 'viability' of those values. Issues raised in this connection included the fact that traditional land-use practices had been interrupted and dislocated due to the impact of European settlers, the fact that the traditional owners no longer lived in the site, and the small number of traditional knowledge holders. ICOMOS recommended that the nomination be deferred and Australia asked

---

74 Larsen and Wijesuriya (n 24) 10; K Buckley and T Badman, 'Nature+Culture and World Heritage: why it matters!' in Ch Cameron and J Herrmann (eds), *Exploring the Cultural Value of Nature: a World Heritage Context* (Proceedings of Round Table, Université de Montréal, 12-14 March 2014) 105, 116.

75 WHC Decision 35 COM 8B.4 (2011) para. 2d.

76 UNESCO, Report on the twentieth session of the WHC (Merida, 1996) WHC-96/CONF.201/21, 60.

to improve the Park's management framework with a view to 'sustaining traditional Aboriginal communities in the Park' and maintaining the intangible cultural heritage associated with the landscape.[77] However, rather than deferring the entire nomination as recommended by ICOMOS, the WHC deferred only the cultural part and inscribed Purnululu under natural criteria. Some hope that Purnululu's indigenous values may eventually be recognized can be found in the fact that the Committee explicitly noted 'the outstanding universal cultural and natural value' of the Park when listing it and in 2008 requested Australia to 'pursue the on-going consideration of indigenous cultural values of the property'.[78]

A less hopeful case is that of the Ngorongoro Conservation Area ('NCA') in Tanzania, a multiple land-use area excised from Serengeti National Park in 1959 to provide a home for Maasai pastoralists who were being evicted from the Serengeti. Listed as a natural site in 1979, it was in 2009 re-nominated under cultural criteria for its significance as an archaeological site and Maasai cultural landscape. However, while the WHC approved the inscription as an archaeological site, it rejected recognition as a Maasai landscape due to a highly negative evaluation by ICOMOS, which held that the Maasai values did not satisfy the conditions of integrity and authenticity and were neither 'unique' nor 'exceptional' enough to be of OUV:

> The Maasai are described in the nomination dossier as pastoralists and nomads who move around with their animals in search of grazing grounds and water sources... [T]he reality is now that the much larger community of Maasai... presently inhabit a number of densely populated villages and only a small percentage spend part of the year in isolated 'bomas'... The largely settled communities now rely for food on agricultural produce as well as on resources from their animals... The Maasai, although extremely interesting in terms of their cultural traditions, are therefore, in ICOMOS's view, neither a unique nor an exceptional testimony to such pastoralist traditions... [T]heir distinctive pastoralism within the Conservation area has now been significantly changed into agro-pastoralism through the impact of population growth and other factors... ICOMOS does not consider that at the present time the conditions of integrity and authenticity have been met for the Maasai pastoral landscape.[79]

---

77 ICOMOS, *Evaluations of Cultural Properties 2003*, WHC-03/27COM/INF.8A, 7.

78 Decisions 27 COM 8C.11 (2003) and 32 COM 7B.8 (2008).

79 ICOMOS, *2010 Evaluations of Cultural Properties*, WHC-10/34.COM/INF.8B1, 65-69. It is a bitter irony that the changes in the pastoralists' lives which ICOMOS considers are com-

The listing of the NCA for its natural and archaeological values, but not its indigenous values, has led to a significant rearrangement of management priorities and undermined the multiple land-use philosophy at the expense of the Maasai residents, who have been subjected to a host of restrictions on their livelihood activities as a result of World Heritage status and the involvement of UNESCO, IUCN and ICOMOS. The recent inscription as an archaeological site has in effect sidelined the already marginalized Maasai community even further in the NCA's decision-making processes.[80]

The questionable requirement by which indigenous peoples' relationship with their ancestral lands and resources has to be 'exceptional' in order to form an integral part of a World Heritage site's recognized value, is also a key issue in the (ongoing) mixed site nomination of Pimachiowin Aki. The cultural part of the nomination was deferred in 2013 because ICOMOS found that the relationship between the Anishinaabeg and the land in the nominated area was 'not unique and persists in many places associated with indigenous peoples in North America and other parts of the world', and that it had not been demonstrated 'how this strong association… can be seen to be exceptional – in other words of wider importance than to the Anishinaabeg themselves'.[81] Since ICOMOS considered, however, that Pimachiowin Aki might have the potential to demonstrate OUV for its cultural values, it recommended that Canada be given an opportunity to explore, together with ICOMOS, 'whether there is a way that the spiritual relationship with nature that has persisted for generations between the Anishinaabe First Nations and Pimachiowin Aki, might be considered exceptional'.[82] The resolution of this issue is complicated by the fact that the Anishinaabeg have emphasized, out of respect for other indigenous peoples, that they 'do not wish to see their property as being "exceptional" as they did not want to make judgements about the relationships of other First Nations' with their lands and thus make comparisons'.[83]

---

promising the authenticity and integrity of the 'pastoral landscape' are in many ways the result of restrictions imposed by conservation measures, such as the fact that the Maasai 'no longer live and move across the whole Conservation Area'. Ibid, 65.

80 W Olenasha, 'A World Heritage Site in the Ngorongoro Conservation Area: Whose World? Whose Heritage?' in Disko and Tugendhat (n 10) 189.

81 ICOMOS, *2013 Evaluations of Nominations of Cultural and Mixed Properties*, WHC-13/37.COM/INF.8B1, 39.

82 Ibid, 46.

83 Ibid, 39.

Whatever the outcome of this case,[84] the need for indigenous peoples to claim and demonstrate that their connection to land is exceptional and 'superior' to that of other indigenous peoples in order for it to be recognized as part of a World Heritage site's OUV, is seen as highly inappropriate – even 'insulting' – by some indigenous representatives.[85] Indigenous representatives have also raised the fundamental question how the heritage values ascribed to the ancestral territory of an indigenous people can be considered as 'universal' if they are not inclusive and respectful of the indigenous people's own values and perspectives and may even run counter to those values. For instance, the Maasai lawyer William Olenasha has recently remarked in relation to the 'World Heritage' status of the NCA:

> The local communities' disenfranchisement and marginalization from decision-making processes begs the questions of whose world and whose heritage are being safeguarded and protected under this label, and whether the concept of 'mankind as a whole' that is embedded in the World Heritage Convention includes the pastoralists living in the Ngorongoro Conservation Area.[86]

Similar questions have been posed by indigenous representatives and others on many occasions throughout the history of the Convention and present a problem which UNESCO is forced to address if it wants to protect the Convention's credibility as an instrument representing the interest of 'all the peoples of the world'[87] and its own credibility as an organization committed to cultural

---

84 In its 2015 revised nomination, Canada referred to the connection between Anishinaabeg and their land as a 'compelling example of the inseparability of an indigenous culture and its local environment that can inspire people around the world' and describes Pimachiowin Aki as 'an exceptional expression of the cultural tradition of *Ji-ganawendamang Gidakiiminaan* ['Keeping the Land']'. 'As mentioned earlier, decision was deferred after Ontario's Pikangikum First Nation withdrew its support and in January 2017, Canada submitted a new proposal for recognition of a smaller area as World heritage Site.

85 See R Feneley, 'Indigenous leaders told of "insulting" UN rule on World Heritage listing', *Sydney Morning Herald* (28 May 2013) <http://www.smh.com.au/national/indigenous-leaders-told-of-insulting-un-rule-on-world-heritage-listing-20130527-2n7ac.html> accessed 1 October 2015; or S Titchen, 'On the construction of outstanding universal value' (DPhil thesis, Australian National University 1995) 245.

86 Olenasha (n 80) 217. Similarly, Sing'Oei (n 73) 181 in relation to Lake Bogoria National Reserve.

87 World Heritage Convention, preamble.

diversity, equality and mutual understanding and respect of peoples.[88] From UNESCO's records it is clear that the WHC has long been aware of this necessity. For instance, the seminal Nara Document on Authenticity, adopted at a UNESCO conference in 1994, refers to the WHC's desire to 'accord full respect to the social and cultural values of all societies, in examining the outstanding universal value of cultural properties proposed for the World Heritage List' and recognizes that '[c]ultural heritage diversity… demands respect for other cultures and all aspects of their belief systems'.[89] Moreover, noting that 'judgements about values attributed to cultural properties… may differ from culture to culture', the Nara Document underlines that 'the respect due to all cultures requires that heritage properties must be considered and judged within the cultural contexts to which they belong'.[90] Also noteworthy is a 2005 UNESCO expert meeting on the concept of OUV in Kazan, Russia, which emphasized that '[t]he identification of outstanding universal value of a site needs wide participation by stakeholders including local communities and indigenous people'.[91] Following this meeting, the WHC adopted a decision recognizing that OUV 'is a concept that shall embrace all cultures, regions and peoples, and does not ignore differing cultural interpretations of outstanding universal value because they originate from minorities, indigenous groups and/or local peoples'.[92] It instructed the World Heritage Centre and the Advisory Bodies to create guidance manuals on the concept and application of OUV, emphasizing that the manuals should '[s]pecifically include the utilization of, or note the obvious omission of the values of minorities, indigenous and/or local peoples' in past Committee decisions.[93]

Despite these insights, intentions and efforts, however, indigenous peoples' perspectives and values continue to be routinely ignored when the OUV of World Heritage sites is defined, as many recent nominations and listings

---

88 Constitution of the United Nations Educational, Scientific and Cultural Organization (adopted 16 November 1945, entered into force 4 November 1946) 4 UNTS 275, preamble and art 1.

89 Nara Document on Authenticity, paras. 2, 6. Reproduced in Operational Guidelines 2015, annex 4.

90 Para. 11. Similarly, Operational Guidelines 2015, para. 81. While the Nara Document only relates to cultural properties, it logically follows that the judgment whether a property is treated as a 'cultural' or 'natural' property would likewise need to be made within the cultural context to which it belongs.

91 UNESCO, 'Recommendations of the Expert meeting on OUV' (Kazan, Russian Federation, 6-10 April 2005). Contained in Doc WHC-05/29.COM/9, 3, para. 7k.

92 Decision 30 COM 9 (2006) para. 3.

93 Ibid, para. 7e.

show.[94] There is no reason to believe that this situation will change unless the dichotomy between nature and culture is finally overcome and significant adaptations are made to the way OUV is defined and determined. A key question that needs to be asked in this regard is whether it is appropriate to base the decision whether or not to give recognition to the values indigenous peoples themselves attach to their ancestral territories on such concepts as 'exceptionality', 'authenticity' and 'integrity'. Put differently, when establishing the OUV of World Heritage sites, is it appropriate to disregard or discount the values of indigenous peoples who have occupied and nurtured those places for centuries (unless it is the genuine will of the indigenous peoples themselves)? Who should be defining the values of World Heritage sites located in indigenous peoples' ancestral territories and deciding which criteria are applied?

Under the current regulations the OUV of a World Heritage site is defined through a process involving the relevant State Party (i.e. the government agencies who prepare the nomination), the Advisory Bodies IUCN and/or ICOMOS (i.e. international heritage experts), and the government delegates in the WHC (nowadays predominantly career diplomats).[95] Whether and to what extent affected indigenous peoples are involved in this process is completely at the discretion of the nominating States. Despite the United Nations' commitments to ensuring participation of indigenous peoples on issues affecting them,[96] the involvement of affected indigenous peoples in the nomination of World Heritage sites is not a mandatory requirement under the Operational Guidelines. Due to the lack of recognition and respect for indigenous peoples' rights in many countries, this means in practice that they are often excluded.

94 Recent examples include, among others, the Sangha Trinational, the Ngorongoro Conservation Area, the Okavango Delta (Botswana), and the Kaeng Krachan Forest Complex (Thailand).

95 Meskell (n 66) 485; C Brumann, 'Shifting tides of world-making in the UNESCO World Heritage Convention: cosmopolitanisms colliding' (2014) 37(12) *Ethnic and Racial Studies* 2176, 2185-88.

96 See, in particular arts 18, 19, 41, 42 of the UNDRIP and the outcome document of the 2014 World Conference on Indigenous Peoples, A/RES/69/2, paras. 3, 20, 33, 40. UNESCO's Medium-Term Strategy 2014-2021 states that the Organization will implement the UNDRIP 'across all relevant programme areas'. Doc 37 C/4 (2014) para. 20.

Lack of Regulations to Ensure Meaningful Participation of Indigenous Peoples in Decision-Making Processes under the World Heritage Convention

Not surprisingly considering its date of adoption, the text of the World Heritage Convention 'does not give any recognition to indigenous peoples' rights over cultural and natural heritage'.[97] Even though the Preamble recognizes that cultural and natural heritage belongs to 'peoples' rather than States, the Convention grants States ultimate control over determining which heritage sites on their territories may fall under the Convention's regime and entrusts them with all responsibilities concerning the nomination, management and protection of World Heritage sites. 'Little to no mention is made of community involvement in protecting heritage, and… in determining what their heritage actually is', as Lucas Lixinski notes; peoples and local communities 'are assumed to be fairly represented by States' in the Convention's processes.[98]

The only reference to communities in the Convention text is a provision according to which each State Party 'shall endeavor, in so far as possible, and as appropriate for each country… to adopt a general policy which aims to give the cultural and natural heritage a function in the life of the community'.[99] The Convention also calls on States to develop educational and information programmes in order to 'strengthen appreciation and respect by their peoples of [World Heritage sites]' and to 'keep the public broadly informed of the dangers threatening this heritage and of activities carried on in pursuance of this Convention'.[100] The rationale for these provisions is not a recognition of the need to involve local populations in decisions affecting them, but the consideration that their engagement is to some extent necessary to ensure an effective conservation of World Heritage. This is underscored by the fact that the Convention does not establish an active role for affected peoples and communities in its processes, but mentions them only as passive recipients of information and policies. This lack of a role for local communities contrasts with

97 International Law Association, Committee on the Rights of Indigenous Peoples, 'Rights of Indigenous Peoples: Final Report' (Sofia Conference 2012) 17.

98 L Lixinski, 'Heritage for Whom? Individuals' and Communities' Roles in International Cultural Heritage Law' in Federico Lenzerini and AF Vrdoljak (eds), *International Law for Common Goods: Normative Perspectives on Human Rights, Culture and Nature* (Hart Publishing 2014) 193, 196.

99 Art 5(a).

100 Art 27.

the important role given to experts, which is central to the operation of the instrument.[101]

While the WHC has over the years increasingly recognized the importance of involving local communities in the protection of World Heritage sites, and included several references to local communities (and more recently also to indigenous peoples) in the Operational Guidelines, their involvement continues to be largely seen as a means to an end, rather than an end in itself. This is because 'the communities at World Heritage sites and their destinies are not the Convention rationale' as Christoph Brumann writes. 'Instead, it is the physical conservation of the sites and the buildings, natural features, or wildlife found on them... [P]resent-day local populations often come in only as a disturbing factor... It is then protection "from," rather than "for," the communities that moves to the forefront'.[102] Even in the case of cultural landscapes, where the ongoing interaction of local communities with the landscape is often the primary reason for World Heritage listing, 'the manuals and programmatic texts prepared by the World Heritage Center and ICOMOS... focus on communities most of all as a tool. It is important to involve them, but they are construed neither as the supreme experts about the sites nor their rightful owners.'[103]

The first time that references to local communities appeared in the Operational Guidelines was in 1994, when a new sentence was included in the section on the nomination process stating that 'Participation of local people in the nomination process is essential to make them feel a shared responsibility

101 See Lixinski (n 98) 196-97. Besides the key role assigned to the expert advisory bodies IUCN, ICOMOS and ICCROM, several provisions in the Convention express an expectation that States discharge their duty of protecting World Heritage sites under their jurisdiction with the active assistance of scientific and technical experts (preamble; arts 4, 5, 22, 24). Indigenous peoples' representatives have repeatedly criticized the expertise provided under the Convention as inadequate for the safeguarding of indigenous heritage, and called on the WHC to create an indigenous advisory mechanism to complement the other expert groups. See, e.g., the much-discussed, unsuccessful 2000 'WHIPCOE' proposal (n 20); and the more recent 'Call to Action' of the International Expert Workshop on the World Heritage Convention and Indigenous Peoples (Copenhagen, 2012), para. 4, available at <http://www.iwgia.org/iwgia_files_news_files/0678_Call_to_Action_plus_Annexes.pdf> accessed 21 October 2015.

102 C Brumann, 'Community as Myth and Reality in the UNESCO World Heritage Convention' in N Adell and others (eds), *Between Imagined Communities and Communities of Practice: Participation, Territory and the Making of Heritage* (Universitätsverlag Göttingen 2015) 274, 277.

103 Ibid, 277-8.

with the State Party in the maintenance of the site.'[104] Additionally, the following sentence was added concerning the nomination of cultural landscapes: 'The nominations [of cultural landscapes] should be prepared in collaboration with and the full approval of local communities.'[105] Both of these provisions can still be found in the current version of the Guidelines.[106] Most other references to local communities in the Guidelines were added during a major revision in 2005, including the following provision, which can be seen as the central provision on community participation:

> States Parties to the *Convention* are encouraged to ensure the participation of a wide variety of stakeholders, including site managers, local and regional governments, local communities, non-governmental organizations (NGOs) and other interested parties and partners in the identification, nomination and protection of World Heritage properties.[107]

Also since 2005, the Guidelines state that local communities and other stakeholders can be 'partners' in the protection and conservation of World Heritage, and encourage a 'partnership approach' to nomination, management and monitoring as a significant contribution to the protection of World Heritage sites.[108] Moreover, 'increas[ing] the participation of local and national populations in the protection and presentation of heritage' and 'enhanc[ing] the function of World Heritage in the life of the community' were included as official objectives (in a new section on 'Encouraging support for the *World Heritage Convention*').[109] Since 2008, the Guidelines also contain the following Strategic Objective: 'Enhance the role of Communities in the implementation of the World Heritage Convention'.[110]

The problem with these provisions is that they do not create procedural obligations for States. Apart from the nomination process for cultural landscapes, no differentiation is made between the participation of local communities and the participation of NGOs, private organizations and other interested parties.

104 Operational Guidelines 1994, WHC/2/Revised, para. 14.

105 Ibid, para. 41.

106 Operational Guidelines 2015, para. 123 (with slight modifications); and annex 3, para. 12.

107 Operational Guidelines 2005, WHC. 05/2, para. 12. Similarly, para. 64 (in relation to the preparation of Tentative Lists) and para. 123 (preparation of nominations).

108 Operational Guidelines 2015, paras. 39, 40.

109 Ibid, para. 211.

110 Ibid, para. 26. This fifth Strategic Objective ('fifth C') was adopted in recognition of 'the critical importance of involving indigenous, traditional and local communities in the implementation of the *Convention*'. See WHC Decisions 31 COM 13A, 13B (2007).

The fact that some stakeholders, in particular indigenous peoples, have a right to be involved in the processes concerned, whereas others do not, is completely ignored. In the end it continues to be at the discretion of States to what extent they involve local communities and indigenous peoples in decisions regarding the nomination and protection of World Heritage sites. The same can be said with regard to the Advisory Bodies, who are in no way obliged to involve or consult with local communities when evaluating nominations or monitoring the state of conservation of listed sites. While IUCN's own procedure for the evaluation of nominations entails on-site consultations with stakeholders and the examination of written comments from NGOs, local communities and indigenous peoples, the procedure adopted by ICOMOS highlights consultations with the nominating State Party, site managers, specialist academics and research institutes, but makes no mention of consultations with local communities and indigenous peoples.[111]

Given these inadequacies and shortcomings, it is no surprise that indigenous peoples continue to voice concerns about violations of their participatory rights in the processes of the World Heritage Convention. The recurrent violations have increasingly drawn the attention of international human rights bodies and mechanisms in recent years, most notably the African Commission on Human and Peoples' Rights ('ACHPR'), the UNPFII, the EMRIP and the Special Rapporteur on the Rights of Indigenous Peoples. Since the adoption of the UNDRIP in 2007, all of these have repeatedly urged UNESCO and the WHC to take corrective action and align the implementation of the Convention with the UNDRIP.[112] For instance, EMRIP has issued the following advice to the Committee, drawing attention to the obligations of UN agencies, intergovernmental organizations and States under Articles 41 and 42 of the UNDRIP:[113]

> robust procedures and mechanisms should be established to ensure that indigenous peoples are adequately consulted and involved in the man-

111 See Operational Guidelines 2015, annex 6 (Evaluation procedures of the Advisory Bodies for nominations). There are also significant concerns regarding the transparency of the Advisory Bodies' evaluation processes. For instance, the ICOMOS procedure states that the dates and programs of on-site missions 'are agreed in consultation with States Parties, who are requested to ensure that ICOMOS evaluation missions are given a low profile so far as the media are concerned'. Ibid.

112 For details, see S Disko, H Tugendhat and L García-Alix, 'Introduction' in Disko and Tugendhat (n 10) 3; EMRIP, Study on cultural heritage (n 1) paras. 38-41.

113 Arts 41 and 42 of the UNDRIP establish a special obligation of UN agencies and intergovernmental organizations to implement the provisions of the UNDRIP and establish ways and means of ensuring the participation of indigenous peoples on issues affecting them.

> agement and protection of World Heritage sites, and that their free, prior and informed consent is obtained when their territories are being nominated and inscribed as World Heritage sites...[114]

EMRIP therefore encouraged the Committee to establish a process to elaborate, with the full and effective participation of indigenous peoples, changes to the Operational Guidelines and other appropriate measures to ensure that the implementation of the World Heritage Convention is consistent with the UNDRIP and that indigenous peoples can effectively participate in decision-making processes affecting them.[115] Similar recommendations have been made by the other two UN mechanisms on indigenous issues,[116] the ACHPR,[117] the 2012 IUCN World Conservation Congress[118] and the 2014 IUCN World Parks Congress.[119] The need for revising the Operational Guidelines to ensure respect for indigenous rights in World Heritage processes has also repeatedly been stressed by indigenous peoples themselves, for instance in the Alta Outcome Document[120] and in a 'Call to Action' adopted by an international expert workshop on the World Heritage Convention and indigenous peoples held in Copenhagen in 2012 during the Convention's 40th anniversary.[121]

While the WHC has so far not established an adequate, participatory process for reviewing and revising the Guidelines in cooperation with indigenous peoples, UNESCO has become increasingly responsive to indigenous peoples' concerns and there have been some efforts by the World Heritage Centre towards aligning the implementation of the World Heritage Convention with the

114 EMRIP, Report on its fifth session (n 4) 7. Similarly, Study on cultural heritage (n 1), paras. 35, 45 and annex, para. 30.

115 Ibid.

116 See n 5.

117 Resolution 197, Protection of indigenous peoples' rights in the context of the World Heritage Convention and the designation of Lake Bogoria as a World Heritage site (2011).

118 Resolution 5.047, Implementation of the UNDRIP in the context of the UNESCO World Heritage Convention.

119 The Promise of Sydney: Innovative Approaches for Change, <http://worldparkscongress.org/about/promise_of_sydney_innovative_approaches.html> accessed 21 October 2015. See in particular Recommendation 5 under the World Heritage theme, and Recommendation 8 under Stream 7: Respecting indigenous and traditional knowledge and culture.

120 Outcome Document of the Global Indigenous Preparatory Conference for the World Conference on Indigenous Peoples, Alta, Norway, 10-12 June 2013, UN Doc A/67/994, Theme 2, para. 9.

121 Copenhagen Call to Action (n 101), para. 1. For the report of the expert workshop, see <http://whc.unesco.org/document/122252> accessed 21 October 2015.

UNDRIP.[122] Due to these efforts, the WHC at its 39th session in July 2015 in Bonn for the first time included references to indigenous peoples in the Operational Guidelines. The Guidelines now mention indigenous peoples among the list of potential 'partners' in the protection of World Heritage, and encourage States to obtain their free, prior and informed consent ('FPIC') when nominating World Heritage sites:

> Participation in the nomination process of local communities, indigenous peoples, governmental, non-governmental and private organizations and other stakeholders is essential to enable them to have a shared responsibility with the State Party in the maintenance of the property. States Parties are encouraged to prepare nominations with the widest possible participation of stakeholders and to demonstrate, as appropriate, that the free, prior and informed consent of indigenous peoples has been obtained, through, inter alia making the nominations publically available in appropriate languages and public consultations and hearings.[123]

The adoption of this provision is a positive step towards enhancing respect for the participatory rights of indigenous peoples in the context of World Heritage nominations. However, involving affected indigenous peoples in the preparation of nominations and obtaining their FPIC is still not obligatory for States but merely recommended practice, and from the discussions at the WHC's 39th session it is clear that there are significant reservations within the Committee about making this a mandatory requirement.[124] The session also clearly demonstrated that the Committee will presently not insist on the consent of indigenous peoples: in the case of the nomination of the Kaeng Krachan Forest Complex (Thailand), it explicitly voted against requesting Thailand to obtain the FPIC of the Karen communities living within the area, although the Office of the UN High Commissioner for Human Rights and local NGOs had raised

122 Disko, Tugendhat and García-Alix (n 112) 32-33.

123 Operational Guidelines 2015, para. 123.

124 Endorois Welfare Council, Saami Council and IWGIA, 'Joint statement on indigenous rights and World Heritage', EMRIP, 8th session, 22 July 2015, available at <http://www.iwgia.org/news/search-news?news_id=1234> accessed 23 October 2015. Several States even contested the very concept of 'indigenous peoples', including some States that have endorsed the UNDRIP such as France, Mali or Senegal. For the French position, also see UNESCO, 'States Parties' comments to the Draft Policy for the integration of a Sustainable Development Perspective into the Processes of the World Heritage Convention' (2015), WHC-15/20.GA/13, 8-9.

concerns about serious conflicts between conservation authorities and the Karen.[125] The Committee also decided against adopting a rule to make all nominations publically accessible once UNESCO receives them.[126] Therefore, unless States Parties publish the nomination documents voluntarily, they are not accessible to affected communities or the public at large before sites are listed. Indigenous peoples and human rights organizations have repeatedly criticized this remarkable lack of transparency as inconsistent with indigenous peoples' right to FPIC, as well as State obligations to ensure public participation in environmental decision-making.[127]

Hope that the WHC will eventually adopt guidelines making respect for indigenous peoples' participatory rights mandatory in Convention processes derives from UNESCO's awareness of its obligations to implement the UNDRIP and to establish ways and means of ensuring the participation of indigenous peoples on issues affecting them. The organization is currently in the process of developing a house-wide policy on engaging with indigenous peoples,[128] and although this policy will not be directly binding on the WHC (as a largely autonomous intergovernmental treaty body), the WHC has decided to re-examine the role of indigenous peoples in Convention processes following the adoption of this policy.[129] Moreover, the General Assembly of the States Parties to the World Heritage Convention in November 2015 adopted a Policy for the integration of a sustainable development perspective into the processes of the World Heritage Convention (prepared at the request of the WHC under the guidance of the World Heritage Centre), which underlines that recognizing indigenous rights is at the heart of sustainable development and calls on States Parties to ensure the effective participation and FPIC of indigenous peoples

125 The draft decision prepared by IUCN therefore requested Thailand to 'achieve a consensus of support for the nomination that is fully consistent with the principle of FPIC'. This sentence was deleted at the request of Viet Nam, whose delegate stated that 'we are here at a prestigious Committee of culture and heritage, we are not in Geneva on the Human Rights Council'. Only one Member State (Portugal) spoke up against this notion. Ibid.

126 Endorois Welfare Council, Saami Council and IWGIA (n 124).

127 E.g. EMRIP, Study on cultural heritage (n 1) para. 51; IWGIA and others, 'Joint Submission on the lack of implementation of the UNDRIP in the context of UNESCO's World Heritage Convention' (2012) <http://www.forestpeoples.org/sites/fpp/files/publication/2012/05/joint-submission-unpfii.pdf> accessed 23 October 2015.

128 See UNESCO, 'Report on the achievement of the goal and objectives of the Second International Decade of the World's Indigenous Peoples' (2014) <http://www.un.org/esa/socdev/unpfii/documents/2014/unesco.pdf> accessed 23 October 2015.

129 Decisions 39 COM 11 (2015) para. 10; 37 COM 12.II (2013) para. 7.

where World Heritage processes affect them.[130] Over the next few years, the Centre and the Advisory Bodies are supposed to develop proposals for specific changes to the Operational Guidelines to translate the principles of the policy into specific operational procedures.[131]

Conclusion

The adoption of the UNDRIP, which all UN agencies and intergovernmental organizations are required to promote and apply in their work, has resulted in greatly increased attention to the recurring violations of indigenous peoples' rights in the nomination, declaration and management of World Heritage sites. Cases such as the 2011 World Heritage listing of Lake Bogoria National Reserve without the FPIC of the Endorois people, only two years after a landmark ruling of the ACHPR affirming the traditional ownership rights of the Endorois over Lake Bogoria, have attracted the notice of human rights bodies and the international conservation community alike,[132] and highlighted the urgent need for measures to ensure that the implementation of the World Heritage Convention is consistent with the UNDRIP. Much of this discussion, including the advocacy of indigenous peoples themselves,[133] has focused on the need for appropriate regulations and mechanisms to be put in place to ensure the effective participation of indigenous peoples in relevant decision-making processes under the Convention. As a result of this, the WHC in July 2015 inserted references to indigenous peoples into two paragraphs of the Operational Guidelines dealing with stakeholder participation, including a reference to the FPIC of indigenous peoples in the context of World Heritage nominations. While these provisions are couched in non-obligatory language and the involvement of indigenous peoples continues to be left at the discretion of States, it can be hoped that the forthcoming UNESCO policy on indigenous peoples and the Convention's new sustainable development policy will eventually lead to the adoption of regulations making respect for indigenous peoples' participatory rights, including their right to FPIC, a mandatory requirement in World Heritage decision-making processes.

130 Doc WHC-15/20.GA/INF.13, paras. 21-22. The policy was adopted by Resolution 20 GA 13 of the twentieth General Assembly.

131 General Assembly Res 20 GA 13, para. 8; WHC Decision 39 COM 5D (2015), para. 10.

132 See e.g. ACHPR res 197 (n 117); World Conservation Congress res 5.047 (n 118).

133 E.g. IWGIA and others (n 127).

The existence of such regulations would no doubt go a long way in making the World Heritage Convention more meaningful for indigenous peoples and in preventing the most serious violations of their human rights, especially at the nomination stage when the influence and leverage of the WHC and its Advisory Bodies are greatest. However, for the Convention to play a consistently positive role for indigenous peoples and the protection of their cultural heritage and rights, additional measures are needed. In particular, measures must be taken to ensure that indigenous peoples' own views and interpretations of their cultural and natural heritage can be, and are, consistently respected, recognized and reflected when the OUV of World Heritage sites in indigenous territories is defined.

Of fundamental importance in this regard is a reassessment by the WHC of the way the concept of 'heritage' is interpreted in the implementation of the Convention. As EMRIP has noted, the Convention's categorization of heritage into 'cultural' and 'natural' heritage is inappropriate in the case of indigenous peoples, for whom 'cultural and natural values are inseparably interwoven and should be managed and protected in a holistic manner'.[134] Considering that most World Heritage sites in indigenous peoples' territories are classified as purely 'natural' sites, in disregard of their cultural, spiritual and economic significance for the indigenous peoples concerned, it is clear that there is an urgent need for a renewed discussion – in which indigenous representatives should be centrally involved – on how the Convention's separation between nature and culture can be overcome, so that interconnections are consistently recognized.[135] The urgent necessity of action in this regard is also highlighted in the 'Promise of Sydney' agreed at the 2014 IUCN World Parks Congress, which includes the following recommendation/target:

> By 2020 the conceptual and management gap between natural and cultural World Heritage Site designations is eliminated, and a comprehensive approach taken towards the conservation of natural and biocultural heritage and knowledge systems in all designated sites.[136]

---

134 Study on cultural heritage (n 1) para. 8 and annex, para. 7.

135 Representatives of UNESCO and the Advisory Bodies have repeatedly noted the need for a rethink in this area in recent years. See, e.g., K Rao, 'Editorial' (2015) 75 *World Heritage* 1; Leitão and Badman (n 23) 87-88; Larsen and Wijesuriya (n 24) 13; Buckley and Badman (n 74).

136 Promise of Sydney, Innovative Approaches for Change (n 119), Respecting indigenous and traditional knowledge and culture, Recommendation 7.

This recommendation revives the suggestion of the 1996 and 1998 UNESCO expert meetings at la Vanoise and Amsterdam that the distinction between 'cultural', 'natural' and 'mixed' sites be abandoned in favor of a unified identity for all World Heritage sites, a suggestion that was at the time supported by all three Advisory Bodies and should now be revisited.[137] The WHC should also reconsider the recommendation made at the Amsterdam meeting that references to links between people and nature be reinserted into the text of the natural criteria (now criteria vii-x).[138] As the Director of IUCN's World Heritage Programme, Tim Badman has recently remarked, with the deletion of the references to human interaction with the environment and combinations of cultural and natural elements from the natural criteria in 1992, 'something was lost in terms of potential for the World Heritage Convention to bring together integrated practice from both "nature" and "culture" and has not yet been fully regained. It is now time to resume this discussion....'[139]

Perhaps most important for ensuring that OUV adequately and consistently reflects indigenous peoples' own values and interpretations of World Heritage sites in their territories, however, is a reassessment by the WHC of the way the concept of OUV is interpreted and applied. Under the existing regulations, indigenous cultural values are routinely brushed aside and disregarded when they are deemed as not 'exceptional', 'unique', 'intact' or 'authentic' enough by government agencies, ICOMOS and/or the WHC. Consequentially, the values and priorities of heritage experts, bureaucrats and academic specialists assume greater importance than – and in many ways replace and undermine – the values attached to the sites by the traditional owners and custodians, who have inhabited, shaped and protected the respective areas for generations and whose lives and cultures are inextricably connected to them. To remedy this situation, EMRIP has offered the following advice to the WHC:

> The World Heritage Committee should adopt changes to the criteria and regulations for the assessment of 'outstanding universal value' so as to ensure that the values assigned to World Heritage sites by indigenous

137 See n 41. Leitão and Badman also note that this suggestion remains valid. Leitão and Badman (n 23) 87.

138 See n 36.

139 Leitão and Badman (n 23) 88. Elsewhere Badman has noted: 'If such a proposal was made today – to eliminate people from nature in the World Heritage criteria – it would be out of tune with nature conservation practice, and there would not be support for such a move within IUCN.' Buckley and Badman (n 74) 114.

> peoples are fully and consistently recognized as part of their outstanding universal value.[140]

Similarly, the Promise of Sydney recommends:

> The World Heritage Convention should fully and consistently recognize Indigenous Peoples' cultural values as universal, and develop methods for recognition and support for the interconnectedness of natural, cultural, social, and spiritual significance of World Heritage sites, including natural and cultural sites and cultural landscapes.[141]

These recommendations are not meant to suggest that all heritage sites in indigenous peoples' territories should be considered as having OUV and do not challenge the idea of the World Heritage List as a select list and the prerogative of the WHC to make the final judgment on whether a given site merits inscription or not. What they do challenge, however, is the authority of the WHC, States and the Advisory Bodies to redefine, reinterpret and reinvent the significance of the indigenous heritage sites that *are* inscribed on the List without respecting the views of the indigenous peoples, and at the expense of their livelihoods and rights to protect, exercise and develop their cultural heritage and expressions. The existing requirement by which indigenous peoples' cultural and spiritual relationship with their lands and natural resources must be shown to be 'exceptional' or 'unique' in order to be recognized as an integral part of a World Heritage site's OUV is inappropriate and not compatible with the WHC's stated desire to 'accord full respect to the social and cultural values of all societies' and respect the 'cultural contexts to which [heritage properties] belong'.[142] To be consistent with these principles, the focus should be on finding ways to recognize and reflect indigenous peoples' own values and interpretations of their heritage sites, not on comparative analyses regarding their significance in a global context. Nor should the conditions of 'integrity' and 'authenticity' provide a justification for not respecting indigenous peoples' perspectives when the OUV of World Heritage sites in their territories is defined – all the more so as the interpretation of these concepts by the WHC,

---

140 Study on cultural heritage (n 1) annex, para. 29.

141 Promise of Sydney, Innovative Approaches for Change (n 119), World Heritage theme, Recommendation 6.

142 Operational Guidelines 2015, annex 4 (Nara Document on Authenticity) paras. 2, 11.

the Advisory Bodies and States Parties is often incompatible with indigenous understandings.[143]

An in-depth discussion of the interpretation and application of the concepts of integrity and authenticity in the implementation of the World Heritage Convention is beyond the scope of this chapter. It is evident, however, that the practice of assessing the integrity of a landscape's natural values in isolation from the integrity and authenticity of associated indigenous cultural values is highly inadequate considering that for indigenous peoples these values are inseparably interwoven.[144] To be meaningful for indigenous peoples and compatible with their perspectives, the notion of integrity would need to reinforce and protect indigenous peoples' relationship with their territories, their rights to their land and resources and the roles and responsibilities of traditional owners and custodians, no matter whether a site is classified as a cultural, natural or mixed site. In other words, it would need to be consistent with and reinforce indigenous peoples' right to cultural integrity.[145] However, the reality is that the notion of integrity is frequently used to justify the imposition of restrictions on indigenous peoples' traditional land use activities and then serves to undermine their rights in World Heritage sites, in particular those listed as natural sites.

The application of the concept of authenticity to indigenous heritage is also often not consistent with indigenous peoples' own perspectives. Despite the WHC's endorsement of the Nara Document on Authenticity, it continues to be heavily influenced by Western notions, which 'require that indigenous people must match a perceived ideal of indigenousness that is ahistorical, un-

143 The Native Hawaiian lawyer Mililani Trask has remarked that 'UNESCO and its affiliates IUCN, ICOMOS and ICCROM, impose their own interpretations of "outstanding universal value", "integrity" and "authenticity" rather than ensuring that the cultural values of Indigenous people are included and addressed.' Quoted in the report of the Copenhagen expert workshop (n 121) 12.

144 As Andrews and Buggey note in relation to Aboriginal cultural landscapes in Canada: 'Aboriginal cultural landscapes are expressions of a worldview that... regards humans as an integral part of the land, inseparable from its animals, plants and spirits... Considerations of wholeness or intactness, the defining conditions of integrity..., must situate within this cultural context.' T Andrews and S Buggey, 'Authenticity in Aboriginal Cultural Landscapes' (2008) 39(2-3) *APT Bulletin* 63, 68.

145 The right of indigenous peoples to cultural integrity 'refers to a bundle of inter-related human rights such as rights to culture, subsistence, livelihood, and religion, which all support the protection of land rights as an important aspect of the cultural survival of indigenous peoples'. See Gilbert (n 10) 59.

changing, and pure from foreign influences'.[146] For indigenous peoples their lands and territories are not relics but living cultural landscapes (as well as economic, spiritual and social landscapes) in which dynamic change is inherent and integral to the cultural value. 'Any test of authenticity, therefore, must recognize, expect and endorse change', as Thomas Andrews and Susan Buggey emphasize.[147] This corresponds with the interpretation of indigenous peoples' right to the enjoyment of their own culture in international human rights law, which is based on a recognition that:

> The right to enjoy a culture is not 'frozen' at some point in time when the culture was supposedly 'pure' or 'traditional'. The enjoyment of culture should not be falsely restricted as a result of anachronistic notions of the 'authenticity' of the culture.[148]

In 2011, a broad coalition of indigenous and human rights organizations submitted a joint statement to both the WHC and the UNPFII in which they expressed concern that the concepts of OUV, integrity and authenticity are 'interpreted and applied in ways that are disrespectful of Indigenous peoples and their cultures, inconsiderate of their circumstances and needs, preclude cultural adaptations and changes, and serve to undermine their human rights'.[149] Indigenous representatives have repeatedly called on the WHC to proactively engage with indigenous peoples in order to find a solution to these issues. For

146 Andrews and Buggey (n 144), 69. See for example the case of the Ngorongoro Conservation Area (text to n 79).

147 Ibid, 70. Also see Australia ICOMOS, 'The Asia-Pacific Regional Workshop on Associative Cultural Landscapes: Report' (1995) Doc WHC-95/CONF.203/INF.9, 12, where it is underlined that authenticity 'must not exclude cultural continuity through change, which may introduce new ways of relating to and caring for the place' and 'may mean the maintenance of a continuing association between the people and the place, however it may be expressed through time'.

148 Aboriginal and Torres Strait Islander Social Justice Commissioner, *Native Title Report 2000* (Human Rights and Equal Opportunity Commission 2001) 58. For details see J Gilbert, 'Custodians of the land: Indigenous peoples, human rights and cultural integrity' in M Langfield, W Logan and MN Craig (eds), *Cultural Diversity, Heritage and Human Rights* (Routledge 2010) 31, 37-38.

149 Endorois Welfare Council and others, 'Joint Statement on continuous violations of the principle of free, prior and informed consent in the context of UNESCO's World Heritage Convention' (2011) <http://www.forestpeoples.org/sites/fpp/files/publication/2012/04/joint-statement-indigenous-organizations-unesco-2.pdf> accessed 23 November 2015, fn 13.

instance, the indigenous participants at the 2012 expert workshop on the World Heritage Convention and indigenous peoples in Copenhagen recommended:

> [C]omprehensive amendments to the Operational Guidelines are… necessary for enabling the World Heritage Convention to become an instrument that appropriately reflects and embraces the worldviews, values and heritage of Indigenous peoples, on an equal footing and with the same emphasis as it reflects and embraces the worldviews, values and heritage of the other peoples of the world. To achieve these ends, the Guidelines must be carefully reviewed, through an open and transparent process with the full and effective participation of Indigenous peoples.[150]

Additionally, the WHC should undertake a comprehensive review of the World Heritage List to identify the sites incorporating indigenous peoples' traditional territories and reassess, together with the indigenous peoples concerned, whether their OUV adequately reflects indigenous perspectives and whether their management frameworks are adequate for the safeguarding of indigenous heritage and in line with international standards regarding indigenous rights. Considering UNESCO's mission and its commitments to human rights, cultural diversity and cultural pluralism, it is obvious that addressing these questions is important not only for the credibility of the World Heritage Convention, but also for the credibility of UNESCO as a whole.

150 Copenhagen Call to Action (n 101), annex 3, p. 1.

Towards Sámi Self-determination over Their Cultural Heritage: The UNESCO World Heritage Site of Laponia in Northern Sweden

Leena Heinämäki, Thora Herrmann and Carina Green

1 Introduction

The World Heritage Site of Laponia is a 9,400 square kilometer area, situated just above the Arctic Circle in the north of Sweden (Fig 1). The area obtained its World Heritage status in 1996. Stretching to the Norwegian border, the area consists of the national parks *Stora Sjöfallet/Stuor Muorkke, Sarek, Padjelanta/Badjelánnda,* and *Muttos/Muddus* and the nature reserves *Sjaunja/Sjávnja* and *Stubba* (Fig. 1).

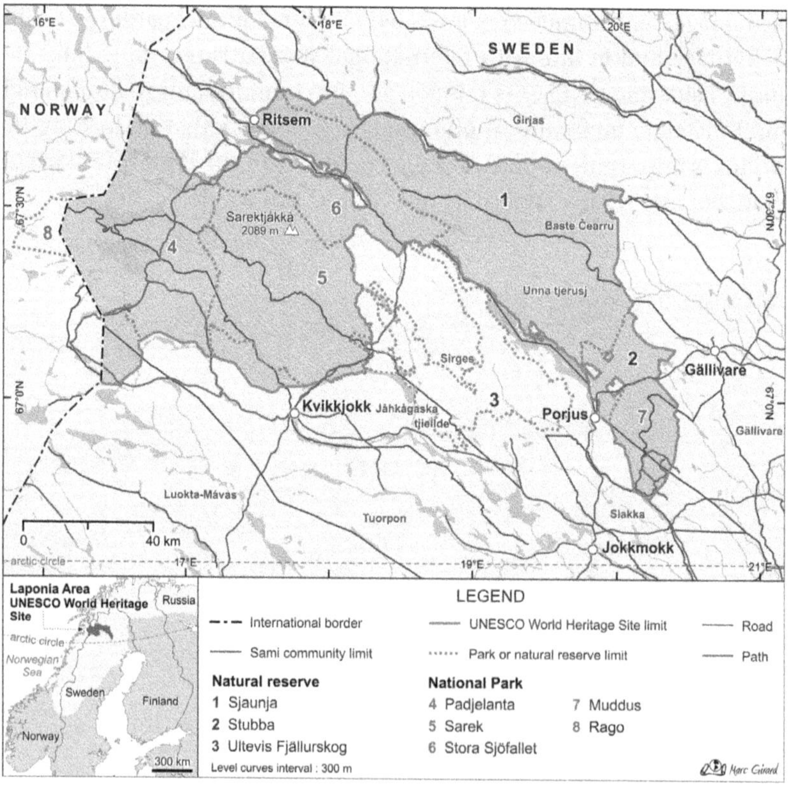

FIGURE 1 *Location of Laponia UNESCO World Heritage Site. Cartography: Marc Girard, Université de Montréal, 2015*

Xanthaki, Valkonen et al. (eds.), *Indigenous Peoples' Cultural Heritage: Rights, Debates and Challenges.*

Both the natural qualities of the area and the local Sámi reindeer herding culture are included in the justification for the status of this site as a World Heritage area. Seven samebys[1] have parts of their lands inside the World Heritage area: *Báste, Unna tjerusj, Sirges, Jåkkåkaska tjiellde, Tuorpon, Luokta-Mavas,* and *Gällivare skogssameby*. Two others, *Slakka* and *Udtja*, only use small segments of land within the borders of Laponia for grazing their reindeer at certain periods of the year. No-one lives within the World Heritage area permanently, but each summer many reindeer herding families move up to the mountains to be close to the reindeer grazing on the summer pastures.

In 1972, UNESCO adopted the *Convention Concerning the Protection of the World Cultural and Natural Heritage*,[2] or *The World Heritage Convention*,[3] as it is commonly called, in order to identify, safeguard, protect, and preserve natural areas and cultural sites that are unique from a global perspective.[4] According to UNESCO, World Heritage sites "belong to all the peoples of the world, irrespective of the territory on which they are located" (UNESCO, World Heritage Centre).[5] Sites may be nominated on the basis of natural, cultural or mixed criteria. Laponia was nominated in both categories, and was officially selected as a mixed World Heritage site under the natural criteria (i), (ii) and (iii) and under the cultural criteria (iii) and (v). Laponia has a unique management organisation called *Laponiatjuottjudus*. The organisation has a strong Sámi influence and consists of representatives from the local Sámi samebys, the regional and local authorities and the Swedish Environmental Protection Agency.

During the past twenty years, international law relating to Indigenous Peoples' human rights has gone through a profound transformation. Not only new instruments, such as the United Nations Declaration on the Rights of Indigenous Peoples[6] (UNDRIP) and the Convention on Biological Diversity[7] (CBD)

---

1 The sameby (the literate translation being *Sámi Village*) is an economic association for a group of reindeer herders that jointly use a certain geographical area. For the historical background and juridical and structural organization of the samebys, see also Beach 1981:360-393.

2 http://whc.unesco.org/en/conventiontext/ (accessed on 12 November 2015).

3 UNESCO World Heritage List : http://whc.unesco.org/en/list/ (accessed on 12 November 2015).

4 UNESCO, *World Heritage Information Kit*, UNESCO World Heritage Centre, 2008, Paris.

5 UNESCO, World Heritage Centre : http://whc.unesco.org/en/about/ (accessed on 12 November 2015).

6 The United Nations Declaration on the Rights of Indigenous Peoples, 7 September 2007, Sixty-first Session, A/61/L.67.

7 The Convention on Biological Diversity, adopted 5 June 1992, entered into force 29 December 1993, 1760 UNTS 79.

expand the recognition of Indigenous Peoples' rights; national constitutions and legislation have also widened the enforceability of Indigenous Peoples' rights to an unparallelled degree. Meanwhile, far-reaching decisions of treaty bodies, national courts and regional human rights bodies have demonstrated judicial willingness to interpret and apply Indigenous Peoples' human rights in an expansive fashion. This includes recognition of rights to their lands, traditional territories, natural resources, cultural heritage and, most importantly, self-determination.[8]

This chapter, first, looks at the recent developments of the Indigenous Peoples' right to self-determination as it relates to their cultural and natural heritage. Indigenous Peoples' self-determination is inherently connected to the rights of Indigenous Peoples to their lands and traditional territories, natural resources, culture, cultural heritage and "way of life", as well as to self-identification and to participation in decision-making processes affecting them.[9] In the context of world heritage, an important element of the right to self-determination is the right of Indigenous Peoples to manage, for their own benefit, their own cultural and natural resources.[10]

After discussing international legal developments towards the recognition of the right of Indigenous Peoples to self-determination, we will take a closer look at the extent to which the structures of co-management of Laponia's World Heritage translate to Sámi control over their tradional lands. On what grounds is Laponia to be preserved, and what were the elements in need of "preservation" and "conservation" in Laponia? We will examine how one could possibly preserve a "living culture" such as the local Sámi reindeer herding culture, and conserve a "living landscape" such as reindeer pastures that were part of the justification for the designation of Laponia. We will analyse what place is given to the Indigenous Peoples who have rights of ownership, access or use to these sites in the different strands of activities related to heritage management. More specifically, the crucial question addressed in this chapter is: Are the local Sámi involved in the designation process and management/ protection of their heritage site and if so, at what level? Since it was situated on their traditional territory and the actual justification was based on both the nature and the local Sámi reindeer herding culture, one would assume that they would play a vital role in the local discussions on how best to manage this

8 See, Tobin, B, *Indigenous peoples, Customary Laws and Human Rights – Why Living Law Matters*, (Routledge, New York 2014), 1.

9 Tobin, at 33.

10 EMRIP 2011, Final Report of the study on Indigenous Peoples and the right to participate in decision-making. UN Doc.A/HRC/18/42, Annex, para. 18.

newly achieved status of the area. The chapter aims to view how influential the local Sámi have been in the appointment work, and whether governance, policy and management practices draw upon and integrate indigenous conservation practices and State conservation practice in safeguarding this area.

The participation of Indigenous Peoples in environmental management is inherently linked to their right to self-determination.[11] We will explore whether and to what extent the engagement of Indigenous communities in managing World Heritage sites is in line with their right of self-determination. More specifically, we will analyse to what extent Laponia's co-management reflects the Sámi people's right to self-determination, especially concerning their tangible and intangible cultural heritage and natural ressources, which are inseparable since culture and lands and its resources cannot be viewed as two separate entities in the case of Indigenous Peoples.

Through the analysis of the Laponia World Heritage area in Norrbotten, Sweden, this chapter argues that the nomination of Laponia as a UNESCO World Heritage site and the establishment of the co-management of the site have been active processes for the Sámi community aimed at (re)gaining control over their cultural and natural heritage and the associated cultural landscape they have been using for generations. Control over their cultural heritage and traditional territories is a crucial component of Indigenous Peoples' right to self-determination.

2 Indigenous Peoples' Right to Cultural Heritage

Although framing their claims within the language of human rights, Indigenous Peoples' efforts to protect their cultural heritage have been drawn into the realm of cultural and intellectual property rights. Tobin notes that applying the concept of "cultural property" to aspects of Indigenous Peoples' tangible and intangible culture is highly controversial for a number of reasons, including the inherent difference of legal approach between customary law and positive legal regimes.[12] These include conflicts related to perceptions on

11 Li, TM, 'Locating Indigenous Environmental Knowledge in Indonesia', in R Ellen, P Parkes and A Bicker (eds.), *Indigenous Environmental Knowledge and its Transformations. Critical Anthropological Perspectives*. (Routledge, New York 2000) 144.

12 Tobin, B, 'Redefining Perspectives in the Search for Protection of Traditional Knowledge: A Case Study from Peru', *Review of European Community and International Environmental Law*, (2001), 10(1): 47-64.

individual versus collective rights,[13] as well as gaps between property ownership versus stewardship responsibilities.[14]

Barsh, opposing the property rights approach, argues that it leads to a distortion of the very nature of indigenous cultures, and of the relationship between Indigenous Peoples and their lands.[15] According to Barsh, this is due to an artificial distinction in Western thought between nature and culture reflected in the assumption that cultural and intellectual property can be completely detached from the landscapes in which they arose.[16] This fails to recognize that land and knowledge are so closely interlinked that the use of property-based terms such as "land tenure" completely distort indigenous conceptions of law.[17] This conflict has led many authors to prefer the concept of cultural heritage.[18]

Daes, using the term "collective heritage" of Indigenous Peoples,[19] covering both their cultural and intellectual property, defines "heritage" as: "everything that belongs to the distinct identity of a people and which is theirs to share, if they wish, with other peoples. It includes all those things, which international law regards as the creative production of human thought and craftsmanship, such as songs, stories, scientific knowledge and artworks. It also includes inheritances from the past and from nature, such as human remains, the natural features of the landscape, and naturally occurring species of plants and animals with which a people has long been connected."[20] Janke, in her research on Indigenous Peoples' cultural and intellectual property in Australia, sets a more comprehensive list of heritage rights, which includes rights to: "own, control and define what constitutes Indigenous Cultural and Intellectual Property and/or Indigenous heritage; have protection based on self-determination;

13 Tsosie, R, 'Cultural Challenges to Biotechnology: Native American Genetic Resources and the Concept of Harm', *Journal of Law, Medicine & Ethics*, (Fall 2007): 396-411, 397-398.

14 Coombie, RJ (2009), 'The Expanding Purview of Cultural Properties and their Politics', *Annual Review of Law and Social Sciences* (2009) 2: 293-412.

15 Barsh, RL, 'How Do You Patent A Landscape? The Perils of Dichotomizing Cultural and Intellectual Property', *International Journal of Cultural Property* (1999) 8(1):14-47, 15.

16 Ibid., 16.

17 Ibid., 20.

18 Coombie (2009), supra note 14; Janke, T (1999); *Our Culture: Our Future – Report on Australian Indigenous Cultural and Intellectual Property Rights* (Michael Frankel & Co, Sydney 1999); Prott, L and O'Keefe, P (1992), '"Cultural Heritage" or "Cultural Property"', *International Journal of Cultural Property*, 1(2): 307-320.

19 Daes, EI (1993), *Discrimination Againsta Indigenous Peoples: Study on the Protection of the cultural and Intellectual Property of Indigenous Peoples*, E/CN.4/Sub.2/1993/28, UNCHR, Geneva, para. 23.

20 Ibid., para. 24.

be recognized as guardians and interpreters of their culture; collective ownership of cultural and intellectual property rights; authorize or refuse rights for commercial use in accordance with their own customary law; require prior informed consent for access and use; and maintain secrecy over Indigenous knowledge and other cultural resources."[21]

As rightly pointed out by Tobin, it is nowadays a commonplace to see the term cultural heritage utilized as an umbrella term to cover all aspects of indigenous culture, including traditional knowledge, traditional cultural expressions as well as their intellectual and cultural property.[22] Tsosie, however, distinguishes cultural property, which she defines as: "items that are part of the cultural heritage of a tribal government or native people and which are significant to the native nation's survival as a distinctive people and culture from commercial products, which are items intentionally manufactured and created by native artists for the purpose of economic development."[23]

Tsosie's distinction may be relevant in terms of emphasizing the economic development aspect. If we acknowledge, however, Indigenous Peoples' right to self-determination regarding their cultural heritage, the economic development naturally also falls into this framework. In this respect, the recent study of the United Nations Expert Mechanism on the Rights of Indigenous Peoples (EMRIP) related to the promotion and protection of their cultural heritage[24] rightly emphasizes the principle of self-determination in defining the cultural heritage. It states that "Indigenous Peoples' cultural heritage includes tangible and intangible manifestations of their ways of life, world views, achievements and creativity, and should be considered an expression of their self-determination and their spiritual and physical relationships with their lands, territories and resources."[25]

Legal and administrative measures adopted to secure Indigenous cultural heritage include full property rights, *sui generis* regimes, co-management systems and the establishment of obligations to consult and/or seek prior informed consent from Indigenous Peoples for access to, holding of or use of

21 Janke (1999), supra note 18, 47-48.

22 Tobin, supra note 8, 147.

23 Tsosie, R, 'An Argument for Indigenous Governance of Cultural Property', in CB Graber, K Kuprecht and JC Lai, *International Trade in Indigenous Cultural Heritage: Legal and Policy Issues* (Edward Elgar, Cheltenham 2012), 237.

24 UN Human Rights Council, Expert Mechanism on the Rights of Indigenous Peoples, *Study and advice on the promotion and protection of the rights of indigenous peoples with respect to their cultural heritage*, A/HRC/EMPRIP/2015/2.

25 Ibid., para. 7.

elements of aspects of their cultural heritage.[26] Both co-management and consultation including free, prior and informed consent, can be seen as important steps towards the actualization of Indigenous Peoples' self-determination, as will be discussed below. This is not to say that many indigenous peoples might want to go beyond co-management, aiming rather for full autonomy or self-government over their lands and internal matters. Free, prior and informed consent is currently an evolving principle in international law that is still all too often interpreted as "a genuine attempt to reach an agreement" rather than a right to say no to developments that are against the wishes of Indigenous Peoples.[27]

2.1 *Indigenous Peoples' Right to Self-determination over Their Cultural Heritage*

It has become a common point that the right of Indigenous Peoples to self-determination is a fundamental human right, upon which the subsequent rights of Indigenous Peoples depend. For centuries, Indigenous Peoples have been resisting the colonial powers and national authorities and have repeatedly framed this resistance in the form of a demand for self-determination. It has been said that for Indigenous Peoples, recognition of their right to self-determination does not amount to the grant of new rights; rather, it is the recovery of rights denied by states that have assumed power over their affairs; whether states acting as colonial powers, settlers and other post-colonial state authorities or states that deny the existence of Indigenous Peoples in their territories. Indigenous Peoples view the struggle for self-determination as first and foremost a struggle for recovery of their ancestral sovereign rights.[28]

The realization of the right of Indigenous Peoples to self-determination can take a variety of forms. Shin Imai has suggested four categories of self-determination: sovereignty and self-government, self-management and self-admin-

26 Tobin, supra note 8, 146; See also, Carpenter, K A, Katyal, S and Riley, A, 'In Defense of Property'. *Yale Law Journal* 118 (2009), 1022-125.

27 See, an analysis of the indigenous peoples' right to free, prior and informed consent in L Heinämäki 'Global Context – Arctic Importance: Free, Prior and Informed Consent – An Emerging Paradigm in International Law Related to Indigenous Peoples' in TM Herrmann and T Martin (eds.) *Indigenous Peoples' Governance of Land and Protected Territories in the Arctic* (Springer 2016) 209-240; L Heinämäki 'The Rapidly evolving International Status of Indigenous Peoples: The Example of the Sami People in Finland' in C Allard and S Funderug Skogvang (eds.), *Indigenous Rights in Scandinavia* (Ashgate 2015) 189-204.

28 Tobin, supra note 8, 33.

istration, co-management and joint management, and participation in public government.[29] He explains:

> [t]he 'sovereigty and self-government' option leads to more autonomy for the Indigenous community to control its own social, economic and political development. The 'self-management and self-administration' option leads to greater control of local affairs and the delivery of services within a larger settler government legislative framework. The 'co-management and joint management' model institutionalizes indigenous participation in the management of lands and resources. The 'participation in public government' option provides a means to influence the policies of the settler government through Indigenous-specific institutions.[30]

In this chapter, we aim to have a particular look at the co-management aspect of self-determination. We do not necessarily hold the view that co-management exhausts the applications of self-determination, but rather see it as an important first step towards it. The fundamental question of the general right of Indigenous Peoples to self-determination in international law falls beyond the scope of this chapter, but has been discussed extensively in the legal literature.[31] Rather, this chapter aims to look at particular aspects related to

29 Imai, S, 'Indigenous Self-Determination and the State', in BJ Richardson, S Imai and K McNeil (eds.), *Indigenous Peoples and the Law: Comparative and Critical Perspectives* (Hart Publishing, Oxford 2009) 292-306.

30 Ibid., 292.

31 See generally, J Anaya *Indigenous Peoples in International Law*, 2nd edn (Oxford, Oxford University Press, 2004); E-IA Daes, 'The Right of Indigenous Peoples to "Self-Determination" in the Contemporary World Order' in D Clark and R Williamson (eds.), *Self-Determination: International Perspectives* (Houndmills, MacMillan Press, 1996) 47; A Xanthaki, Indigenous Rights and UN Standards: Self-determination, Culture, Land (CUP, 2010); P Thornberry, Indigenous rights in international law (Machester University Press, 2002); M Davis, 'Indigenous Struggles in Standard-Setting: The United Nations Declaration on the Rights of Indigenous Peoples' (2008) 9 *Melbourne Journal of International Law* 1; T Koivurova, 'From high hopes to disillusionment: Indigenous Peoples' struggle to (re)gain their right to self-determination' (2008) 15 *International Journal on Minority and Group Rights* 1; T Koivurova, 'Alkuperäiskansojen itsemääräämisoikeus kansainvälisessä oikeudessa' ['The right of selfdetermination of Indigenous Peoples in international law'] in M Aarto and M Vartiainen (eds.), *Oikeus kansainvälisessä maailmassa* [*Law in a changing world*] (Edita Publishing Oy, Lapin yliopiston oikeustieteiden tiedekunta (Faculty of Law at the University of Lapland), 2008) 249; LS Vars, *The Sámi People's Right to Self-determination* (University of Tromsö, 2009); GS Alfredsson, 'The Greenlanders and their human rights choices' in M Bergsmo (ed.), *Human Rights and Criminal Justice for the Downtrodden* (Lei-

self-determination such as control of Indigenous Peoples over their lands, and, related to this, the evolving right to free, prior and informed consent as articulated in international instruments, and as actualized in cultural heritage matters, including our case study of the Laponia World Heritage area.

3 UNDRIP and the Draft Nordic Sámi Convention

As pointed out by Tobin, Indigenous Peoples' rights to self-determination and cultural survival are both dependent upon and threatened by natural resource use. On the one hand, Indigenous Peoples' daily subsistence, development, spiritual and cultural well-being is interwined with the natural environment and biodiversity. On the other hand, natural resource exploitation is the single biggest threat to their territorial and cultural integrity and in some cases to their very existence. Effective and sensitive control of resource use is, therefore, crucial for the realization of their human rights and the protection of their territorial, environmental and cultural integrity and enjoyment of their cultural heritage and way of life.[32]

Regarding the UN Declaration on the Rights of Indigenous Peoples (UNDRIP), it has become a commonplace to state that the instrument did not establish any new rights for Indigenous Peoples but rather codified the existing rights.[33] However, according to the present authors, this does not do justice to the ambitious Declaration which celebrates a paradigm shift: not only does it explicitly recognise, for the first time, the right to self-determination of Indigenous Peoples, but it also guarantees stronger participatory rights than any earlier instrument, including the free, prior and informed consent (FPIC) in relation to decision-making concerning natural resources and other crucial mat-

---

den, Martinus Nijhoff Publishers, 2003) 453; GS Alfredsson, 'Minorities, Indigenous and Tribal Peoples, and Peoples: Definitions of Terms as a Matter of International Law' in N Ghanea and A Xanthaki (eds.), *Minorities, Peoples and Self-Determination* (Leiden, Martinus Nijhoff Publishers, 2005) 163; M Åhren, *The Saami traditional dress and beauty pageants: Indigenous Peoples' rights of ownership and self-determination over their cultures*, Avhandling leverert for graden Philosophiae Doctor I rettsvitenskap (Thesis supplied for the degree of Philosophiae Doctor of Law) (2010) (unpublished).

32 Tobin, supra note 8, 120.

33 The Ministry of Justice of Finland has also noted that the UN Declaration does not establish new rights. See, Government Bill: Hallituksen esitys eduskunnalle itsenäisten maiden alkuperäis- ja heimokansoja koskevan yleissopimuksen hyväksymisestä sekä laiksi yleissopimuksen lainsäädännön alaan kuuluvien määräysten voimaansaattamisesta (20 May 2014).

ters.[34] Although the UNDRIP is not strictly a legally binding instrument,[35] human rights monitoring bodies have already started to apply it as a legal source and as a basis for the rights of Indigenous Peoples.[36] However, the national implementation of UNDRIP will be a challenging process, especially in relation to issues where states should give up their interests in indigenous peoples' traditional lands and related natural resources.

The right to self-determination, as understood in the UNDRIP, does not afford Indigenous Peoples total freedom to determine their political status, since it is also concerned with protection of the territorial integrity of sovereign states.[37] Fitzmaurice states that: "the definition of self-determination in the Declaration is considered a compromise between the aspirations of Indigenous Peoples and the reluctance of States to grant a broadly understood right to self-determination."[38] Thus, according to the UNDRIP, self-determination does not entail the right to secession. However, the UNDRIP does recognize full self-determination in terms of the economic, social and cultural development of Indigenous Peoples. The Declaration guarantees the right to self-determination in internal and local matters, including the protection of Indigenous Peoples' cultural heritage.[39] Article 31 of UNDRIP recognises, in very clear terms, the Indigenous Peoples' right to tangible and intangible heritage,

---

34 See Articles 3, 19 and 32 of the UNDRIP.

35 The binding or semi-binding nature of the Declaration is widely discussed amongst international lawyers. It has been argued, at least partly, to already express customary international law or at least generally accepted principles related to Indigenous Peoples. See, Anaya, J, Report of the Special Rapporteur on the rights of Indigenous Peoples, A/68/317 (14 August 2013) 16-18 http://daccess-dds-ny.un.org/doc/UNDOC/GEN/N13/427/10/PDF/N1342710.pdf?OpenElement. (accessed 20 August 2015). See also, International Law Association (ILA), 75th conference, resolution No 5/2102, para. 2 (5 August 2012); International Law Association, Committee on the Rights of Indigenous Peoples, Final Report (2012).

36 See, *Saramaka People v Suriname*, Inter-American Court of Human Rights, Judgment of 28 November 2007, Series C, No 172. The Supreme Court of Belize made a decision relating to the rights of the Maya community to their lands and resources, applying the Declaration. *Aurelio Cal v Attorney-General of Belize Claim* 121/2007 (18 October 2007) Supreme Court of Belize http://www.elaw.org/node/1620 (accessed 19 January 2014).

37 See UN Doc E/CN.4/Sub2AC.4/1992/3 Add 1 (1992) 5. See Article 46 of the UN Declaration on the Rights of Indigenous Peoples, which explicitly protects the territorial integrity of states.

38 See Fitzmaurice, M, 'The New Developments Regarding the Saami Peoples of the North' (2009) *16 Journal on Minority and Group Rights* 67-156, 151. See generally, Allen, S and Xanthaki, A (eds.), *Reflections on the UN Declaration on the Rights of Indigenous Peoples* (Hart Publishing 2011).

39 Article 4.

and obliges states to take effective measures to recognize and protect the exercise of this right.[40]

In addition, effective and meaningful participation – the right to consultation or even FPIC with respect to land and resource use and other important matters, such as participation in international decision-making – plays a key role in the determination of economic, social and cultural development, including the maintenance and protection of cultural heritage.

The right to FPIC has been seen as a part of the "new" understanding of self-determination of Indigenous Peoples. However, to what degree the FPIC works as intended and how it works in practice, and how it affects local communities are issues that are not yet well documented.

Effective realization of Indigenous Peoples' rights to self-determination is closely linked to their right of self-identification, as well as to their involvement in decision-making processes and implementation of requirements for their free, prior and informed consent under international human rights law.[41] Self-determination also entails recognition of the inextricable link between Indigenous Peoples' human rights and the protection of their natural environment and their cultural and economic way of life.

It is important to note that the UN Human Rights Committee has applied Article 1 of ICCPR (the right of peoples to self-determination) on Indigenous Peoples in several concluding observations to States' reports.[42] On the 2009 re-

---

40 Article 31 of UNDRIP.

41 Doyle, C and Carino, J, 'Making Free, Prior and Informed Consent a Reality: Indigenous Peoples and the Extractive Sector', PIPLinks and Middlesex University School of Law 2013, available at www.piplinks.org/system/files/Consortium+FPIC+report+-+May+2013+-+web+version.pdf (accessed 10 June 2014), at 7.

42 Article 40 of the CCPR requires States Parties to submit reports on measures taken to give effect to the rights defined therein. An initial report is to be submitted one year after the state ratifies the CCPR, and further reports are required periodically (normally every five years). State reports and the Concluding Observations of the UN Human Rights Committee, http://www.unhchr.ch/html/menu2/6/hrc/hrcs.htm (accessed 5 March 2007). See Concluding Observations of the Human Rights Committee on Canada UN Doc. CCPR/C/79/Add.105 (1999). Explicit references to either Article 1 or to the notion of self-determination have also been made in the Committee's Concluding Observations on Mexico, UN Doc. CCPR/C/79/Add.109 (1999); Norway, UN Doc. CCPR/C/79/Add.112 (1999); Australia, UN Doc. CCPR/CO/69/Aus (2000); Denmark, UN Doc. CCPR/CO/70/DNK (2000); Sweden, UN Doc. CCPR/CO/74/SWE (2002); Finland, UN Doc. CCPR/CO/82/FIN (2004); Canada, UN Doc. CCPR/C/CAN/CO/5 (2005); and the United States, UN Doc. CCPR/C/USA/CO/3 (2006); It should be noted that also the Committee on Economic, Social and Cultural Rights has applied Article 1 on Indigenous Peoples. See, for instance, CESCR Concluding Observations on the Russian Federation, UN doc. E/C.12/1/

port by Sweden, the Committee expressed its concern about the limited extent to which the Sámi Parliament may participate in the decision-making process on issues affecting land and traditional activities of the Sámi people, explicitly referring to the right to self-determination and the right to culture and participation.[43] The Committee addressed a key component regarding the Sámi people's self-determination over their cultural heritage by requesting that the State party should take further steps to involve the Sámi in the decisions concerning the natural environment and necessary means of subsitence for the Sámi people.[44] Without a real possibility to influence the decision-making related to traditional lands and means of subsistence, the Sámi cannot participate in the maintenance of their cultural heritage. The Committee on the Elimination of Racial Discrimination (CERD) has also made an important statement concerning Indigenous Peoples' free, prior and informed consent in relation to the Sámi in Sweden. In 2013, the Committee recommended that Sweden adopt legislation and take other measures to ensure respect for the right of Sámi communities to offer free, prior and informed consent whenever their rights may be affected by projects, including extraction of natural resources, carried out in their traditional territories.[45]

The concerns and the recommendations of the two international human rights monitoring bodies are justified. Regarding Sámi rights in Swedish legislation, it should be noted that the Swedish Constitution, and in particular the Instrument of Government Chapter 1, section 2, mentions the Sámi as a people since the overhaul of the Act in 2010. Before that, the Sámi were only mentioned as an ethnic minority. The provision, however, creates goals for the public and cannot be evoked by persons before courts. It states: "The opportunities of the Sámi people and ethnic, linguistic and religious minorities to pre-

---

Add.94, 2003, paras. 11,39., http://www.unhchr.ch/tbs/doc.nsf/(Symbol)/E.C.12.1.Add.94.En?Opendocument (accessed 19 January 2007). See also CESCR General Comment No. 15, on the Right to Water (ICESCR Arts. 11,12) UN doc. E(C.12/2002/11, at para. 7, http://www.ohchr.org/english/bodies/cescr/comments.htm (accessed 17 January 2007). According the Committee, Article 1, which guarantees peoples' rights, cannot be used in individual communications because the Optional Protocol provides a procedure under which individuals may claim that their individual rights have been violated. *Lubicon Lake Band v. Canada*, supra note 124, para. 32.1.

43 UN Human Rights Committee, Concluding Observations on Sweden, CCPR/C/SWE/CO/6, 7 May 2009, para. 20. Referred articles are 1,25 and 27 of the CCPR.

44 Ibid., para. 20.

45 Committee on the Elimination of Discrimination, Concluding Observations on Sweden, CERD/C/SWE/CO/19-21, 23 September 2013, para. 17.

serve and develop a cultural and social life of their own shall be promoted".[46] However, as explained by Allard, despite the constitutional protection of Sámi culture and way of life, there exist no specific Sámi courts, nor are there specific procedures laid down related to Sámi matters.[47]

Sweden, along with Finland and Norway are currently negotiating a Nordic Sámi Convention, which would, when accepted, create an extensive improvement of the legal situation of the Sámi in all the Nordic countries. On October 2005, the Expert Group, nominated by the governments of Finland, Norway and Sweden and respected Sámi Parliaments, presented a draft Nordic Saami Convention.[48] The Draft Convention, from the outset, makes the Sámi people a legal subject and recognizes their right to self-determination.[49] The acknowledgment of this right fundamentally changes their status of an indigenous people, by making them active actors alongside states, at least in matters that directly concern them.[50]

---

46 Instrument of Government, 1974, ch. 1 s. 2 para. 5. See an English version of the Act at http://www.riksdagen.se/en/How-the-Riksdag-works/Democracy/The-Constitution/The-Instrument-ofGovernment/ (accessed 13 March 2014).

47 Allard, C, Legal Pluralism and the Sámi: an Indigenous People in Europe, Conference Proceedings, Indigenous Peoples' Sovereignty and the Limits of Judicial and Legal Pluralism : American Tribes, Canadian First Nations and Scandinavian Sami, Compared Roberto Toniatti and Jens Woelk (eds.), International Conference Trento, 24-25 October 2013, 49-60, available at http://www.jupls.eu/images/ebook%20JPs%20-%202014.pdf (accessed 27 December 2015).

48 See an analysis of the Draft Convention, Timo Koivurova, 'The Draft Nordic Saami Convention: Nations Working Together', *International Community Law Review* 10 (2008), 279-293. See also, Malgosia Fitzmaurice, 'The New Developments Regarding the Saami People of the North', *Journal on Minority and Group Rights* 16 (2009), 67-156.

49 According to the Convention, the Sámi people is the indigenous people of Finland, Norway and Sweden. The Sámi thus constitutes one people, living across the national borders. The Expert Group were researching the possibility to include the Russian Federation and Sámi people that live in the Russia, but concluded, with the regrets, that it would be too complicated to agree on a strong and effective Sámi Convention if the negotiations should have also included the Russian Federation. See Mathias Åhren, in M Åhren et al. (eds.), "The Nordic Sami Convention: International Human Rights, Self-Determination and other Central Provisions", 3 *Gáldu Cala – Journal of Indigenous Peoples Rights* 8, 2007, 13.

50 See an analysis of the self-determination articles of the Draft Nordic Sami Convention, Leena Heinämäki, 'The Nordic Saami Convention: The Right of a People to Control Issues of Importance to Them', in N Bankes and T Koivurova (eds.), *The Proposed Nordic Saami Convention, National and International Dimensions of Indigenous Property Rights*, (Hart Publishing, Oxford and Portland, 2013), 125-147.

One key aspect of the self-determination closely connected to the management of cultural heritage is the decision-making power related to natural resources. Article 36 of the Draft Convention states that: "before public authorities, based on law, grant a permit for prospecting or extraction of minerals or other sub-surface resources, or make decisions concerning utilization of other natural resources within such land or water areas that are owned or used by the Sámi, negotiations shall be held with the affected Sámi, as well as with the Sámi parliament, when the matter is such that it falls within Article 16" (matters of major importance). Additionally, Article 36 notes that: "permits for prospecting or extraction of natural resources shall not be granted if the activity would make it impossible or substantially more difficult for the Sámi to continue to utilize the areas concerned, and this utilization is essential to the Sámi culture, unless so consented by the Sámi parliament and the affected Sámi." This article creates a strong basis for the Sámi to safeguard their cultural heritage. Although their traditional lands and people's interaction with the lands can be seen as the foundation and expressions and of Indigenous Peoples' cultural heritage, there might be places of significant importance, such as cultural heritage sites, that can be safeguarded and managed only in line with Indigenous Peoples' self-determination when free, prior and informed consent of Indigenous Peoples is applied.

In this respect, the Draft Nordic Sámi Convention would strengthen the commitments created by UNDRIP in relation to FPIC. Article 32 of UNDRIP requires the consent of Indigenous Peoples prior to approval of any project affecting their lands or territories. Additionally, Article 19 requires the consent of Indigenous Peoples before adopting and implementing legislative or administrative measures that *may affect* them. In the Sámi homeland region (in all Nordic countries), this could mean that Sámi parliaments' views should be taken into account in all the relevant decision-making that *directly* affects the Sámi as an indigenous people, such as cultural heritage. This would set a frame for a strong protection of Sámi people's cultural heritage, if the Convention will be ratified.

Importantly, specifically related to the cultural heritage, the Draft Convention states that the states "shall respect the right of the Sámi people to manage its traditional knowledge and its traditional cultural expressions while striving to ensure that the Sámi are able to preserve, develop and pass these on to future generations".[51] Traditional knowledge has been defined to mean the skills and knowledge of flora, fauna and other natural resources and the ways to manage these. Moreover, Sámi cultural heritage is protected via Article 32.

51 Art. 31.

For the Sámi, the cultural landscape has a special meaning, since they have used the environment for generations and thus have created strong connections with their environment. It is this cultural environment which the Sámi have grown into and thus perceive as theirs, and which also consolidates their identity as Sámi.[52] This broad understanding of cultural heritage, including cultural landscape, "shall be protected by law and shall be cared for by the country's Sámi parliament or by cultural institutions in cooperation with the Sámi parliament."[53]

Negotiations of the Draft Nordic Sámi Convention have been set to be finalized by the end of 2016. Time will show whether the three Nordic countries and respective Sámi parliaments will ratify this ambitious instrument. This being the case, the protection of the Sámi people's rights would meet the required standards of the UNDRIP and general international law. In some respects, however, these standards may to some extent already be fulfilled in some particular cases, as will be discussed below.

4 Laponia World Heritage Area

Laponia obtained its World Heritage status during the UNESCO paradigm shift that took place during the late 90s in heritage conservation, which shifted emphasis from the preservation of only lost cultural traditions to the inclusion of living cultures and values.[54] In 1992, the World Heritage Convention became the first international legal instrument to recognize and protect living landscapes, when discussions within UNESCO to expand it to include also the protection of intangible values led to the introduction of a new category called *Cultural Landscape*, which works parallel to the purely natural or cultural criteria. *Cultural Landscape* bridges the traditonal nature-culture dichotomy in the heritage conservation field by comprising elements of what the World Heritage Convention defines as both Nature and Culture. As Rössler rightly stated:

52 See an analaysis, Koivurova. T, 'The Draft for a Nordic Saami Convention', *European Yearbook of Minority Issues* Vol 6, 2006/7: 103-136, 122-123.

53 Art. 32(1), Draft Convention.

54 ÅN Dahlström, *Negotiating Wilderness in a Cultural Landscape. Predators and Saami Reindeer Herding in the Laponian World Heritage Area* (Acta Universitatis Upsaliensis (Uppsala Studies in Cultural Anthropology no 32), 2003 Uppsala). p. 230, in : Carina Green, *Managing Laponia: A World Heritage as arena for Sámi ethno-politics in Sweden*, (2009, Acta Universitatis Upsaliensis. Uppsala Studies in Cultural Anthropology 47. 221 pp. Uppsala. ISBN 978-91-554-7656-4), 79.

"Cultural Landscapes are at the interface between nature and culture, tangible and intangible heritage, biological and cultural diversity – they represent a closely woven net of relationships, the essence of culture and people's identity. Cultural landscapes are a focus of protected areas in a larger ecosystem context, and they are a symbol of the growing recognition of the fundamental links between local communities and their heritage, humankind and its natural environment." [55]

The recognition of living landscapes mirrors the increasing emphasis placed on the interconnection between culture and nature, and on the intrinsic people-place relationships. As such, the category of *Cultural Landscape* has given increased recognition of the various forms of indigenous knowledge that shape landscapes, and the continuing living relationship between Indigenous Peoples with surrounding natural enviroment, including the latter's spiritual, social and identity-shaping values.[56] In the case of Laponia, the area is not protected as a Cultural Landscape by UNESCO but as a mixed site; both cultural and natural criteria has played a crucial role in establishing the co-management of the area with strong Sámi governance.

Although UNESCO itself has no powers to enforce the World Heritage Convention, it is, however, possible for UNESCO to exert pressure on the states parties to respect agreements. It is in this arena that local communities can seek support for their aspirations or rights concerns concerning a World Heritage identification, nomination or establishment. This direct connection between local people who are affected by, or responsible for the protected area or site, and the international community proved to be substantial for the local Sámi in Laponia. With the implementation of a World Heritage nomination, people living in or close to the protected sites have the possibility of building a stronger position vis-à-vis governmental authorities, a position that the local Sámi people in the case of Laponia have not had before, due to colonial history.

4.1 *The Process Leading Up to the Nomination of Laponia*

Laponia gained its World Heritage status in 1996, but the story of how Laponia came to be begins much earlier. Already in the 1980s the Swedish government

55 Mechthild Rössler,'World Heritage cultural landscapes: A UNESCO flagship programme 1992-2006' (2006), 31(4) *Landscape Research*, 334.

56 Thomas Schaaf and Mechthild Rössler 'Sacred Natural Sites, Cultural Landscapes and UNESCO's Action' in Bas Verschuuren, Robert Wild, Jeffrey A McNeely, and Gonzalo Oviedo (eds.), *Sacred Natural Sites Conserving Nature & Culture*, (Earthscan 2010) 161-170; Christina Cameron, and Mechthild Rössler 'World Heritage and Indigenous Peoples. The evolution of an important relationship' (2012), 62 *World Heritage Review*, 44-49.

sought to nominate a World Heritage site in the area that is today Laponia. This was the nature reserve of Sjávnja (today part of Laponia) and the idea was to nominate the site only based on natural criteria. However, the World Heritage Committee did not accept this first application. According to the advisory body, IUCN, the area was not unique enough to meet the standards of the World Heritage list. The Swedish government was recommended to revise the idea and to go for a larger area.[57] During this time, local participation in nature and culture management was being highlighted in many international arenas. As part of this debate, Indigenous Peoples' participation in the management of World Heritage sites that affected them had become an important issue within the World Heritage organization and also among indigenous and nature conservation groups.[58] Other World Heritage sites, such as Tongariro National Park in New Zealand, were adjusting their World Heritage status and incorporating criteria that acknowledged the local indigenous groups' cultural and spiritual links to these sites. In other words, when both the Sámi Parliament in Sweden and several governmental ministries and agencies raised the idea of including a Sámi cultural aspect in the new revised nomination, it came as no surprise. Up until this point, the local Sámi had not been involved in the World Heritage plans on any substantial level but once the idea of including the Sámi cultural aspect in the application was suggested, the local Sámi started to become more directly involved in the process. Representatives from the nine samebys with grazing lands inside the borders of the proposed site were now involved in discussions on how to proceed with the application. However, there was a general feeling that they often were pulling the short straw and that their will to be active in the process was not sufficiently acknowledged. And there was already at this stage some mistrust and mutual suspicion between the samebys and the state agencies.[59] This led many to talk about the "colonial structures" at work within the Swedish bureaucracy, and see the Laponian process as an illustration of this.

A lot of work and effort was put into preparing the application as far as the natural criteria were concerned. Now, the cultural part had to be added to the application text. The assignment of doing this was given to the head of the Sámi museum in Jokkmokk, but they had only about three months to finish

---

57 Dahlström, supra note 252.

58 Carina Green, *Managing Laponia: A World Heritage as arena for Sámi ethno-politics in Sweden*, (2009), Acta Universitatis Upsaliensis. Uppsala Studies in Cultural Anthropology 47. 221 pp. Uppsala. ISBN 978-91-554-7656-4), 80ff.

59 Green, supra note 59, 107ff.

the work before the application had to be submitted.[60] The short amount of time spent on preparing the (Sámi) cultural part of the application in contrast to the amount of time that went into formulating the justifications for meeting the natural part has been bought up by the local Sámi. There was a general feeling that less time and resources were spent on articulating the Sámi cultural interests than the pure ecological importance of the area. The Swedish Environmental Protection Agency (SEPA) and the County Administration of Norrbotten had been in charge of much of the process at this stage, as the agencies responsible for the nature conservation management in Sweden. This disproportionate emphasis on the "culture" vis-à-vis the "nature" in the application was therefore also linked to the disproportionate power between Swedish agencies (the State) and Sámi interests. This imbalance would continue to influence the negotiations concerning the management of Laponia, once the site was established.[61] However, a management philosophy that does not take into account indigenous peoples' (i.e. Sámi) narratives, spiritual values and knowledge that are intrinsically connected to the landscape, fails to ensure an adequate preservation of this world heritage site.

4.2 *How is Laponia to be Managed?*

After its inclusion in the World Heritage list in 1996, a number of local actor-groups got together to discuss the alternatives for managing the site. Because Laponia consists of already well-established national parks and nature reserves, there were regulations and directives on how to conduct the conservation management in place. The regulations for the parks also included changes for the reindeer herders in the parks. But the safeguarding and protection of the cultural criteria in the area was something new, and a fact that had to be taken into account. Although all agreed that the importance of Sámi reindeer herding culture had to be recognized, opinions varied as to the extent and the manner in which Sami reindeer herding culture should be promoted. By that time the representatives from the samebys had recognized the potential of the World Heritage status in terms of increasing Sámi influence of the management of the area and of starting a process of decolonization of the bureaucratic structures. After all, in other areas around the world, different forms of joint management between state authorities and Indigenous Peoples were becoming rather widespread.

---

60 Green, supra note 59, 103.

61 Green 'The Laponian World Heritage area. Conflict and collaboration in Swedish Sápmi' in S Disko H Tugendfeld (eds.), *World Heritage and Indigenous Peoples' rights*, IWGIA, Copenhagen (2014): 90.

In spite of genuine efforts among the local stakeholders to cooperate, it soon became clear that there were differences in opinions that were difficult to bridge. The Sámi representatives were firm in their belief that they had to be equal partners in the negotiations with the other stakeholders and that they were to have a strong say in the future management of Laponia. They stressed the importance of a change to the current conservation management regime, something that was not a priority of the other partners.[62] It was not long before this first attempt at negotiations broke down. From then onwards, the stakeholders that engaged in the future of Laponia formed into three major groups: the country Administration of Norrbotten, the two municipalities of Jokkmokk and Gällivare, and the local samebys. However, very little cooperation was possible at this stage due to the differences in goals and prioritizations. From the samebys side, it was then that they collectively started a more formal collaboration among themselves. They formed an association called "Mijá Ednam" that was to act as the platform for Laponia-related matters and where they could develop an internal discussion on their aims and the objectives of the World Heritage site, and also produced a proposal for a management plan for the area.[63] Many of the representatives of the samebys recognized that Laponia was an arena where many important issues related to self-determination and control of the management of the traditional lands came to the surface: they managed it for generations, and therefore also should be a part in the new management.

In the Mijá Ednam-proposal the samebys argued for indigenous control over the future management of Laponia. They asked for the majority of seats in a future management board. The other actors rejected this idea. The County Administration stated that they had a mandate from the Government to be responsible for the protection and management of these areas, and that they could not give that mandate away without a new governmental decree. However, more unofficially, there were also other reasons behind the refusal to discuss the Sámi claim for majority seats. In essence, the sentiments among many of the politicians and state officials of the agencies were that the local Sámi were not ready for such a responsibility and that they would close off large parts of the mountain areas for non-sameby members.[64]

But the samebys would not drop the claim of achieving majority seats on a future board of management. In fact, they decided not to enter into any nego-

62 Green supra note 59, 111ff.; Green, supra note 62, 91f.

63 Michael Teilus and Karin Lindahl, *Mijá ednam – samebyarnas laponiaprogram* (Samebyarnas Kansli 2000), Jokkmokk.

64 Green, supra note 59, 129.

tiations with the other actors before they approved this claim. A long period of non-communication between the samebys and the other actors followed. During this time, the samebys turned to the international community for encouragement. They were in contact with UNESCO to express their predicaments and they continued to look for good examples of progressive co-management projects in other areas and seek support in international conventions and guidelines. The Sámi representatives also articulated their position and identity as an indigenous people in relation to the other actors.[65]

The samebys had a common strategy not to enter into negotiations before the demand for majority seats on a future board of management were met and to always "speak with one voice".[66] Disagreements and discussions were held within the group. They also were meticulous to put their propositions and written intentions within a framework that can only be described as "correct bureaucratically". They would use a language and a format that would be easily recognizable as being inside the dominant discourse. In this way, the state agencies could not dismiss the statements and suggestions. They were recognized as professional and correct, but spoke of a wish to take on more responsibility for the traditional lands and to work for a transformation of the current "Swedish" conservation management practice.[67]

4.3 *Agreeing on a Management Structure*

Given the locked positions, it was something of a surprise to many when the table suddenly turned and the involved actors announced that they had agreed to start negotiations and go forward to create a new and progressive management plan for Laponia.[68] In the fall of 2005, the representatives of the samebys were called to a meeting by the County Governor to discuss the future management of Laponia. Now there was commitment from the state agencies' side to find ways to implement the idea of Sámi majority on a management board. The new round of discussions resulted in a proposal that was sent to the government in 2006 on how to go forward with the organization structure, signed by all three-actor groups. In this proposal a management plan was outlined that relied on the importance of the reindeer herding practice of the area, and that allowed a strong Sámi responsibility and control.[69] The government commissioned a delegation consisting of representatives from the local actor

65 Green, supra note 59, 152ff.
66 Green, supra note 59, 147ff.
67 Green, supra note 59, 164ff.
68 Green, supra note 59, 207ff.
69 Green, supra note 62, 95.

groups and from SEPA to set up a new management organization. In June 2011, the government gave its formal approval of the new management regime to be established.[70]

In hindsight it seems that the years of disagreement and polarized positions ended surprisingly suddenly. To many of the representatives involved in the process, this new turn of events was quite unanticipated, but also encouraging and positive. It is difficult to pinpoint one simple explanation for this development. Several circumstances contributed to break the dead-lock.[71] Perhaps the most important factor was time. Many years had by now passed since the inscription of Laponia and there was a general feeling, not least among the state agencies (both nationally and locally/regionally) that the management issue concerning Laponia had to be solved. The question was also frequently discussed within World Heritage circles, even if not officially so. Internationally, different forms of co-management schemes were beginning to be increasingly common in regards to conservation on traditional indigenous lands, and this was also a fact that influenced the general attitude in society and among state officials and politicians. Another important factor is that new people entered into the actor groups during these years. This meant that some of the personal conflicts that had been established early on in the process were now consequentially phased out. It is important here also to emphasise the importance of the Sámi strategy, their persistence and determination to push for a Sámi majority on a future management board and to stay unified. Needless to say, there had been many different opinions and aspirations linked to the World Heritage appointment, but the Sámi representatives had a conscious strategy to "speak with one voice" before the other actors in order to be recognized as a convincing and legitimate counterpart in the negotiations.

4.4 *Laponiatjuottjudus*

Many of the claims that the representatives from the samebys fought for during the years of conflict and non-dialogue have in the end been included in the current management plan and organization.[72] There is a clear emphasis on the protection of Sámi cultural values and on the importance of providing conditions for a thriving reindeer herding industry to continue. The protection of natural values is equally important, but not treated as something entirely separate from the protection of a living cultural landscape. The area is viewed

---

70 Ministry of Environment 2011, *Ny Förvaltningsorganisation för världsarvet Laponia*. Press Release, 16 June 2011. http://www.regeringen.se/sb/d/8149/a/170963.

71 Green, supra note 59, 209; Green, supra note 62, 96.

72 Laponiatjuottjudus, *Laponia, Tjuottjudusplána – Management plan* 2012.

as an arena where sustainable development and change is welcome, as long as the cultural and environmental sustainability is not jeopardized. An important standpoint is to include the Sámi language(s) in all forms of written documentation and presentation. Consequently, the new management organization also goes under a Sámi name: *Laponiatjuottjudus.*

The board is made up of nine permanent members, 5 of whom are appointed by the local samebys. The other 4 consists of two representatives from the local municipalities of Jokkmokk and Gällivare, 1 representative from the County Administration of Norrbotten and 1 from SEPA. The Sámi have the majority seats, they also hold the chair. Decisions are, however, to be taken according to the principle of consensus, something that has meant that the importance of majority seats have been reduced. To the Sámi representatives, it is still an important circumstance that signals the leading role of the Sámi community.[73] At present, the chair of the board is held by one of the Sámi representatives.

In many ways the new management plan has many things in common with many other official documents of this sort, but in many ways it is unique. It differs from other 'conventional' documents by partly using a form and language that includes Sámi views and ways of organizing and working. *Laponiatjuottjudus* thus becomes a platform from where a Sámi inspired management based on traditional and local knowledge can be developed, but still very much within normative bureaucratic structures.[74] An open dialogue with the surrounding local society is an outspoken aspiration for the new management organization. Local input is assured by the arrangement or public deliberations – *rádedibme* – held regularly.

The management plan focuses on applying a holistic perspective where the importance of ensuring the integrity of the World Heritage criteria needs to be combined with a sustainable development of the area. Both modern technologies and traditional knowledge are imperative aspects to incorporate when practicing and developing the management of the site.[75] The management plan also includes an emphasis on management as a process, which needs to be revised, improved and made flexible. Laponia is thus seen as an arena for learning (*searvelatnja*) for all involved actors.

One important factor in the management plan is the recognition to not only protect the material heritage of the area. In the Laponia World Heritage Area,

73 Green, supra note 62, 33.

74 Carina Green, and Jan Turtinen 'Indigenous Peoples and world heritage sites: Normative heritage discourses and possibilities for change' *Proceedings of the International indigenous development research conference, Ngä Pae o te Märamatanga*, 2014: 64.

75 Laponiatjuttjudus, ibid.

sacred sites where antlers and other items were placed as offerings, such as the Stálojåhkå sacrificial site, reflect the importance of reindeer for the local Sámi people.[76] Laponia also includes many graves and the names of mountains, lakes and marshes, that bear witness to the way local Sámi people understood the landscape, life and death. These immaterial (intellectual and spiritual) values are equally important to consider. Stories, memories and knowledge are continuously being recorded and highlighted with the agreement of the local communities. Here, the reintegration of the Sámi language(s) is one vital component[77] along with customary laws. Perhaps the most important change inherent in the new management organization is on an operative level. The current staff deliberately work towards implementing local structures and articulating Sámi conservation perspectives and aspirations. This includes a holistic management perspective where both material and immaterial values are protected. There is a closer relationship between the rangers that work out in the field and local sameby members (and other locals) than was the case before, which creates important possibilities for local participation and dialogue.

In short, Laponia has gone from being an arena where disagreement and lack of communication was prominent to being an area where collaboration and strengthened relationships between the indigenous people and the state agencies is evolving. For the Sámi representatives, being engaged in the development of the World Heritage site was all along linked to the idea of more influence and control in general.

Today, the local Sámi peple feel responsible for Laponia, they are involved and take ownership of Laponia management. When new steps are taken in the management process, local Sámi communities call the Management board to be informed. There is real participation in place, which leads to quicker decision-making. Meetings between samebys and authorities now sometimes take place in the Laponia offices, which makes establishing contacts with authorities easier for local communities.

There are still tricky issues addressed on the board where the different representatives voice diverse opinions. And there are still differences in perspectives on how to organise and structure conservation management and how to carry it out practically. At times, the involved Sámi have felt that Sámi initiatives and ways of conducting things are not being acknowledged, or seen as a correct way, by some of the other actors. In other words, notwithstanding the

76 Swedish National Heritage Board, Swedish National Commission for UNESCO, Swedish Environmental Protection Agency, *World Heritage Sites in Sweden*, 2014: 12.

77 Green, supra note 62, 97.

progress made, there is still a feeling that there is room for improvement as far as the de-colonization of current bureaucratic structures is concerned.[78]

A major future challenge ensuring that Sámi engagement in managing Laponia is in line with the right of self-determination lies in the recognition of Sámi toponymes: getting Sámi place names accepted on maps, on road signs and other signalization panels is still an unsolved issue. Another future task for strengthening Laponia management is to widen local participation beyond the nine Sámi communities, which use land within Laponia, and to involve local people from the town of Jokkmokk, a centre of Sámi culture in Lapland. And finally, there is a need for *Laponiatjuottjudus,* which is still a project, to become a real organisation. The funding accorded to Laponia however is small for the amount of work that lies ahead (i.e., priority list every year).

Nevertheless, one should not underestimate the importance of Laponia as a platform for Sámi revitalization and as a milestone in the process of regaining control over the management of their traditional lands. Neither should one underestimate its importance as a milestone for a new form of nature conservation management that has the possibility to inspire governance structures not only in indigenous circles, but beyond.

Conclusion

There is a growing consensus that Indigenous Peoples should be able to manage or at least participate in the management of their cultural heritage. Yet, there is also a large gap between the rhetoric on the international level and the actual political practices on a national and regional level. The UNESCO World Heritage Convention is one model that can, in the best case, assist Indigenous Peoples to (re)-gain their self-determination over their cultural heritage. Although the UNESCO framework has met great difficulties in fully recognizing the unique features of Indigenous Peoples' cultural heritage and their involvement in the nomination process of the heritage sites, our case study of Laponia has illustrated that if the skillful and active strategical planning of Indigenous Peoples is met with the willingness of the related State to advance Indigenous Peoples' rights and participation, it is possible to create a satisfactory outcome. Based on voluntary guidelines and arrangements, similar co-management

78 Carina Green, and Jan Turtinen 'Indigenous peoples and World Heritage sites – contested management regimes in Australia, New Zealand and Sweden' in L Elenius, C Allard, C Sandström (eds.), *Sámi Customary Rights in Modern Landscapes,* Ashgate, London. (forthcoming).

models have recently been successfully created in other places in the world (e.g., Canada).[79]

Without recognition of Indigenous Peoples' self-determination, their cultural heritage cannot be protected in a satisfactory way. As long as Indigenous Peoples are seen as objects of protection, rather than legal subjects, their fundamental views, philosophies and knowledge remains unacknowledged. The establishment of the Laponia World Heritage area, as shown in this chapter, led to a restructuring of the relations between the local Sámi community and the local authorities.

The unique co-management body put in place in Laponia, Laponiatjuottjudus, links to the profound shift that has occurred during the last decades in the way in which Indigenous Peoples' rights are viewed, culminating in the adoption of the UN Declaration on the Rights of Indigenous Peoples, including its direct embrace of Indigenous Peoples' right to self-determination. From the point of view of protection of Indigenous Peoples' cultural heritage, their right to self-determination is a vital component. As stated by EMRIP, Indigenous Peoples' cultural heritage should be considered as an expression of their self-determination and their spiritual and physical relationships with their lands, territories and resources.[80] What Indigenous Peoples' self-determination does or should mean in practice, is, however, far from clear and lacks any comprehensive understanding within the international community. It is possible, anyhow, to identify some areas that are indisputable, at least in the sense of "the best effort." Indigenous Peoples' right to effectively participate in the decision-making concerning matters that are directly related to their cultural core, such as traditional, nature-based livelihoods, is a widely accepted norm within the human rights framework. Although the right to effective participation originally became accepted as a part of Indigenous Peoples' right to a distinct cul-

79 See for example: Thora Herrmann, Leena Heinämäki, Cindy Morin 'Protecting Sacred Sites, Maintaining Cultural Heritage, and Sharing Power: Co-management of the SGang Gwaay UNESCO World Heritage Site in Canada', in L Elenius, C Allard, C Sandström (eds.), *Sámi Customary Rights in Modern Landscapes*, Ashgate, London. (forthcoming).

80 UN Human Rights Council, Expert Mechanism on the Rights of Indigenous Peoples, *Study and advice on the promotion and protection of the rights of indigenous peoples with respect to their cultural heritage*, A/HRC/EMPRIP/2015/2 (para. 7).

ture[81] or collective property,[82] through a recognition of Indigenous Peoples' right to self-determination, the duty of the states or state agencies to consult with Indigenous Peoples has been transformed into an obligation to seek Indigenous Peoples' free, prior and informed consent for actions that have large-scale and far-reaching impacts on Indigenous Peoples' cultures and traditional lands (such as creation of protected areas).[83]

81 *Lubicon Lake Band v. Canada*, Communication No. 167/1984, CCPR/C/38/D/167/1984; *Kitokv. Sweden*, Communication No. 197/1985, CCPR/C/33/D/197/1985 (1988); *Lubicon Lake Band v. Canada*, Communication No. 167/1984, CCPR/C/38/D/167/1984; *I. Länsman et al. v. Finland*, Communication No. 511/1992, UN Doc. CCPR/C/52/D/511/1992 (1994).

82 I/A Court H.R., *Case of the YakyeAxa Indigenous Community v. Paraguay. Merits, Reparations and Costs.* Judgment of June 17, 2005. Series C No. 125, paras. 131, 135, 137. I/A Court H.R., *Case of the Sawhoyamaxa Indigenous Community v. Paraguay. Merits, Reparations and Costs.* Judgment of March 29, 2006. Series C No. 146, paras. 118, 121.I/A Court H.R., *Case of the Plan de Sánchez Massacre v. Guatemala.Reparations and Costs.* Judgment of November 19, 2004. Series C No. 116, par. 85. I/A Court H.R., *Case of the Mayagna (Sumo) AwasTingni Community v. Nicaragua. Merits, Reparations and Costs.* Judgment of January 31, 2001. Series C No. 79, para. 149. IACHR, Arguments before the Inter-American Court of Human Rights in the case of *YakyeAxa v. Paraguay*. Cited in: I/A Court H.R., *Case of the YakyeAxa Indigenous Community v. Paraguay. Merits, Reparations and Costs.* Judgment of June 17, 2005. Series C No. 125, par. 120(j). IACHR, Arguments before the Inter-American Court of Human Rights in the case of *Sawhoyamaxa v. Paraguay*. Cited in: I/A Court H.R., *Case of the Sawhoyamaxa Indigenous Community v. Paraguay. Merits, Reparations and Costs.* Judgment of March 29, 2006. Series C No. 146, para. 113(a).

83 *Poma Poma v. Peru*, Human Rights Committee, Communication No. 1457/2006, Doc. CCPR/C/95/D/1457/2006 of 27 March 2009; I/A Court H.R., *Case of the Saramaka People v. Suriname. Preliminary Objections, Merits, Reparations and Costs.* Judgment of November 28, 2007. Series C No. 172, para. 95. See the analysis by Inter-American Commission on Human Rights, Indigenous and tribal peoples' rights over their ancestral lands and natural resources, Norms and Jurisprudence of the Inter-American Human Rights System, OEA/Ser.L/V/II, Doc. 56/09, 30 December 2009, 67-68.

On Transfer of Sámi Traditional Knowledge: Scientification, Traditionalization, Secrecy, and Equality*

Elina Helander-Renvall and Inkeri Markkula

Introduction

The aim of this chapter is to elaborate how Sámi traditional knowledge is articulated and transferred, especially as part of research activities. As a starting point, we will discuss traditional knowledge and its various understandings. Further on, we will trace and address some of the concerns that Sámi have in relation to how their reality is researched and described. Special attention will be paid to the secrecy surrounding some Sámi traditions and some knowledge in the context of conducting research on such issues; the scientification of Sámi knowledge; the traditionalization (actualization) of various traditions; and the need for equality between scientific and traditional knowledge.

Traditional knowledge (TK) has many definitions. Traditional knowledge may be defined as knowledge that has a long historical and cultural continuity, having been passed down through generations, as Berkes has noted.[1] In the book on traditional knowledge by Porsanger and Guttorm[2] the concept *árbediehtu* (inherited knowledge, a Northern Sámi word) is used to refer to Sámi knowledge. They state that *árbediehtu* is 'the collective wisdom and skills of the Sámi people used to enhance their livelihood for centuries. It has been

---

* We would like to thank Regional Council of Lapland, European Regional Development Fund, and University of Lapland for the financial support for the project Traditional Ecological Knowledge in the Sami Homeland Region of Finland which was conducted at the Arctic Centre, Rovaniemi during 1.1.2014-30.4.2015. The general aim of this project was to promote the status of Sami traditional ecological knowledge through support to the Sami craftswomen. www.arcticcentre.org.

1 Berkes, F. 1993. Traditional Ecological Knowledge in Practice. In: Inglis, J. (ed.). *Traditional Ecological Knowledge; Concepts and Cases*. Ottawa: Canadian Museum of Nature and the International Development Research Centre, 1-9; Berkes, F. 2012. *Sacred Ecology*. Philadelphia: Taylor and Francis.

2 Porsanger, J. and Guttorm, G. 2011. Building up the Field Study and Research on Sami Traditional Knowledge (Arbediehtu). In: Porsanger, J. and Guttorm, G. (eds.). *Working with Traditional Knowledge: Communities, Institutions, Information Systems, Law and Ethics. Diedut* 1/11: 13-57.

Xanthaki, Valkonen et al. (eds.), *Indigenous Peoples' Cultural Heritage: Rights, Debates and Challenges*.
 ISBN 978-90-04-34218-7. PP. 104-129.

passed down from generation to generation both orally and through work and practical experience. Through this continuity, the concept of *árbediehtu* ties the past, present and future together'.[3] In a more limited sense, Traditional ecological knowledge (TEK) refers to cumulative knowledge of the local environment and ecosystems and the ways how to use and manage them. It is knowledge held by Indigenous Peoples or local communities, encompassing language, naming and classification systems, resource use practices, rituals, spirituality and worldview.

Helander-Renvall and Markkula have emphasized the significance of ecological understanding as a central aspect of Sámi traditional knowledge.[4] We think that *transmission* of traditional knowledge is particularly important: the focus should not be in the first place on 'getting information'.[5]

Currently, there is great concern about the worldwide decrease of traditional lifestyles and related knowledge. The knowledge, which is no longer used, documented or passed on from one generation to the next, will disappear. Traditional knowledge is part of intangible cultural heritage, which, according to UNESCO, contains oral traditions, practices and knowledge concerning nature and the universe, and knowledge and skills on how to make traditional handicrafts.[6] Therefore, transfer of traditional knowledge is central in the preservation of indigenous cultural heritage.

Accordingly, TEK is increasingly valued alongside scientific knowledge in research and conservation efforts especially in Arctic areas, where climate change significantly impacts on the traditional livelihoods of Indigenous Peoples. Traditional knowledge is currently also used in revitalization processes, embodied in the production of cultural continuity. Studies integrating TEK and scientific knowledge in the Arctic region are numerous.[7] Many of these

---

3 Ibid. 18.

4 Helander-Renvall, E. and Markkula, I. 2011. *Luonnon monimuotoisuus ja saamelaiset. Biologista monimuotoisuutta koskevan yleissopimuksen artikla 8(j):n toimeenpanoa tukeva selvitys Suomen saamelaisalueella* [Biodiversity and Sami people. Investigation to support the implementation of Convention on Biodiversity article 8 (j) in Sami domicile region in Finland] Suomen ympäristö 12. Helsinki: Suomen ympäristöministeriö; Markkula, I. and Helander-Renvall, E. 2014. *Ekologisen Perinnetiedon Käsikirja* [Traditional Ecological Knowledge Handbook] Arktisen keskuksen tiedotteita 59. Rovaniemi: Lapin yliopisto.

5 Nadasdy, P. 1999. The politics of TEK. Power and the 'integration' of knowledge. In: *Arctic Anthropology* 36 (1-2): 1-18.

6 UNESCO Convention for the Safeguarding of the Intangible Cultural Heritage 2003.

7 Bogoslovskaya, L. 2003. The Bowhead whale off Chukotka: integration of scientific and traditional knowledge. In: McCartney, A.P. (ed.). *Indigenous Ways to the Present. Native Whaling in the Western Arctic.* Edmonton and Salt Lake City: Canadian Circumpolar Insti-

studies research the local adaptation to climate and environmental change. The potential of TEK in climate change research and adaptation to environmental changes has indeed been acknowledged in different studies and reports, including the Arctic Climate Impact Assessment and assessment reports of the Intergovernmental Panel on Climate Change (IPCC).[8] The fourth IPCC report noted that indigenous knowledge is an invaluable basis for developing adaptation and natural resource management strategies in response to environmental and other forms of change, and the fifth IPCC report states that indigenous, local, and traditional forms of knowledge are a major resource for adapting to climate change.[9] Natural resource dependent communities, harboring Indigenous peoples, have a long history of adapting to highly variable and changing social and ecological conditions. The usefulness of indigenous knowledge is already now important for climate research and many inquiries lean on indigenous knowledge.[10]

The value of traditional knowledge was first acknowledged internationally in the (1992) UN Convention on Biological Diversity (CBD). Article 8(j) of the convention obliges the State parties to respect, preserve and maintain the knowledge, innovations and practices of indigenous and local communities that embody traditional lifestyles relevant to the conservation and sustainable use of biological diversity and promote their wider application with the approval and involvement of the holders of such knowledge, innovations and

---

tute and University of Utah Press, 209-254; ACIA 2005. *Impact of a Warming Arctic: Arctic Climate Impact Assessment.* Cambridge: Cambridge University Press; Krupnik, I.I. and Ray, G.C. 2007. Pacific walruses, indigenous hunters, and climate change: bridging scientific and indigenous knowledge. In: *Deep Sea Research* 54: 2946-2957; Magga, O.H., Mathiesen, S.D., Corell, R.W., Oskal, A. 2009. *Reindeer Herding, Traditional Knowledge and Adaptation to Climate Change and Loss of Grazing Land.* Ealat project report. Alta: Fagtrykk Idé AS; Krupnik, I., Aporta, C., Gearheard, S., Laidler, G.J., Kielsen Holm, L. (eds.). 2010. SIKU: *Knowing Our Ice Documenting Inuit Sea Ice Knowledge and Use.*Springer; Weatherhead, E., Gearheard, S. and Barry, R.G. 2010. Changes in weather persistence: Insight from Inuit knowledge. In: *Global Environmental Change* 20: 523-528.

8 ACIA 2005; IPCC 2007. Climate change 2007. Synthesis report; IPCC 2014. Climate Change: Impacts, Adaptation, and Vulnerability. Part A: Global and Sectoral Aspects. Contribution of Working Group II to the Fifth Assessment Report of the Intergovernmental Panel on Climate Change.

9 IPCC 2007; 2014.

10 Lambert, L. 2003. From 'Savages' to Scientists: Mainstream Science Moves Toward Recognizing Traditional Knowledge. In: *Tribal College Journal of American Indian Higher Education* 15(1): 11-12; McGregor, D. 2006. Traditional Ecological Knowledge. In: *Ideas: the Arts and Science Review* 3(1). Online.

practices and encourage the equitable sharing of the benefits arising from the utilization of such knowledge, innovations and practices.

As the value of TEK has been recognized by scientists, it is often collected and integrated in studies in order to fill gaps in knowledge about species distributions or behavior, to collect observations of changes in climate, or to understand traditional management practices and how these contribute to resource conservation.[11] However, if the studies into which TEK is integrated have quantity-oriented objectives, this may lead researchers to code, categorize and typologize the narratives of TEK holders.[12] That can result in a simplified picture of TEK. Gearheard et al. have paid attention to the different implications of knowledge.[13] For example, for Inuit following the traditional lifestyle, knowing the sea ice means that one gets good food and has freedom, as sea ice is the base for hunting and traveling.

This knowledge, gathered through generations and shared with others in the community, is evolving and living knowledge. Moreover, if TEK is coded and simplified, links and connections between nature, traditions and cultural identity may be lost. For example Sakakibara has studied how sea ice, sea ice loss, cultural identity, human-animal relations and drumming traditions of Inupiaq are all connected.[14]

Critical Voices

In the context of Arctic research, the following definition of TEK by Berkes is commonly used: 'TEK is a cumulative body of knowledge and beliefs, handed down through generations by cultural transmission, about the relationship of living beings (including humans) with one another and with their

11 Shackeroff, J.M. and Campbell, L.M. 2007. Traditional Ecological Knowledge in Conservation Research: Problems and Prospects for their Constructive Engagement. In: *Conservation & Society* 5: 343-360.

12 Agrawal, A. 2002. Indigenous knowledge and the politics of classification. In: *International Social Science Journal* 54(173): 287-297.

13 Gearheard, S.F., Kielsen, Holm, L., Huntington, H., Leavitt, J.M., Mahoney, A.R., Opie, M., Oshima, T. Sanguya, J. (eds.). 2013. *The Meaning of Ice. People and sea ice in three Arctic communities*. Hanover and New Hampshire: International Polar Institute Press.

14 Sakakibara, C. 2008. 'Our home is drowning': Iñupiat storytelling and climate change in Point Hope. In: Alaska.Geographical Review 98: 456-475; Sakakibara C. 2009. 'No Whale, No Music': Iñupiaq drumming and global warming. In: *Polar Record* 45: 289-303; Sakakibara C. 2010. Into the whaling cycle: Cetaceousness and climate change among the Inupiat of Arctic. In: *Alaska. Annals of the Association of American Geographers* 100: 1003-1012.

environment'.[15] For Indigenous Peoples themselves, however, TEK is much more than a 'body of knowledge'. McGregor has emphasized that 'body of knowledge' can be considered as something that is separate from the people who hold and practice this knowledge, which is not the case with indigenous knowledge.[16] Moreover, the definition conceptualizes TEK as a set of procedural ecological knowledge, for example the knowledge of animal behavior or plant distributions.[17] Consequently, a 'body of knowledge' can take on a particular meaning and express itself as decontextualized and fragmented. TEK is dynamic and complex and connects biophysical and social processes. All this validates the notion of TEK as indigenous knowledge that is rooted in relationships and participations.[18] As stated by Cruikshank, traditional knowledge is produced and expressed in human encounters, not encapsulated in closed traditions.[19] It is also an aspect of spiritual existence and connection to land.[20] It must also be stressed that traditional knowledge is closely connected to local practices, subsistence activities and survival possibilities; in that sense it is very vulnerable, especially if regarded and used as a commodity.[21] What is more, many researchers avoid using the concept 'traditional' because the term is seen as contrary to change. They prefer the term 'indigenous'. [22] Similarly, Kuokkanen explains: 'talking about "traditional" ways of life or "traditional" culture can suggest racist notions of a frozen culture giving rise to false views

15 Berkes 1993:3.

16 McGregor, D. 2004a. Traditional Ecological Knowledge and Sustainable Development: Towards Coexistence. In: Blaser, M., Feit, H. A., Mc Rae, G. (eds.). *In the Way of Development.* London: Zed Books, 72-91; McGregor, D. 2004b. Coming Full Circle. Indigenous knowledge, Environment, and our future. In: *American Indian Quaterly* 28(3-4): 358-410.

17 Casimirri, G. 2003. Problems with integrating traditional ecological knowledge into contemporary resource management. XII World Forestry Congress, Quebec City, Canada 2003.

18 see: Wilson, S. 2008. *Research Is Ceremony. Indigenous Research Methods.* Halifax and Winnipeg: Fernwood Publishing.

19 Cruikshank, J. 2005. *Do Glaciers Listen? Local Knowledge, Colonial Encounters, and Social Imagination.* Vancouver: UBC Press, 4.

20 Helander-Renvall, E. 2014. Relationships between Sámi reindeer herders, lands, and reindeer. In: Marvin, G. and McHugh, S. (eds.). *Routledge Handbook of Human-Animal Studies.* London and New York: Routledge, 246-258.

21 Helander, E. 1999. Sami subsistence activities. Spatial aspects and structuration. In: *Acta Borealia, A Nordic Journal of Circumpolar Societies* 16(2): 7-25.

22 Porsanger, J. 2011. The Problematisation of the Dichotomy of Modernity and Tradition in Indigenous and Sami contexts. In: Porsanger, J. and Guttorm, G. (eds.). *Working with Traditional Knowledge: Communities, Institutions, Information Systems, Law and Ethics. Diedut* 1/11: 225-252.

of authenticity and "traditional practices". This, for its part, denies development and change in indigenous cultures'.[23]

Increasing use of traditional knowledge including TEK in research has indeed raised many questions and debates as traditional knowledge is an ambiguous term, as explained above. The ACIA-report, for example, notes the difficulties in defining TEK.[24] In addition to the above, scientists have also been criticized for their treatment of TEK as mere data or facts, leaving many aspects of TEK, such as spirituality and ecological relationships, unexplored.[25] This might be because holistic aspects of traditional knowledge can be confusing from a scientific perspective. Berkes admits that TEK is more than just information: it describes the spiritual relationship Indigenous Peoples share with the land, and is a process of gathering knowledge and conclusion drawing.[26] In reality, the concept 'traditional knowledge' refers not only to information or facts but also to ways of knowing.[27] These ways of knowing are based on holistic aspects of indigenous knowledge. Holistic knowledge is relational and, as indicated above, it is strongly rooted in spiritual, cultural and ecological elements of a community's life. These, and similar notions, definitely expand the understanding of the concept.

According to the Assembly of First Nations, indigenous knowledge consists of four interlinked components:

1. creation stories and cosmologies which explain the origins of the earth and its people;
2. codes of ritual and behavior that govern peoples' relationships with the earth;
3. practices and seasonal patterns of resource utilization and management that have evolved as expressions of these relationships;
4. body of factual knowledge that has accumulated in connection with these practices.[28]

---

23 Kuokkanen, R. 2000. Towards an 'Indigenous Paradigm' from a Sami Perspective. In: *The Canadian Journal of Native Studies* 20(2): 411-436.

24 ACIA 2005: 64.

25 Nadasdy 1999; Casimirri 2003.

26 Berkes 2012.

27 Ibid: 8.

28 AFN, Assembly of First Nations, Environment Division. 1995. *The Feasibility of Representing Traditional Indigenous Knowledge in Cartographic, Pictorial or Textual Forms*. Draft Final Report.

The two last components are the types of traditional knowledge which are in all likelihood most extensively documented by scientists during recent years. Numerous studies which integrate TEK and scientific knowledge report Indigenous Peoples' observations and knowledge regarding, for example, animal behavior and migration patterns, traditional weather forecast and changes in sea ice and weather.[29] Furthermore, there are several studies which focus on indigenous classification and knowledge systems.[30] In the ACIA report, TEK is considered to include changes and effects of climate warming observed by Arctic Indigenous Peoples, and their perceptions of climate impacts, such as the effects on everyday life, land and water use, diet, and social and cultural activities.[31] In the context of ACIA, TEK contains observations and, in addition, also the meanings and consequences of climate change.

McGregor writes about sources of indigenous knowledge acquisition, identifying three categories: 1. traditional knowledge, which is passed on from generation to generation; 2. empirical knowledge, which is gained through observation; and 3. revealed knowledge, which is acquired through spiritual means and regarded as a gift.[32] This list is certainly not complete, but useful for our discussion. Empirical knowledge is today frequently used in studies of

29 Bogoslovskaya 2003; George, J.C., Braund, S., Brower Jr., H., Nicholson, C., O'Hara, T. 2003. Some observations on the influence of environmental conditions on the success of hunting Bowhead whales off Barrow, Alaska. In: McCartney, A.P. (ed.), *Indigenous Ways to the Present. Native Whaling in the Western Arctic*. Edmonton and Salt Lake City: Canadian Circumpolar Institute and University of Utah Press, 255-275; Krupnik and Ray 2007; Gagnon, C. and Berteaux, D. 2009. Integrating Traditional Ecological Knowledge and Ecological Science: a Question of Scale. In: *Ecology and Society* 14 (2):19, online; Weatherhead et al. 2010; Gearheard, S., Pocernich, M., Stewart, R., Sanguya, J., Huntington, H. 2010. Linking Inuit knowledge and meteorological station observations to understand changing wind patterns at Clyde River, Nunavut. In: *Climatic Change* 100(2): 239-242; Krupnik et al. 2010.

30 Roturier, S. and Roue, M. 2009. Of forest, snow and lichen: Sami reindeer herders' knowledge of winter pastures in northern Sweden. *In: Forest ecology and management* 258: 1960–1967; Krupnik et al. 2010. Riseth, J. Å., Tømmervik H., Helander-Renvall, E., Labba, N., Johansson, C., Malnes, E., Bjerke, J.V., Jonsson, C., Pohjola, V., Sarri, L-E., Schanche, A., Callaghan, T.V. 2011. Sámi traditional ecological knowledge as a guide to science: snow, ice and reindeer pasture facing climate change. In: *Polar Record* 47: 202-217; Roturier, S. 2011. Sami herders' classification system of reindeer winter pastures – A contribution to adapt forest management to reindeer herding in northern Sweden. In: *Rangifer* 31: 61-69; Roturier 2011. Eira, I.M.G., Jaedicke, C., Magga, O.H., Maynard, J.G., Vikhamar-Schuler, D., Mathiesen, S.D. 2013. Traditional Sámi snow terminology and physical snow classification – Two ways of knowing. In: *Cold Regions Science and Technology* 85: 117-130.

31 ACIA 2005.

32 McGregor 2006.

TEK and indigenous knowledge, especially in those related to climate change. To give an example, *Climatic Change* – an academic journal, published a special issue on Indigenous Peoples' knowledge of climate and weather in 2010. The special issue's articles discussed the local and indigenous knowledge in different parts of the world, regarding seasonal patterns of precipitation and temperature; local traditional climate indicators; observations of meteorological events; changes in wind patterns including variability, speed and direction; the use of indigenous knowledge and meteorological forecasts in traditional farming and local seasonal calendars including changes in behavior of animals and plants.[33]

Documenting indigenous observations of climate change, species distributions and behavior, or indigenous ways in resource conservation can work towards to a greater nature conservation efforts, and can as a matter of fact result in local and indigenous voices be heard. Mainstream recognition of TEK has indeed to a certain extent led to the strengthening of indigenous voices and challenged the hegemony of western science.[34] However, the selection process resulting from the study design and researchers expectations has an effect on what kind of TEK is documented and presented to a wider audience.

Within this context, one needs to be aware of the importance of documentation of Sámi traditional knowledge. Laila. S. Vars explains: 'Documentation of Sámi knowledge is the most urgent issue facing us today… Sámi traditional knowledge encompasses the beliefs, practices, innovations, arts, music, livelihoods, spirituality, and other forms of cultural experience and expression that belong to the Sámi'.[35] Documentation is important as there is a risk that Sámi traditional knowledge fades away. In addition, it is important as part of various cultural, legal and political processes, for instance, in the context of discourses regarding land rights.[36]

It is wise to be aware of research conducted in indigenous societies, as much of it results in texts that will become well-known and provide students and those working with indigenous issues with facts and standpoints. Keep in

---

33 See: Green, D. and Raygorodetsky, G. 2010. Indigenous knowledge of a changing climate. In: *Climatic Change* 100: 239-242, and references therein.

34 See: Shackeroff and Campbell 2007.

35 Vars, L. S. 2008. *The Sámis Should Share Knowledge With Indigenous Peoples*. Available at: http://www.galdu.org/web/index.php?odas=3370&giellai=eng (accessed 5.7.2015).

36 Helander-Renvall, E. 2013. On Customary Law Among the Saami People. In: Bankes, N. and Koivurova, T. (eds.). *The Proposed Nordic Saami Convention. National and International Dimensions of Indigenous Property Rights*. Oxford and Portland, Oregon: Hart Publishing, 281-291.

mind that mainstream research procedure is normally carried out using mainstream reasoning and methodology. Various research activities, 'while they draw on indigenous cultural knowledge, are imagined, conceptualized, and carried out within the theoretical and methodological frameworks of Anglo-European forms of research, reasoning, and interpreting'.[37] Whatever the case may be though, many Indigenous People resent that their knowledge would go through some kind of scientification or scientific validation, that would in the long run change the looks and contents of their knowledge.[38] The scientification may lead to knowledge that is not contextual and open-ended: such knowledge would lack many of Indigenous Peoples' relevant aspects.[39]

For example, one can find many cases in the reindeer herding community which show that the excessively rigid mainstream ordering of reality may create problems for herding. The reindeer herding community is a flexible social and economic unit.[40] Herding is very much dependent on Sámi conceptual understanding and terminology that is developed and used in reindeer herding.[41] Overall, the flexibility of Sámi thoughts and order allows for flexible reindeer herding depending on various variables, such as weather fluctuations and adaptable pasture use; in other words, flexibility gives herders possibilities to cope with uncertainty and maintain resilience.[42] Similarly, one would need to practice flexibility also in research and management as part of epistemological thinking and analysis. If the Sámi ways are restricted through reindeer herding legislation or otherwise in a way that restricts their flexibility too much, the consequences could become very harmful for the herding society. 'Adaptation is a flexible process, not a fact', as Bjerkli has noted.[43]

---

37 Gegeo, D.W. and Watson-Gegeo, K.A. 2001: 'How we know': Kwara'ae rural villagers doing indigenous epistemology. In: *The Contemporary Pacific* 13: 55-88.

38 Helander-Renvall, E. 2011. Traditional Knowledge and Participatory Research – Barriers and Openings. Paper. *ARKTIS seminar*, Arctic Centre, Rovaniemi April 4-5, 2011.

39 Smith L.T. 2012. *Decolonizing Methodologies. Research and Indigenous Peoples*. London: Zed books. Wilson 2008.

40 Pehrson R. N. 1964. *The Bilateral Network of Social Relations in Könkämä Lapp Distict*. Oslo: Samiske samlinger 7.

41 Eira, R.B.M. 2012. *Using Traditional Knowledge in Unpredictable Critical Events in Reindeer Husbandry. The case of Sámi reindeer husbandry in Western Finnmark, Norway and Nenets reindeer husbandry on Yamal peninsula, Yamal-Nenets AO, Russia*. Master thesis. Tromsø: University of Tromsø; Eira et al. 2013.

42 Gaup Eira, I.M. 2012. *The Silent Language of Snow. Sámi traditional knowledge of snow in times of climate change*. Tromsø: Universitetet i Tromsø, 5.

43 Bjerkli, B. 1996. Land Use, Traditionalism and Rights. In: *Acta Borealia* 13(1): 3- 21.

In Sámi reindeer herding we can see that herding practices are partly linked to knowledge as 'a set of improvisational capacities called forth by the needs of the moment'.[44] After all, indigenous knowledge 'is the way of living within contexts of flux, paradox, and tension'.[45] It goes without saying that the mainstream society wants to fix too alterable activities and strategies of the Sámi people for more strict management and control. The challenges of Arctic reindeer herding are: the interface between reindeer herders' traditional knowledge and modern understanding of ecology, economy, sociology, land use, and management. At the same time, if we are looking at specifically the land use rights of Sámi people, then, there is a need to codify the customs and customary rules through which one can affirm the existence of earlier land use and thus the continuity of certain valued rights and customs.

Still, we are in the presence of positive changes as more and more projects impacting indigenous communities are carried out with the active participation of Indigenous Peoples. What is more, with the help of time, indigenous societies will educate their own students and teach them indigenous methodologies. In a general way, this is an essential and urgent task for educational institutions. Within the domain of indigenous research, there are several elements regarding methods of indigenous projects. Smith has confirmed that most progressive among indigenous methodologies are those which are based on indigenous worldviews and research paradigms.[46] The aim of such knowledge methods is not to reject western theories and methods, but rather to focus on indigenous concerns and perspectives.[47]

Equal Treatment of Various Knowledge Systems

TEK is increasingly incorporated into the negotiation and implementation of international agreements, decision-making processes and land-use planning. In Canada, for example, TEK is a required part of various environmental impact assessments.[48] When TEK is integrated into science and used in decision-

44 Richards, P. 1993. Cultivation: knowledge or performance? In: *An Anthropological Critique of Development: The Growth of Ignorance*. New York: Routledge, 61-78.

45 Battiste, M. and Henderson, J. 2000. *Protecting Indigenous Knowledge and Heritage*. Saskatoon Sk: Purich Publishing, 42.

46 Smith 2012.

47 Ibid.

48 Usher, P.J. 2000. Traditional Ecological Knowledge in Environmental Assessment and Management. In: *Arctic* 3: 183-193.

making, power relations between different actors, such as Aboriginal people and states, impact on the processes. In some cases, western experts accept only certain types of information. What is more, Indigenous People feel that their knowledge is too often required to fit into an existing framework of western ideas.[49] Many think that diverse knowledge systems should be acknowledged and treated as equal to non-indigenous.[50] Novel approaches for the inclusion of diverse knowledge systems have been unraveled. They include dual based evidence and knowledge co-production. The dual based evidence is an approach where science and other knowledge systems are validated in parallel using separate protocols. Co-production of knowledge is a process where research questions are formulated after co-operation between indigenous and western scientists, and collaborative methods are used for data gathering.[51] These approaches require that indigenous knowledge be recognized as a discipline or methodology in its own right.

Integration of TEK into decision-making processes, scientific programs and studies is often done through a validation process. This is based on the idea that indigenous knowledge can only benefit societies, if it has gone through scientific validation, while science remains the gatekeeper of knowledge.[52] Again, validation processes have an impact on how TEK is understood, presented and documented. However, novel approaches to TEK integration, such as the co-production of knowledge, require science to be reflected on itself as a cultural practice.

There are different types of knowledge validation designs:

- Empirical validation: if it works, it is good;
- Moral validation: why are things done in a certain way;
- Cultural validation: is the knowledge in accordance with the given worldview;
- Technical validation: if the right tools and devices are used in the experimentation, the result is true;

---

49 See: Nadasdy 1999; McGregor 2004a, 2004b.

50 Helander-Renvall 2011; Tengö, M., Malmer P., Borras, B., Cariño, C., Cariño , J., Gonzales, T., Ishizawa, J., Kvarnström, M., Masardule, O., Morales, A., Nobrega, M., Schultz, M., Soto Martinnez, R, Vizina, Y. (eds.). 2012. Dialogue workshop on Knowledge for the 21st Century: Indigenous knowledge, traditional knowledge, science and connecting diverse knowledge systems. Usdub, Guna Yala, Panama, 10-13 April 2012. *Workshop Report*. Stockholm: Stockholm Resilience Centre, 15.

51 Armitage, D., Berkes, F., Dale, A., Kocho-Schellenberg, E., Patton, E. 2011. Co-management and the co-production of knowledge: Learning to adapt in Canada's Arctic. In: *Global Environmental Change* 21: 995-1004; Tengö et al. 2012: 15-16.

52 Tengö et al. 2012: 15.

- Procedural validation: validation comes from the protocols which are previously tried and which have worked.[53]

The last two types are those on which scientific experimental knowledge is built.[54] This goes against the traditional model. For validation of traditional knowledge, cultural and moral aspects are central. In consequence, when TEK and scientific knowledge are integrated and TEK is validated, it is important to ask, whose perception of validation is used and whose knowledge counts, and in which context.[55]

It should be noted that indigenous communities may also use traditional knowledge in combination with western science. For example, Sámi reindeer herders combine both types of knowledge tradition in decision-making processes and when responding to unpredictable weather events.[56] In this context, scientific information is evaluated from an indigenous perspective. So, the consideration is whether the given knowledge is useful from a community's point of view. Simpson asks the following question as she ponders the role of traditional knowledge in relation to western science: 'How can researchers become allies with Aboriginal Peoples who are advancing their interests?'[57] She notes: 'Researchers need to examine their internal environment. They need to critically examine and challenge their own biases and assumptions, and most of all, they need to listen to the numerous Aboriginal voices already present in the literature'.[58]

It is already suggested earlier that TEK is not solely information or data; it is for example also the life TEK holders are living, it is much more than an observation, it is something you do, and the way you do it.[59] Partly because of its intricate nature, there are challenges in the transfer of TEK in research and documentation. Krupnik and Ray noted 'bottlenecks' in knowledge transfer in studies integrating TEK with science.[60] These bottlenecks include the following: 1. scientists regard TEK as data, and document only the type of TEK which is valuable to their own research, for example observations regarding

53 Tengö et al. 2012: 15-16.

54 Tengö et al. 2012: 21-23.

55 Ibid.

56 Eira 2012: 74.

57 Simpson, L. 1999. *The construction of traditional ecological knowledge: issues, implications and insights.* A thesis. Faculty of Graduate Studies. Winnipeg, Manitoba: University of Manitoba, 95.

58 Ibid: 96.

59 See: McGregor 2004a; 2004b.

60 Krupnik and Ray 2007.

animal behavior and weather patterns, or changes in the local environment; 2. TEK holders are willing to share only part of their knowledge. For example, knowledge which is regarded as sacred, is not fully shared. This may have as a result that those components of TEK which are relevant to scientists and those knowledge parts that TEK holders are willing to share, will in due time constitute official TEK. This authenticated TEK is then acknowledged and used further in other situations, such as in land use planning or other decision-making processes. These components of TEK will be documented and preserved, while many other knowledge parts, those difficult to document for various reasons, will be excluded from studies, databases and various epistemological displays.

Another challenge in documenting TEK is constant change. All cultures change. TEK is living and evolving knowledge. When TEK is documented, it easily becomes 'frozen' in time. However, TEK includes both old and new knowledge and its continuity is rooted in the past. When discussing traditions (here 'tradition' is considered to include TEK), also the stability of these traditions should be taken into account.[61] Today in Arctic regions, the temporality of TEK is partly determined by the climate warming: Arctic nature is changing fast and therefore knowledge founded on it changes at the same rate. In the era of climate change, it might even be that indigenous knowledge, which is based on constant observations, changes faster than scientific knowledge.[62] Smith has noted that 'traditional' and 'new' are interpretive terms, and 'new' can take on symbolic value as 'traditional'.[63]

Silence and Secrecy Surrounding Traditional Knowledge

Many Native Americans and Indigenous People elsewhere use silence as a natural and integrative part of their daily communication. Basso writes about the function of silence among the Apache people who in social communication use silence as a legitimate way of dealing with people.[64] On some occasions, such as meeting strangers or meeting someone who has lost a loved one, one is expected to be silent. Aboriginal people in Australia are comfortable

61 Noyes, D. 2009. Tradition: Three Traditions. In: *Journal of Folklore Research: An International Journal of Folklore and Ethnomusicology* 46. 233-268.

62 See Krupnik and Ray 2007 on Inuit hunter's knowledge.

63 Smith, M.E. 1982. The Process of Sociocultural Continuity. *Current Anthropology* 23: 127-141.

64 Basso, K. H. 1972. 'To Give Up Words': Silence in Western Apache Culture. In: *South Western Journal of Anthropology* 26(3): 213-230.

with staying silent during long periods of time.[65] Often, silence is preferred; for example, in learning situations one is expected to take in information by remaining quiet. In this chapter, however, instead of looking at silence as related to intercommunication, we will outline some aspects of secrecy in the Sámi society, mainly in the context of research procedures regarding tradition and traditional knowledge. There is secrecy, and the use and maintenance of it depends largely on the fact that certain knowledge has definite substantial values and other aspects (e.g. spiritual, ecological, identity-related, ethical, economic, etc.) linked to it. Secrecy is part of the traditional Sámi way of interaction. Therefore secrecy is a frequent tool of communication for Sámi in the present-day contexts as well.

Tacit knowledge is something we know but cannot put it into words. Such unvoiced knowing is tacit to such a degree that it is difficult to document or transfer to others by verbalizing it. In this sense, 'we know more than we can tell'.[66] Much of the Sámi traditional knowledge is learned through a person's own observations, experiences, practices and activities within a variety of contexts, and by imitating knowledge holders such as one's own parents. This knowledge is without doubt linked to or based on tacit understandings and may not be easily explained and visible to others because it is not formally constituted as explicit knowledge expressed for instance through words. It is striking that, in many cases, the holders of traditional Sámi knowledge are not willing to share their knowledge. In this way, tacit knowledge as part of traditions is maintained and culturally disconnected from external view. Naturally, this may lead people from outside the Sámi society to think that Sámi are deliberately silent when asked questions.

Another reason for this secretiveness of Sámi relates to the risk that outsiders misappropriate their traditional knowledge, as soon as this knowledge becomes oral or published in print, and therefore measures are taken locally to prevent the flow of information from the traditional knowledge holders to non-members of a Sámi community. As a matter of fact, there is no adequate legislation protecting the heritage of Indigenous Peoples from external exploitation: their cultural heritage is considered public domain. As a result, parts of traditional knowledge become endangered. McGregor writes: 'While people did (and do) share knowledge and while such knowledge changes over time, there are often very specific rules that govern this process of knowledge acquisition and transmission. It has never been a trivial matter. In contempo-

65 Walsh, M. 1991. Conversational styles and intercultural communication: An example from northern Australia. In: *Australian Journal of Communication* 18 (1): 1-12.

66 Cf. Polanyi, M. 1966. *The Tacit Dimension*. Chicago: The University of Chicago Press, 4-5.

rary times, however, the rules around knowledge acquisition and sharing have changed, and it has become necessary to protect our knowledge'.[67]

The lack of legal protection of the cultural heritage including its epistemological components may have negative impacts on the documentation, transfer and maintenance of traditional knowledge. A recent project, the aim of which was to give support to traditional ecological knowledge of Sámi craftswomen in Enontekiö in Western Lapland, made apparent that those working with Sámi handicraft and participating in the project limited access to their knowledge in concrete communication situations within the project. This occurred even if the researcher interacting with these knowledge holders was originally from the same area. The main reason for not answering fully the questions and sharing traditional knowledge was obviously because issues of intellectual property rights and pattern and design ownership of the participating craftswomen. They felt that there was not enough protection in the Finnish legislation for the Sámi handicraft and traditional understandings governing it.[68] Consequently, there seemed to exist a need to regulate the access to their knowledge as secrecy is an effective tool in protection of traditional knowledge. Let us not forget that their handicraft items and knowledge have commercial value which can be lost if people from outside the local handicraft community know the same things as the members of that community.

Furthermore, in many parts of the Arctic, TEK and TK have been heavily politicized and used for instance in resource management, environmental movement and climate change argumentation. Many contradictory premises, propositions and assessments regarding traditional knowledge may make Indigenous People concerned when asked about their knowledge. Actually, they are to some extent also concerned about the rationality and monopoly of scientists, cultural specialists, and administrators.

Knowledge of healing and some other aspects of spirituality have not been part of public information among the Sámi. Generally speaking, knowledge of healers and practitioners of shamanism belongs to the spiritual reality, and such knowledge is a constituent of sacred epistemology of truths, manifesting itself through subtle spiritual experiences and practices. Accurate healing knowledge is normally revealed only to some specific individuals of the community. Hætta writes how healing knowledge of Sámi is maintained and used

---

67 McGregor 2006.

68 Helander-Renvall, E., Alakärppä, I., Markkula, I., Labba, M. 2015. *Ekologinen perinnetieto Suomen saamelaisalueella. Hankkeen loppuraportti* [Traditional ecological knowledge in Sami homeland region in Finland. Project final report] Arctic Centre, University of Lapland.

by chosen individuals, those who 'know more than others'.[69] Those who know are often reluctant to talk openly about their insights. This is because healing knowledge is handed down from parents to their children, and those who become knowledge holders are specifically advised not to reveal their skills to cultural outsiders because it may result in loss of power to heal.[70] Also, Sexton and Stabbursvik underline that Sámi healers hesitate to talk about their healing experience because it is regarded as an inner experiential knowledge, and according to the same conviction, one should not openly talk about it.[71]

These examples highlight that some members of a local community can actually become excluded from parts of traditional knowledge. However, the secrecy is negotiable to some extent. As Hætta explains: The border between what is held in secret and what uninitiated people get insight into is not fixed [...] Even if there is a general norm against claiming to have healing abilities, there are researchers and journalists who have actually gotten insight into relatively deep information about traditional healing practices. This line between the secret and the open can be stretched both ways and how much the knowledge holders are willing to reveal about these things seems to be dependent on, among other things: the local tradition, who is asking, and the person who is asked'.[72]

Locations of sacred places are additional examples of information to which outsiders do not necessarily have access.[73] Documentation of sacred sites of Sámi is a good example of how concepts of secrecy and protection should be taken into account when collecting TEK. Within the Sámi homeland region, locations of sacred sites are widely documented and registered in databases. The aim of these databases is to protect the sites. However, opinions among Sámi are contradictory. Some feel that a sacred place loses its value or might perish if exposed, especially if the site becomes a tourist attraction. Therefore, the best way to protect the sites is to keep the locations secret. As claimed by Norberg

---

69 Hætta, A.K. 2010. *Secret Knowledge. The management and transformation of traditional healing knowledge in the Marka Sámi villages*. Master thesis. Tromsø: University of Tromsø, 48-49.

70 See Hætta 2010: 48-49.

71 Sexton, R. and Buljo Stabbursvik, E. A. 2010. Healing in the Sámi North. *Culture, Medicine and Psychology* 34(4): 571-589.

72 Hætta 2010: 71.

73 Hætta 2010; Äikäs, T. 2013. *'Kelle se tieto kuuluu, ni sillä se on.' Osallistava GIS Pohjois-Suomen pyhien paikkojen sijaintietoon liittyvien näkemysten kartoituksessa*. [The one knowledge belongs to, has it. Participatory GIS in documenting views on localizing sacred sites in Northern Finland] Master thesis. Oulu: University of Oulu. http://herkules.oulu.fi/thesis/nbnfioulu-201306011417.pdf.

and Fossum, it is possible to make the cultural heritage the group's own by keeping it secret.[74] Others argue that it is not possible to protect sacred sites or take them into account in land-use planning, if their locations are not known. Also, if knowledge regarding the locations and meanings of sacred sites is not passed on to younger generations, and is not registered, secrecy may lead to loss of sacred knowledge.[75]

In the Sámi contexts, in particular, registration of sacred *sieidi* is controversial.[76] *Sieidi* are for instance sacred rocks, cliffs and wooden objects to which Sámi earlier regularly used to make offerings. They are located in places such as islands and mountain slopes or in places where people hunt and fish, and where reindeer migrate. According to a Finnish archaeologist, Antti Lahelma, in Northern Finland, there are approximately 100 '*sieidi*' sacred sites.[77] Their exact number is however difficult to estimate or count. To some extent even today, Sámi continue to have contact with these revelatory places.[78] Sacred places are still in use. Äikäs writes that, at sacred sites, among the findings of post-1950s, there are for instance coins, candles, personal objects, quartzite, cigarettes and alcohol.[79] In Finland, the National Board of Antiquities maintains a database of antiquities, including many sacred Sámi *sieidi*. There is open access to this information. Traditionally among the Sámi, there have been strict rules about the use and access rights of sacred *sieidi*. Currently, there is no exact reliable information regarding these issues. Many questions are open, such as who should have the right to visit *sieidi* rocks, how much information should be revealed about them and whether everything should be kept hidden.

As a general rule, it can be claimed that dealing with secrecy and its norms can require that a researcher is an active member of the community he or she is studying, and that he or she has a relevant knowledge-based and experience-related position within the community: what would be shared would be knowledge learned by living in the local community and through being

74 Norberg, E., and Fossum, B. 2011. Traditional Knowledge and Cultural Landscape. In: Porsanger, J. and Guttorm, G. (eds.). *Working with Traditional Knowledge: Communities, Institutions, Information Systems, Law and Ethics. Diedut* 1/11: 193-223, 207.

75 Äikäs 2013: 28-33.

76 Norberg and Fossum 2011.

77 Lahelma, A. 2008. *A Touch of Red: Archaelogical and Ethnographic Approaches to Interpreting Finnish Rock Paintings.* Vaasa: Waasa Graphics Oy. 127.

78 Helander-Renvall 2014: 249-250.

79 Äikäs, T. 2012. Archaeology of sieidi stones. Excavating sacred places. In: *The Diversity of Sacred Lands in Europe. Proceedings of the Third Workshop of the Delos Initiative.* Inari/Aanaar, Finland, 1-3 July 2010. IUCN and Metsähallitus, 47-57.

involved in the local livelihood activities, such as herding and handicraft.[80] Simpson describes her traditional knowledge as internal environment: 'Anishinaabe knowledge is part of my internal environment, it is part of who I am and it comes to me through relationships with family, Elders, spiritual leaders, and interactions with the spiritual to world.'[81] For older Sámi people, it is challenging to distribute their knowledge to younger Sámi, if these two groups do not share those experiences, values and knowledge components that are necessary for grasping fully the contents of traditional knowledge.[82] Similarly, many aspects of traditional knowledge can be challenging or even impossible to describe to a cultural outsider: 'If you were born by the sea ice, played as a child on the sea ice, raised a family on your own by the sea ice, depend on it, work with it, think and dreamed about it, day in and day out – how do you describe such an integral part of your life, something exotic to most people but so familiar to you?'[83]

Eira who has conducted climate studies in reindeer herding discusses the researcher's position and its impact on collecting TEK.[84] According to her own experience, TEK holders are usually eager to talk to a researcher who originates from the community. Eira has pointed out though that an insider researcher may not be able to ask as detailed and descriptive questions as an outsider researcher.[85] Some parts of TEK can be so familiar and self-evident to an insider that information is actually left out from the documentation or study. On the other hand, an insider may be able to discover the key facts and hidden reali-

80 Helander 1999; Jernsletten, J. 2010. *Bissie dajve. Relasjoner mellom folk og landskap i Voengel-Njaarke sïjte* [Relations between people and landscape in Voengel-Njaarke village]. Avhandling levert for graden Philosophiae Doctor [Ph.D. Dissertation. Tromsö: University of Tromso]. Tromsö: Universitetet i Tromsö; Jernsletten, J. 2000. *Dovletje Jirreden. Kontesktuell verdi formidling i et sørsamisk miljø* [Contextual mediation within a Southern Sami environment.]. Hovedfagsoppgave I Religionshistorie [Master's degree in theological history]. Tromsø: Universitetet i Tromsø.

81 Simpson, L. 2001. Aboriginal peoples and knowledge: decolonizing our processes. In: *The Canadian Journal of Native studies* 21(1): 137-148.

82 Cf. Dunfjeld Aagård, M. 1989. *Symbolinnhold i Sørsamisk Ornamentikk* [Symbol contents in Southern Sami Ornaments]. Hovedfag i duodji. Oslo: Statens Lærerhøgskole i forming [Master's degree in Handicraft. Oslo: State Teacher College in Design], 154-155; Jernsletten 2010: 123-126; Norberg and Fossum 2011.

83 Gearheard et al. 2013: xxxiii.

84 Eira 2012: 15.

85 Eira 2012: 14-16.

ties of a culture.[86] Also, as we have seen for instance in the context of a project among the Sámi in Enontekiö, a researcher's ethnic or local background does not necessarily guarantee favorable interview conditions. Other factors may strongly influence these situations. For instance, Eira's comments are about climate research. It is obvious, that in relation to some specific topics, people are more willing to share and hand out their traditional knowledge openly to others.

Traditionalization

It has become common to state that traditions refer to those customs and beliefs that are handed down from previous generations. Within the Sámi culture there are features which are indeed regarded as traditions. They include the Sámi language; reindeer herding, handicraft and other traditional occupations; relationship to land; worldview; and cultural expressions, such as songs, stories, myths, and symbols. Sámi traditions constitute practices, understandings, features and particularities that continue to be important for the survival of the Sámi as a people.

A tradition should not be defined mainly in terms of boundedness, givenness or essence. Hymes chooses the term 'traditionalization' to purge the concept of tradition of its static, naturalistic implications':[87] 'But what constitutes 'tradition' to a people is ever-changing. Culture is not static, nor is it frozen in objectified moments in time'.[88]

In order to protect and guarantee continuity to culture, traditions are reinterpreted and recreated, and as we have seen above, for the same reason, they may also become disarticulated and kept secret. Change has always been there: in this sense, a tradition is an adaptive and selective process of continuity and transformation. We can see this clearly in relation to the Sámi reindeer herding terminology. There are words in Sámi that are several thousands of years old, and they originally describe circumstances related to the hunting of wild reindeer. But their meaning is now different, and the old words are used in

86 Menzies, C. R. 2001. Reflections on research with, for, and among indigenous peoples. In: *Canadian Journal of Native Education*. 25(1): 19-36.

87 Hymes, D. 1975. Folklore's Nature and the Sun's Myth. In: *Journal of American Folklore* 88: 345-69; Handler, R. and Linnekin, J. 1984. Tradition, Genuine or Spurious. In: *The Journal of American Folklore* 385: 273-290.

88 Trask, H. K.1991. Natives and Anthropologists: The Colonial Struggle. In: *The Contemporary Pacific* 3(1): 159-167.

different contexts, as the ways of harvesting reindeer have changed. In the similar way, the Sámi relationship to land and the rules governing this relationship have been maintained even if the land ownership and usage have changed.[89]

Tradition can be understood as a symbolic process that both presupposes past symbolisms and creatively reinterprets them.[90] Cocq considers tradition as a basic cultural process which has the political and cultural power to influence various issues of a society.[91] In other words, there may exist political claims behind the use and labeling of traditions and traditional practices. All this validates the argument that traditionalization can have a significant impact on the ways TEK is presented and maintained, as traditionalization is a process which involves reinterpreting and through which people select valued aspects from the past for cultural articulation and custodianship in the present.[92] Traditionalization is a self-conscious scheme or act which presupposes actors and agents.[93]

In this context, it is interesting to get a glimpse of how Indigenous People disarticulate certain traditions and remove them from public display as part of their postcolonial strategy. One example is the removal of the Iroquois *Ga:goh:sah,* false face masks from most of the museums of North America.[94] The masks are important for the wellbeing and overall strength of the Iroquois people. Accordingly, the masks, symbolize the increasing importance of traditional knowledge and the need to maintain its spiritual and epistemological paradigm (e.g. secrecy) for the empowerment and autonomy of Indigenous People and their culture. The act of removal of these masks from public display, and the usage of them in native ceremonials shows that the masks are a living tradition: 'they can be read as attempts to return to earlier traditions that turn out not, after all, to be lost'.[95]

In some cases, modern traditionalization activities are lifted up to the level of institutions and political organizations, where they can get and offer moral, financial and legislative support. Simultaneously, some traditions and know-

89 Helander 1999; Helander-Renvall 2013.

90 Handler and Linnekin 1984.

91 Cocq, C. 2014. Traditionalisation for revitalisation: *Tradition* as a concept and practice in contemporary Sámi contexts. In: *Folklore: Electronic Journal of Folklore* 57/14: 79-100.

92 Mould, T. 2005. The Paradox of Traditionalization: Negotiating the Past in Choctaw Prophetic Discourse. In: *Journal of Folklore Research* 42(3): 255-294.

93 Handler and Linnekin 1984: 287.

94 Phillips, R. B. 2004. Disappearing Acts: Traditions of Exposure, Traditions of Enclosure, and Iroquois Masks. In: M. Phillips and G. Schochet (eds.). *Questions of Tradition*. Toronto, Buffalo, London: University of Toronto Press, 56-87.

95 Phillips 2004.

ing linked to them become known far beyond local contexts, a development which reinforces the meanings of the original and transformed traditions as unique, grounded and worth keeping.[96] In this manner, as Kuutma states: 'Objects and elements of previous cultural experience are transformed into heritage as fragments that are decontextualised, in order to recontextualise them in a novel situation of representation that transforms them into national or ethnic symbols'.[97] Kuutma mentions Sámi traditional music, yoik, as an example of traditionalization, which when lifted up communicates Sámi heritage, identity and cultural knowing both in the Sámi society and outwards towards international spheres. Traditions and traditional knowledge are in this sense used in cultural revitalization.[98] Propelled into the Sámi cultural life are many new modes of expressions (e.g. theatre, film, modern pop music, advanced information technology, festivals, innovative Sámi clothing, ideas from social media), which after a while are or will become entangled with traditions.

Already in the Sámi cultural and political programs of the early 1970s and 1980s, there were certain cultural features that became stronger: as official core cultural values have since then been proclaimed, among others, the Sámi language, history and origins, and traditional livelihoods. It is obvious that traditions worth traditionalization and support are selected from the main cultural categories of the Sámi people. It is worth keeping in mind that they are or have been living traditions, not invented fabrications. One of their tasks, as already explained, is to effectuate and present continuity.

However, the role of traditions as identity marker is important as well. Sámi handicraft, *duodji* is an example on traditionalization, as *duodji* is a powerful identity marker and generator of many traditions, such as language, social relationships, knowledge of nature, customary rules, production techniques, aesthetic understanding, just to mention a few. Duodji skills and experiences are passed on from generation to generation through practice: teaching and learning may take place for instance when several generations make handicraft together. On the other hand, currently some craftspersons also take courses to learn from other knowledge holders or teachers, and some learning takes place through formal education. Ways of *duodji* have changed in Sámi society in line with changes in society as a whole. Dunfjeld Aagård has described how old Sámi patterns and symbols have survived in the Southern Sámi handicraft tradition and how these representations are reproduced and reinterpreted in the

96 Cf. Handler and Linnekin 1984.

97 Kuutma, K. 2006. Changing Codified Symbols of Identity. In: *FF Network for the folklore* fellows 31:7-11.

98 Cf. Berkes 2012:35.

present.[99] These activities have taken place for various reasons through 'a practical selection'.[100] It is important to understand that some traditions just keep living on. For example, Sámi sacred symbols are persistent, as Dunfjeld Aagård has shown. What has changed is how symbols are interpreted, and the contexts in which they are articulated or grounded, as we already have explained regarding the reindeer herding language.

Misuse of Sámi handicraft by the non-Sámi in tourism industry is common in Finland. Cheap mass-produced Lapland items are regarded by many Sámi as a threat to genuine Sámi handicraft. Especially the Sámi handicraft organization *Sámi Duodji* and Sámi cultural workers, have been actively criticizing this type of appropriation. Today, it is challenging to work as a full-time craftsperson, for example due to the income tax which creates further obstacles for the survival of traditional knowledge. Furthermore, many areas where materials have earlier been gathered for handicraft, are now open to external land-use activities causing additional problems. Be that as it may, in many ways, *duodji* is one of those cultural occupations that have gone through a traditionalization process: it has become a powerful cultural and political force. Many of *duodji*'s elements have been selected and reintegrated into the current Sámi society. TEK gets a new and varied meaning due these types of actualizations.

Regarding the political sphere '[t]he recognition of Indigenous Knowledge coincides with the increasing assertion by Indigenous people of their rights and the recognition of these rights by the international community', as McGregor explains.[101] However, it needs to be emphasized that traditionalization does not mean that things taking place are only or mainly political: 'a dynamic tradition includes many diverse activities'.[102] Harris has written an article on temporalities of traditions, in which she counts three different moments or options which describe 'how tradition may be conceptualized'.[103] Harris mentions the modernist moment, the structuralist moment and the postmodern moment. Hawaiian Lilikala Kame'eleihiwa contributes with indigenous temporality, in which time has no straight direction.[104] Trask explains: 'In our language, the past (*ka wa mamua*) is the time in front or before; the future (*ka wa mahope*) is

99 Dunfjeld Aagård 1989.

100 Clifford, J. 2004. Traditional futures. In: M. Phillips and Schochet, G. (eds.). *Questions of Tradition*. Toronto, Buffalo, London: University of Toronto Press, 152-168.

101 McGregor 2004: 389.

102 Clifford 2004.

103 Harris, O. 1996. The temporalities of tradition. Reflections on a changing anthropology. In: V. Hubinger (ed.) *Grasping the changing worlds*. London: Routledge, 1-16.

104 Lilikala Kame'eleihiwa 1986.

the time that comes after'. [105] Here different western temporalities are blurred, and accordingly: 'Loyalty to a traditional past is, in practice, a way ahead, a distinct path in the present'.[106] Thus, traditions continue to live and flourish in many temporalities, places and ways.

In some cases, Sámi people bring back old traditions. One example is a project of *Sámi Duodji* called in Sámi '*Láhppon duojit*' (Vanished handicraft), the aim of which is to seek time-worn handicraft objects in the museums for reproduction, reintroducing simultaneously old knowledge linked to them.[107] In some other cases, Sámi have developed their handicraft to attune into the modern society. One example is the *náhppi*, a wooden reindeer milking vessel. Reindeer milking in most Sámi areas has been abandoned. The original milking bowls were produced by men and their form was round and deep and the handle was shaped for holding the vessel while milking a reindeer doe. The milking bowl is still in use, albeit with a different style and purpose.[108] It is reintroduced to fit as a bowl in a modern household to place sugar, plants, and other objects into it or as a home decoration. Furthermore, the *náhppi* has been transformed into a piece of art and beyond that also into a commodity. Accordingly, it is used in the context of commercial activity as a souvenir or a collector item. In fact, today's Sámi handicraft is to a certain extent produced for trade. As the use of *náhppi* has been changed, it is now constructed in a slightly altered way. For example, the handle is different as the bowl is no longer used for milking and does not need a strong and particular handle to support the milking activity. Worth mentioning is that these days there are bowls made also by women.

A central point here is that the decoration of *náhppi* has become more important than earlier, whereas tradition-based understanding of the *náhppi*'s quality has been kept as one of its main criteria. But *náhppi* are handmade in the manner of old times. Thus, one still needs to know how to bring about a wooden object: what kind of material is needed and what is the technique of production. Consequently, TEK continues to be linked to the production of *náhppi*.

In the Sámi society there are several institutions that keep an eye on Sámi handicraft. The *Sámi duodji* association was established in 1975 to promote the

---

105 Trask 1991: 164.

106 Clifford 2004: 156.

107 Inarilainen. 2014. Kadonneen saamelaiskäsityön jäljillä [In search of disappeared Sami handicraft]. In: *Inarilainen* [Inari local newspaper] 10.12.2014.

108 Guttorm, G. 2014. *Náhppi, a ladle for milking reindeer.* http://senc.hum.helsinki.fi/wiki/Náhppi.

interests of the Sámi craftsmen, to strengthen the position of handicraft and to monitor the commercial activities related to crafts. It gives advice, arranges exhibitions and helps to sell handicraft products. *Sámi duodji* trademark is a brand name that was established in 1980s. In Finland, the *Sámi duodji* organization manages the handicraft trademark. The use of the trademark indicates to a buyer that a handicraft object is a genuine Sámi artifact and the producer of the object is a Sámi. The trademark also reveals the viability of Sámi handicraft activity and knowing. By the power of the trademark, the quality of Sámi handicraft traditions have been maintained and even improved. There are certain criteria linked to the right to use the Sámi handicraft trademark. In this way, the Sámi handicraft association as the managing organization is able to select and interpret certain works and workings, and bring handicraft traditions from the past to the present.

In line with *Sámi Duodji*'s understandings, there are persons within the Sámi society who regard themselves as guardians of traditions.[109] In the context of *duodji*, these persons are willing to accept and sustain the rules and ways of the Sámi society, and they give their contribution to the efforts of protecting and maintaining the traditions. However, many of them also make innovative experiments, even if such activities can be kept vague. Sámi clothing is especially much discussed within the Sámi cultural circles: *gákti*, the national dress, giving continuity to the Sámi identity, is a very important group marker. The making, style, use, customs, and social meaning of *gákti* turn in discussions and practices into a very complex issue whereby many understandings come together, coexist and compete. What is more, there are handicraft workers who are not willing to fully adopt the Sámi society's traditional discourse as such. Functioning in the borderland between the modern and the traditional can be a blessing for them in some ways, and force and help them to be more alert and reflective in terms of innovation, skills, traditional knowledge, and ethnic identity.[110]

---

109 Magga, S-M. 2010. *Vapauden rajat ja ulottuvuudet. Kirjoittamattomat säännöt duodjin ja saamelaisen muotoilun mahdollisuuksina ja rajoittajina* [Limits and dimensions of freedom. Unwritten rules in duodji and Sami desing] Master thesis. Oulu: Oulun yliopisto.

110 Cf. Magga 2010: 71; see also the interviews of a Sami handicraft person, Jenni Laiti, in Sami media, Sápmi 29.1.2015.

Concluding Remarks

As argued above, there are parts in traditional knowledge (TK) that are not easy to get a hold of. There is tacit and secret knowledge. On the other hand, it seems, that there is lots of information about traditions and traditional knowledge to which local people, researchers and others get effortlessly access. Researchers who collect and study traditional knowledge, impact the ways such knowledge is presented and transferred. If traditional knowing is removed from its natural ground, a living life, it may become scientifically rationalized and transformed into a 'body of data', which may be rather inflexible from an Indigenous vantage point. Researchers may consider TK only as data, and as consequence document only the type of TK which is valuable to their own research. Furthermore, we have been urging that TK needs to be acknowledged as a knowledge system equal to mainstream science. In addition, there is reason to support the indigenous strivings to protect TK through legislation as it is strongly endangered. What is more, researchers educated in mainstream institutions need to reflect on their own theoretical assumptions and methodological tools. Indigenous traditional knowledge may help to update western science into a wider and deeper understanding of reality for the better future.

The actualization (traditionalization) of specific traditions and ways of knowing, seems also to be for Indigenous People a way to manage their knowledge. Traditionalization is a cultural process, in which people choose valued aspects from the past for attention in the present. When a tradition is used in cultural revitalization, the traditionalization process is central. Various actualizations take place on different levels of the Sámi society. We have described Sámi handicraft, *duodji*, to exemplify issues regarding traditionalization. Sámi handicraft has been developed into a central Sámi identity marker, modern cultural activity, and commercial enterprise. Furthermore, *duodji* as organizing unit of various activities related to handicraft has consciously selected some components to safeguard and give support to, whereby the knowledge linked to it has gained a renewed meaning. Maintenance and delivery of tacit and secret knowledge are embedded in this selection approach.

The reflections in this article hopefully show that continuity and change, traditions and modernity, are not necessarily opposite powers: in Sámi society they take place simultaneously, in contesting and incorporating ways. They are not linear either: there does not necessarily exist a straight road from the past into the present or future regarding traditions and traditional knowledge. Tradition is not a wholesale return to past ways either. It is a question of maintenance, continuous development, multi-dimensional orientation, action, reaction, interpretation, reinterpretation, articulation, rearticulation and disarticulation. In conclusion, there is a need to study and manage traditional knowledge in new ways and with respect in order to elaborate how to make traditional knowledge more adaptable, accepted and accessible for the future generations. Traditions and traditional knowledge play a significant role in empowerment of Indigenous People.

Indigenous Creativity and the Public Domain – *Terra Nullius* Revisited?[1]

Mattias Åhrén

1 Introduction

This chapter attempts to draw an analogy between the *terra nullius* doctrine and its effects on indigenous peoples' capacity to control their traditional territories, and the notion of a so-called public domain and its impact on who can access indigenous peoples' respective cultural heritages.

To what extent indigenous peoples[2] have established rights over land through inhabitation and traditional use has been a concern of international law since its inception. It is generally held that the roots of the contemporary international legal system can be traced back to the second half of the 1600s. The international normative order that then gradually emerged did not only support the colonization of indigenous territories. It was indeed developed largely for facilitating European imperialism. Section 2 explains how the European states invoked the principle of state sovereignty to proclaim the so-called *terra nullius* doctrine law, a theory that professed that indigenous peoples – due to the nature of their cultures – can hold no rights over land. Since the classical international legal system did not embrace human rights norms that could place checks and balances on the exercise of sovereignty, it was from an international legal perspective unproblematic that states invoked the *terra nullius* doctrine in order to make legal claims to indigenous territories.

Section 3 articulates, however, how matters changed when, following the establishment of the United Nations, human rights, including the right to equality, were integrated into the international legal system. This development chal-

1 This chapter draws from a smaller part of a doctoral dissertation defended by the author in 2010 at The Arctic University of Norway – UiT, titled *The Saami Traditional Dress and Beauty Pageants–Indigenous Peoples' Ownership and Self-Determination Over their Cultures*. The chapter further borrows from another work by the author; *Indigenous Peoples' Status in the International Legal System* (Oxford University Press, 2016).

2 To be precise, indigenous property rights over land most often vest with indigenous communities within an indigenous people, rather than with the people as such. See further Åhrén, ibid. Section 9.1. For consistency, this chapter nonetheless employs the term 'peoples' throughout.

Xanthaki, Valkonen et al. (eds.), *Indigenous Peoples' Cultural Heritage: Rights, Debates and Challenges.*

lenged the authority of the *terra nullius* doctrine, and required a re-evaluation of whether indigenous peoples *per se* lack capacity to hold property rights over territories traditionally used.

Sections 4-7 focus on indigenous intellectual property (similar) rights (IPRs), or perhaps rather on the lack thereof. The Sections place a particular focus on whether an analogy can be drawn from recent developments within the sphere of indigenous land rights, i.e. they survey whether these developments are, or should be, translatable into the sphere of indigenous peoples' potential rights over their creativity. Section 4 sketches the basic contours of the intellectual property (IP) system. In particular, the section explains how IP protection, generally speaking, does not extend to works (i) that are not sufficiently new/original, (ii) anonymous, and (iii) from an IP perspective old. Section 5 proceeds to articulate the basic characteristics of indigenous creativity, while Section 6 subsequently explores the compatibility between (i) the core features of IP, and (ii) the characteristics of indigenous creativity. Finally, Section 7 addresses the question posed by the title, i.e. it compares the effects of *terra nullius* doctrine on indigenous peoples with those of the notion of a public domain, viewed through the prism of the right to equality.

2 Classical International Law's Position on Indigenous Land Rights – *The Terra Nullius* Doctrine

2.1 *Generally on the* Terra Nullius *Doctrine*

It is generally submitted that the seed to the international legal system we know today was planted in Europe in the post-Westphalian era. Resting heavily on its constitutional principle – that of state sovereignty – the international legal order that now took form not only supported colonization of indigenous lands, but was actually created for the precise purpose of facilitating and legalizing European control over foreign territories.[3] The European realms unilaterally declared, as was their sovereign right to do, that under international law indigenous peoples – due to the very nature of their societies – lack capacity to hold rights over land. In other words, the European sovereigns declared indig-

3 W Kymlicka, 'Beyond the Indigenous/Minority Dichotomy?', in S Allen and A Xanthaki (eds.), *Reflections on the UN Declaration on the Rights of Indigenous Peoples* (Hart Publishing, 2011) 183; J Crawford and M Koskenniemi, *International Law* (Cambridge University Press, 2012) 15; G Simpson, 'International law in diplomatic history', in Crawford and Koskenniemi, ibid. 27.

enous territories *terra nullius*, i.e although factually inhabited, empty for legal and political purposes.[4]

The *terra nullius* doctrine has two elements. The first relates to a population's capacity to hold political, or sovereign, rights over a territory, the second to its capability of establishing private rights to land. Here, it is the second element that is relevant. It professes that to establish private rights over land, one must improve on, or add value, to it. British philosopher John Locke is often associated with this line of thought. According to him, uncultivated land cannot constitute property. Man must transform such land into valuable and productive property in order to claim rights thereto. Concepts such as 'uncultivated', 'improve upon', and 'add value to' are, however, clearly not terms of art. They are culturally relative, i.e. they only acquire meaning in a particular cultural context. Proponents of the *terra nullius* doctrine were, however, ignorant to this fact. Locke held that only such lands had been improved upon, and thus constituted property, that were used for European style agrarian practices. Lands used in other, less 'civilised' (i.e. non-European) manners were, by definition, 'uncultivated', and their inhabitants as a consequence uncivilized, incapable of holding rights.[5]

In summary, the European realms invoked the principle of sovereignty to proclaim the *terra nullius* doctrine law. Putting the norm they had thus created into action, they subsequently unilaterally determined that indigenous peoples could hold no rights to land as their land uses were 'uncivilized', i.e. not sufficiently 'European'. One can say that international law of the era professed a 'dynamic of difference' to justify denying indigenous peoples rights over land.[6]

---

4 While *terra nullius* with time became the term for a legally and politically empty territory, Andrew Fitmaurice points to that initially the term was employed to describe territories that were not only politically, but in fact literally, uninhabited, most often in a Polar context. See A Fitzmaurice, 'Discovery, Conquest, and Occupation of Territory', in B Fassbender and A Peters (eds.), *The Oxford Handbook of the History of International Law* (2012) 9-11. Still, since *terra nullius* seemingly is the general term of choice, this chapter will employ it as well.

5 J Tully, *Strange Multiplicity: Constitutionalism in an Age of Diversity* (Cambridge University Press, 1995) 72; L Obregón Tarazona, 'The Civilized and the Uncivilized', in Fassbender and Peters (n 4) 2, 7; Fitzmaurice (n 4) 8; J Gilbert, *Indigenous Peoples' Land Rights under International Law* (Transnational Publishers, 2007) 3, 24-26; P Fitzpatrick, 'Terminal Legality: Imperialism and the (De)composition of Law', in D E Kirby and C Coleborne (eds.), *Law, History Colonialism, The Reach of Empire* (Manchester University Press, 2001) 14.

6 A Anghie, 'Finding the Peripheries: Sovereignty and Colonialism in Nineteenth-Century International Law' [1999] Harvard International Law Journal 40 24-28.

2.2 *Further on the 'Dynamic of Difference'*

More specifically, the 'dynamic of difference' argument consisted of two main elements.

First, generally speaking, indigenous cultures aspire to leave few marks on lands used. Clearly, this feature of indigenous cultures sits badly with the Lockean understanding of value-adding. As seen, John Locke and his contemporary scholars (and sovereigns) defined valuable land – and thus property – in terms of European style agrarian lands. In other words, improving on the land was – by definition – an exercise of substantially altering the land compared with its natural state. Through their practices, indigenous peoples had, on their part, in the minds of the Europeans not altered the land in any legally relevant manner. That indigenous peoples treasured the land in its natural stage lacked importance. As mentioned, Locke and his colleagues were blind to cultural relativism in that sense.

As to the second part of the 'dynamic of difference' formula, indigenous cultures normally orient around the collective, rather than around individual members of the group, in manners western cultures, generally speaking, are alien to.[7] Thus, indigenous lands and natural resources are commonly communally used, and lands and natural resources are also perceived to vest with the collective,[8] insofar the people think of lands in terms of rights at all. Also this aspect of indigenous land uses squares badly with the Western/European idea of land uses and rights. As Western/European cultures are more individual-centric, rights to land are largely perceived to vest with individuals, or at least with identifiable groups thereof.[9] As a consequence, when the Europeans observed indigenous communal land uses and failed to associate particular indigenous individuals with particular land areas, it, in their view, allowed them to infer that no private rights attached to the land.

To conclude, the method used for maintaining that indigenous land uses can *per se* not result in private rights to land was one of differentiation between cultures. The European sovereigns took upon themselves to unilaterally

---

7 S Von Lewinski, *International Copyright Law and Policy* (Oxford University Press, 2008) 528.

8 J Gibson, *Community Resources* (Ashgate Publishing, 2005) 15-19, 29-30, 104.

9 Some might question this assertion with reference to commons. Still, it would appear incorrect to refer to commons as recognition of collective property rights over territories. Rather, commons can probably, generally speaking, be better described as areas to which no private title apply. With regard to commons see, generally, B H Weston and D Bollier, *Green Governance; Ecological Survival, Human Rights, and the Law of the Commons* (2014); P Linebaugh, *The Magna Carta Manifesto* (UC Press, 2009).

declare that international law provides that their way of using land results in property rights, while land uses not sufficiently similar to their own practices, common to indigenous cultures, do not.

3 Rejection of the *Terra Nullius* Doctrine

3.1 *The Emergence of the Right to Equality*

As seen, under classical international law, who could hold private rights over land was from an international legal perspective largely a political issue. States invoked their sovereign right to 'subjectively' determine who could be eligible for such rights and who could not, without it being a concern to international law.

During this era, human rights simply did not form part of the international legal system.[10] Only following the establishment of the United Nations did human rights become an integral part of the international legal system in earnest.[11] Within the contemporary human rights normative order that now gradually took form, everyone's equal value was from the outset considered a cardinal principle and norm. Consequently, international law came to outlaw practices that discriminate based on among other reasons racial, cultural, and ethnic background. The right to equality appears in the Bill of Rights in a manner that underscores the principal importance of the right,[12] something that is further emphasized by the fact that an entire human rights treaty – the Convention on the Elimination of Racial Discrimination (CERD) – was devoted to the right.

Thus, in sharp contrast to its classical counterpart, the contemporary international normative order now came to call for equal treatment in absence

10 See M Koskenniemi, *The Gentle Civilizer of Nations* (Cambridge University Press, 2001) 55; A Cassese, *International Law* (2nd edn., Oxford University Press, 2005) 23-24. That said, one might note in passing that already during the classical era, scholars in Europe developed civil rights theories that with time became an integral part of liberalism (A Eide, 'Economic, Social and Cultural Rights as Human Rights', in A Eide, C Krause, and A Rosas (eds.), *Economic, Social and Cultural Rights – A textbook* (2nd edn., Martinus Nijhoff Publishers, 2001) 12-13). For considerable time, however, these theories by and large remained precisely theories, rather than forming part of the international normative order (Koskenniemi, ibid. 55).

11 Cassese (n 10) 143.

12 Universal Declaration on Human Rights (UDHR), arts 2, 7; International Covenant on Civil and Political Rights, arts 2.2, 26; International Covenant on Economic, Social and Cultural Rights, art 2.2.

of objectively justifiable reasons for differentiation. Seemingly, the emergence of such a norm should create obstacles for states wishing to maintain that indigenous peoples – simply by the nature of their cultural practices – lack the capacity to hold rights over land. The difficulties associated with pursuing such a line of argument becomes even more apparent if one considers the nature of the right to property.

3.2 *The Nature of the Right to Property*

As the right to equality, the right to property was incorporated into the contemporary human rights system at its inception. It for instance appears in UDHR Article 17 and CERD Article 5 (d) (v).

It follows from the manner in which the right has been articulated in the mentioned and other human rights instruments that the right to property known to international law is not a right to be provided with property. Rather, it is a right to acquire property on equal basis with others, and, once property has been thus acquired, a right not to be arbitrarily deprived of the same.[13] International law hence largely accepts any domestic position as to what extent matter can be subject to private property rights – provided that the law is non-discriminatory. In other words, the right to property is at its core a particular aspect of the right to equality.

3.3 *Implications for Indigenous Communities' Possibilities to Establish Property Rights over Land*

As the above alludes to, the inclusion of the right to equality into the international normative order, and its intrinsic connection to the right to property, should reasonably render it difficult for states to maintain that certain segments of society, simply by the very nature of their cultures, lack the capacity to establish property rights over land. On the face of it, the right to equality is simply incompatible with a position that leaves states free to unilaterally decide that indigenous peoples', but not other peoples', lands are *terra nullius*.

Consequently, following the incorporation of the right to equality into international law, domestic and regional human rights courts and institutions commenced to formally firmly reject the *terra nullius* doctrine as inherently discriminatory.[14] It became generally accepted that indigenous peoples' tradi-

13 Compare R Lillich, 'Global Protection of Human Rights', in T Meron (ed.), *Human Rights in International law: Legal and Policy Issues* (Clarendon Press, 1984 (reprint 1992)); C Krause, 'The Right to Property', in Eide, Kause, and Rosas (n 10) 191-2.

14 For an elaboration on the rejection of the *terra nullius* doctrine, see further Åhrén (n 1) Section 8.3, with references.

tional land uses in accordance with their own cultural practices do carry the capacity to establish property rights. The key word here is 'traditional'.

The significance of the qualifier 'traditional' becomes clear if one examines to what extent indigenous peoples, at this point in time, managed to convert the mentioned *formal* recognition into acknowledgement in *practice* of property rights over territories traditionally used. Because even with the emergence of the right to equality as a fundamental international norm, indigenous peoples continued to experience great difficulties when seeking to have property rights over land realized. The reason is to be found in how the right to equality was understood when it emerged as an international norm.

At the time of its incorporation into the human rights system, the right to non-discrimination only provided for formal equality. It was sufficient (indeed expected) that the state provided one educational system, one set of health care service etc., if only all citizens, irrespective of their ethnic and cultural background, had equal access to such services. In short, the right to non-discrimination only called for equal treatment of equally situations.

The applicability of this principal understanding of property was not limited to spheres such as education. It also extended to property right law and policy. Although states were no longer allowed to have property laws and policies in place that *formally* excluded indigenous cultures from establishing property rights over land, a right to non-discrimination that merely calls for equality in law still does not require states to accustom property rights laws and policies so to provide indigenous peoples with *factual equality* when it comes to the capacity to establish such rights through traditional use. The difference between equality in law and in fact can be illustrated with a practical example. When the right to non-discrimination merely calls for equal treatment of equal situations, it is non-discrimination if a Scandinavian farmer and an indigenous Sami reindeer herder have equal opportunities to establish property rights over land through purchasing a cattle-herd, place that herd within a fence, and allow it to graze there for a relevant time period. With this understanding of equality, Scandinavian jurisdictions need not extend property right protection to land uses that are not 'sufficiently similar' to those that are common to the majority culture.

More recently, however, the right to equality has evolved to take on a second facet. The right no longer only provides that equal cases be treated equally. In addition, those with a different background compared with the majority population are entitled to treatment accustomed to their cultural identity.[15] This evolved understanding of equality has a profound impact on indigenous peo-

---

15 Åhrén (n 1) Section 6.3, with references.

ples' possibilities to have property rights over land recognized. Now, domestic jurisdictions may no longer employ property laws and policies derived only from land uses common to the majority culture. Rather, such laws and policies must recognize that if a group has historically used a land area *in manners common and traditional to its particular culture*, this results in property rights. This new norm can be illustrated by returning to the Sami reindeer herding example. Now, it is no longer non-discrimination if a Sami reindeer herder has merely the same possibility to establish property right over land through engaging in Scandinavian style agrarian practices as a farmer of Scandinavian decent. Rather, it is equality if the Sami reindeer herder has the same opportunity to establish a property right over land through practicing nomadic reindeer herding in the Sami traditional manner as a Scandinavian farmer has through stationary farming.[16]

The question then becomes, what relevance, if any, does, or should, this development within the sphere of land rights have on indigenous peoples' rights over their creativity?

4 Generally on Intellectual Property Rights (IPRs)

4.1 *The Origin of and Basic Nature of IPRs*

IP is no modern invention. For instance, already in 1474 the Republic of Venice protected a technique for glass-making particular to the republic from the use of others,[17] arguably an early form of patent. As to the other IP element of central relevance here, copyright, the notion that printed works should be subject to legal protection emerged essentially in tandem with the invention of the printing press.[18] The world's first copyright act, the Statute of Anne, was subsequently enacted in Britain in 1709, followed a few decades later by the first proposal for an international treaty on copyright protection.[19] As to the history of national legislation pertaining to patents, the first domestic patent

16 Numerous international legal sources affirm that the articulated new understanding of equality forms part of international law, as well as that it has the described impact on indigenous peoples' property rights over lands and natural resources. See Åhrén (n 1) Chapters 7 and 8, with references.

17 G Dutfield and U Suthersanen, *Global Intellectual Property Law* (Edward Elgar, 2008) 6, 106; By (author) World Intellectual Property Organization, *Introduction to Intellectual Property, Theory and Practice* (1997) 17.

18 By (author) (n 17) 23; G Gregory Letterman, *Basics of International Intellectual Property Law* (Transnational Publishers, 2001) 259; Dutfield and Suthersanen (n 17) 66.

19 Von Lewinski (n 7) 13-14; By (author) (n 17) 24; Dutfield and Suthersanen (n 17) 68.

act was arguably the English Statute of Monopolies of 1624. Some time later, both France and the United States adopted their first national patent laws almost immediately after their respective revolutions.[20] The first international patent treaty – the Paris Convention – was subsequently adopted in 1883.[21]In the present day, IP has been broadly defined as legal rights which result from human intellectual creativity.[22] However, regardless how one defines 'IP', such property is by no means a term of art. There is nothing inherent or mandatory that prescribes what forms of human creativity, if any, should be subject to rights. On the contrary, to ascribe rights to creativity is a purely subjective decision by a lawmaker. IP does not 'occur naturally'. Rather, it exists only if explicitly provided for by law.[23] Dutfield's and Suthersanen's observation that the term (although not necessarily the concept) actually lacks meaning in its own right and is thus, despite attempts to the contrary, in fact objectively undefinable can therefore be described as an apt one.[24]

Already at this point, it is pertinent to underscore that instantly during the era when liberals formulated the *terra nullius* doctrine and the European sovereigns rendered it law, the notion that creativity – as land and natural resources – should be subject to individual monopoly rights was not only entertained but also practiced. Moreover, as with indigenous territories, it was up to the sovereign to decide who was bestowed with rights over creativity. In its inherently subjective nature, IP resembles the *terra nullius* doctrine. As

---

20 By (author) (n 17) 18-19; Dutfield and Suthersanen (n 17) 106-07.

21 Letterman (n 18) 170.

22 By (author) (n 17) 3.

23 Letterman (n 18) 2-3. It falls outside the scope of this chapter to discuss why, against the backdrop of the just stated, norms have been created that extend legal protection to human creativity. For discussions of the most common arguments for (and against) the existence of IP, see, generally, ibid. 165-73, 256-65; Dutfield and Suthersanen (n 17) 51-60, 109-112; Gibson (n 8) 85-89; more generally, P Drahos, *A Philosophy of Intellectual Property* (Ashgate Publishing, 1996).

24 See Dutfield and Suthersanen (n 17) 6, 13-16, 18, 48, 78, and compare also Gibson (n 8) 129. This feature of the IP system carries an additional implication. It means that this chapter's presentation of the general contours and features of this system must necessarily be an oversimplification. The fact that there is no, and indeed cannot be, any universally applicable definition of IP implies that each jurisdiction may, and does, define IP differently. To present the IP system in a generalized and simplified manner is, however, not a problem for the present chapter, as its ambition is precisely to measure this system's basic and general features and elements–and in particular the notion of a public domain–against recent developments within the sphere of indigenous land and natural resource rights.

touched upon, the chapter returns to this similarity between the two categories of rights below.

4.2 *The General Elements and Features of IPRs*

It is common to divide IP into two broad categories; 'industrial property' and 'copyrights'. While the subject of copyright protection should be self-explanatory, it might be worth pointing out that the former category includes IP mechanisms such as patents and trademarks.[25] Copyright, patents, and trademarks are generally considered the three most central IP tools. Of these, copyrights and patents are the ones most often discussed in an indigenous rights context,[26] and are also the main focus of this chapter. Very briefly, the basic features of these two IP-mechanisms can be described as follows.

Copyrights largely relate to artistic expressions,[27] such as music, paintings, and clothing. However, not all such creations are copyrightable; rather, only new, or original, creations enjoy copyright protection.[28] In other words, the creation must be sufficiently dissimilar to already existing works. If a work meets the originality criterion and thus is copyrightable, put simply, and setting certain exceptions aside, a copyright awards the creator with an exclusive right to make copies of the work and make those available to the general public, and/or to perform or recite the work.[29] If a work is copyrightable, copyright protection does, however, like most IPRs, not last in perpetuity.[30] From the point in time when a work is made publically available, such protection normally expires in a number of years defined by domestic law following the passing away of the creator of the work.[31]

---

25 By (author) (n 17) 3.

26 See Dutfield and Suthersanen (n 17) 13. That said, one might perhaps discern a trend among scholars to direct increased attention to trademarks as a IP tool that could potentially protect indigenous creativity. See, generally, D Zografos, *Intellectual Property and Traditional Cultural Expressions* (Edward Elgar, 2010) 50-103.

27 By (author) (n 17) 5.

28 Megan M Carpenter, 'Intellectual Property Law and Indigenous Peoples: Adapting Copyright Law to the Needs of a Global Community' [2004] Yale Human Rights Law & Development Law Journal, Vol 7 69; By (author) (n 17) 9, 256; Dutfield and Suthersanen (n 17) 79-80.

29 Von Lewinski (n 7) 55; Letterman (n 18) 2-3, 257-8; By (author) (n 17) 5.

30 Letterman (n 18) 8-9.

31 A Sterling, *World Copyright Law* (Sweet & Maxwell, 2003) 193-194; Dutfield and Suthersanen (n 17) 8, 79-80, 97; Letterman (n 18) 257-58.

For its part, patents provide, similar to copyrights, the inventor with a sole right to utilize her or his invention in ways he or she see fit.[32] However, as with copyrights, only inventions that are new, or novel, i.e. sufficiently dissimilar compared with already existing inventions, can be the subject to patent protection.[33] Further, patent protection too, is time-limited. It is normally valid for 20 years following the filing for registration, with the possibility to file for subsequent protection for an additional 20-year period.[34]

In addition, both copyright and patent protection only extend to works that can be attributed to an individual creator or, alternatively, to an identifiable number of creators.[35]

4.3 *Conclusions as to the Basic Contours of IPRs – The Notion of a So-called Public Domain*

We have thus established that IP is not a term of art. The lawmaker determines what forms of human creativity, if any, are worthy of legal protection based on political choice. Creativity that the lawmaker decides should not be protected – either not at all or after a certain time-period – is from an IP perspective considered to fall into the so called public domain, and thus free for everyone to use, also against the creator's will. The fact that IP law is as much about deciding *what should not be protected* as about what should be implies that the notion of a public domain is integral to the IP system.[36]

As further described, when determining the scope of IP protection – and as a consequence at the same time conversely that of the public domain – lawmakers have (in addition to deciding that certain forms of creativity should not be protectable *per se*) generally held that creativity with certain characteristics shall be disqualified from IP protection. First, generally speaking, IPRs do not lend themselves to anonymous works. IP-protection presupposes an identifiable creator or group of creators where the membership is known. Second, IP-protection does not extend to creativity that is not sufficiently original or novel – as measured against already existing and known human creativity. Or to put it differently, one may not receive IP protection with regard to works that have

32 Letterman (n 18) 166.

33 Carpenter (n 28) 69; Letterman (n 18) 5, 9, 165.

34 Dutfield and Suthersanen (n 17) 112-13, 128; Letterman (n 18) 166.

35 David Lea, *Property Rights, Indigenous Peoples and the Developing World: Issues From Aboriginal Entitlement to Intellectual Ownership Rights* (Martinus Nijhoff Publishers, 2008) 263; Dutfield and Suthersanen (n 17) 12.

36 A Chander and M Sunder, 'The Romance of the Public Domain' [2004] California Law Review, Vol 92 1340; Letterman (n 18) 257.

not sufficiently 'improved upon', i.e. are not sufficiently dissimilar compared with, the bulk of already existing creativity. Finally, even if a work did at a time qualify for IP-protection, the protection will normally expire following the passing of a certain time-period. As a consequence, central elements of a particular culture will in all likelihood most often not enjoy IP-protection today, since one can expect such elements to be 'old', for IP purposes.

The question then becomes, how well do the articulated basic contours of IPRs match the characteristics of indigenous creativity?

5 The General Characteristics of Indigenous Creativity

Indigenous creativity tends to be a result of continued reworking of already available and known material. Generally speaking, it is marked by a dynamic interplay between old and new, evolving at 'slow pace'. As a consequence, indigenous 'new' collective creativity often contains substantial elements of already existing and from an IP perspective already disseminated 'works',[37] with relatively marginal additions being made at any given time. Innovation is restricted, as faithful reproduction of the indigenous people's culture is often important. Art can be viewed as a means to communicate history, culture etc. wherefore the artist is bound by respect for the tradition and is not given free rain for inspiration, sometimes to the extent that it is not even possible to discern a 'new work' from the existing bulk of cultural elements springing from the indigenous people in question.[38]

That said, it should be underlined that the above is a general description of indigenous creativity, perhaps even overly so. Clearly, there are examples of indigenous individuals creating matter that might be inspired by the individual's

37 The same knowledge of for instance the properties of a plant, and also other forms of creativity, can of course be generated by more than one indigenous people independent of one another when the same plant or other properties are found in several indigenos territories. Legal issues pertaining to such 'shared' knowledge or expressions is, however, outside the scope of this chapter.

38 T Kongolo, *Unsettled International Intellectual Property Issues* (Kluver Law International, 2008) 42; Carpenter (n 28) 54, 69-70; T Cottier and M Panizzon, 'A New Generation of IPR for the Protection of Traditional Knowledge in PGR for Food, Agricultural, Pharmaceutical Uses', in S Biber-Klemm and T Cottier (eds.), *Rights to Plant Genetic Resources and Traditional Knowledge: Basic Issues and Perspectives* (CABI, 2006) 216; Von Lewinski (n 7) 529-30; A Lucas-Schloetter, 'Folklore', in S Von Levinski (ed.), *Indigenous Heritage and Intellectual Property: Genetic Resources, Traditional Knowledge and Folklore* (2nd ed, Kluver Law International, 2008) 384-85.

cultural background, but which are still distinctly different from already existing 'works' in that culture.

Further, as mentioned, indigenous cultures tend to place significant emphasis on the collective, in a manner and to an extent not usually found within other societies. This aspect of indigenous cultures and societies is no less present within the sphere of creativity. As seen, indigenous authorship and innovations can, generally speaking, be said to have a collective dimension, in the sense that the individual creator normally build on and remains true to the pre-existing culture. Against this background, it is only natural that indigenous peoples, including the individual author, often view elements of their creativity to vest with the collective, rather than with individual members thereof.[39] As Michael Blakney observes, with reference to the cultures of the Aboriginal peoples of Australia, 'if the beliefs and practices of Australian indigenous peoples are any guide, authorship may reside in pre-human creator ancestors... [a]uthorship is replaced by a concept of interpretation through initiation.'[40]

As a consequence of these aspects of indigenous creativity it might be difficult, indeed impossible, to attribute elements of an indigenous culture to one or more identifiable individuals within the group. Indeed, since individual authorship tends to be of limited relevance to indigenous cultures where creativity is often distinguished by it being attributable to the community,[41] elements of such peoples' creativity are not uncommonly of anonymous origin, i.e. the individual creator/s is/are unknown.

6 Compatibility between the Basic Features of IP and the Characteristics of Indigenous Creativity

If one compares the basic features of IPRs and the general characteristics of indigenous creativity, it would appear clear that that the former legal framework is not particularly suited to protect the latter form of creativity, for three, but

39 See Von Lewinski (n 7) 528; S Biber-Klemm and D Szmura Berglas, 'Problems and Goals', in Biber-Klemm and Cottier (n 38) 18-19; Gibson (n 8) 104; G Dutfield, *Intellectual Property, Biogenetic Resources and Traditional Knowledge* (Earthscan, 2004) 101. Again, this might be somewhat of an oversimplification. The fact that indigenous peoples tend to view their creativity to west with the collective need not preclude that customary norms prescribe that certain elements of the creativity are to be controlled by groups or individuals within the indigenous society. See e.g. Dutfield, ibid. 95.

40 M Blakney, 'The Protection of Traditional Knowledge under Intellectual Property Law' [2000] European Intellectual Property Review, Vol 22 251-52.

41 Von Lewinski (n 7) 529-30.

interrelated, reasons which are all rooted in the collective nature of indigenous creativity, as opposed to the individualistic focus of conventional IPRs.

First, the fact that indigenous creativity tends to be marked not so much by original ideas of the individual author, but rather by a slow reworking of already existing material, wherefore a 'new' work regularly contains substantial elements of material that already exists within that particular indigenous culture necessarily results in an apparent risk that the work is not considered sufficiently original or novel for IP purposes. As a consequence, it will not be eligible for IP protection.[42]

Second, the collective dimension of indigenous peoples' creativity, resulting in it often being difficult to attribute particular elements of indigenous cultures to one or more identifiable individuals, may often lead to the conclusion that the author of the work is unknown for IP purposes and as such not IP protectable.[43]

In addition to the miss-match between conventional IPRs and indigenous creativity caused by their individualistic and collective nature, respectively, the fact that most IPRs are time-limited also renders much indigenous creativity ineligible for IP protection. The slow speed at which indigenous cultures evolve, where small bricks are added to existing bulk of creativity, results in, generally speaking, that major parts of indigenous creativity have been created 'long ago', if measuring against an IP yardstick, and are as a result in the public domain. Moreover, this bulk is likely to include the most central, and most culturally important, elements of indigenous peoples' culture, as these are presumably the fundamental building blocks upon which the small bricks of creativity have subsequently been added. As a consequence, the IP-system leaves the underlying creative mass of indigenous peoples' cultures unprotected.[44]

The conclusion thus becomes that for the outlined reasons, indigenous creativity is largely ineligible for IP protection, but rather falls into the so called public domain. As a consequence, irrespective of that the cultural elements can be clearly attributed to a particular indigenous people, non-indigenous lawmakers have decided that such elements shall nonetheless be free for everyone to use, also against the direct objection of the indigenous people.

---

42 Dutfield (n 39) 104.

43 Dutfield (n 39) 101, 104; Carpenter (n 28) 54, 67-68; Von Lewinski (n 7) 529-30; Cottier and Panizzon (n 38) 216-18; Kongolo (n 38) 43; Lucas-Schloetter (n 38) 386-88; Biber-Klemm and Szmura Berglas (n 39) 18-19.

44 Dutfield (n 46) 101, 104; Gibson (n 12) 8-9, 118, 124; Kongolo (n 45) 42; Carpenter (n 34) 54, 69-70; Cottier and Panizzon (n 45) 216; Lucas-Schloetter (n 45) 384-85; Von Lewinski (n 11) 531.

Generally speaking, the articulated conclusion finds support in the doctrine. Johanna Gibson infers, with reference to copyright, that IP 'is an inadequate means of protection [for indigenous creativity] because of its limited duration, its attachment to individual authors... and its requirement of originality'.[45] In the same vein, Silke Von Lewinski notes that as a rule, '[indigenous traditional cultural expressions are] not protected by classical intellectual property rights'.[46] Terri Janke contrasts rights over creativity in indigenous customary legal systems with IP law. She notes that while the latter legal system 'grants economic rights which are individual rights', indigenous peoples' rights tend–in accordance with their own legal traditions–to be collective in nature...'.[47] Similarly, Peter Drahos notes that '[p]roperty rules, more than most rules, are rooted in the fundamental morality of a given society. Western copyright laws, for instance, reflect a view of art that promotes the importance of individual creativity and individual rights...'.[48] See in this context also some of the references already referred to above.[49]

In summary, the property rights regime that governs what forms of human creativity should be subject to property rights – the IP regime – takes the same position towards indigenous creativity today as it did historically, i.e. it largely leaves such creativity unprotected. The question then becomes; how well does this position – and in particular the notion of a public domain – sit with the contemporary understanding of the right to equality?

---

45 Gibson (n 8) 77, 123 (quote from this page), 124.

46 Von Lewinski (n 7) 527, 534 (quote from this page).

47 T Janke, 'Don't Give Away Your Valuable Cultural Assets: Advice for Indigenous Peoples' [1998] Indigenous Law Bulletin 8 9.

48 Drahos (n 23) 15.

49 That the present IP regime is not well equipped for protecting indigenous creativity is further reflected in the deliberations undertaken under the auspices of the World Intellectual Property Organization's (WIPO) Intergovernmental Committee on Genetic Resources, Traditional Knowledge and Folklore (IGC). Within the IGC, member states are negotiating legal instruments that, if adopted, would extend IP *similar* protection to traditional knowledge and traditional cultural expressions generated by indigenous peoples. Clearly, such an undertaking had not been necessary had it been generally held that conventional IPRs do sufficiently protect indigenous creativity. See reports from the IGC sessions, WIPO documents WIPO/GRTKF/IC/1-29. In this context see also, more generally, Gibson (n 8) 73-126.

7 The Compatibility between the Right to Equality and the Notion of a Public Domain as Applied in an Indigenous Peoples' Context

7.1 *Introduction*

As seen, the right to equality did not form part of classical international law, which left sovereigns free to politically formulate a law that professed that indigenous peoples were incapable of possessing property rights over land. By a similar token, we further saw that to what extent rights should vest in human creativity was also a political decision, and that the IP system that emerged in parallel with the *terra nullius* doctrine became geared towards Western, rather than indigenous, forms of creativity. The justification used in both instances was one of distinction. Argued dissimilarities between both indigenous land uses and forms of creativity, on one hand, and Western practices, on the other, was used to disqualify the former from property rights, although, as touched upon, the argument was more explicitly made in the land rights context.

As further seen, however, equality emerging as a fundamental principle and right has, within the sphere of land rights, resulted in a conclusion that to what extent indigenous peoples hold property rights over lands and natural resources is no longer only a matter of the will of the sovereign, but predominantly of human rights. This development begs the question; if the extent to which indigenous peoples may exercise control over lands traditionally used has become a question of equality, should it not the same be true with regard to creativity traditionally created? In other words, is there any legally relevant rationale that motivates that one distinguishes between the two categories of subject matter? Unless such a rationale can be identified, one can perhaps expect international law to recognise indigenous peoples' right to control not only their traditional lands, but also their traditional knowledge and traditional cultural expressions?

7.2 *On the Relevance of Comparing Property Rights over Land and IP*

At first glance, it might appear far-fetched to compare IPRs with property rights over lands and natural resources in the suggested manner on the ground that lands, on one hand, and human creativity, on the other, are two fundamentally different subject matters. And indeed, from a factual point of view it is difficult to imagine two subject matters more distant from one another. The former is rock steady, while the latter need not necessarily even be fixed in a tangible form. Many forms of creativity can be reproduced in infinity,[50] where

50 P Cullet et al., 'Intellectual Property Rights, Plant Genetic Resources, and Traditional Knowledge', in Biber-Klemm and Cottier (n 38) 113-14.

each copy is equally representative of the creator's production. A real estate, on the other hand, is a unique piece of property. It cannot be reproduced or otherwise copied. There is simply only one 'version' of it. It is surely possible to make the list over differences between lands and creativity longer.

Irrespective of how long the list, however, the distinction between land and human creativity remains one of fact, and not law. As seen, the right to property is at its core a particular aspect of the right to equality, where each legislator stands free to determine what sorts of subject matter should be eligible for property rights. Once the legislator has identified the subject matters to which property rights may attach, the right to property must however – under the right to equality – apply equally to all such thus identified categories of subject matters, irrespective of how factually different they may be. One could perhaps say that in a 'pre-property right stage, subject matter differ widely, but once the legislator have made the various forms of matter subject to property rights, they are from a legal perspective generic. It follows that it is simply the role of domestic law to determine whether land, human creativity, and other subject matter, are so fundamentally different that one should be subject to property rights and the other not. To conclude, the fact that human creativity *factually* distinguishes itself from lands and natural resources is not necessarily a rationale for *legally* distinguishing between the two categories of subject matter.

The just inferred would seem to argue for that, as it has been firmly argued for here everyone – indigenous and non-indigenous alike – must have the same possibility to establish property rights over land, the same should be true with regard to creativity, insofar the legislator determines that both categories can in general be subject to private rights.

7.3 *The Public Domain* – Terra Nullius *Revisited?*

As touched upon, different compared with the *terra nullius* doctrine, little suggests that the public domain was deliberately construed to accommodate for 'legal' European acquisition of elements of other peoples' cultures. Irrespective of a lack of *intent*, however, the public domain has a very similar *effect* on indigenous peoples' rights over their collective creativity, compared with the effects the *terra nullius* doctrine has had on their rights over lands and natural resources. As with classical real estate law, framing IPRs with the structure and social patterns of the European society in mind has resulted in such rights offering limited protection to human creativity common to indigenous cultures. The result is that the idea of a public domain caters for misappropriation of indigenous peoples' collective creativity, in a fashion comparable to how the notion of *terra nullius* allowed the 'legal' occupation of indigenous territories by others. Indeed, the contact areas between the *terra nullius* doctrine and the notion of a public domain are even broader. As alluded to, the 'dynamic of difference' that has been applied to indigenous lands and creativity, respectively, is largely the same.

As seen, the *terra nullius* doctrine professes that to establish property rights over land, the use must have 'improved' on the land, i.e. the land must have been made sufficiently distinguishable – or 'original' if one wants – compared with the land prior to use. There is a clear resemblance between this criterion and the IP novelty/originality criterion, which requires that a work is sufficiently distinguishable from pre-existing works for a right to attach to it. The comparison limps, in the sense that under real estate law one judges whether the work is sufficiently 'original' based on a comparison with a particular object, i.e. that particular land-patch prior to use. By contrast, in an IP context the measurement is with all previously existing creativity. But the comparison is on the mark in that in both instances, it is the indigenous people's work that is deemed not sufficiently original to result in rights. In the context of 'Western' real estate law, the indigenous people's work does not render the land area sufficiently original compared with the land area prior to the indigenous people working on it. In the context of IPRs, the work is not sufficiently original compared with the indigenous people's previous 'works'.

In addition, we saw how the fact that indigenous peoples' land uses tend to be communal in nature where it is often not possible to attribute a particular land area to a particular individual or groups of individuals squared badly with more individualistic non-indigenous agrarian practices. This was what the European states used to 'legitimise' declaring these territories *terra nullius* as the Europeans failed to identify the individual right-holders intrinsic to their legal systems. Comparably, we further saw how indigenous creativity too tends to be communal in nature. As a consequence, it is often not possible to attribute a particular cultural element to an individual or an identifiable group of individuals within the indigenous people. Against this backdrop the creativity is from an IP perspective deemed anonymous and not eligible for protection. Rather, it is held to be in the public domain.

Again, similar observations have been made previously. Graham Dutfield notes the parallels one can draw between *terra nullius* and the public domain. He observes that the collective nature of indigenous creativity has led non-members to treat such as '*res nullius*', a term otherwise normally associated with land, before being 'discovered' by others.[51] Johanna Gibson concurs that IP leaves indigenous creativity without protection through 'criteria set by west-

51 G Dutfield, 'The Public and Private Domains' [2000] Science Communication, Vol 21 No 3.

ern styles of knowledge generation and western concepts of innovation and creativity'.[52] Also, Megan M Carpenter draws a direct parallel between jurisprudence pertaining to property rights to land, on one hand, and to IPRs, on the other.[53]

In this context, it is worth noting that John Locke's theory that each owes the products of her or his labour was in fact not restricted to land. Rather, Locke's argument was a more general one, and embraces creativity. According to him, if one adds value to the existing bulk of creativity, one ought to be in possession of a property right, based on the same basic principle that adding value to land results in a property right to such subject matter.[54] As John Locke's theory was previously held equally relevant to indigenous lands and creativity, respectively, perhaps it is time to acknowledge that it is eqaually irrerelevant to these two forms of subject matter today?

In conclusion, within the sphere of land rights, the *terra nullius* doctrine has recently been rejected as inherently discriminatory. Rather, it has been established that the right to equality requires that property right protection extend also to indigenous peoples' traditional land uses. That indigenous land uses are collective in nature and do not significantly 'improve' on the land from a conventional western legal perspective is no longer a legally relevant argument for leaving the land unprotected. There is seemingly no valid argument that speaks for – and this is the main argument of this chapter – that in a corresponding manner, the right to non-discrimination should not equally guide our understanding of property rights over indigenous creativity. The only rational conclusion seems to be that, in an indigenous context, the public domain should face a destiny similar to that of the *terra nullius* doctrine. Recent developments within international law seem to provide that the nature of indigenous creativity is no longer a legitimate reason to declare such to be in the public domain and free for others to misappropriate. The logical conclusion seems rather to be that indigenous peoples' *traditional* manners in generating creativity are equally worthy of protection as practices common to non-indigenous cultures.

52 Gibson (n 8) 130.

53 Carpenter (n 28) 64-66.

54 Von Lewinski (n 7) 37; Dutfield and Suthersanen (n 17) 259.

An Ontological Politics of and for the Sámi Cultural Heritage – Reflections on Belonging to the Sámi Community and the Land

Sanna Valkonen, Jarno Valkonen and Veli-Pekka Lehtola

1 Introduction

The aim of this chapter is to consider certain particular practices of belonging as integral aspects of the intangible cultural heritage of the Sámi, an Indigenous people. The two practices to be discussed are vital social and customary law institutions[1] of the Sámi: the kinship-based practice of ethnic recognition and the particular relation of the people to the land. Both institutions have become heavily politicized and objects of external definition during recent decades in Finland. We analyse them both in the light of the discourse on international legal cultural heritage and as fundamental ontological elements of Sámi society. Our analysis draws on the work of R. Harrison,[2] who in studies of Indigenous Australians has examined safeguarding of the cultural heritage as ontological politics, a politics in which choices are made from the past, in the present, for the future. Following Harrison, we consider protection of the Sámi cultural heritage as ontological politics, as politics for assembling a particular future.

The general aim of preserving cultural heritage is to maintain cultural diversity in the face of growing globalization.[3] The importance of the cultural heritage is seen as lying not in its manifestations but rather in the wealth of knowledge and skills that is transmitted through it from one generation to the

1 About the concept of institution, see A. Giddens, *The Constitution of Society: Outline of the Theory of Structuration* (Polity Press 1984).

2 R. Harrison (2015) 'Beyond "Natural" and "Cultural" Heritage: Toward an Ontological Politics of Heritage in the Age of Anthropocene' [2015] *Heritage and Society*, Vol. 8 No. 1, 24-42; See also R. Harrison, *Heritage: Critical Approaches* (Routledge 2013).

3 UNESCO Universal Declaration on Cultural Diversity (2001) <http://portal.unesco.org/en/ev.php-URL_ID=13179andURL_DO=DO_TOPICandURL_SECTION=201.html> accessed 8 January 2016; UNESCO Convention for the Safeguarding of the Intangible Cultural Heritage (2003) <http://portal.unesco.org/en/ev.php-URL_ID=17716andURL_DO=DO_TOPICandURL_SECTION=201.html> accessed 78 January 2016; F. Lenzerini (2011) 'Intangible Cultural Heritage: The Living Culture of Peoples *The European Journal of International Law* Vol. 22 no. 1., 101-120.

Xanthaki, Valkonen et al. (eds.), *Indigenous Peoples' Cultural Heritage: Rights, Debates and Challenges.*
 ISBN 978-90-04-34218-7. PP. 149-174

next.[4] In addition, it is often argued that heritage needs to be preserved to ensure that future generations can remember where they come from.[5] The purpose of preserving the cultural heritage is to transmit the heritage from past to present in a manner that ensures its future survival.

The principal focus in safeguarding a people's cultural heritage is generally on identifying past customs which clearly reflect the people's tradition. This orientation manifests itself in the ways in which the cultural heritage is dealt with and understood in the institutional practices that seek to safeguard the cultural heritage and that thus confine the discourse to that frame. For example, the UNESCO Convention for the Safeguarding of the Intangible Cultural Heritage stipulates that states are to preserve, identify, document and prepare inventories of the intangible cultural heritage and to protect and foster its enhancement.[6] Thus, an intangible cultural heritage worth safeguarding comprises only elements that can be classified, measured, quantified, documented, and inventoried. These practices are the ways in which a heritage is rendered "safeguardable".

The process of safeguarding a cultural heritage thus involves interpretations and, finally, produces common understandings of what a cultural heritage is and how it can be managed. This approach prompts the question whether the safeguarding of a cultural heritage is predominantly preserving elements, traditions and practices which existed in the past and which in the present are considered important for the particular group's identity and existence. Or is what we see here rather the construction of the relation between the present and the future? It will be our contention in this chapter that safeguarding a people's cultural heritage is primarily a process of producing the future; that is, it can be seen as an ontological politics for the future. Building on the work of R. Harrison, we approach preservation of heritage as ontological politics, fundamental for which is the recognition of ontological plurality, namely, "that different forms of heritage practices enact different realities and hence work to assemble different futures."[7]

This kind of approach emphasizes the fundamental contingency of the cultural heritage – heritage is "neither 'fixed' nor 'inherent, but emerges in dia-

4 F. Lenzerini, 2011, 102.

5 E.g. Promotion and protection of the rights of indigenous peoples with respect to their cultural heritage. Study by the Expert Mechanism on the Rights of Indigenous Peoples. A/HRC/EMRIP/2015/2.

6 Unesco Convention for the Safeguarding of the Intangible Cultural Heritage (2003), art. 2, para. 3; art. 11; art. 12.

7 R. Harrison, 2015, 24.

logue among individuals, communities, practices, places, and things".[8] Heritage is thus always a present-day phenomenon, a history of the present.[9] Whenever heritage is defined and interpreted, assumptions are made about the past from the perspective of the present. Yet, as Harrison persuasively brings out, interpretation of heritage is never innocent: the perspective of the present allows us to choose a range of histories. In other words, the values and power relations that prevail in the present determine what we choose as a representation of the past in the present as well as what we hope to preserve in the future.[10]

This conception of safeguarding means protecting cultural features whose function does not bear on the present as much as it does – and above all does – on the question of what kinds of futures communities want for themselves. Traditional elements, traditions and practices selected from the past and considered worthy of sustaining in the present form a particular assemblage of practices and objects, which is called "the cultural heritage". When this assemblage of practices and objects is engaged in and within everyday life, rituals or institutional settings, the heritage is materialized as concrete realities for people. Accordingly, the different practices of which the heritage is formed constitute a different reality and thus always involve the assembling of a particular future.[11]

In this chapter, we view certain particular practices of belonging to Sámi community as integral facets of the cultural heritage of the Sámi people that are, as we argue, essential in assembling Sámi communities' future(s). In other words, we examine the ontological politics of the Sámi cultural heritage through an analysis of two vital social and customary law institutions: the kinship-based practice of ethnic recognition and group-making, and the particular relation of the Sámi to the land. As these are also constitutive parts of the political and legal ordering of Sámi society within the mainstream society of the nation-state, efforts have been made to render the institutions objectively definable, recognizable and legally valid, and thus viable bases for decisions affecting Sámi society. From the Sámi perspective, recognition of these traditions is important, as they are regarded as having sustained Sámi society in the past and as doing so in the present and future: they form the ontological basis of the Sámi community. The struggle for the recognition and acceptance

8 Ibid., 35; H. Cornelius, and G. Fairclough, 'The New Heritage and Re-shapings of the Past', in A. González-Ruibal (ed.) *Reclaiming Archaeology: Beyond the Tropes of Modernity* (Routledge 2013), 197-210.

9 See M. Foucault, *Discipline and Punish. The Birth of the Prison* (Penguin Books [1975] 1991).

10 R. Harrison, 2015.

11 Ibid.

of the two traditions can thus be seen as an ontological politics that will shape the future of Sámi culture and Sámi communities.

In the analysis to follow, we discuss the impact of neoliberal rationalities on establishing and defining Indigenous subjectivity and Sámi rights in Finland. I. Altamirano-Jiménez,[12] who has analysed the relations between neoliberalism, indigeneity, the environment and gender in Mexico and Canada, argues that "neoliberal understandings of the self, difference, the economy, and the environment have shaped state practices and articulations of indigeneity". Inspired by her work, we consider the politicization of belonging to the Sámi community and to the land as an interplay of the complex colonial relations and the influence of neoliberal rationalities inscribed both in the Finnish state's policy towards the Sámi and in certain interpretations of indigeneity in the country. These developments seem to question the ontological basis of Sámi communities by offering a different kind of understanding of being Indigenous.

2 The Rationale for Safeguarding the Indigenous Cultural Heritage

The UNESCO Convention for the Safeguarding of the Intangible Cultural Heritage, in paragraph 1 of Article 2, defines intangible cultural heritage as follows:

> practices, representations, expressions, knowledge, skills – as well as the instruments, objects, artefacts and cultural spaces associated therewith – that communities, groups and, in some cases, individuals recognize as part of their cultural heritage. This intangible cultural heritage, transmitted from generation to generation, is constantly recreated by communities and groups in response to their environment, their interaction with nature and their history, and provides them with a sense of identity and continuity, thus promoting respect for cultural diversity and human creativity.[13]

The second paragraph of the article states: "The 'intangible cultural heritage', as defined in paragraph 1 above, is manifested inter alia in the following domains: (a) oral traditions and expressions, including language as a vehicle of the intangible cultural heritage; (b) performing arts; (c) social practices, ritu-

12 I. Altamirano-Jiménez, *Indigenous Encounters with Neoliberalism. Place, Women, and the Environment in Canada and Mexico* (UBC Press 2013).

13 UNESCO Convention for the Safeguarding of the Intangible Cultural Heritage (2003), art. 2, para. 1.

als and festive events; (d) knowledge and practices concerning nature and the universe; (e) traditional craftsmanship".[14] Significantly, the elements chosen for consideration in the Convention are confined to those that are "compatible with existing international human rights instruments, as well as with the requirements of mutual respect among communities, groups and individuals, and of sustainable development".[15]

Finland ratified the Convention in 2013. The instrument obligates states parties to preserve, recognize, document and draw up inventories of the intangible cultural heritage. Safeguarding also requires protection, research and enhancement of that heritage. Implementation of the Convention in Finland is the responsibility of the National Board of Antiquities. However, the former president of the Sámi Parliament, Juvvá Lemet (Klemetti Näkkäläjärvi) has proposed that management of the Sámi intangible cultural heritage should be entrusted to the Sámi Parliament, arguing that the Finnish Constitution, the UN Declaration on the Rights of Indigenous Peoples (2007) and Article 1 of the International Covenant on Civil and Political Rights (1976) point to such an arrangement. He has also pointed out that "the intangible cultural heritage in the case of Sámi culture cannot be safeguarded merely by storing documents telling about it or other archival and museum records or by doing research on Sámi culture. The protection of the Sámi intangible cultural heritage requires that its maintenance be supported through funding, administrative solutions and improved legislation".[16]

A study by the Expert Mechanism on the Rights of Indigenous Peoples (EMRIP) study titled "Promotion and protection of the rights of indigenous peoples with respect to their cultural heritage"[17] has noted that one can see increased attention to and recognition of the relationship between communities and cultural heritage. The report also points out that the Council of Europe Framework Convention on the Value of Cultural Heritage for Society defines cultural heritage as "a group of resources inherited from the past which people

14 UNESCO Convention for the Safeguarding of the Intangible Cultural Heritage (2003), art. 2, para. 2.

15 F. Lenzerini, 2011.

16 Juvvá Lemet, K. Näkkäläjärvi. Puhe eduskunnan sivistysvaliokunnalle Unescon aineettoman kulttuuriperinnön suojelusopimuksen ratifioimisesta 15.11.2012 [Speech about the ratification of the UNESCO Convention for the Safeguarding the Intangible Cultural Heritage to the Parliament Committee in 15 November 2012] <http://www.samediggi.fi/index.php?option=com_docmanandtask=cat_viewandgid=209andItemid=99999999andmosmsg=Yrit%E4t+p%E4%E4st%E4+sis%E4%E4n+ei+hyv%E4ksytyst%E4+verkko-osoitteesta.+%28www.google.fi%29> accessed 16 November 2015.

17 A/HRC/EMRIP/2015/2/A/4.

identify, independently of ownership, as a reflection and expression of their constantly evolving values, beliefs, knowledge and traditions. It includes all aspects of the environment resulting from the interaction between people and places through time".[18] For her part, the Special Rapporteur in the field of cultural rights has noted that "cultural heritage should be understood as resources enabling the cultural identification and development processes of individuals and communities which they, implicitly or explicitly, wish to transmit to future generations".[19]

The documentation and classification of cultural heritages referred to in international legal discourse has been considered problematic in Indigenous contexts.[20] It has been stated in many connections that the distinction between tangible and intangible and between cultural and natural heritages is unworkable and even absurd in the case of Indigenous peoples.[21] This is also noted in the EMRIP study cited above, which goes on to describe "[i]ndigenous cultural heritage is a holistic and inter-generational concept based on common material and spiritual values influenced by the environment".[22]

We argue that if there is a true will to safeguard the cultural heritages of Indigenous peoples such that future generations can engage with the heritage and feel a connection to previous generations, it must be understood that indigeneity entail to a different way of conceiving of reality and the world; that is, the reality of an Indigenous people is based on a different ontology than that underlying the Western way of seeing the world.[23] This being the case, efforts to safeguard the cultural heritage of an Indigenous people should be predicated expressly on the people's own ontologies and on respect for those ontologies.

---

18 Council of Europe Framework Convention on the Value of Cultural Heritage for Society, art. 2. Faro, 27.X.2005 Council of Europe Treaty Series – No. 199; A/HRC/EMRIP/2015/2/A/4.

19 Report of the independent expert in the field of cultural rights, F. Shaheed. A/HRC/17/38, paras. 4 and 6; A/HRC/EMRIP/2015/1/A/5.

20 See e.g. S. Disko in this volume.

21 E.g. ibid.; See also P. Magga and E. Ojanlatva (eds.) *Ealli biras – Elävä ympäristö. Saamelainen kulttuuriympäristöohjelma* [Living Environment – Sámi Cultural Environment Program] (Sámi museum – Saamelaismuseosäätiö 2013).

22 A/HRC/EMRIP/2015/2/B/6.

23 See M. Blaser, 'Ontology and Indigeneity: On the Political Ontology of Heterogeneous Assemblages' [2014] *Cultural Geographies*, Vol 21(1), 49-58; T. Ingold, *The Perception of the Environment. Essays on Livelihood, Dwelling and Skill* (Routledge 2000), 132-152.

3 Belonging to the Sámi Community – the Kinship-based Practice of Ethnic Recognition as Part of the Sámi Cultural Heritage

The kinship-based system of ethnic recognition is an oral and embodied tradition and a living practice in Sámi society that tells us who we are, where we come from and who belong to us.[24] The system is a traditional way of knowing, maintaining and regulating the cohesion, togetherness and boundaries of Sámi communities and is transferred from generation to generation. In its richness and subtleness, it can be considered an Indigenous knowledge system that is still a functioning cultural practice despite modernization and the social change that has occurred in many local Sámi communities.

In the past, groups who were linguistically and culturally Sámi lived rather far apart from each other. Importantly, old sources reveal how different Sámi groups felt ethnic solidarity even before the Sámi started to organize themselves as a political community, as one people, in a movement that began in the 1950s. For example, the Deatnu River Sámi described their relationship with the Aanaar Sámi using the term *lapinsuku* (lit. family of Lapps), meaning that they felt they represented the same ethnicity. Finns who were familiar with Lapland referred to the phenomenon as a "feeling of nationality" shared by different groups of Sámi.[25] The basis for experiencing a common ethnicity was kinship: the different groups located themselves as Sámi through their extended families.[26] Kinship-based ethnic recognition figures quite prominently and is very well documented in, among other practices, the Sámi *yoik* tradition[27] and the reindeer earmarking system.[28]

---

24 See e.g. S. Valkonen, 'The Embodied Boundaries of Ethnicity' [2014] *European Journal of Cultural Studies*, Vol. 17(2) 209-224; S. Valkonen, *Poliittinen saamelaisuus* [Political Sáminess] (Vastapaino 2009), 219-226.

25 V.-P. Lehtola, *Saamelaiset suomalaiset. Kohtaamisia 1896-1953* (The Sámi and the Finns. Encounters in 1896-1953) (SKS 2012), 30-31.

26 Ibid.

27 M. Jouste, *Tullâčalmaaš kirdâččij 'tulisilmillä lenteli'. Inarinsaamelainen 1900-luvun alun musiikkikulttuuri paikallisen perinteen ja ympäröivien kulttuurien vuorovaikutuksessa* [*The Interplay of Tradition and Surrounding Culture of the Inari Sámi Music Culture in the Beginning of 1900's*] (Tampere University Press 2011); M. R. Järvinen, 'Saamelaisten musiikit ja musiikkien tutkimus' [The Music and Music Research of the Sámi] [2011] in I. Seurujärvi-Kari, P. Halinen & R. Pulkkinen (eds.), *Saamentutkimus tänään* (SKS 2011), 330-331.

28 K. Näkkäläjärvi, *Jauristunturin poropaimentolaisuus. Kulttuurin kehitys ja tietojärjestelmä vuosina 1930-1995* [Reindeer Herding in Jauristunturi. The Development of Culture and its Knowledge System in 1930-1995](Näkkäläjärvi 2013); K. Näkkäläjärvi, 'Poron korvamerkit yhteisöjärjestelmän perustana' [The reindeer Earmarks as a Basis of Communal Life]

To this day, the practice continues to be one of the principal distinguishing characteristics of the Sámi sense of community in addition to the Sámi languages; a considerable body of research can be cited illustrating this, such as that on the ethnic identification of the Sámi living in urban environments.[29] The Sámi family and a sense of belonging to it, as well as the Sámi language, carry a strong emotional charge. Clearly, not all Sámi know one another personally beyond the community level, but family networks provide effective links to Sámi living farther field.

The practices of kinship-based ethnic recognition and a sense of community are materialized and manifested (and documented) in North Sámi personal names. In addition to official names, and even in place of them, Sámi have known one another best through a family-based name. An example would be Lásse-Biera-Sámmol-Máhte, the name of a man named Máhte who is known through his father as Sámmol's son but also through his grandfather (Biera) and great grandfather (Lásse). The name one is given by one's parents does not always necessarily come from the father's side of the family. A son might also be named after his mother if she was better-known in the community or in the environment in which the boy is spoken about. An example would be Gádjá Nilla: Gádja was a well-known and strong reindeer woman in her community in the 19th century, and her son Nilla followed in her footsteps. The same naming practices apply in the case of girls and women, an example being Jovnna-Máreha-Máret.[30]

Although the European practice of using patronyms has become common among the Sámi, Sámi read kinship in another way as well, that is, by male and female ancestors going farther back. For example, the Aikios and Helanders of the Utsjoki district (family surnames) are known among the Sámi as the descendants of Vulleš, who lived in the 1800s; the men and women descended from him are all referred to as "vulležat", a name one can often see in a Sámi given name, an example being Vulleš-Jovnna-Máreha-Máret. The Niittyvuopio (surname) family is known as the "Niillasaččat" family, that is, Niillas's de-

---

[1999] in J. Pennanen and K. Näkkäläjärvi (eds.), *Siiddastallan. Siidoista kyliin. Luontosidonnainen saamelaiskulttuuri ja sen muuttuminen.* (Inarin saamelaismuseon julkaisuja 2000), 171.

29 See e.g. A.-R. Lindgren, *Helsingin saamelaiset ja oma kieli* [The Sámi of Helsinki and Own Language] (SKS 2000), 166-190; A. Amft, 'Etnisk identitet hos samerna i Sverige – en complex bild' [Ethnic identity of the Sámi – A Complicated Picture] in M. Autti, S. Keskitalo-Foley, P. Naskali and H. Sinevaara-Niskanen (eds.), *Kuulumisia: feministisiä tulkintoja naisten toimijuuksista* (Lapin yliopisto 2007), 66-101; S. Valkonen, 2009.

30 V.-P. Lehtola, *Saamelainen evakko* [A Sámi Evacuee] (Kustannus-Puntsi 2004), 7.

scendants. Sámi characteristically have detailed knowledge of kinship going back three or four generations.

The Sámi naming practice is also a living practice in modern Sámi social institutions, as seen in the news broadcasts of Yle Sápmi, the Finnish Sámi's own radio service, which often refer to people using their Sámi names in addition to their official names. For example, the president of the previous Sámi Parliament was consistently called Juvvá Lemet (Finnish name: Klemetti Näkkäläjärvi).[31] The rap artist Nikke Ankara (Niiles Hiirola), who comes from southern Finland, was identified as a Sámi and located in his extended family through his Sámi name, Niillas Niillasa Káre-Márjjá Merja Niillas.[32]

Kinship-based ethnic identification is thus a means by which individuals identify with and locate themselves in their community through their family and by which the community, for its part, identifies and locates individuals as its members, most often over two or three generations, but over as many as five when a young person is involved (Niillas Niillasa Káre-Márjjá Merja Niillas). Sámi communality – being Indigenous in a Sámi sense – is therefore connected both to the near history and to the present day sense of community which the kinship-based practice of ethnic recognition well indicates. This being the case, the system of kinship-based ethnic recognition can be considered a central element of the living Sámi heritage.

3.1 *The Politicization of Being Indigenous – the Question of Sáminess in the Era of Neoliberal Governance*

The Sámi in Finland have a constitutionally safeguarded status as an Indigenous people. One concrete realization of this status in Finland is cultural autonomy in the Sámi Homeland,[33] provided for in the Act on the Sámi Parliament of 1995 and implemented by the Sámi Parliament.[34] During the dec-

---

31 See e.g. YLE Sápmi 8 October 2014: Juvvá Lemet ja Hánno Heaiká leaba duđavaččat vuođđoláhkaváljagotti gullamii [Juvvá Lemet and Hánno Heaiká are satisfied with the hearing of the Constitutional Law Committee] <http://yle.fi/uutiset/juvva_lemet_ja_hanno_heaika_leaba_duavaccat_vuoolahkavaljagotti_gullamii/7515677> accessed 16 November 2015.

32 See Yle Sápmi 18 July 2014: Ođđa rap-lohpádus Nikke Ankara lea sápmelaš [The new rap talent Nikke Ankara is a Sámi] <http://yle.fi/uutiset/oa_rap-lohpadus_nikke_ankara_lea_sapmelas/7364149> accessed 16 November 2015.

33 The Sámi Homeland of Finland is situated in Northern Finland and in the area of four Finnish municipalities.

34 Finnish Constitution/2/paragraph17 <http://www.finlex.fi/fi/laki/ajantasa/1999/19990731>, accessed 16 November 2015; The Act on the Sámi Parliament/1995/974/paragraph 25 <https://www.finlex.fi/fi/laki/ajantasa/1995/19950974> accessed 16 November 2015.

ades after the Sámi in Finland acquired the status of an Indigenous people recognized by the state as well as established their own decision-making body for managing their autonomy, the issue of definition – how 'Sámi' and thus members of the Indigenous people should be defined – has become strongly politicized.

Before their status was laid down in the Finnish Constitution and the Sámi Parliament was established, Sámi affairs were managed by the Sámi Delegation, set up in 1973. The Decree on the Sámi Delegation contained a definition of a Sámi which has basically not been questioned by any parties whereby a Sámi means a person one of whose parents or grandparents has learned Sámi as his or her first language and any of that person's descendants. A person also had to feel that he or she was a Sámi, as no one could be considered a Sámi against his or her will.[35] This definition emphasized that a person defined as a Sámi had to have a close connection to Sámi-speaking society over a period of three generations. A Sámi did not have to know the Sámi language, one reason being that after World War II the schools, among other institutions, alienated many Sámi from their language. In effect, the definition involved kinship-based ethnic recognition: in practice, families were considered Sámi if Sámi had been a living, spoken language for them at least up until the post-war period.[36]

In the 1995 Act on the Sámi Parliament, an addition was made to the Delegation's definition of a Sámi whereby a person was also considered a Sámi "if he is a descendent of a person who has been entered in a land, taxation or population register as a mountain, forest or fishing Lapp". The aim was to make it possible to identify who was a Sámi also on the basis of the 1875 or later land and taxation records.[37] The purpose of the addition was to reinforce the connection of the Sámi to the land through the letter of the law. The records from 1875 and thereafter were seen as guaranteeing that the addition would apply principally to the contemporary ethnic Sámi, not contemporary ethnic Finns. However, the Finnish Constitutional Law Committee dropped the date (1875), as its inclusion would have required that a decree be issued. The Sámi Delegation was not asked for its position on the changed definition. The end result of the process was that the definition based on historical documents had no

---

35 Committee Report 1973:46, 6.

36 See e.g. V.-P. Lehtola, 2012, 434; S. Valkonen, 2009, 237.

37 See V.-P. Lehtola, *Saamelaisten parlamentti. Suomen saamelaisvaltuuskunta 1973-1995 ja Saamelaiskäräjät 1996-2003* [The Sámi Parliament. The Finnish Sámi Delegation 1973-1995 and The Sámi Parliament 1996-2003] (Saamelaiskäräjät 2005).

temporal limit.[38] This then meant that the language-based definition covered three generations but the definition based on historical records went back perhaps hundreds of years: anyone who could find even one ancestor who was a documented resident of a Lapp village, perhaps centuries ago, could insist that he or she be considered a member of the Sámi people and demand the legal and political rights accorded the Sámi, such as the right to vote and to stand for election to the Sámi Parliament.

The Sámi communities in general do not consider this so-called Lapp criterion to be a legitimate one for proving that one is a Sámi, as it is not based on the Sámi's conception of the membership of their communities.[39] Nor has the Sámi Parliament, the people's representative body, approved the addition. In fact, from its establishment, the Sámi Parliament's policies have stressed the self-determination of the Sámi and the definition of a Sámi as based on the language criterion which mostly is feasible with the kinship -based ethnic recognition.[40]

From the outset, the Sámi Parliament has proceeded from the principle that the Sámi, as an Indigenous people, must be allowed to define "who we are" on the basis of Sámi traditions and practices.[41] The right of an Indigenous people to define itself is safeguarded in article 33 of the UN Declaration on the Rights of Indigenous Peoples:

1. Indigenous peoples have the right to determine their own identity or membership in accordance with their customs and traditions. This does not impair the right of indigenous individuals to obtain citizenship of the States in which they live.

---

38 See L. Heinämäki et al., *Saamelaisten oikeuksien toteutuminen: kansainvälinen oikeusvertaileva tutkimus* [Actualizing Sámi Rights: International Comparative Research]. Publications of the Government's analysis, assessment and research activities 4/2017 (Prime Minister's Office, 25.1.2017), 187-194.

39 See e.g. L. Heinämäki et al., 2017, 176-223; V.-P. Lehtola, *Suomen saamelaiskiista. Sortaako Suomi alkuperäiskansaansa?* [The Sámi Conflict of Finland. Does Finland Oppress its Indigenous People?] (Into-Kustannus 2015).

40 See L. Heinämäki et al., 2017, 86-216; S. Valkonen, 2009, 155-172; V.-P. Lehtola, 2015, 214-215.

41 See e.g. Saamelaiskäräjät [The Sámi Parliament], Saamelaiskäräjien lausunto perustuslakivaliokunnan pykälämuutosehdotuksista saamelaiskäräjistä annetun lain muuttamiseen [Statement on the Changes in the Act on the Sámi Parliament] 10.12.2014 Dnro: 565/D.a.4/2014. <http://www.samediggi.fi/index.php?option=com_docmanandtask=cat_viewandgid=259andItemid=165> accessed 3 February 2016; L. Heinämäki et al., 2017, 176-223.

2. Indigenous peoples have the right to determine the structures and to select the membership of their institutions in accordance with their own procedures.[42]

Finland intended to amend the Act on the Sámi Parliament in 2015, as the law was considered to be outdated and ineffective in many particulars. A key point to be reformed was the definition of a Sámi. The bill, drafted by a working group established by the Ministry of Justice that comprised representatives of the Sámi Parliament, the Finnish government and other experts, put forward kinship and socialization into Sámi culture (to complete the Lapp criterion) as the key criteria in addition to language.[43] Expressly incorporating kinship into the definition is a sign that kinship-based ethnic recognition is not only a traditional practice, but also one that is very much present today; it is a living means for constituting the Sámi community and one that the people wish to see continue in the future.

The bill, and particularly the definition it contained, met with extensive opposition by many different, mostly non-Sámi parties.[44] The fear was that legal Sámi subjectivity defined by the Sámi kinship would lead to arbitrary decisions as to who is a Sámi and who is not and exclusion at the hands of the dominant Sámi families. The reference to kinship in the definition in the Act was considered too vague and unclear. In fact, doubts were expressed as to the existence of the practice of kinship-based recognition or it was deemed to be nothing but a political tool by which the Sámi elite could wield exclusionary power.[45] It was the Finnish Members of Parliament from Lapland in particular who found allowing the Sámi to exercise self-determination in the question of who is a Sámi to be very problematic. They considered – and this view has persisted in the debate during recent decades – that the Sámi way to define who the Sámi are runs contrary to the definitions of "Indigenous people" in

---

42 UNDRIP 2007, Article 33 <http://www.un.org/esa/socdev/unpfii/documents/DRIPS_en.pdf>, accessed 8 January 2016.

43 Ministry of Justice, Saamelaiskäräjälakityöryhmän mietintö [Government bill] 55/2013 <http://www.oikeusministerio.fi/fi/index/julkaisut/julkaisuarkisto/1382513081296/Files/OMML_55_2013_MIETINTO_196_s.pdf> accessed 23 November 2015.

44 About the political mobilization and complex debate related to defining Sáminess in Finland see V.-P. Lehtola, 2015; J. Valkonen, S. Valkonen and T. Koivurova, 'Groupism and the Politics of Indigeneity: A Case Study on the Sámi Debate in Finland' [2016] *Ethnicities* June 19, 2016.

45 See V.-P. Lehtola, 2015.

international law, particularly that found in ILO Convention No. 169.[46] Their opposition ultimately led to the bill being rejected in the Finnish Parliament and to the previous definition of Sámi, the one strongly opposed by the Sámi Parliament, remaining in force.[47]

Lenzerini writes about the philosophical rationale for preserving the intangible cultural heritage, which has a firm basis in the presence of self-identification by the group concerned as one of the heritage's constitutive elements. This differs radically from the definition of material cultural heritage, which is based on "an objective evaluation of its outstanding worth from the standpoint of a presumed universally valid appreciation of value".[48] The nature of intangible cultural heritage, by contrast, "rests in the self-recognition of it as part of the cultural heritage of the communities, groups, and (if the case) individuals concerned".[49] According to Lenzerini, "the presence of self-identification among its constitutive elements makes intangible cultural heritage valuable in light of the subjective perspective of its creators and bearers, who recognize the heritage concerned as an essential part of their idiosyncratic cultural inheritance, even though it may appear absolutely worthless to external observers."[50]

A second inherent characteristic of the intangible cultural heritage cited by Lenzerini, one also closely linked to self-identification, is "its deep connection with the identity and cultural distinctiveness of its creators and bearers".[51] He notes that the connection is well evidenced by the definition in Article 2 of the Convention for the Safeguarding of the Intangible Cultural Heritage, which describes the intangible cultural heritage as an entity that gives communities and groups a sense of identity and continuity. Lenzerini goes on to conclude that this is probably the principal value of the intangible cultural heritage.[52]

Clearly, the system of kinship-based ethnic recognition fulfils the criteria of self-identification by the community and deep connection with the identity and cultural distinctiveness of its creators and bearers. The system is a living reality that has adapted to the historical and social evolution of the Sámi but without losing its character as an element of collective customary law in de-

46 See V.-P. Lehtola 2015, 179-233; The ILO Convention No. 169 concerning Indigenous and Tribal Peoples in Independent Countries (1989), art. 1. <http://www.ilo.org/dyn/normlex/en/f?p=NORMLEXPUB:12100:0::NO::P12100_ILO_CODE:C169.> accessed 24 March 2015.

47 V.-P. Lehtola, 2015, 179-223.

48 F. Lenzerini, 2011, 108.

49 Ibid.

50 Ibid.

51 Ibid.

52 Ibid., 109.

fining the boundaries of the community and the subjects belonging to that community. Defining the boundaries of a community is a collective practice which evolves as the community does; the practice lives and is understandable within the particular culture and community.

The reform of the Sámi Parliament and particularly the (Finnish) debate on the definition of Sámi revealed clearly that a culture's internal, immaterial and intangible practices and mechanisms, ones based on the culture's internal dynamic and its institutions, often go unacknowledged or there is no interest in acknowledging them in the mainstream society. Yet, for Sámi culture it is precisely such practices, however hard to define, that are crucial if the culture is to survive. It is these practices that sustain the core of the culture and sense of community; they are essential in defining and maintaining membership in, the interrelationships within and the boundaries of the community. In other words, the practices are crucial for the ontological foundation of the community, whereby the system of kinship-based recognition of ethnicity is a constitutive element of Sámi society.

Why is it then that accepting kinship-based identification with the community as a part of Sámi autonomy – and thus as a form of the Sámi cultural heritage, which enjoys statutory protection – has been so difficult and prompted such resistance? We suggest that one central aspect of the answer lies in the limitations of the prevailing political institutions and ideologies; they seem to be infiltrated by the pervasive influence of neoliberal governance, making them unable to understand and acknowledge a conception of community and of membership in a community that is predicated on a different type (non-Western) of ontology.[53]

Neoliberalism is a global economic, political and social phenomenon and political rationality that emphasizes and is based on deregulation, privatization, individualization and transformation of the state-citizen relationship. It entails "practices, knowledge, and ways of inhabiting the world that emphasize the market, individual rationality, and the responsibility of entrepreneurial subjects".[54] Neoliberalism also "shapes the constitution of identity and com-

53 About neoliberalism and Indigenous peoples, see e.g. I. Altamirano-Jiménez, 2013; F. E. McCormack, 'Levels of indigeneity: the Maori and neoliberalism' [2011] *Journal of the Royal Anthropological Institute*, 17(2), 281-300; M. Mora 'The Politics of Justice: Zapatista Autonomy at the Margins of the Neoliberal Mexican State' [2015] *Latin American and Caribbean Ethnic Studies* Vol. 10:1, 87-106.

54 C. R. Hale, 'Does Multiculturalism Menace? Governance, Cultural Rights, and the Politics of Identity in Guatemala' [2002] *Journal of Latin American Studies* 34 (3), 136-46; I. Altamirano-Jiménez, 2013, 70.

modification of nature"[55] and thus has "cultural, social and political effects that exceed its surface".[56]

Embracing the definitions of "Indigenous" in international law, the Finnish debate on the definition of Sámi places considerable emphasis on the rights and identity of the individual. The salient questions in discussing and implementing politics in Finland are who at the individual level are Indigenous, who are entitled to indigenous rights and how "indigeneity" is to be defined. I. Altamirano-Jiménez writes that "the adoption of global discourses of indigeneity at the local level, although politically empowering, raises a number of extremely political questions. Who defines 'Indigenous' and what is 'authentic' or 'traditional'?"[57] The emergence of these questions, as has happened in the Sámi context in Finland, illustrates how the global discourses and developments related to Indigenous peoples' rights and political position, while being Indigenous resistance against a colonial world order and the legitimacy of state powers, are at the same time constrained by those very power structures.[58] They are part of the complex legacy of colonialism, in which the emergence of neoliberal rationalities is producing new forms of governance that rest on "old", existing injustices and unequal structures.

Although Indigenous peoples themselves are shaping and producing global articulations of indigeneity, "the sites involved create a complex field in which Indigenous peoples negotiate a balance between local needs and global wants."[59] In Finland, the discussions among some established researchers and certain politicians on the definition of Sámi have foregrounded the rights and the identity of the individual as the basis of indigeneity; being a member of an Indigenous people is seen as a right of an individual and, in keeping with the reading of international Indigenous law, it becomes necessary to "find" the in-

55 I. Altamirano-Jiménez, 2013, 70; N. Laurie, R. Andolina and S. Radcliffe, 'The Excluded "Indigenous"? The Implications of Multi-ethnic Policies for water Reform in Bolivia', in R. Sieder (ed.), *Multiculturalism in Latin America: Indigenous Rights, Diversity and Democracy* (Palgrave MacMillan 2002), 252-76.

56 W. Brown, *Politics Out of History* (Princeton University Press 2001); I. Altamirano-Jiménez, 2013, 70.

57 I. Altamirano-Jiménez, 2013, 7.

58 Cf. J. Clifford, 'Indigenous Articulations' [2001] *Contemporary Pacific* 13 (2), 472; Altamirano-Jiménez 2013, 4; see also C. Sturm, *Becoming Indian: The Struggle over Cherokee Identity in the Twenty-first Century* (SAR Press 2010); A. Simpson, *Mohawk Interruptus: Political Life Across the Borders of Settler* States (Duke University Press 2014).

59 I. Altamirano-Jiménez 2013, 4.

dividuals who can belong to a given Indigenous people.[60] The question "Who is a Sámi?" has also become a question of an individual's identity, meaning that the right to membership in an Indigenous people is considered to be bound up with an individual's identity as he or she personally experiences it.[61] This line of reasoning is at odds with Sámi conceptions of communality and the Sámi custom of defining the group based on group identification. After all, it is an interpretation that originates in the political rationalities of modern societies, which places the rights of the individual at the core of society. What is more, it hampers efforts to secure political acceptance of the Sámi ontology as the foundation of a political community.

The decades-long deliberation of the definition of Sámi and, in particular, the discussions in 2015 surrounding the amendment of the Act on the Sámi Parliament and the ratification of the ILO Convention no. 169 reflect, among other things, the power relations and asymmetrical power structures that impact efforts to define "Indigenous cultural heritage" and by extension an "Indigenous people"; those processes also reveal the deeply political condition of Indigenous self-determination within the mainstream society. Although kinship-based ethnic recognition satisfies both the community's own criterion for self-identification and the elements of deep identity and cultural uniqueness defined by its creators and bearers, it is difficult to accurately verify and document in a manner that would enable political actors from outside Sámi society to understand it.

4 Belonging to the Land: The Sámi in Their Environment

An integral part of an Indigenous people's cultural heritage is their special relationship to the land and the closely connected traditional ecological knowledge and tradition of cultural landscape.[62] The relationship to the land is a fundamental question of existence for Indigenous peoples, as cultures grow

60 T. Joona, 'Ihmisoikeusnäkökulma ILO-sopimukseen No. 169' [A Human Rights Perspective on ILO Convention No. 169][2013] *Agon* 37-38, 6-12; J. Joona, 'Kuka kuuluu alkuperäiskansaan – historian vastauksia tämän päivän kysymyksiin' [Who Belong to an Indigenous People – Answers of History to Contemporary Questions], *Lakimies* 4/2013, 734-755; See also Lehtola 2015, 202-207.

61 Cf. E. Sarivaara, *Statuksettomat saamelaiset. Paikantumisia saamelaisuuden rajoilla* [Sámi without a Status. On the Edge of Sámi Culture] (Dieđut 2, Sámi allaskuvla).

62 P. Magga, 'Mikä tekee kulttuuriympäristöstä saamelaisen?' [What makes an Environment Sámi], in P. Magga and E. Ojanlatva (eds.), *Ealli Biras. Saamelainen kulttuuriympäristöohjelma* (Sámi Museum – Saamelaismuseosäätiö 2013), 10-13.

from the land and in places. The relationship to the land bears on the place where an indigenous people dwells, where its members practice their traditional livelihoods and what the people's broader cultural conception is of itself, its identity and its past.[63]

The connection to the land in Sámi culture is an ethnic underpinning of all Sámi groups and the foundation on which Sámi culture rests. According to the anthropologist J. Pennanen, undergirding the Sámi feeling of ethnic identity is the conception that they belong to the same language family and share a nature-bound cultural background comprising the hunting, fishing and gathering livelihoods and reindeer herding.[64] Sámi culture has a connection to a historical place defined through their life practices, to the ethnic ties and social relations which prevail in that place, to memories and to biographical experiences of place. The connection to the land produces and sustains Sáminess and through the connection a Sámi today can experience an affinity with Sámi who lived millennia ago.[65]

Any examination of the Sámi connection to the land must take into consideration that the connection involves both the intangible and material cultural heritage. The Sámi worldview makes no distinction between nature and culture, nor are the two mutually exclusive. Accordingly, the connection to the land is seen as including not only a material bond but also elements of the intangible heritage, such as place names and the oral tradition. In the Sámi worldview, the human being is not an agent who manipulates or exploits nature; rather, the relationship entails a deeper awareness of, belonging to and obligation towards a place.[66] The Sámi connection can be aptly described as "ecological connectivity", a term coined by D. Rose. It indicates a "mode of existence" in which the land is not only a place or object but also a subject (or "agent") in its own right.[67] According to Rose, for Indigenous peoples, the land

63 See T. Ingold, 2000, 148-150.

64 J. Pennanen, 'Ihmisen ja luonnon vuorovaikutus saamelaiskulttuurin lähtökohtana' [Human-Nature Interaction as a Basis of Sámi Culture], in J. Pennanen and K. Näkkäläjärvi (eds.), *Siidastallan. Siidoista kyliin. Perinteinen luontosidonnainen saamelaiskulttuuri ja sen muuttuminen* (Inarin saamelaismuseon julkaisuja 2000), 13-18.

65 See J. Valkonen and S. Valkonen, 'Contesting the Nature Relations of Sámi Culture' [2014]. *Acta Borealia* 31(1), 25-40.

66 E. Helander-Renvall, 'Saamelainen tapaoikeus' [The Sámi Customary Law] [2013], in P. Magga and E. Ojanlatva (eds.) 2013, 132-134.

67 D. Rose, *Sharing Kinship with Nature: How Reconciliation is Transforming the NSW National Parks and Wildlife Service* (NSW National Parks and Wildlife Service 2003); D. Rose, D. James, and C. Watson, *Indigenous Kinship with the Natural World.* (NSW National Parks and Wildlife Service 2003).

is "nourishing terrain… a living entity with a yesterday, today and tomorrow, with a consciousness, and a will toward life. Because of this richness, country is home and peace; nourishment for body, mind, and spirit; heart's ease".[68]

In R. Harrison's view, the ontological basis of Indigenous peoples' connection to the land hampers efforts to safeguard their intangible cultural heritage. He asserts that the protection of Indigenous cultural heritage is based on a Western, anthropocentric mentality that emphasizes a distinction between culture and nature and a pre-eminence of human beings over nature. In indigenous ontologies, by contrast, there is no boundary between nature and culture; rather, they emphasize that the two are intertwined and that culture is everywhere. Indigenous peoples' connection to the land and notions of protecting their cultural heritage proceed from a wholly different ontological basis, making protection of such heritages challenging.[69]

The Sámi researchers E. Helander-Renvall, A. Schanche and P. Magga have recognized and identified special and distinctive features of the Sámi cultural environment.[70] To Sámi a natural landscape can be a cultural landscape regardless of whether it bears traces of human activity. These scholars argue that the Sámi cultural environment has not, to date, fit neatly into any of the public categories used in defining and managing cultural environments.[71]

Management of the environment in the Sámi homeland of Finland is governed for the most part by the Wilderness Act and the Conservation Act, which are essential elements of the Finnish system. In contrast, sites in the Sámi cultural environment, in particular cultural usufruct areas, have not been given any particular consideration. Yet, given that Sámi usufruct of the landscape and environment differs from the Finnish, it easily remains invisible. It lives in

68 D. Rose, *Nourishing Terrains: Australian Aboriginal Views of Landscape and Wilderness* (Australian Heritage Commission 1996).

69 Harrison 2015, 30.

70 E. Helander, 'Sámi Subsistence Activities – spatial aspects and structuration' [1999] in *Acta Borealia* 2, 7-25; A. Schanche, 'Horizontal and vertical perceptions of Saami landscapes' [2004] in *Dieđut* 3, 1-10; P. Magga and T. Elo, 'Johdanto' [Introduction] [2007] in Tiina Elo and Päivi Magga (eds.) *Eletty, koettu maisema: näkökulmia saamelaiseen kulttuurimaisemaan* (Lapin ympäristökeskus 2007); E. Helander-Renvall, 'On customary law among the Saami people' [2013] in N. Bankes and T. Koivurova (eds.), *The proposed Nordic Saami Convention: national and international dimensions of indigenous property rights* (HART 2013), 281-291; P. Magga, 2013; E. Helander, 'The nature of Sami customary law' [2014] in T. Koivurova, T. Joona and R. Shnoro (eds.), *Arctic governance* (University of Lapland 2014), 88-96.

71 Ibid.

the cultural knowledge of small communities and, inasmuch as it has not been articulated and asserted verbally, it is ignored in decision-making.[72]

The Sámi cultural environment is defined flexibly in keeping with the situation at any given time; it is a whole consisting of the seen and unseen. The special feature of the Sámi conception of the cultural landscape is that the human being is not accorded a special status as a shaper and manipulator of nature; rather, a landscape may look like a natural landscape but nevertheless bear values and meanings associated with a cultural landscape. One implication of this, however, is that the content of that landscape is not readily understood by an outsider; it appears to be wilderness, uninhabited and unused.

As the Sámi conceive it, nature is linked to everyday life, the use of resources and travelling from place to place. In this way the concept broadens in the direction of intangible culture heritage. Place names tell how the areas are used and encompass the settlements, the routes people use in getting from place to place as well as invisible boundaries. The place names and locations that live in the oral tradition cannot necessarily be found on maps. Other elements to be found in oral history, such as the *yoik* tradition, also reflect the people's knowledge and use of nature. These have been shaped for generations by customary law: the knowledge of resources such as good cloudberry picking sites and fishing waters was often shared and their use agreed on jointly. The Sámi landscape also includes mystical sites, such as old places of worship and *sieidi* (sacred sites), sacred fells and burial places. It is difficult to translate the oral tradition into a form that can be understood by others; there is a fear that information on sacred places will end up being misused.[73] However, the new Sámi cultural environment unit, established at the Sámi Museum Siida in 2011, took as its starting point that even though the "coordinates" of a sacred landscape must be withheld to some extent, the landscape, along with other archaeological cultural heritage, has to be recorded so that it is taken into account in land-use planning, forestry and other land uses.

In Finland, the Sámi have continually sought recognition of their connection to the land as part of the safeguarding of the Sámi cultural heritage. The need for this recognition derives from the powerlessness the Sámi have experienced when it comes to the policies that steer the use of the land in the Sámi Homeland. Since the beginning of the 1990s, one has seen a series of legal reports and committees in Finland that have tried to determine how the Sámi could hold the rights to their lands and how these rights could be safeguarded without their infringing the legal rights of the other local residents of the area.

---

72 See P. Magga and E. Ojanlatva (eds.), 2013.

73 Ibid.

The impetus for these efforts is Finland's commitment to ratifying ILO Convention No. 169. Ratification has been put off numerous times due to "ambiguities" where the land rights of the Sámi are concerned. The key issue that has emerged is who could be the subjects of the land rights on the individual level.[74]

Sámi claims to the lands and waters in their region have been interpreted in terms of the legal and governance discourse; this requires that a legal basis be demonstrated for the connection to the land, a demand that makes it difficult to take the Sámi connection to the land into account in land-use policies in the Sámi Homeland. According to Sámi researcher A. Nuorgam, Finnish legislation contains no definitions of the concept "cultural environment", let alone "cultural landscape". The landscape in the Sámi region is classified essentially in its entirety as a natural landscape, although large tracts of it are areas in which the traditional Sámi livelihoods are practiced.[75] E. Helander-Renvall points out that the Sámi connection to the land is based on customary rights that are integrated in the form of an oral tradition into the daily practices of the local community"[76] The members of the Sámi community do not even conceive of these as rules; the practices are renegotiated if someone for one reason or another departs from the land-use practices established by custom. Helander-Renvall takes the view that the use and applicability of traditional legal notions are further eroded by the fact that there is a constant collision between them and national legislation and orders issued by government authorities. Moreover, the non-Sámi population in the Sámi region does not necessarily adhere to or even know the Sámi's traditional norms as regards use of the land, a situation which might even prompt some members of the Sámi community to depart from the norms.[77] What is more, as T. Kurttila and T. Ingold have shown, the Sámi's traditional system of knowledge that underlies their use of the land is very difficult, if not impossible, to express in concrete terms, for it is far too dynamic and practically oriented and adapts too readily to the situation at hand.[78]

---

74 See e.g. J. Joona, 2013.

75 A. Nuorgam, 'Saamelaisia koskeva lainsäädäntö ja sopimukset' [The Legislation and Convention Pertaining to the Sámi], 220, In P. Magga and E. Ojanlatva (eds.) 2013, 220-225.

76 E. Helander-Renvall, *Saamelaisten perinnetieto, tapaoikeudet ja biologinen monimuotoisuus* [The Sámi Traditional Knowledge, Customary Law and Biodiversity. 2011, 3. <http://www.ymparisto.fi/download.asp?contentid=127691andlan=fi> accessed 24 November 2015.

77 E. Helander-Renvall, 2014, 133-134.

78 T. Ingold, and T. Kurttila, 'Perceiving the environment in Finnish Lapland' [2001] *Body and Society*, 6, 183-196.

The nature of Indigenous peoples' connection to the land, including the underpinnings of that connection in customary law, has led to its not necessarily being accepted – or accepted at all – as equal to what is set out in the written legislation of the state. Yet, this does not mean that rules deriving from customary law cannot be taken as the basis for legislation or as part of it. There are many examples internationally of how customary law has been taken into account in legal proceedings and negotiations dealing with Indigenous peoples' land rights.[79] According to Helander-Renvall, acknowledging the customary rights indicating in a state's land-use policies the connection of an Indigenous people to the land requires active elaboration of that connection through different practices and discourses so that the rights will be recognized more broadly and become part of society's commitments.[80]

The implementation of the UNESCO Convention for the Safeguarding of the Intangible Cultural Heritage requires Finland to define, among other things, the different elements of the intangible cultural heritage in the Sámi Homeland and to do so in cooperation with communities, groups and the relevant civic organizations. According to Nuorgam, where Indigenous peoples are concerned, it is problematic that the UNESCO conventions do not recognize ownership or possession of the traditional knowledge of Indigenous peoples; rather, the process of documentation and inventorying changes the status of cultural heritage such that it is seen as benefiting all of humankind.[81]

In our view, as regards bringing the connection to the land within the scope of the protection of cultural heritage, a more daunting problem than ownership or possession is how the Sámi connection to the land can be rendered in a form that the discourse on safeguarding cultural heritage is ready to recognize. As P. Magga, a researcher who has done work on the Sámi cultural environment, points out: "The concepts and vocabularies that define the cultural environment have not been directly applicable in the Sámi region, whereby it was essential to start the work [on definition of the Sámi cultural environment] from these and ask what they mean in the Sámi context". According to Magga, it is difficult to explain fully what landscape and the environment mean from the Sámi perspective. "To a Sámi the landscape is more than an object nor is the environment merely an object of one's actions; it is a person's partner –

79 See Helander-Renvall, 2014, 132; See also M. de la Cadena, 'Indigenous Cosmopolitics in the Andes: Conceptual Reflections beyond Politics' [2010] *Cultural Anthropology* 25(2), 334-70; M. Blaser, 'Ontology and Indigeneity: on the Political Ontology of Heterogeneous Assemblages' [2014] *Cultural Geogra* Vol 21(1), 49-58.

80 E. Helander-Renvall, 2014, 132.

81 A. Nuorgam, 2014, 222.

another subject with whom one has to act properly and wisely, because one's own survival depends on it".[82] As the Sámi conception of the landscape incorporates a cognitive dimension, religiousness, myths, tales and communality in addition to the values and meanings it entails it is difficult to inventory and to convert into discrete pieces of information in a database. Yet, safeguarding of the cultural heritage requires this to some degree, as the UNESCO Convention for the Protection of the Intangible Cultural Heritage, for example, obligates Finland to document and inventory the cultural heritage that the state wishes to preserve and sustain.[83]

In addition, the conflicts associated with the governance of land use in the Sámi region have brought with them pressures to play down attention to the Sámi connection to the land in administration. The state-controlled land and water areas in the Sámi Homeland are managed by *Metsähallitus* (National Forest Service), which controls some 90 per cent of the land and water areas in the region. Approximately 80 per cent of this area is set aside for conservation under either the Conservation Act or the Wilderness Act. The Metsähallitus Act prescribes that the management, use and protection of the natural resources under the control of Metsähallitus in the Sámi Homeland must be coordinated such that the Sámi are guaranteed the conditions necessary for enjoying their culture. The government of Finland is amending the Metsähallitus Act and the special provisions on the Sámi Homeland have been removed. These stipulated that the plans and projects of the Metsähallitus could not detract from the Sámi's opportunities to engage in traditional Sámi livelihoods. The removal of these special provisions is the result of demands of many actors in the Sámi Homeland, including the municipalities of Inari and Enontekiö. For example, the former municipal manager of Enontekiö, now a member of the Finnish Parliament, has called for "a comprehensive and independent mapping of conditions in the region that would determine in what way the position of the Sámi is weaker than that of the region's other population or entrepreneurs". Only after that can it be considered whether special Sámi provisions are needed in the legislation.[84]

As in the reform of the Metsähallitus Act, the criticism of the special status of the Sámi as users of the land often culminates expressly in how the connection of the Sámi to the land is understood. Due to their particular relationship

---

82 P. Magga, 2013, 10.

83 A. Nuorgam, 2014, 222.

84 M. Kärnä, Uusi Suomi Blog, 9.5.2014 <http://mikkokarna.puheenvuoro.uusisuomi.fi/167651-kolme-syyta-vastustaa-esitettya-metsahallituslakia> accessed 16 November 2015; About the reform of the Metsähallitus Act, see also L. Heinämäki et al., 2017, 34-50.

to nature, the Sámi have been expected to act in harmony with nature; when these expectations have not been fulfilled, conclusions have been drawn on the state of modern Sámi culture. For example, it has been claimed that over-grazing of reindeer, the attitude towards predators and the increased use of technology show how the culture of Sámi reindeer herding has become "dislocated", "alienated from itself" and "lost its special nature as a culture". The solution to this that has been proposed is a return to "the old" and "Indigenous" practices, which would mean giving up technology, a money economy and other elements of the modern world.[85]

Interpretations of the Sámi connection to the land have thus had their impact on policies regarding nature in Finland. The Sámi connection to the land is a significant factor in considering the Sámi cultural heritage and its protection, for without a connection to the land the culture would end up with no concrete basis, jeopardizing its prospects for continuing in the future.

5 Conclusions

In this chapter, referring to the work of R. Harrison[86] we have considered protecting Sámi cultural heritage as ontological politics, that is, a process of assembling a particular future for Sámi communities. Central to this approach is that cultural heritage is understood above all as a present-day phenomenon: selection of elements representing that cultural heritage, in other words elements worth protecting for the future, is made from the present-day perspective and under and constrained by contemporary power conditions and discourses, such as international legal discourses.

We have examined two social institutions of Sámi related to customary law that are closely linked to the questions of Indigenous belonging, the system of kinship-based ethnic recognition and the Sámi connection to the land, as elements of the cultural heritage whose recognition and acknowledgement are extremely important for the continued existence of the Sámi and of the special features of Sámi communities and Sámi culture. Each of the institutions has become highly politicized in recent decades as efforts have been made by the Finnish government to stabilize the status of the Sámi as an Indigenous people by granting them cultural autonomy – managed through the Sámi Parliament – in their homeland. Interestingly, the global legal discourse on Indigenous

85 See J. Valkonen, *Lapin luontopolitiikka* [The Nature Politics of Lapland] (Tampere University Press 2003), 171-194.

86 R. Harrison, 2015.

peoples and interpretations of it that have taken on a neoliberal bent have made it possible to call into question the Sámi's own forms of group-making and thus the ontological basis of Sámi communities. Safeguarding the political status of the Sámi as an Indigenous people within the state system has involved making membership in the Sámi community and the Sámi connection to the land facets of individual rights (and identity), which must be proven legally with documents. Such developments can be seen as part of a complex colonialist situation in which both the political foundations of the Sámi community and the international legal discourse on Indigenous rights and cultural heritage are constrained by structural relations of domination.

The UNESCO Convention for the Safeguarding of Cultural Heritage recognizes the threat to intangible cultural heritage posed by globalization, social change and intolerance. Where the existence of Indigenous peoples is concerned, the principal threat is the inability and reluctance of the Western system and the prevailing political ideologies to recognize that the intangible cultural heritage of Indigenous peoples and thus their very existence is based on a special ontology, one which is difficult to grasp, translate and document in terms of the Western system. In a word, it seems that although the UNESCO Convention emphasizes the importance of a group's self-identification in defining a cultural heritage that is to be preserved and safeguarded, in reality what is essential is how well the legislation of the mainstream societies and those who shape it are able to recognize and deal with the different forms of intangible cultural heritage. The upshot of this is that only forms of the cultural heritage that are recognizable and comprehensible by the mainstream society as cultural heritage and tradition, such as different cultural performances or *duodji* (traditional Sámi handicraft), can be seen as cultural heritage that should be safeguarded. In this way ontological interpretations are made on the nature of a culture, interpretations that may be blind to the Indigenous people's own ontology.

One problem is that because, on the one hand, the concept of cultural heritage, as a Western category, demands recognisability, a making visible and documentation and, on the other, Western legislation entails the requirement of legal recognition and transparency, it seems to be difficult, or impossible, to protect social institutions such as the Sámi connection to the land and the practice of group identification using legislation (of the mainstream society). When efforts are made to give a living, situational and ongoing practice a concrete form and to demand precision in observing it, the practice loses its flexibility, logic and origin, whereupon it appears to be political and susceptible to political caprice.

The EMRIP study 'Promotion and protection of the rights of indigenous peoples with respect to their cultural heritage' provides the following guidance to states as regards safeguarding of cultural heritage: "States should recognize the value and livelihood aspects of the cultural heritage of Indigenous peoples. States should recognize that the cultural heritage of Indigenous peoples is not limited to the protection of specific manifestations, symbols or objects, but also includes tangible and intangible manifestations of their ways of life, achievements and creativity, and of their spiritual and physical relationships with their lands, territories and resources."[87]

Safeguarding of the Sámi cultural heritage for the future requires that the people's own understanding of the world and of its place in that world is taken seriously; the idea must be accepted that Sáminess is based on an ontology of its own, one that creates a Sámi reality. In that case, the political community should be established and built with due consideration for and reliance on the ontology. Safeguarding the Sámi cultural heritage would then play out precisely as it was intended to, that is, as the preservation of Indigenous peoples as distinctive, separate groups.

Can kinship-based ethnic recognition and connection to the land (in themselves) provide a foundation for government and politics where Sámi culture is concerned? Discussions on Sámi autonomy have cast serious doubt on this, because the two are considered far too vague and thus cannot, for example, function as a basis for a law. Making kinship-based recognition the basis of the definition of Sámi in a law would require setting down objective criteria describing the practice. The concern here is that without such criteria the Sámi could decide arbitrarily who is accepted as a Sámi and who is not.[88]

Doubts as to the applicability of the Sámi's own practices in government and politics have their origin in the disparity between the Sámi minority and the mainstream society. According to E. Helander-Renvall, the majority population determines the discursive conditions in Indigenous politics, and it is in these terms that issues are considered, ascribed meaning and interpreted. It is often the case that the majority discourse does not – or perhaps does not even want to – engage with the reality in which a particular Indigenous people lives. She cites the example of conflicts in Norway and Sweden relating to overgrazing in reindeer herding. In her view government officials in Norway readily use the term "overbetning" (overgrazing) and "beitedyr" (grazing animal) when discussing the problems of reindeer herding and pastures in a political context. However, the Sámi language has no clear references to overgrazing nor is there

87 A/HRC/EMRIP/2015/2/Annex/B/9.

88 See V.-P. Lehtola, 2015.

a term "grazing animal".[89] Thus overgrazing does not exist in the Sámi reindeer herding culture in the same sense as that intended by Norwegian officials. Sámi reindeer herding examines questions of grazing in terms of its own knowledge practices, which official discourse does not recognize as knowledge at all.

The example put forward by Helander-Renvall shows how the majority population sets the conditions in political discussions and decision making for what is knowledge. In doing so, it imposes a semantic field of sorts on Indigenous politics, with this field then forming the context in which an Indigenous people's demands are assessed. It is also important to note that what is considered knowledge at any given time is never detached from the political prevailing situation. In political struggles, knowledge, politics and economics become closely intertwined and determine what is possible and what is not.

The importance of the Sámi system of kinship-based ethnic recognition and of the people's connection to the land is determined in relation to the conflictual situation which prevails in Finland. In other words, the political situation determines how viable the traditional institutions of the Sámi are seen as being. Before Sámi subjects had political rights associated with them – that is before the status of the Sámi as an Indigenous people was safeguarded – the traditional Sámi kinship-based practice of recognition was accepted as a viable way to recognize a person as belonging to the Sámi people. The connection to the land was not a problem either, at least to the extent that it did not directly challenge land use plans of the majority culture. Clearly, the present, highly politicized situation greatly impacts how the traditional institutions of the Sámi are assessed and interpreted. This in turn shows that if the Sámi practices that have evolved as elements of customary law were to be examined in different contexts, they could be seen as forming a rational basis for politics and governance pertaining to Sámi culture.

The ontologies of Indigenous peoples are heterogeneous assemblages which as such trouble the established political conception of how issues and the relationships between people should be organized. The idea that Sámi society could be organized on the basis of and with respect for the people's own ontology poses a challenge to what is a closely guarded colonialist and Eurocentric way of categorizing people and the world.

89 E. Helander-Renvall, *Sámi Society Matters* (Lapland University Press, 2016).

Links between Lands, Territories, Environment and Cultural Heritage – The Recognition of Sámi Lands in Norway

Øyvind Ravna

1 Introduction[1]

Indigenous peoples are generally characterized as constituting a minority within the national states where they have their origin and traditional lands, and sharing culture, languages and religions that have been suppressed and assimilated over a long period.[2] This implies that indigenous peoples' cultural heritage is in a particularly vulnerable situation. International society has become aware of this situation, and by adopting the 2007 United Nations Declaration on the Rights of Indigenous Peoples, UN states expressed a willingness to protect indigenous cultural heritage.[3]

Indigenous peoples have largely based their livelihoods on *traditional use of lands* and *natural resources*. This is noted by the UN Human Rights Committee, which has stated that there is a clear link between land resources and cultural – and thereby cultural heritage. The Committee has explained this link as follows:

---

1 This chapter is elaborated from a presentation on the UN Expert Seminar on the Promotion and Protection of the Rights of Indigenous Peoples with Respect to their Cultural Heritage at University of Lapland, Rovaniemi, February 26 and 27, 2015. Thanks to Seamus Ryder for excellent proof reading and useful advices on the text. Chapter 2 and 3 is in parts also elaborated on Øyvind Ravna, 'ILO 169 and Securing of Sámi Rights to Lands, Nature-based Livelihood, and Natural Resources', *Understanding the Many Faces of Human Security*, eds. K. Hossain and A. Petréti, Brill-Nijhoff, Leiden, Boston 2016, 173-189.

2 For a general description of the concept of 'indigenous peoples', see José Martinez Cobo, 'Study of the Problem of Discrimination Against Indigenous Peoples', *UN Docs* E/CN.4/Sub.2/476; E/CN.4/Sub.2/1982/ E/CN.4/Sub.2/1983/21 (1981-1983). See also the Indigenous and Tribal Peoples Convention No. 169, Convention concerning Indigenous and Tribal Peoples in Independent Countries (ILO 169) Article 1 (1) (b). The Convention was adopted in Geneva, 76th ILC session (27 June 1989) and entered into force 5 September 1991. It is currently ratified by 22 countries. Full text to be found here: <www.ilo.org/dyn/normlex/en/f?p=NORMLEXPUB:12100:0::NO::P12100_ILO_CODE:C169> accessed 22 April 2015.

3 United Nations Declaration on the Rights of Indigenous Peoples, 61/295, Article 31 (1) and (2), adopted at the UN 107th plenary meeting 13 September 2007, see <www.un.org/esa/socdev/unpfii/documents/DRIPS_en.pdf>, accessed 10 March 2015.

Xanthaki, Valkonen et al. (eds.), *Indigenous Peoples' Cultural Heritage: Rights, Debates and Challenges.*
 ISBN 978-90-04-34218-7. PP. 175-198

> With regard to the exercise of the cultural rights protected under article 27, the Committee observes that culture manifests itself in many forms, including a particular way of life associated with the use of land resources, especially in the case of indigenous peoples. That right may include such traditional activities as fishing or hunting and the right to live in reserves protected by law. The enjoyment of those rights may require positive legal measures of protection and measures to ensure the effective participation of members of minority communities in decisions which affect them.[4]

The statement shows that traditional ways of life of indigenous peoples, and the lands needed for such life, are protected under the concept of culture in International Covenant on Civil and Political Rights (ICCPR), article 27. Such lands are thus crucial for the protection of indigenous cultural heritage.

In addition, a statement from the Expert Mechanism on the Rights of Indigenous Peoples (EMRIP) underlines the significance of land and natural resources for indigenous peoples:

> Indigenous peoples' cultural heritage… should be considered [as] an expression of their self-determination and their spiritual and physical relationships with their lands, territories and resources. While the notion of heritage encompasses traditional practices in a broad sense, including language, art, music, dance, song, stories, sports and traditional games, sacred sites, and ancestral human remains, for indigenous peoples the preservation of heritage is deeply embedded and linked to the protection of traditional territories.[5]

The link between land, resources and culture is also reflected in the state obligations under the International Labour Organization Convention No. 169 (ILO 169).[6] See e.g. Article 4 (1) and 5 (a). Consequently, the obligation to promote indigenous cultures, including by identifying the lands on which they depend, is strengthened, as it can be subsumed under each of these independent, binding international conventions, and the interaction between them.

---

4 Human Rights Committee, General Comment 23, Article 27 (Fiftieth session, 1994), para. 7.

5 Human Rights Council, 30th session, Human rights bodies and mechanisms, 'Promotion and protection of the rights of indigenous peoples with respect to their cultural heritage', EMRIP, A/HRC/30/53 (2005), para. 6.

6 See supra note 2.

The topic of this chapter is connected to lands and resources. More precisely, the aim is to discuss and analyze how the international legal obligations to identify, recognise, and secure the indigenous peoples lands, natural resources, and livelihood, as a basis for exercising culture, are implemented in relation to the Sámi people. The protection of Sámi cultural monuments and sites will not be given specific attention.[7] Although the Sámi have their homelands in both Finland, Norway, Sweden and the Russian Federation, and meet the criteria of the ILO 169 definition of 'Indigenous Peoples' included in article 1 (1) b, Norway is the only state among these four that has ratified the ILO 169.[8] In addition, Norway has sought to implement the obligations of the ILO 169 through internal legislation – namely through the Finnmark Act.[9] This chapter is therefore limited in scope to examining the situation in Norway, which is highlighted as a significant example for other Nordic countries.[10] The fact that other Nordic countries such as Finland, are in a process of ratifying ILO 169, makes the subject of this chapter particularly topical.

2 The Legal Commitments to the Sámi Undertaken by Norway

2.1 *The Legal Basis for Protecting Sámi Lands and Culture in Norway*

Norwegian Sámi policy is based on the recognition that Norway is established on the territory of two peoples the Sámi and the Norwegians, as expressed by

---

7 Act 9 June 1978 no. 50 Act Concerning the Cultural Heritage [Lov om kulturminner] Article 4 automatically protects 'Sami monuments and sites of the kinds described above that are over 100 years old'. An English translation of the Act can be found here: <www.regjeringen.no/en/dokumenter/cultural-heritage-act/id173106/> accessed March 10, 2015. More about the Norwegian Act Concerning the Cultural Heritage, see Marit Myrvoll, Alma Thuestad, Elin Rose Myrvoll and Inger Marie Holm-Olsen, 'Unpredictable Consequences of Sámi Self-determination: Rethinking the legal protection of Sámi cultural heritage in Norway', *Arctic Review on Law and Politics*, vol 3, 2002, 30-50.

8 Ratified by Norway June 19, 1990, see supra note 2.

9 Act 17 June 2005 No. 85 relating to legal relations and management of land and natural resources in the county of Finnmark (The Finnmark Act) [Lov 17. juni 2005 nr. 85 om rettsforhold og forvaltning av grunn og naturressurser i Finnmark fylke (finnmarksloven)], An English translation of the Act can be found here: <www.ub.uio.no/ujur/ulovdata/lov-20050617-085-eng.pdf>, accessed March, 10, 2015.

10 James Anaya, *The situation of the Sámi people in the Sápmi region of Norway, Sweden and Finland*, <http://unsr.jamesanaya.org/docs/countries/2011-report-sapmi-a-hrc-18-35-add2_en.pdf> accessed March 10, 2015, para. 44.

H.M. King Harald as he opened the third Sámi Parliament in 1997.[11] The ratification of ILO 169 implies that the government has also acknowledged that the State of Norway is established on the territory of two peoples; the Sámi and the Norwegians, and that the Sámi are the indigenous people of Norway. The ratification also implies that the government is committed to identify, recognise, and secure Sámi lands lying within Norwegian territory.

The Constitutional amendment of 1988, Article 108, which commits Norway to 'create conditions enabling the Sámi people to preserve and develop its language, culture and way of life', also strengthens the state's commitment to identify Sámi land and user rights as part of the basis for Sámi culture. In addition, Norway has passed the Human Rights Act in 1999, which incorporates the ICCPR, and gives precedence to the terms and effect of the latter instrument in the event of any conflict with existing national law. Together, the ILO 169, Article 108 of the Norwegian Constitution, and Article 27 of the ICCPR, form the basis for the protection of Sámi culture, language and livelihood in Norway, and thus the legal basis for Norwegian Sámi policy. Norway has also endorsed the UN Declaration on the Rights of Indigenous Peoples – itself triggering relevant obligations and commitments – and has promoted it actively.[12]

The following section will analyse ILO 169 – the main binding instrument under international law committing Norway to identify and recognize Sámi lands. In addition, the chapter will review Article 27 of the ICCPR, which clearly protects and promotes the cultures of minorities, including the Sámi. The chapter will then discuss how these international commitments are implemented and applied in Norwegian national law.

2.2 *ILO Convention 169 Concerning Indigenous and Tribal Peoples in Independent Countries*

The ILO 169, which Norway ratified as the first state in the world, is of major significance for state parties to the convention, when it comes to securing Sámi rights to lands and natural resources. Notable are the introductory provisions of Articles 1 and 2, which define indigenous peoples and establish the general purposes of the Convention. Of significance is also Article 6, which safeguards the rights of indigenous peoples to be consulted; Article 7, which safeguards the rights of indigenous peoples to decide their own priorities, and

11 St.meld. nr. 55 (2000-2001) [A white paper] Om samepolitikken, 17.

12 The space, scope and aim of this chapter does not allow for a separate discussion of the UN Declaration on the Rights of Indigenous Peoples, although it is highly relevant to the protection of indigenous peoples' cultural heritage. However, at the end of section 2.2, there are some considerations of the UN Declaration.

to participate in 'the formulation, implementation and evaluation of plans and programmes for national and regional development which may affect them directly'; and Article 8, which protect indigenous customs and customary law and obligates governments to respect these.

However, it is Chapter II, entitled *Land*, which is the most significant part of the Convention in relation to identifying and securing Sámi traditional lands and livelihood.[13] It is not without reason that Article 14 is the most referred among the seven articles forming the land chapter. Article 14 (1) reads:

> The rights of ownership and possession of the peoples concerned over the lands which they traditionally occupy shall be recognised. In addition, measures shall be taken in appropriate cases to safeguard the right of the peoples concerned to use lands not exclusively occupied by them, but to which they have traditionally had access for their subsistence and traditional activities. Particular attention shall be paid to the situation of nomadic peoples and shifting cultivators in this respect.

Paragraph (2) and (3) of article 14 contains key provisions, too, stating that:

> Governments shall take steps as necessary to identify the lands which the peoples concerned traditionally occupy, and to guarantee effective protection of their rights of ownership and possession.

and:

> Adequate procedures shall be established within the national legal system to resolve land claims by the peoples concerned.

In spite of its unambiguous wording, there has been intense discussion on whether Article 14 requires the states to recognize ownership of indigenous peoples to traditional lands, or whether it is sufficient that strong use rights are recognized.[14] Today, the prevailing opinion seems to favour a close following to the wording of the convention: i.e. that indigenous communities have rights to

13 NOU 1993: 34 Rett og forvaltning av land og vann i Finnmark, 70.

14 Geir Ulfstein, 'Indigenous Peoples Right to Land', *Max Planck* UNYB 8 (2004): 21-23. See also the discussion in NOU 1993: 34, 70-72 and NOU 1997: 5 Urfolks landrettigheter etter folkerett og utenlands rett, 33-37; the latter with an interpretation more consistent with the current view that indigenous peoples are entitled to ownership.

collectively own their traditional lands.[15] Article 14 is therefore of great significance, not only for identifying lands to which the Sámi can claim ownership, but also in defining areas where the Sámi have rights of use.

Although Article 15 has not received the same attention as Article 14, it is no less significant for safeguarding Sámi rights to natural resources, particularly in relation to extractive industries within indigenous lands. The provision poses four obligations on state authorities: a general obligation to involve potentially-affected indigenous peoples in decision-making processes, and three more specific commitments in cases where the state retains the ownership of mineral or sub-surface resources, or rights to other resources pertaining to traditional indigenous lands. These latter commitments include establishing or maintaining procedures for consultations with indigenous peoples, before undertaking or permitting any programmes for the exploration or exploitation of such resources pertaining to their lands; providing indigenous peoples with benefits (royalties) of such activities; and ensuring fair compensation for any damages which they may sustain as a result of such activities.

Moreover, Article 15 (1) reads:

> The rights of the peoples concerned to the natural resources pertaining to their lands shall be specially safeguarded. These rights include the right of these peoples to participate in the use, management and conservation of these resources.

This *participation obligation* safeguards and clarifies the terms of participatory rights, such as those ensured in Article 7, by clearly stating that indigenous peoples have rights to participate in the use, management, and conservation of the resources pertaining to their traditional areas.[16] *Hans Petter Graver* and *Geir Ulfstein* maintain that the provision implies that the indigenous peoples shall be represented in the bodies that make decisions and are responsible for management of natural resources in indigenous areas. However, they argue that since the provision uses the word 'participate', it may not require that the management must be left to the indigenous peoples, or that they should be given conclusive influence in matters concerning resources pertaining to their

---

15 James Anaya, *Indigenous Peoples in International Law* (Oxford University Press, 2nd ed., 2004), 143 and Mattias Åhren, *Indigenous Peoples' Status in the International Legal System* (Oxford University press 2016), 175.

16 NOU 2007: 13 Den nye sameretten, 850.

areas. If one looks at the ILO 169 in conjunction with UN Declaration on Rights of Indigenous Peoples, this becomes even clearer.[17]

Nonetheless, this means that decisions, such as those made according to the Planning and Building Act, the Nature Conservation Act, and other Norwegian domestic legislation, cannot be settled without Sámi representation in the bodies that make such decisions or exercise the management of the resources.[18]

Further, Article 15 (2) reads:

> In cases in which the State retains the ownership of mineral or sub-surface resources or rights to other resources pertaining to lands, governments shall establish or maintain procedures through which they shall consult these peoples, with a view to ascertaining whether and to what degree their interests would be prejudiced, before undertaking or permitting any programmes for the exploration or exploitation of such resources pertaining to their lands. The peoples concerned shall wherever possible participate in the benefits of such activities, and shall receive fair compensation for any damages which they may sustain as a result of such activities.

The *consultation obligation* safeguarded in the first sentence of Article 15 (2), is imposed on the government when planning the extraction of mineral resources that the state retains the ownership of, which is the case in Norway.[19] Whether or not the provision requires the government to establish special consultation arrangements to determine the extent to which the indigenous interests would be prejudiced as a result of exploration of mineral resources can be debated. However, the case law of the ILO bodies, in the complaints procedure, do not draw any distinction between the obligations derived from Article 6, on

17 In a more binding relationship, participation includes the concept of *Free, Prior and Informed Consent,* which is ensured in the UNDRIP (articles 10, 11 (2), 19, 28, 29 (2), 32 (2)). It can be strongly argued that the ILO 169 commitments of Norway must be interpreted in accordance to the UNDRIP. However, the space and aim of this chapter, do not allow me to elaborate on it here.

18 Hans Petter Graver og Geir Ulfstein, *Folkerettslig vurdering av forslaget til ny Finnmarkslov* (November 3, 2003), see <http://www.regjeringen.no/nb/dep/jd/dok/rapporter_planer/rapporter/2004/folkerettslig-vurdering-av-forslaget-til/3.html?id=278380> accessed March 10, 2015. The Sámi Rights Committee will not extend the provision so far, see NOU 2007: 13, 1044.

19 See lov [Act] 19 June 2009 nr. 101 om erverv og utvinning av mineralressurser (mineralloven) (The Mineral Act) Section 7, para. 1.

one hand, and those derived from Article 15 (2), on the other.[20] The fact that there is a special provision for consultations in Article 15 (2) next to the general rule in Article 6, may be reason to suggest that it is particularly important that the governments implement consultations 'in good faith', and prior to exploitation of natural resources that states have retained ownership of in indigenous traditional territories.[21] Article 15 (2) is also designed more specifically than Article 6, since it poses a particular obligation of consultation regarding plans to allow the exploitation of natural resources to which the state claims ownership. In such a way, it strengthens the obligations for consultations settled in Article 6 (1).

The second sentence of Article 15 (2), introduces a *benefit sharing commitment,* stating that the indigenous peoples 'shall wherever possible participate in the benefits of such activities'. This is in addition to a *compensation commitment,* also provided for in Article 15 (2), which states that the indigenous peoples concerned 'shall receive fair compensation for any damages which they may sustain as a result of such activities'.[22] Together, these benefit sharing and compensation commitments establish that indigenous peoples not only should be financially compensated for damages and losses, but also should partake in the benefit of the profits of the industry 'wherever possible'.

The Norwegian government has not only acknowledged the above mentioned commitments and obligations by ratifying the ILO 169 in 1990; it has also moved to fulfil them by adopting and implementing the 2005 Finnmark Act, which 'shall apply with the limitations that follow from ILO Convention No. 169 Concerning Indigenous and Tribal Peoples in Independent Countries'.[23] The Norwegian authorities also signed the UN Declaration on Rights of Indigenous Peoples and actively participated in the work of the declaration since its inception in 1984. On the government's web page, one can read:

> The government's goal has been a declaration that can contribute to a strengthened legal protection for the world's indigenous peoples. In the

20 Graver and Ulfstein, supra note 18 and the Sámi Right Committee in NOU 2007: 13 Den nye sameretten, 1044.

21 The Sámi Rights Committee in NOU 2007: 13, 1044.

22 When it comes to compensation for damages, loss, and inconvenience as a result of intervention, the Sámi, and others, are secured by the Constitution § 105, Expropriation Act (23 October 1959 no. 3) and other laws including the European Convention on Human Rights, Protocol 1 Article 1 to receive full compensation for interference. This is not discussed further here.

23 The Finnmark Act section 3, see supra note 9.

> work, the government has cooperated closely with the Sámi Parliament, which consistently has been represented in the Norwegian delegation to the negotiations at the United Nations on the Declaration.[24]

That Norway has signed the Declaration, and actively promoted it, is not without obligations. It strengthens the legal obligations to the country's own indigenous people, both in terms safeguarding the rights to land, water and cultural heritage.

How Finnmark Act implements and safeguards the legal obligations under ILO 169, I will return to below.

2.3 *The significance of the relation between the International Covenant on Civil and Political Rights and the Norwegian Constitution Article 108*

The International Covenant on Civil and Political Rights (ICCPR) also commits Norway.[25] For the topic of this chapter, Article 27, which protects the rights of minorities' cultural practices, is of particular interest.[26] What makes Article 27 particularly interesting in relation to securing lands, resources and cultural heritage of indigenous peoples, as mentioned in the introduction, is that the Human Rights Committee interprets it to protect the substantial basis for a minority's culture; i.e. the particular way of life associated with the use of land resources.[27] In this way, the provision establishes a threshold for interferences in lands and natural resources of the kind that could threaten the exercise of Sámi culture and livelihood – both at the individual and community level. Interferences exceeding this threshold will violate Article 27.

The Norwegian government acknowledges this understanding as it endorses the report of the Ministry of Labour and Social Inclusion: "In relation to the Sámi as an indigenous people, it is a common interpretation that the provision

24 See FNs erklæring om urfolks rettigheter <www.regjeringen.no/no/tema/urfolk-og-minoriteter/samepolitikk/internasjonalt-urfolksarbeid/fns-erklaring-om-urfolks-rettigheter/id87024/> accessed 12 Oct. 2016.

25 Lov [Act] 21. mai 1999 nr. 30 om styrking av menneskerettighetenes stilling i norsk rett (menneskerettsloven) [The Human Rights Act] incorporates the ICCPR with precedence in front of National legislation.

26 Article 27 reads: 'In those States in which ethnic, religious or linguistic minorities exist, persons belonging to such minorities shall not be denied the right, in community with the other members of their group, to enjoy their own culture, to profess and practise their own religion, or to use their own language'.

27 See the quotation in section 1, reference given in supra note 4.

[Article 27] includes the substantive bases for the Sámi total cultural practices, also referred to as a natural basis for Sámi culture".[28]

Case law from the Human Rights Committee also clarifies that modern ways of exercising traditional culture-related industries, such as coastal fishing with modern gear or reindeer herding with motor vehicles, enjoy protection under Article 27.[29]

Article 27 of the ICCPR constitutes a significant legal obligation in securing the natural resources and lands used by the Sámi, insofar as it sets up a framework that limits interventions. Seen in the context of Norwegian Constitution Article 108,[30] which protects Sámi language, culture and livelihood and is modelled on the ICCPR Article 27,[31] establishes a special protection of the Sámi culture. The link between these two provisions helps to strengthen the mutual obligations. Moreover, Article 108 must be interpreted in accordance with the 'requirements of international law committed to the Norwegian authorities'.[32] The implication is that Article 108 not only creates a legal obligation for the Norwegian authorities as regards the implementation of the country's Sámi policy, but also contributes in protecting lands, natural resources and cultural heritages as a basis of Sámi culture.

3 The Implementation of ILO 169 in National Legislation

3.1 *The Legislative Story of the Finnmark Act*

Norway has taken an active approach in respect of the ILO 169 commitments to ensure the Sámi's rights of ownership and possession over their traditional lands, implementing such commitments through national legislation by adopting a particular law for the most central Sámi areas known as the *2005*

---

28 St.meld. nr. 28 (2007-2008) Samepolitikken (Recommendation to the Parliament from the Ministry of Labor and Social Inclusion on the governmental Sámi Policy), 33. (Translation of quotations here and below, except for the sections of the Finnmark Act, is done by the author).

29 Apirana Mahuika v. New Zealand, Comm. 547/1993, U.N. Doc. CCPR/C/55/D/547/1993 (HRC 1995). See also Ravna, supra note 1. 179-180.

30 Article 108, which protects Sámi language, culture and livelihood, reads: The authorities of the state shall create conditions enabling the Sámi people to preserve and develop its language, culture and way of life. Translation from<www.stortinget.no/globalassets/pdf/english/constitutionenglish.pdf> accessed October 12, 2016.

31 NOU 1984: 18 ibid., 441.

32 Sámi Rights Committee II in NOU 2007:13, 191.

Finnmark Act.[33] Before examining how the ILO 169 commitments are implemented and applied in practice, I will briefly explore the background and the legislative history of this Act.

Notwithstanding the discourses in the 1980s that acknowledged the Sámi as an indigenous people who were entitled to ownership of their traditional lands, the question of Sámi rights to lands and waters remained highly controversial. This was clearly evident when it came to the implementation of the ILO 169 in national legislation. Although the Sámi Rights Committee had proposed a rather more far-reaching way of meeting the relevant ILO 169 obligations, including, *inter alia*, by identifying local community-owned lands to be governed by the those communities,[34] the government, through the 2003 bill of a Finnmark Act, submitted that the ILO obligations could be met by transferring the state-held lands to a regional body only.[35] The Sámi rights to ownership and participation were to be ensured by letting the Sámi Parliament appoint three of the six board members. In such a way, the Sámi were supposed to enjoy substantial participation in the governance of all former state lands, including the Coastal sector with a traditional Norwegian population. Consequently, the government did not see any need to identify local community lands, or particular lands to which the Sámi Community could claim collective ownership to, as Article 14 of ILO 169 prescribes.

The government bill was met with broad opposition, not least from the Sámi Parliament, which argued, alongside others, that the bill was contrary to international law.[36] As a result of this criticism, the legislature asked for an independent assessment of the draft, which was a unique occurrence in the history of Norwegian legislation. The law professors Geir Ulfstein and Hans Petter Graver were engaged to undertake the assessment. They concluded that the draft bill was, on a number of key points, insufficient in meeting the requirements of ILO169, including, *inter alia*, when it came to the identification and recognition of specific Sámi lands:

> Should the Finnmark Act meet ILO Convention requirements for recognition of land rights, the decision rules must be changed so that the Sámi

---

33 See supra note 9. The county of Finnmark, which is the northernmost county of Norway, is the area with the most significant concentration of traditional Sámi lands and settlements.

34 NOU 1997: 4 Naturgrunnlaget for samisk kultur, 239-268.

35 Ot.prp. nr. 53 (2002-2003) Om lov om rettsforhold og forvaltning av grunn og naturressurser i Finnmark fylke (Finnmarksloven) [The Finnmark Act], 90-91.

36 Innst. O. nr. 80 (2004-2005), 17.

> are secured the control according to an ownership position. If this is not relevant for the entire county, the particular Sámi areas need to be identified with a view to ensure the Sámi the control and rights to these areas.[37]

The broad criticism in the report of Graver and Ulfstein served to trigger consultations between the Parliamentary Standing Committee of Justice, the Sámi Parliament and the Finnmark County Council. During these consultations, the legislature acknowledged that Norway was required to identify the rights to specific lands and waters in Finnmark in order to meet the ILO 169 obligations under Article 14.[38] Accordingly, legal identification and recognition had to be included as a key element in the Finnmark Act.

Instead of addressing the identification and recognition process through the ordinary courts or through a specialized land tribunal, the legislature proposed that the rights to lands and waters in Finnmark should be identified in two steps: First, by a commission mandated to investigate rights to lands and waters; and second, by a special court mandated to settle disputes concerning those rights arising from the investigation of the commission. This proposal is now formalized in the Finnmark Act, section 5, para. 3. From the preparatory work, it is not clear why the legislature chose this two-step solution. However, it can partly be reasoned in the criticism that was directed at *Uncultivated Land Commission for Nordland and Troms,* where the same body both investigated the case and ruled the trials that arise.[39] That the procedure chosen in the Finnmark Act, consumed twice more time, was not in the mind of the legislators.[40]

There is also reason to inquire why the focus of identification and recognition of land rights is on private property rights, rather than the two categories prescribed in the ILO 169 Article 14.[41]

---

37 Graver and Ulfstein, supra note 14.

38 Innst. O. nr. 80 (2004-2005), 17.

39 *The Uncultivated Land Commission for Nordland and Troms* (1985-2004) had the task to clarify boundaries between state land and private property in Troms and Nordland, including usage rights that rested on state lands. The Commission were severely criticized by the Sami Parliament, which argued that it was not an adequate procedure within the national legal system to resolve land claims by indigenous peoples: see Sámi Parliament meeting protocol, case 61/1993 (May 10 and 11, 1993).

40 See Øyvind Ravna, 'The Finnmark Act 2005 Clarification Process and Trial "Within a Reasonable Time"', *Nordic Journal of Human Rights,* 29 (2011): 184-205.

41 See Innst. O. nr. 80 (2004-2005) p. 28, where the Sámi Parliament proposed to include identification land categories according to the categories of ILO 169 Article 14 (1), which

The Finnmark Commission aimed 'to establish the scope and content of the rights held by Sámi and other people on the basis of prescription or immemorial usage', and the Uncultivated Land Tribunal for Finnmark aimed 'to settle disputes concerning such rights', were both established to fulfil the commitment in respect of ILO 169, particularly Article 14. Consequently, these two bodies stand as the most prominent institutions established to meet the legal commitments Norway has undertaken by signing ILO 169.

Another controversial topic addressed during the consultations was the removal of legal protection for the interests of the public living outside the county of Finnmark, which the government bill sought to protect in its preamble.[42] The intention of such removal was to strengthen the local communities' control and management of the nearby outlying areas and natural resources.

In relation to the theme of this anthology, it is worth mentioning that Sámi cultural heritage provided minimal attention in the government's 2003 bill to the Finnmark Act.[43] Cultural heritage is only mentioned in a proposal for a provision that the *Finnmark Estate*[44] may not claim compensation when expropriating land or resources for a number of public purposes, including cultural heritage projects. The proposal was not adopted by the legislature.

The fact that Sámi cultural heritage received minimal treatment in the draft bill that formed the basis for the Finnmark Act is recognized by the Ministry of Environmental Protection, but further discussion of cultural heritage is generally absent.[45]

3.2 *The Finnmark Act and the Obligations under ILO 169*

The 2005 Finnmark Act is established as a result of the development of Sámi rights that occurred towards the end of the last millennium. It has an aim to include the Sámi in the governance of land and renewable resources in the County of Finnmark in order to fulfil Norway's various obligations under ILO 169.

In its preamble (section 1), the act pronounces that:

> The purpose of the Act is to facilitate the management of land and natural resources in the county of Finnmark in a balanced and ecologically

is 'rights of ownership and possession' and 'right… to use lands (not exclusively occupied by them)'.

42 Innst. O. nr. 80 (2005-2006), 32.

43 Ot.prp. nr. 53 (2002-2003), supra note 35.

44 *The Finnmark Estate* (Finnmarkseiendommen) is the legal entity that shall administer the land and natural resources that it owns on behalf of the peoples of Finnmark.

45 Ot.prp. nr. 53 (2002-2003), 24.

> sustainable manner for the benefit of the residents of the county and *particularly as a basis for Sami culture, reindeer husbandry, use of non-cultivated areas, commercial activity and social life* (my emphasis).[46]

The Finnmark Act incorporates the ILO 169 into Norwegian law. This is established in Section 3, which reads:

> The Act shall apply with the limitations that follow from ILO Convention No. 169 concerning Indigenous and Tribal Peoples in Independent Countries. The Act shall be applied in compliance with the provisions of international law concerning indigenous peoples and minorities and with the provisions of agreements with foreign states concerning fishing in transboundary watercourses.

This is a partial incorporation,[47] limited to the jurisdictional area covered by the Finnmark Act. It is important to be aware that the Parliamentary Standing Committee of Justice[48] emphasizes that the phrase 'the limitations' implies that the ILO 169 prevails over the Finnmark Act in case of conflicts. On the other hand, if one finds, on the basis of the ILO 169, that the Act lacks provisions on a certain topic, the Committee states that it will be a task for the legislature to address such a gap. The Courts shall, in other words, not rely on the ILO 169 to determine rules that are not specified in the Finnmark Act.[49]

The Finnmark Act Section 3 and the rationale in the preparatory works have recently been discussed by the Supreme Court of Norway, which has interpreted the incorporation narrowly.[50] The Court finds that ILO 169 only has priority over the provisions of the Finnmark Act. Thus, ILO 169 is not incorporated in

46 Translation here and below of sections of the Finnmark Act is taken from <http://app.uio.no/ub/ujur/oversatte-lover/>, see supra note 9.

47 The Parliamentary Standing Committee of Justice in Innst. O. nr. 80 (2004-2005), 33.

48 Parliamentary Standing Committee of Justice is one of the committees of Parliament. It hears matters related to the Judiciary of Norway, the Police and Correctional Services, Prosecutors, general administrative law, criminal law, procedural law and general civil law. Consequently, the Committee had parliamentary responsibility for completing the preparatory work of the Finnmark Act.

49 Innst. O. nr. 80 (2004-2005), 33.

50 The Norwegian Supreme Court, Stjernøy Reindeer Husbandry district and Johan J. Sara et al. vs. the Finnmark Estate, 28 Sept. 20016, HR-2016-2030-A, para. 76. See also Ø. Ravna, 'Norway and its obligations under the ILO 169 – some considerations after the recent Stjernøy Supreme Court Case', *Arctic Review on Law and Politics* (7) no. 2 2016.

front "jurisdictional area of the act" and does not take precedence over property law to be applied as a result of the Finnmark Act.

Section 4, which sets out guidelines for the Sámi Parliament regarding changes in the use of uncultivated land, allows the Sámi Parliament to adopt guidelines for changes in the use of outlying fields and mountainous areas. Such guidelines were in fact adopted in 2007.[51] It is among these guidelines that we find the only consideration of Sámi cultural heritage related to the Finnmark Act. The relevant guideline requires public authorities, including Finnmark Estate, to conduct a thorough and proper assessment of the potential effects on Sámi culture, reindeer herding, areas, commercial activity and social life before making a decision in matters concerning changes in the use of land in Finnmark. Section 7 (of the Guidelines) states that, in particular, it shall be taken into account that the measures or plans are not unsightly, and do not infringe upon *Sámi sacred sites, burial sites and other places of special cultural significance,* see the Act Concerning the Cultural Heritage.[52]

Returning to the Finnmark Act itself, the most substantial commitment to the Sámi is pronounced in Section 5, paragraph 1, which reads:

> Through prolonged use of land and water areas, the Sámi have collectively and individually acquired rights to land in Finnmark.

Paragraph 1 reflects the commitment of the ILO 169, Article 14 (1), which ensures the rights of ownership and possession of the Sámi over the lands which they have traditionally occupied. The Parliamentary Standing Committee of Justice has noted that the provision explicitly prescribes that the Sámi have acquired rights to lands in Finnmark. This is a principled and political recognition of the occurrence of such rights.[53]

Paragraph 2 and 3 of Section 5 are also certainly of significance:

> This Act does not interfere with collective and individual rights acquired by Sami and other people through prescription or immemorial usage. This also applies to the rights held by reindeer herders on such a basis or pursuant to the Reindeer Herding Act.

---

51 Sametingets retningslinjer for vurderingen av samiske hensyn ved endret bruk av meahcci/utmark i Finnmark [The Sámi Parliament's guidelines for the assessment of Sámi considerations for changes in the use of uncultivated land (meahcci) in Finnmark], regulation 11 June 2007 no. 738.

52 For the full reference of the Act, see supra note 7.

53 Innst. O. nr. 80 (2004-2005), 37.

> In order to establish the scope and content of the rights held by Sami and other people on the basis of prescription or immemorial usage or on some other basis, a commission shall be established to investigate rights to land and water in Finnmark and a special court to settle disputes concerning such rights, cf. chapter 5.

Paragraph 2 clearly establishes that the act cannot intervene in established use and ownership rights, for example through the regulatory regime that is established under Chapter 3, or through the surveying and identification of legal rights under Chapter 5. Paragraph 3 reflects the commitments in ILO 169, Article 14 (2), which provide that governments shall take steps as necessary to identify the lands that indigenous peoples have traditionally occupied by establishing and guaranteeing effective protection of their rights of ownership and possession. It also reflects Article 14 (3) which provides that adequate procedures shall be established within the national legal system to resolve land claims from the indigenous peoples.

It is noteworthy that the majority of the Parliamentary Standing Committee of Justice stated that the assessment of evidence in recent case law has been satisfactory. Newer Norwegian jurisprudence, especially the Selbu- and Svartskog cases, provide insight on how traditional Sámi use shall be considered as a basis for the acquisition of rights. They are important sources of law for the Commission and the Court.[54] In the precedent-setting Selbu- and Svartskog cases,[55] the Supreme Court of Norway acknowledged Sámi pastoral rights on private land (in the former case), and title to an area of uncultivated land the local Sámi population had used over centuries (in the latter case).

Protection of Sámi cultural heritage was not a topic in the Selbu Case. However, the importance of such heritage was in focus as evidence of Sámi presence in earlier times. In this context, the Supreme Court refers to a survey of 1985, where it was stated:

> An overall consideration of the scope of cultural heritage in this area reveals a Sámi dwelling and usage area with long traditions… The Sámi's cultural heritage extends throughout the whole project area.

Based on this report, the Supreme Court rejected the assertion of landowners that there was no Sámi cultural heritage in the disputed area: 'Even if it is just

54 Ibid., 36.

55 Published in Norsk Retstidende (NRt) 2001, 769 ff. and 1229 ff., respectively.

a field report, it does at least exclude conclusions that there is no Sámi cultural heritage in the area.'[56]

Chapter 2 includes Sections 6 and 7. Section 6 prescribes that *Finnmarkseiendommen* ('the Finnmark Estate') is an independent legal entity seated in Finnmark, which shall administer the land and natural resources that it owns in compliance with the purpose of this Act. According to the government, the provision forms the legal basis for the establishment of the new governing system, and stipulates that the body is a separate legal entity within the framework of the act.[57]

Section 7 is an important provision, which governs the composition of the board of the Finnmark Estate. It provides that the Finnmark County Council and the Sámi Parliament shall each elect three members, in addition to personal deputies, for a total of six board members – in line with the arrangement to fulfil the obligations of ILO 169 that was originally envisioned by the government in its 2003 law bill. The provision must also be seen as a follow-up to Article 15 (1), which, as previously discussed, safeguards 'the right of these [indigenous] peoples to participate in the use, management and conservation of these resources'. However, it has yet to be formally established whether locals who have historical rights in the nearby outlying areas, both Sámi and non-Sámi, can participate in its governance and management.

Chapter 3 (Sections 21-27), which defines the rights of the municipality and the county's population, respectively, and provides the Finnmark Estate a broad right to regulate the use of natural resources, is not discussed further. However, one should note that the statutory regulatory regime shall not include acquired-use rights or property rights.

Chapter 5, entitled 'Survey and recognition of existing rights', includes Sections 29 and 36, which grant authority to the Finnmark Commission and the Uncultivated Land Tribunal for Finnmark, respectively. These bodies are a direct consequence of the recognition of the obligations under ILO 169, Article 14 (2) and (3). However, the entire Chapter, which was drawn up during the consultations between the Sámi Parliament, the Finnmark County Council and Parliamentary Standing Committee of Justice, must be seen in this light.

56 NRt. 2001, 769 at 808. More about the Selbu- and Svartskog cases, published in NRt 2001, p. 769 et seq. and p. 1229 et seq, respectively, see Øyvind Ravna, 'The Process of Identifying Land Rights in parts of Northern Norway: Does the Finnmark Act Prescribe an Adequate Procedure within the National Law?' in *Yearbook of Polar Law*, vol. 3, 2011, 423-453 at 429-432.

57 Ot.prp. nr. 53 (2002-2003), 123. The Parliamentary Standing Committee of Justice has no further comments to the provision.

More specifically, Section 29 imposes a particular duty on the Finnmark Commission, on the basis of current national law, to 'investigate rights of use and ownership to the land to be taken over by Finnmark Estate pursuant to Section 49'. The preparatory works show that 'current national law' implies that Sámi customary law must be emphasized as a source of law,[58] in line with Norway's commitments under ILO 169, Article 8.

The above-explained review is not exhaustive.[59] However, it demonstrates that the Finnmark Act has a broad range of provisions intended to address Norway's obligations under ILO 169. Nevertheless, the identification process established under Chapter 5 can be criticized, given that it has a private-law focus, rather than representing an initiative to identify the categories of lands listed in ILO 169, Article 14. Whether the Commission should be obliged to take such an initiative is worthy of further attention, particularly in light of the fact that the ILO 169 enjoys priority over the Finnmark Act. A further review of Chapter 5 will also show that it contains unusual and unsuitable procedural regulations.[60]

3.3 *The Application of the Finnmark Act in Relation to Identifying and Securing Sámi Lands and Collective Use Rights*

The process of legally identifying Sámi lands, aimed at defining the ownership and use rights provided under the Finnmark Act, Section 5, paragraph 1, started in March 2008 when the Finnmark Commission was first established. This process is not only of regional or national interest, but also of international interest, as it demonstrates how the first state to sign the ILO 169 fulfils its commitments to the Sámi. In addition, the five reports of the Finnmark Commission published to date,[61] are the first specific documents to clarify the rights of the Sámi to particular land areas, and arose after many decades of investigation and political discussions on Sámi land rights.

---

58 Inst. O. nr. 80 (2004-2005), 19.

59 Among other things, the relatively complicated procedural requirements have not been discussed: On this, see Øyvind Ravna, 'The Process of Identifying Land Rights in parts of Northern Norway: Does the Finnmark Act Prescribe an Adequate Procedure within the National Law?', *Yearbook of Polar Law*, 3 (2011): 423-453 at 437-450.

60 More about this, see Ravna, supra note 59, 444-450.

61 Finnmarkskommisjonen, *Rapport felt 1 Stjernøya/Seiland*, March 20, 2012 (Report 1), *Rapport felt 2, Nesseby*, February 13, 2013 (Report 2), *Rapport felt 3 Sørøya*, October 16, 2013 (Report 3), Rapport felt 5, Varangerhalvøya Øst, June 24, 2014 (Report 5) and Rapport felt 6, Varangerhalvøya Øst, October 16, 2015 (Report 6), see <http://www.domstol.no/no/Enkelt-domstol/Finnmarkskommisjonen/Felt-1---3/Avsluttede-felt/>, accessed December 10, 2015.

The first report concerns the islands of *Stjernøya* and *Seiland* in the Alta Fjord in West Finnmark.[62] The area covered by the report is inhabited by both Sámi and non-Sámi coastal populations. It is also used as summer pastures for nomadic Sámi reindeer-herders. In addition, the *Sibelco Nordic* mining company produces the valuable mineral nepheline syenite on one of the two islands.

While taking position on substantive questions concerning the local Sámi, the non-Sámi population, and the nomadic Sámi reindeer-herders' usage and ownership-rights on the two islands, the Finnmark Commission found that none of the land users had acquired collective property rights. However, the Commission found that there *are* established use rights with an independent legal basis. Nonetheless, this finding does not imply that the local population have rights to use the natural resources without permission from the Finnmark Estate or to participate in the management and conservation of these rights as the ILO 169, Article 15 (1) prescribes. In fact, neither the locals nor the reindeer herders were acknowledged to enjoy any rights beyond those that these groups already enjoy under the 2007 Reindeer Husbandry Act and the Finnmark Act, Sections 22 and 23.[63]

Remarkably, the Commission refused to take a position on whether or not the Sámi herders are entitled to benefits derived from Sibelco Nordic's mining activities on their pastoral lands. The reason for this is that the question must be settled on the basis of international law, i.e. ILO 169 solely, which, according to the Commission, is not within the scope and mandate of the legal clarification process.[64] However, the ILO 169 prevails the Finnmark Act in case of contradictions.

The assessments in the Report 1 have been heard by the Uncultivated Land Tribunal for Finnmark and the Supreme Court of Norway. In both instances, the Courts held that the Sámi reindeer herders had not acquired title to Stjernøya. As shown above, the Supreme Court constricted the importance of ILO 169 in relation to the Finnmark Act.[65] However, the Supreme Court highlights the so-called "presumption principle". This principle says that Norwegian law as far as possible shall be interpreted in accordance with international law.[66]

---

62 Ibid., Report 1.

63 For more reading, see Øyvind Ravna, 'The First Investigation Report of the Norwegian Finnmark Commission', *International Journal on Minority and Group Rights* 20 (2013), 443-457.

64 Supra note 61, Report 1, 50.

65 Supra note 50.

66 Ibid., para. 77.

In the second report, published in February 2013, which covers the Sámi municipality of Nesseby in the eastern parts of Finnmark, the conclusions reached in relation to collective rights are substantially the same, although the landscape, location, and evidence of use varied significantly from the circumstances under focus in the first report.[67] Consequently, not a square meter of collective ownership was recognized for the inhabitants of the Sámi Community of Nesseby. However, as was the case in the earlier report, it was assumed that both locals and reindeer herders had use rights with an independent legal basis. In the report, however, it was more clearly articulated why the rights holders were not entitled to dispose of or exercise control over their own usage rights. The reason for this involved the allocations of the government, which through its governance and management, has established a right to rule over the local population's use rights.[68] To be denied control over their own usage rights is contested by the locals, who have brought the case before the Uncultivated Land Tribunal for Finnmark. A judgement in the case is expected in late autumn 2016.

Report 3 and 5, published in October 2013 and June 2014 respectively, confirm the 'case law' regarding collective rights as established in the previous two reports.[69] So does Report 6, published in October 2015.

However, there is an exception in Report 6. In the small abandoned Coastal Sámi village Gulgofjord by the Tana fjord, the Finnmark Commission found that the people who moved away from the village in 1970, and their ancestors, have pursued such an extensive use while government allocations have virtually been absent, which means that they hold title to an outlying area of 30 square kilometers.[70] The Commission, however, concluded that since the village is abandoned, the Finnmark Estate have the title until the residents reportedly move back to the village, which has neither infrastructure, shops or schools. The Finnmark Estate has called this as a "sleeping ownership," to which it opposes.[71]

It is worth noting that within the preparatory works of the Finnmark Act, the legislature assumed that the two precedent Supreme Court cases of Selbu and Svartskogen[72] were examples to be followed:

67 Supra note 61, Report 2.

68 Supra note 61, Report 2, 122.

69 Supra note 61, Report 3 and 5.

70 Supra note 61, Report 6, 158-172.

71 Protocol of the chair meeting of Finnmark Estate 20 and 21 June 2016, para. 9.4.

72 Published in NRt. (2001), 769 ff. and 1229 ff., respectively.

> It is opinion of the majority [of the Parliamentary Standing committee of justice] that the assessment of evidence in recent case law has been satisfactory. Recent Norwegian case law, especially the Selbu- and Svartskog cases, have given instructions on how traditional Sámi use shall be considered as the basis for the acquisition. It will be important sources of law for the commission and the court.[73]

The Finnmark Commission has found that the local peoples' use of lands in all the five fields investigated was extensive, flexible, and long-lasting – similar to that of the locals in Manndalen,[74] who won the title to land in the Supreme Court Case of Svartskogen.[75] However, the Commission did not conclude in accordance with the latter judgment. Instead, it argued that the state's allocations as proprietor, and administrative deeds as authority, had been so extensive in all the four fields that they had extinguished the collective property rights of the local people – even though they had been there prior to 1775, when the state began to survey and register private land plots.

When it comes to use rights, they have in principle survived, but are of little significance because the right holders are not granted any exclusive protection from outsiders. In addition, the right holders are not permitted to use the rights without the permission of Finnmark Estate, nor can they participate in management or benefit from dividends.

Rather than emphasising Sámi use of lands or Sámi customary law, as the legislature prescribed in the preparatory works for the Finnmark Act,[76] the Finnmark Commission has identified the governmental exercises of authority and ownership, together with lack of local, informal management of natural resources, to be of significance for law-making. Thus, it is not lack of continuous and intensive use of land and natural resources in good faith, as prescribed in the rules of immemorial usage that prevent people from acquiring their rights, but rather place heavy emphasis on the state's former colonial legal regime and associated land transactions and allocations.

Accordingly, colonial state ownership, the very thing that the Finnmark Act aims to abolish, is the same thing preventing the Norwegian state from upholding its commitment to the Sámi under the same act, in Section 5 – that is, that 'the Sámi have collectively and individually acquired rights to land in Finnmark'. That the Commission has, to a very limited extent, taken into ac-

73 Inst. O. nr. 80 (2004-2005), 36.

74 Supra note 61, Report 1, 64, Report 2, 65 and Report 3, 51.

75 Nrt. (2001), 1229 ff. The case is referred in 3.2 (above).

76 Innst. O. nr. 80 (2004-2005), 19.

count the varying situations between the islands in western Finnmark and a municipally in eastern Finnmark, which have a living Sámi culture, both in terms of the local population use and management, and government dispositions, is a part of the case.

Notably, the UN Special Rapporteur on the Rights of Indigenous People, in her report on the human rights situation of the Sámi people in the Sápmi region of Norway, Sweden and Finland, have criticized the weight the state's earlier dispositions as the claimant of property rights in Finnmark in the reports of the Finnmark Commission.[77] She proposes instead that a starting point for any measures to identify and recognize indigenous peoples' land and resource rights "should be their own customary use and tenure systems". She also highlights the management of areas, nature and *cultural heritage* is therefore important to ensure the basis for preserving and developing Sámi culture.[78]

4 Summary

This chapter deals with land and resources as a part of cultural heritage. More precisely, it analyzes how the international legal obligations to identify, recognise, and secure indigenous peoples' lands, natural resources, and livelihoods – as provided for under the ILO 169 – are met in Norway. Based on this analysis, one can clearly argue that the Finnmark Act could give stronger guidance as to how the usage and ownership rights to the former state lands of Finnmark are to be identified. The Act could also better safeguard the identification of lands in accordance with the established categories under ILO 169. To assume that the Sámi have sufficient influence on their traditional lands by letting the Sámi Parliament appoint three out of six board members, may also seem naive. The Act can consequently also be criticized for its limited consideration and protection of Sámi cultural heritage.

Notwithstanding, the review above shows that the legislature has endeavoured to implement provisions in the Finnmark Act that allow the law to meet commitments under the ILO 169. Bearing in mind that the Act resulted from a compromise between many interests, one has to admit that the legislature probably came as far as it was possible in 2005. To complete the implementa-

---

77 Report of the Special Rapporteur on the rights of indigenous peoples (Victoria Tauli-Corpuz) on the human rights situation of the Sami people in the Sápmi region of Norway, Sweden and Finland, *Human Rights Council, A/HRC/33/42/Add.3*, para. 24.

78 Ibid., para. 27 (my emphasis).

tion, there have to be a focus on the application of the law in relation to both the Finnmark Act and the ILO 169.

The application of the law, as conducted by the Finnmark Commission has not had this focus, but rather, has emphasized other considerations. By placing heavy weight on governmental exercises of ownership and authority, in the five areas that are have been investigated, the Commission has prevented the local inhabitants – both Sámi and non-Sámi – from acquiring recognition of both collective property rights and use rights beyond what is already provided in the Finnmark Act. Particularly noteworthy is the statement that even though the locals are acknowledged to possess original use rights with an independent legal basis, the state's exercises as land owner and executive authority in the past, has implied that the locals do not have the rights to control or manage their use rights. The fact that the Commission argues that the communities have not exercised a local, customary-based governance and management of lands, contributes to strengthening the assertion that the locals do not have the right to control and manage the usage rights of their own traditional lands.

In addition, when taking into account the special guidelines for the legal identification and clarification process embedded in the preparatory work, including reference to the Selbu and Svartskogen Cases, it becomes necessary to ask whether the governmental exercises and the presumed absence of local governance – in method and in actual fact – is too heavily emphasized. This is, as mentioned, pointed out by the UN Special Rapporteur on Rights of Indigenous Peoples in her 2016 Report on the human rights situation of the Sámi People.

Giving significant weight to state allocations and lack of local governance will effectively imply that it is not possible to achieve the aim of the Finnmark Act. In other words, a 'significant historic shift to local control',[79] will not take place – despite the fact that the language of the ILO obligations is relatively well implemented in the Finnmark Act itself, including Section 5 (1) and (2).[80]

Nor does this manner of application contribute to advancing the legislature's intentions regarding the strengthening of Sámi rights to participate in the use, management, and conservation of the natural resources pertaining to their lands.

---

79 Ot.prp. nr. 53 (2002-2003), 7.

80 (1) Through prolonged use of land and water areas, the Sámi have collectively and individually acquired rights to land in Finnmark, (2) This Act does not interfere with collective and individual rights acquired by Sámi and other people through prescription or immemorial usage.

Admittedly, the methodological and practical challenges the Finnmark Commission has faced have not been easy to meet. Assessing the significance of Sámi customary use, control, and governance of lands in a context of varying factual circumstances is no small feat, especially where the state has exercised broad public governance over a long period. However, it does not justify the current application of the law. By a general, proprietary law approach, the landowner's allocations must obviously be heavily emphasized. Nevertheless, the situation in Finnmark is different: The state's position as landowner in the Sámi areas has long been both unclear and disputed,[81] and the government has acknowledged that it is 'difficult to conclude for sure that state ownership can be fully maintained'.[82] A responsibility to both the Sámi and the non-Sámi population in Finnmark has also been recognized by the statement that 'there is a need for a clear recognition of the independent rights on ordinary property law basis, not because the legal situation has to be altered or modified, but to make it clear that the former position of the state as landowner, has not been an obstacle to obtaining such rights'.[83]

Accordingly, the law cannot be applied in such way that the former position of the state, based on a colonial doctrine, prevents Norway from identifying Sámi collective rights to lands and waters, and thereby fails in ensuring Sámi rights to lands, traditional nature-based livelihood and natural resources. Such an application of the law not only implies that international law obligations are in danger of being violated; it also means that the Sámi are not free to enjoy their cultural rights or have necessary control over their cultural heritage.

81 See inter alia Nrt. (1979), 492 (Varfjell-Stifjell) where Sámi reindeer herders were not affected by the statute of limitations as a result of uncertainty about the ownership of the unregistered land in Finnmark.

82 Ot.prp. nr. 53 (2002-2003), 43.

83 Ibid., 96.

The Self-Governing of Inuit Cultural Heritage in Canada: The Path so Far

Violet Ford

Introduction

For the last few decades, indigenous peoples around the world have sought opportunities and methods to govern their own cultural heritage. In the previous administration, President Obama acknowledged this struggle: on a visit to Alaska, he changed the name of Mount McKinley back to the historical traditional name that the indigenous peoples of Alaska had given to this highest mountain peak in North America – Denali, which means 'the High One'.[1] This step by a world leader to acknowledge the cultural heritage of an indigenous people is positive, as indigenous peoples have faced many challenges regarding the misappropriation and misuse of their cultural heritage. UN bodies continue to look at indigenous cultural heritage, and scholars are currently studying and discussing the many issues that indigenous cultural heritage raises. The goal of this chapter is to discuss how indigenous peoples in the Arctic are governing their cultural heritage. The chapter argues that the Inuit in Canada are governing their cultural heritage to varying degrees and with various results.

The United Nations Educational, Scientific and Cultural Organization (UNESCO) refers to culture as 'the whole complex of distinctive spiritual, material, intellectual and emotional features that characterize a society or social group. It includes not only the arts and letters but also modes of life, the fundamental rights of the human being, value systems, traditions and beliefs.'[2] Cultural heritage, then, may be defined as both the physical, tangible forms of lifestyle and the expression of culture, including buildings, landscapes, artifacts, and archaeological remains, and the intangible expressions of culture, including values, customs, traditional skills, language, and artistic expressions.

1 Roberta Rampton, 'Obama Changing Name of Alaska's Mount McKinley to Denali' Reuters (Washington, 31 August 2015) <www.reuters.com/article/2015/08/31/us-usa-obama-alaska-idUSKCN0QZ0YZ20150831?feedType=RSS&feedName=politicsNews>.

2 United Nations Educational, Scientific and Cultural Organization (UNESCO), *Constitution of the United Nations Educational, Scientific and Cultural Organization(UNESCO)*, 16 November 1945.

Xanthaki, Valkonen et al. (eds.), *Indigenous Peoples' Cultural Heritage: Rights, Debates and Challenges.*
 ISBN 978-90-04-34218-7. PP. 199-217

Indigenous peoples' right to their cultural heritage is now clearly recognized under the United Nations *Declaration on the Rights of Indigenous Peoples*.[3]

Numerous academics, advocates, and stakeholders have studied and written about cultural heritage. Joffe highlights the connection between the principle of free, prior and informed consent (FPIC), a cornerstone of the United Nations *Declaration on the Rights of Indigenous Peoples*, and the protection of cultural heritage,[4] while Prosper argues that the study of cultural landscapes can lead to alternative ways of seeing heritage value centered around relationships.[5]

The relationship between archaeologists and indigenous peoples has been a matter of concern over the last years. Clifford looks at the limits of collaborative work between archeologists and the community.[6] Chirikure and Pwiti rightly suggest that community archaeology empowers previously disenfranchised peoples such as indigenous peoples and local communities that had lost their rights to their heritage through colonialism.[7] They argue that community involvement in archaeology and cultural heritage management has created in some areas a positive relationship between archaeologists and communities. At the same time, they recognize that heritage management and the relinquishment of control by heritage managers and archaeologists has been a challenge; and working towards an equal partnership between the indigenous community and scientists remains a challenge.[8] Specifically on the Inuit, Marianne Stenbaek notes that although the they have faced many cultural changes

3 UN General Assembly, *United Nations Declaration on the Rights of Indigenous Peoples: resolution/adopted by the General Assembly*, 2 October 2007, A/RES/61/295, *see* Articles 11, 12, 13, and 14.

4 Paul Joffe, 'Canada's Opposition to the UN Declaration: Legitimate Concerns or Ideological Bias' in J Hartlet et al. (eds.) *Realizing the UN Declaration on the Rights of Indigenous Peoples: Triumph, Hope, and Action* (2010) 70, 81.

5 Lisa Prosper, 'Wherein Lies the Heritage Value? Rethinking the Heritage Value of Cultural Landscapes from an Aboriginal Perspective' (2007) *The George Wright Forum*, vol 24, no 2, 117.

6 James Clifford, 'Looking Several Ways: Anthropology and Native Heritage in Alaska' (2004), *Current Anthropology* vol 45, no 1, 5.

7 Shadreck Chirikure and Gilbert Pwiti, 'Community Involvement in Archaeology and Cultural Heritage Management: An Assessment from Case Studies in Southern Africa and Elsewhere' (2008) *Current Anthropology* vol 49, no 3, 467.

8 Ibid.

due to the influx of peoples from southern regions, the Inuit culture maintains its strength as a culture of a transnational region.[9]

Traditional knowledge is very important to Inuit. It is a body of knowledge in its own right that reflects who the Inuit are and the worldview that they hold. In their paper, Andrew Stewart, Darren Keith, and Joan Scottie propose that traditional knowledge is played out in the archaeological landscape.[10] Inuit place names are another aspect of Inuit cultural heritage and describe physical or cultural features of the landscape.[11] George Wenzel posits that traditional knowledge has become a political concern because of the appropriation of this knowledge and argues for closer ethical treatment through intellectual property.[12]

What remains rather unexplored in the literature is how the governance of cultural heritage by indigenous peoples within the context of land rights is progressing to date, particularly at the domestic level. Therefore, the question explored in this chapter is the extent to which the protection and promotion of Inuit cultural heritage can be reached under Inuit land claims agreements and the self-government arrangements flowing from these agreements. Its purpose is to look at Inuit governance and the legal arrangements that provide for governance and how these arrangements have created a path for the Inuit control over and management of their cultural heritage.

Inuit in Canada are located in four regions: the western Arctic, the central Arctic, Northern Quebec, and Northern Labrador. Part one provides a sample of the activities that Inuit are carrying out in the governing of their cultural heritage under various legal arrangements. Part two examines other legal arrangements that pertain to the issue of governing and protecting Inuit legal rights. Finally, part three discusses more in depth these findings.

---

9 Marianne Stenbaek, 'Forty Years of Cultural Change among the Inuit in Alaska, Canada and Greenland: Some Reflections' (1987) *Arctic* vol 40, no 4, 30.

10 Andrew Stewart, Darren Keith, and Joan Scottie, 'Caribou Crossings and Cultural Meanings: Placing Traditional Knowledge and Archaeology in Context in an Inuit Landscape' (June 2004) *Journal of Archaeological Method and Theory* vol 11, issue 2, 183.

11 Inuit Heritage Trust, <www.inti/eng/placenames/pp.index.html>.

12 George W. Wenzel, 'Traditional Ecological Knowledge and Inuit: Reflections on TEK Research and Ethics' (1999) *Arctic* vol 22, no 2, 113.

PART ONE: MAKING A PATH FOR INUIT GOVERNANCE OF CULTURAL HERITAGE

First, the paper will examine the legal arrangements under Inuit land claims agreements, the accompanying self-government regimes, and the related land claims provisions. All these agreements have had a direct impact on the protection of Inuit cultural heritage and have allowed the development of cultural institutions where the Inuit have control over the management of their cultural heritage.

Inuit Land Claims Agreements

Before Canada's *Constitution Act* of 1982 came into existence, the Aboriginal Peoples in Canada were not protected. Section 35(1) of Canada's *Constitution Act, 1982*, recognized and affirmed existing Aboriginal and treaty rights of the Aboriginal peoples of Canada. Section 35(3) states that the treaty rights referred to in section 35(1) include 'rights that now exist by way of land claims agreements or may be so acquired'. Therefore, the Inuit land claims agreements are protected. As such, the Inuit land claims agreements are intended to define resource rights and to improve the social, cultural, and economic well being of the Aboriginal people concerned by providing long-term certainty and clarity for land and resource use and management.[13] Self-government goes hand in hand with the constitutional rights reflected in the Land Claims Agreement. The Government of Canada recognizes the inherent right of self-government as an existing Aboriginal right under section 35 of the Constitution.[14] Recognition of inherent rights is based on the view that the Aboriginal peoples of Canada have the right to govern themselves in matters that are internal to their communities; integral to their unique cultures, identities, traditions, languages, and institutions; and pertaining to their special relationship to their land and resources.[15]

---

13 Land Claims Agreements Coalition <www.landclaimscoalition.ca> accessed 15 September 2015.

14 Ibid.

15 The government acknowledges that the inherent right of self-government may be enforceable through the courts and that there are different views about the nature, scope, and content of the inherent right. However, litigation over the inherent right would be lengthy and costly and would tend to foster conflict. In any case, the courts are likely to provide general guidance to the parties involved, leaving it to them to work out detailed arrangements. This includes federal self-government policy.

Rather than trying to define self-government in abstract terms, the government of Canada has developed an approach to implementation that focuses on reaching practical and workable agreements on how self-government will be exercised. There are a number of subject matters where Aboriginal governments or institutions have no or limited law-making authority under these self-government arrangements – for example in the area of intellectual property, such as copyright or trademarks. These are the areas where laws and regulations tend to have impacts that go beyond individual communities; therefore, primary law-making authority remains with the federal or provincial governments, and their laws would prevail in the event of a conflict with Aboriginal laws.[16] However, in practice, to the extent that the federal government has jurisdiction in these areas, it is prepared to negotiate some measure of Aboriginal jurisdiction or authority. Of course, in such areas where impacts are within individual communities, the jurisdiction remains with the Aboriginal authority. In some cases, detailed arrangements are required to ensure the harmonization of laws, while in others, a general recognition of Aboriginal jurisdiction or authority may be sufficient. There are also a number of areas where Aboriginal governments or institutions have no law-making authority at all under these self-government arrangements. These can be grouped under two headings: powers related to Canadian sovereignty, defense, and external relations; and other national interest powers. In these areas, it is essential that the federal government retain its law-making authority.

Let us now have a brief overview of the Inuit land claims agreements and the measures that Inuit have taken to protect and govern their cultural heritage.

The James Bay and Northern Quebec Agreement

In 1975, the Inuit of Nunavik in Northern Quebec signed the James Bay and Northern Quebec Agreement (JBNQA),[17] the first comprehensive Land Claims Agreement in Canada between Aboriginal people and the federal government. Nunavik comprises 14 Inuit communities on the eastern shore of Hudson Bay and Hudson Strait and extends over 560,000 square kilometers. The JBNQA gave rise to new institutions, controlled by Inuit in Nunavik, that include es-

16 Subject matters in this category would include environmental protection and assessment, pollution prevention, fisheries co-management, and migratory birds co-management.

17 This agreement provides provisions that define the land regime as well as Aboriginal rights to resource management and environmental protection. See also *The James Bay and Northern Quebec Settlement Act* S.C 1976-77, c.32 Assented to 1977-07-14.

sential powers related to the management, conservation, and development of Inuit territory and resources.

Following this agreement, the Avataq Cultural Institute, the Inuit cultural organization of Nunavik, was established in 1990 and tasked with protecting and advancing the language and culture of all the Inuit of Nunavik.[18] This institute received its mandate from the Elders. Initiatives taken by this institute include, for example, the production and sale of Northern Delights, an Inuit herbal tea made from plants found in the Nunavik territory. This tea project serves both to preserve and to promote Inuit culture: in the description of its mandate, the Avataq Cultural Institute has expressed that 'We, the Inuit, believe that our ways and this earth must be protected. As such, we are prepared to share our knowledge even as we hold on to our values.'[19] The sale of this tea provides financial resources that may be used to further promote Nunavik Inuit culture. Prior to the launch of the project, the Inuit communities in Nunavik were consulted to ensure the project would reflect Inuit values.[20]

Another interesting example of Inuit cultural heritage and its governance can be found in the area of education. Since 1978, the Inuit of Nunavik have had their own school board – namely the Kativiq School Board. Within this structure, they have placed the learning of mathematics in the context of the Inuit culture and have therefore created a curriculum that demonstrates how mathematics can be linked to the Inuit culture.[21] The existing mathematics curriculum created a challenge for non-Inuit teachers because of a lack of knowledge of Inuit culture. In addition, the curriculum is aligned with the Quebec official curriculum. However, the cultural differences have created various challenges for the schools, such as a disconnection between the mathematics taught in Nunavik schools and the daily experience of Inuit students. For example, the concept of probability means in the Inuit culture a guess, an estimate, whereas in Quebec it is taught as a frequency or an evaluation. Concerns about the differences in indigenous and non-indigenous cultures led to further reflection on how mathematics could be taught in a way that allows Nunavik students to relate to their culture.[22] The lesson development that responded to

18 <www.avataq.qc.ca/en/Home>.

19 <http://deliceboreal.com/avataq-social-entrepreneurs/>.

20 Ibid.

21 Annie Savard, Dominic Manuel, and Terry Wan Jung Lin, 'Incorporating Culture in the Curriculum: The Concept of Probability in Nunavik Inuit Culture' (2014) in *education* vol 19, no 3, 152 <www.//ineducation.ca/ineducation/article/view/125/627> accessed 14 September, 2015.

22 Ibid, p. 3.

this challenge resulted in incorporating cultural objects and moving them into a mathematical context. The mathematical concept of probability for example is related to the Inuit students' environment such as weather patterns, and places survival at the core of their thinking. It was felt by the Kativik School Board that these concepts should be incorporated into the maths curriculum. As a result, the Inuit students study mathematics as a tool of critical thinking and learn to apply mathematics to aspects of Inuit society and culture. This approach was inspired by other theoretical frameworks in which the socio-cultural context bridges the contexts of mathematics and citizenship.

Inuvialuit Land Claims Settlement Act

The Inuvialuit Final Agreement[23] was settled in 1984 between the Inuit of the western Arctic – the Inuvialuit – and Canada. Fully aware of the potential threats of development, the Inuvialuit wanted a strong voice in resource development decisions. Therefore, the agreement includes the state's obligation to provide certainty and clarity in the rights to ownership and use of lands and resources and to take measures to realize the rights for Inuit to participate in decision-making concerning the use, management, and conservation of land, water, and resources, including the offshore. Under this agreement, many bodies exist that allow the Inuvialuit to have genuine input into decisions that affect them. For example, the Inuvialuit Regional Council established the Inuvialuit Cultural Resource Centre, targeted to the Inuit in the Inuvialuit region specifically; the centre's mandate is to preserve and promote the Inuvialuktun language and to provide support for its inclusion in the curriculum.[24] The centre has also produced several books for both children and adults in the Inuvialuktun language. Another example of the activities undertaken by Inuvialuit includes the efforts to examine and document the Inuit artifacts that are now in museums, such as those in the Smithsonian Institute in Washington, D.C.; to explore the relevant collections and to inspect the artifacts. The group's goal is to expand their knowledge on curation of the artifacts, to develop relationships with institutions such as the Smithsonian, to consult with those institutions in order to develop educational projects relating to indigenous cultures, and to disseminate knowledge about the artifacts to both Inuvialuit communities and the wider public.[25] The group from the Inuvialuit Cultural

23 *Agreement Between the Inuit of the Inuvialuit Settlement Area and Her Majesty the Queen in Right of Canada* (Ottawa: Indian and Northern Affairs and Northern Development, 1984) [hereinafter Inuvialuit Final Agreement].

24 <www.irc.inuvilauit.com/community/cultural.html>.

25 Maia Lepage, 'Museums and Mukluks' (Winter 2010) *Tusaayaksat*, 29, 37.

Resource Centre has already paid a visit to the Smithsonian Institute, and this trip launched a broader program of outreach with Inuvialuit youth, Elders, and community members, allowing the Inuvialuit "to connect their old culture to the present."[26] The project is now launched in collaboration with the Smithsonian Institute Arctic Studies Center, which focuses on cultural research and education and seeks to bring researchers from the Arctic Studies Center together in collaborative explorations.

Also, the Inuvialuit Self-Government Agreement in Principle[27] has now been signed between the Inuvialuit of the western Arctic, represented by the Inuvialuit Regional Corporation; the government of Canada; and the government of the Northwest Territories. The work is ongoing. The agreement could affect more than 5,000 Inuvialuit and non-Inuit in the Beaufort Delta region, as Aboriginal government will have control over the management of a variety of areas, including culture and heritage.[28] The agreement provides the Inuvialuit with jurisdiction and a broad scope to manage their cultural heritage in ways that they see as appropriate for their particular needs; developing cultural heritage through educational activities is one example.

The Nunavut Land Claims Agreement and the Nunavut Act

The creation of the Territory of Nunavut presupposed a model of self-government where mainstream institutions such as legislatures and courts are tools of Aboriginal government. This region became a self-governing territory in April 1999, following the signing of the Nunavut Land Claims Agreement (NLCA)[29] on May 25, 1993, by the government of Canada, the government of the Northwest Territories, and the Tunngavik Federation of Nunavut, and the enactment of the Nunavut Act. Inuit culture is a cornerstone of both the NLCA and Inuit self-government. According to Paul Okalik, a former premier of Nunavut, 'If Inuit self-government is to manifest itself through the public govern-

---

26 <www.inuvilauit living history> accessed 10 September 2015.

27 www.irc.inuvialuit.com/publications/pdf. This is an agreement between the Inuvialuit Regional Council, the Government of Canada, and the Government of the Northwest Territories.

28 <www.aadnc-aandc.gc.ca/eng/> This agreement will be legally binding when it is ratified by the Inuvialuit Regional Council, the Government of Canada, and the Government of the Northwest Territories.

29 *Agreement Between the Inuit of the Nunavut Settlement Area and Her Majesty the Queen in Right of Canada* (Ottawa: Indian and Northern Affairs and Northern Development, 1993) [hereinafter Nunavut Land Claims Agreement].

ment, Inuit culture will have to become apparent in policies and operation.'[30] The Nunavut Department of Culture and Heritage was established with a mandate to develop and implement policies to strengthen culture, language, and heritage for all people in Nunavut.[31]

The preamble of the NLCA points out that 'the *Constitution Act, 1982* recognizes and affirms the existing aboriginal and treaty rights of the aboriginal peoples of Canada, and treaty rights includes rights that may be acquired by way of land claims agreements.' The articles in the NLCA provide principles for the various aspects of Inuit cultural heritage in Nunavut. Article 33 recognizes the connection that the archeological record has with Inuit spirit, culture, and education. It recognizes the rights and interests of Inuit in the archaeological areas and provides that Nunavut Inuit will manage the archaeology of the territory, including Inuit involvement in the design of policies and legislation.[32]

Section 33.4.1 of the NCLA establishes a heritage trust with certain powers and functions to manage the Inuit cultural heritage, including the facilitation of the conservation and display of archaeological sites. The trust's mandate is to preserve, enrich, and protect Inuit cultural heritage and identity embodied in archeological sites, ethnographic resources, and traditional place names. Section 33.5.1 establishes a permit system with respect to the protection of archaeological sites. This provision gives the trust the ability to control archaeological activities on Inuit lands and manage the activities surrounding archaeological sites within the Nunavut territory, under section 33.5.9 of the land claims agreement. Enacted under the authority of the *Nunavut Act*,[33] pursuant to subsection 51(1) of that act, the Nunavut Archaeological and Palaeontological Sites Regulations provide for the protection of archaeological sites in Nunavut. Under section 4 of the regulations, permits are required for projects. Under section 13, archaeological and paleontological sites must be returned to their original state after completion of an excavation. And under section 14, permit holders are required to submit reports to the Inuit Heritage Trust, the appropriate minister in the Government of Nunavut, and the Canadian Museum of Civilization.

Part 9 of Article 33 of the NLCA specifies that the Inuit Heritage Trust can and will review the official names of locations, geographic features, and landmarks in the Nunavut Settlement Area and may change these official names – that is, the names imposed by non-Inuit colonizers – back to the traditional

30 Ibid, 7.

31 <www.ch.gov.nu.ca/en/home.aspx>.

32 Article 33.3.1, Part 2.

33 S.C.1993, c 28.

names that the Inuit used. The Inuit Heritage Trust which is comprised of Inuit members from Nunavut is now gathering information from Elders about traditional place names.[34] So far, over 8,000 names have been collected.

Further, Nunavut has developed a human remains policy that states that any archaeological investigation or analysis of human remains will be carried out in a way that is sensitive to Nunavummiut[35] values and ethical and scientific principles and that complies with all applicable laws, codes of conduct, and conventions.[36] This policy is based on respect for the dead and the spiritual and cultural interests and views of Inuit under Article 33 of the ILCA. The policy specifies that "'the excavation of human remains will be permitted only under exceptional circumstances', and only after consultation with land claims authorities.[37]

The NLCA also established the Nunavut Wildlife Management Board (NWMB), under Articles 5 and 15 of the NLCA. According to Article 5.9.5, the NWMB's duties include establishing and managing harvest levels; allocating resources to other residents; identifying wildlife management zones; approving plans for managing wildlife habitats within conservation areas, territorial parks, and national parks; providing advice about compensation by commercial and industrial developers that cause damage to wildlife habitats; and regulating access to wildlife in Nunavut. The NWMB also allows the Inuit to regulate harvesting practices among members, including, for example, assessing the specific harvesting needs in the community for food and trade. The NLCA also established the Nunavut Impact Review Board (NIRB) to screen, assess, and recommend or not development project proposals and to monitor projects to assess their eco-systemic and socio-economic impacts. According to Article 12.2.24 of the NLCA, in doing its work, the NIRB is to be guided by 'the broad application of the principles of natural justice and procedural fairness' and specifically to 'give due regard and weight to the tradition of Inuit oral communication and decision-making'.

The government of Nunavut has developed policies to protect and promote its intangible cultural property. In particular, Inuit Qaujimajatuqangi (IQ) is a

34 Nick Walker, 'Mapping Traditional Place Names in Canada's North' (July /August 2013) <www.canadiangeographic.ca/magazine/ja13/Inuit_heritage>.

35 Nunavummiut are the people inhabiting the territory of Nunavut.

36 Department of Culture, Language, Elders and Youth: Culture and Heritage Program (Archaeology): Human Remains Policy <http://www.gov.nu.ca/sites/default/files/files/Human%20Remains%20Policy.pdf>.

37 Ibid.

form of knowledge, 'a new organic way of knowing',[38] understanding and explaining Nunavut. IQ is Inuit traditional knowledge gained and passed down through generations now being applied to social and economic development, governance, and education, based on the principle that better, far more relevant and palatable solutions to some modern issues can and will flow out of closer adherence to ancient Inuit wisdom. IQ goes further than contextualizing traditional knowledge. It is, by one definition, 'a living technology, a means of rationalizing thought and action, a means of organizing tasks and resources, a means of organizing family and society into coherent wholes.'[39]

IQ embodies and reflects Inuit traditional knowledge and values, including the relationship of the Inuit to the land and nature, is responsive to the needs of Inuit in Nunavut, and is a vehicle to shape policy, guiding the government in its framing of decisions, policies, and laws that reflect the key philosophies, attitudes, and practices of the Nunavummiut. Indeed, IQ has been integrated into the policies of new self-government arrangements. An IQ working group in the Nunavut's Department of Sustainable Development defined six guiding principles for policy and program development based on IQ:[40]

1. *Pijitsirniq* (or the concept of serving). This principle lays out the roles and relationships between the organization and the people it serves;
2. *Aajiiqatigiingniq* (or the concept of consensus decision-making). Tied in with this concept is the need to develop a standardized consultation process for the government of Nunavut and the Inuit organizations;
3. *Pilimmaksarniq* (or the concept of skills and knowledge acquisition). This concept was added to ensure a meaningful capacity-building adjunct to all government community-empowerment exercises. More research into teaching and learning practices needs to be done;
4. *Piliriqatigiingniq* (or the concept of collaborative relationships or working together for a common purpose). The initial research that Joelie Sanguya, an Inuit consultant from Clyde River, conducted with Inuit Elders for Sustainable Development suggested strongly that the communities

38 Larry Simpson, 'An Inuit Way of Knowing and the Making of Nunavut' (1 August 2004) *Policy Options* <http://policyoptions.irpp.org/issues/social-policy-in-the-21st-century/an-inuit-way-of-knowing-and-the-making-of-nunavut/>.

39 Jaypetee Arnakak, 'Commentary: What is Inuit Qaujimajatuqangit?' (25 August 2000) *Nunatsiaq News* <http://www.nunatsiaqonline.ca/archives/nunavut000831/nvt20825_17.html>.

40 The following principles are quoted from Arnakak, 'Commentary: What is Inuit Qaujimajatuqangit?'

wanted to be full and meaningful partners in all community and social development activities;
5. *Avatimik Kamattiarniq* (or the concept of environmental stewardship);
6. *Qanuqtuurunnarniq* (or the concept of being resourceful to solve problems). There is no single defining factor of being Inuit, but this comes close. Inuit culture is qanuqtuurniq.

Such principles are now reflected in Nunavut's *Wildlife Act*,[41] which points out in its preamble that IQ 'means traditional Inuit values, knowledge, behavior, perceptions, and expectations'.[42] It is evident that the government of Nunavut, armed with the Nunavut Land Claims Agreement, has developed a complex approach to protecting and advancing Nunavummiut cultural heritage in the day-to-day administration decision-making and practices.

The Labrador Inuit Land Claims Agreement

The Labrador Inuit Land Claims Agreement (LILCA)[43] provides similar opportunities for Nunatsiavut, the Inuit area in the Canadian province of Newfoundland and Labrador. In its first chapter, entitled 'General Definitions and Interpretation', the agreement clarifies that 'Inuit Law' means law of the Nunatsiavut government and includes both subordinate legislation under law of the Nunatsiavut government and any Inuit customary law that is proclaimed, published, and registered in accordance with the registry of laws, thus acknowledging the role of customary laws. The agreement states that the Nunatsiavut government shall 'maintain a public registry of the Labrador Inuit Constitution, Inuit Laws, including Inuit customary laws in respect of matters within the jurisdiction of the Nunatsiavut government, and Bylaws.' The aim of these provisions is to provide a sense of cultural well-being and to ensure the Nunatsiavut government governs activities on its homelands.

The Nunatsiavut government 'has the exclusive authority to establish, impose and collect fees, charges, rents and royalties for commercial Harvesting of Plants in Labrador Inuit Lands.' The principle of free, prior and informed consent (FPIC) is applied through the Torngat Wildlife and Plants Co-Management Board, which is comprised of seven members. Three of the members are appointed by the Nunatsiavut government and are Inuit. Two are appointed

41 SNu 2003, c.26.

42 Ibid.

43 *Agreement between the Inuit of Labrador and Her Majesty the Queen in Right of Canada* (Ottawa: Indian and Northern Affairs and Northern Development, 2005) [hereinafter Labrador Inuit Land Claims Agreement].

by the provincial government and one is appointed by the Canadian government. This board has the power and responsibility to make recommendations regarding the conservation and managements of wildlife, plants, and habitat, and the research activities that may be carried out in areas of important biological activity. Labrador Inuit have the right to harvest wildlife and plants subject to Inuit laws – and the Nunatsiavut government can make laws regarding the collection and publication of Inuit traditional knowledge about wildlife, plants, and habitat, such as laws in relation to the quantities of plants that may be harvested in Labrador Inuit lands. According to the LILCA, harvesting in the Labrador Inuit Settlement Area is also subject to legislation implementing the terms of an international agreement that was in effect at the time the LILCA came into effect. Like other land claims agreements, the LILCA acknowledges the significance of cultural material, such as archaeological material. Under the agreement, the federal government must consult with the Nunatsiavut government with respect to archaeological activities and national parks, for example, and the provincial government of Newfoundland and Labrador must assist in the recovery of Inuit cultural heritage.[44] The Nunatsiavut government has jurisdiction and control over the creation of laws to protect archaeological and cultural material.[45] Furthermore, Canada and Newfoundland and Labrador must consult the Nunatsiavut government prior to passing legislation in this area.[46]

As is the case in Nunavut, in Nunatsiavut, permits for archaeological activities are required.[47] With respect to human remains, the agreement specifies that the cultural affiliation of human remains must be determined as Inuit, not Inuit, or not able to be determined.[48] The Nunatsiavut government currently does not have an approved policy on the repatriation of human remains and burial objects from archeological sites in Nunatsiavut.[49] However, the Nunatsiavut government has given a mandate to its department of Culture, Recreation and tourism the mandate to carry out consultations.[50]

The LILCA provides the Inuit of Labrador with opportunities to undertake cultural heritage activities and to play a role in the management of Inuit cul-

44 Ibid., ch. 15.2.3.

45 Ibid., ch. 15.3.1.

46 Ibid., ch. 15.5.1.

47 Ibid., ch. 15.6.

48 Ibid., ch. 15.7.2.

49 See www.nunatsiavut.com/article/public-consultations.

50 Ibid.

tural heritage.[51] As a past Inuit leader in Nunatsiavut said, 'Heritage is so important; our history is what made us who we are today. It surrounds and binds us together...'[52] To date, the Nunatsiavut government has taken a number of steps, including adding previously unrecorded archaeological sites to the government's archeological database so that these sites are considered before any future development.

The Nunatsiavut government has also taken steps to repatriate the remains of Labrador Inuit located outside the territory. In 2010 the remains of Labrador Inuit located in a Chicago museum were returned and reburied in Labrador, and the Nunatsiavut government is now holding public consultations to determine whether the human remains of an Inuit found in the French Natural History Museum in Paris will be brought back to their original homeland.[53]

The Nunatsiavut government's Department of Culture and Tourism is responsible for the Torngasok Cultural Centre, which focuses on the preservation, protection, promotion, and advancement of the Labrador Inuit language and culture. One of the centre's initiatives is the Illisautikka Inuttitut Initiative, which involves the development and distribution of learning tools. The learning tools are intended to preserve, protect and promote Inuit language and culture.[54]

The Nunatsiavut government, along with other organizations in the province, including among many others the Labrador Heritage Society, Parks Canada, and the government of Newfoundland and Labrador, participates in the Nunatsiavut Heritage Forum, which began in 2010. The first Heritage Forum launched the Inuksuit Project, in which Elders talk about how inuksuit[55] are being constructed and also express concern that inuksuit are losing their meaning. More than 100 sites of inuksuit have been located so far.[56]

---

51 Ibid., ch. 15.2.1.

52 Patty Pottle, Minister of Aboriginal Affairs for the Government of Newfoundland and Labrador, speech at the 2011 Heritage Forum in Hopedale. The Heritage Forum is part of province-wide initiative and is a community-based gathering.

53 CBC News, 'Remains of Abraham Ulrikab May Be Returned to Labrador' (13 May 2015) <http://www.cbc.ca/news/canada/north/remains-of-abraham-ulrikab-may-be-returned-to-labrador-1.3072310> retrieved 9/9/2015.

54 www.nunatsiavut.com/department/cultural centre.

55 *Inuksuit* is the plural of *inukshuk*.One of their purposes is to provide direction in the harsh arctic environment.

56 Jon Beale and Jamie Brake, *Heritage Forum 2011 Report* (2012) Nunatsiavut Government, 15 <http://www.nunatsiavut.com/wp-content/uploads/2014/02/Heritage-Forum-Report-2011.pdf>.

The LILCA is the most recent Inuit land claims agreement to be settled. The agreement provides opportunities for Inuit in this land claims region to participate in the governing of their cultural heritage, including through consultations with the Nunatsiavut government under the principle of FPIC. The initiatives and activities undertaken so far offer insight into how this land claims agreement is actually working to provide Inuit with governance over their cultural heritage. However, it may too soon to draw any conclusion about the extent to which they may be able to govern their cultural heritage in the future.

PART TWO: OTHER LEGAL ARRANGEMENTS THAT PERTAIN TO THE GOVERNANCE AND PROTECTION OF INUIT LEGAL RIGHTS

Beyond the land claims agreements, other Canadian legislation has a bearing on the question of cultural heritage. Intellectual property legislation in particular is important for the protection of intangible cultural heritage. However, Canada's intellectual property regime does not reflect the many views and values of indigenous communities and other aspects that possibly comprise what indigenous peoples' intangible cultural heritage is. Neither does the existing legal regime take into account, for example, the protocols that indigenous peoples apply and practice in their respective communities when these types of heritage are considered.

Canada's *Copyright Act*[57] provides the legal framework within which creators and other rights holders are entitled to recognition and control of and payment for the use of their work. The objective of the *Copyright Act* is to grant rights to authors to ensure their work is properly credited. The legislation covers only the expression of the ideas in a particular work and does not include the ideas that are conveyed by the actual artistic work. Copyright establishes the economic and moral rights of creators and other rights holders to control the publication and commercial exploitation of their works to protect the integrity of their endeavors and ensure that they are properly remunerated. For a work to be protected by copyright, it must be original and contain an expression of the author's creativity. Copyright protects expressions but not ideas, procedures, processes, systems, and methods of operation, concepts, principles, or discoveries. This legislation encourages individual interests and individualistic values that are dominant in mainstream society. Case law is another place to look for support for the rights of indigenous people to govern

57 *Copyright Act*, R.S.1985, c. C-46.

their cultural heritage. In Canada, case law provides for a duty to consult when Aboriginal rights are claimed. In the *Sparrow* decision, the Supreme Court of Canada stated that the crown is *obliged to consult* with First Nations who assert the existence of rights under section 35 of the *Constitution Act, 1982*.

The higher courts have also set down the conditions of duties to consult under land claims agreements specifically. In the case of *Nunavut Tunngavik v. Canada*,[58] the Court held that in light of the provision of the agreement, there must be activities and results that reflect the intent of the agreement, including meaningful inclusion in the decision-making process before any decisions are made. In this case the Inuit used Article 5 of the Nunavut land claims agreement that set out the principles of the relationship between Canada and the Nunavut Inuit.

The 1998 *Makivik Corp v. Canada (Minister of Canadian Heritage) (T.D.)* was about the comprehensive claims negotiations that Nunavik Inuit and the Labrador Inuit Association had been engaged with the federal government. A framework agreement had been negotiated between the Nunavik Inuit and the federal government, which recognized the claims of the Nunavik Inuit without any ultimate resolution of the issue of their Aboriginal rights or title in Labrador. The federal policy for the establishment of national parks purported to operate within the framework of protection for Aboriginal interests. The Labrador Inuit had participated in the five-stage process for the creation of a park, while the Nunavik Inuit were excluded. The position of the Nunavik Inuit was that they were not requesting a determination of any Aboriginal rights to land in Labrador, but rather recognition of the procedural obligations of the federal government flowing from its agreements to negotiate a treaty in settlement of a comprehensive land claim. The federal government held that the Crown's fiduciary duty could be satisfied by the involvement of Aboriginal peoples in decisions with respect to their lands and that this gives rise to a duty of consultation. The nature and scope of the duty would vary with the circumstances. The establishment of a national reserve might have a minimal impact on Aboriginal title. The Federal Court used the following principles in granting the declaratory relief: first, the Court held that the fiduciary relationship that exists between the Crown and Aboriginal peoples may be satisfied by the involvement of Aboriginal peoples in decisions taken with respect to their lands. In addition, there is a duty of consultation, and consultation must be done in good faith and with the intention of substantially addressing the concerns of the Aboriginal peoples whose rights and lands area at issue. Also, the Court held that all Aboriginal nations that have a stake in the territory claimed

58 (1997) 134 F.T.R.246 (F.C.T.D.) 269.

should be included in the negotiations; and, pursuant to section 35(1) of the *Constitution Act*, Aboriginal rights that existed and were recognized under the common law are elevated to constitutional status. Therefore, according to the Court, the federal government had a duty to consult with Nunavik Inuit prior to establishing a park reserve, which included the duty to inform and listen. It also had a duty to consult and negotiate in good faith the Nunavik Inuit claims to Aboriginal rights prior to the establishment of a national park.

PART THREE: THE PATH SO FAR

This paper examined to what extent a Canadian legal regime of Inuit land claims agreements, the existing intellectual property law, and case law can provide Inuit with governance over their cultural heritage. The next section evaluates the role of Inuit land claims agreements in the governing of Inuit cultural heritage and the ongoing matters that require further attention in the ongoing efforts to govern Inuit cultural heritage.

Land Claims and Self-Government

In a broad sense, the Inuit land claims agreements have been a response to the political struggles that Inuit have experienced as a result of colonization. Part of the colonization process was the loss of control over their cultural heritage. Now, the Inuit land claims provisions and accompanying Inuit self-government arrangements are providing a legal framework from within which Inuit may begin to govern their own cultural heritage. The land claims agreements and legislation flowing from these agreements and accompanying self-government arrangements have provided Inuit with a response to the misuse of their cultural heritage. The different Inuit land claims agreements and their respective provisions determine how cultural heritage will be governed and what aspects of cultural heritage will be advanced and how they will be promoted and protected. As shown in this chapter, the activities undertaken by the respective land claim agreements vary among the land claims regions. This chapter also suggested that the land claims agreements truly are providing Inuit with the ability to determine for themselves how they want to govern their cultural heritage. At this time of transition to Inuit self-governance, challenges to further efforts to protect their cultural heritage are ongoing, the dominant society's views and archeologists' beliefs are largely unchanged, and relationships between communities and archeologists are sometimes frail.

The Canadian Intellectual Property Regime

Even though the rights of Inuit to their cultural heritage are affirmed and protected under Canada's Constitution, protection of their intangible property, such as cultural expression, remains unchanged. Inuit intellectual property is now in the public domain, and so the federal government has taken the position that it does not require protection.[59] The history of copyright law in Canada dates back to before Confederation, before 1867.[60] This legislation encourages the individual interests and individualistic values that are dominant in mainstream society. The existing intellectual property legislation, such as the *Copyright Act*, illuminates the relationship among knowledge, power, and authority in that it still represents the values and interests of the dominant society. The existing intellectual property regime remains grounded within a white, patriarchal, middle-class system of values that reflect the traditional image of legal liberalism, the rule of law, and, therefore, the status quo.

Canada's intellectual property legislation limits the extent to which Inuit can protect their intangible cultural heritage. The *Copyright Act* cannot fully protect Inuit rights to their intangible property or provide a means for governance over it. This lack of protection may be due in part to a lack of shared understanding between the dominant society's perspectives and the values that Inuit hold toward their cultural heritage, the meaning and value of this type of cultural heritage, and the different relationships that Inuit have to their cultural symbols. The existing intellectual property regime does not reflect the views and perspectives of Inuit and does not reflect the other legal obligations that Canada has under the Inuit land claims agreements.

Case Law

Although Canada's intellectual property legislation does not see Inuit intangible property as something that can or should be protected under existing intellectual property legislation, Canada's higher courts have nevertheless acknowledged that steps must be taken when legislation infringes on existing Aboriginal rights. The case law affirms that when an Aboriginal right can be claimed, based on the section 35 rights, the government is obligated to consult with Aboriginal peoples according to this right. In examining other legal rights that Inuit are provided through their land claim agreements, it can be argued strongly that the intellectual property regime interferes with the Aboriginal

59 WIPO, *Intergovernmental Committee on Intellectual Property and Genetic Resources, Traditional Knowledge and Folklore* 2nd Sess, UN Doc.GRTKF/IC/2/16 Prov., 41.

60 David Vaver, *Copyright Law* (Irwin Law Inc. 2000) 2-4.

rights of the Inuit and interferes with the goals and objectives of the Inuit land claim agreements.

The case law indicates that when negotiating with Aboriginal groups in Canada, the government must be mindful of the overlap between different Aboriginal groups; each group must be respected based on its Aboriginal rights under its land claim agreement. Thus, the legal principle emerging from this jurisprudence has been seen as a triggering mechanism to further involve Inuit in legislation that has an impact on their Aboriginal rights, such as their Aboriginal rights to the protection of their intangible property. Because the Inuit land claims are a section 35 right, the protection of Inuit cultural heritage rights must be heeded, especially if they are to be involved in any laws that affect this right. Copyright legislation does not reflect the obligations of government as set out under the Inuit land claims agreements.

Conclusions

Some progress has been made in terms of Inuit regaining control over their cultural heritage. The goals and aspirations of indigenous peoples can be achieved when the values and beliefs of a single cultural grouping are identified and there is a shared understanding of what is important and a recognition that relationships with others – for instance, archaeologists – are important to maintain for mutual benefit. However, it is important to note that all Inuit cannot be painted with the same brush; the different regions have their own goals and aspirations. Cultural heritage is tied to the land, and there is a two-way relationship between protecting and promoting cultural heritage and furthering the Inuit's ability to survive on the land. Cultural heritage is also significant for language and education.

The findings of this chapter show that Inuit have gained governance over their tangible cultural heritage, which is both a generator and a product of decolonization. However, Inuit still do not have control over their intangible property, and therefore the control and governance over their cultural heritage has been extended only within the context of the various land claims agreements.

The steps to be taken to ensure that Inuit rights to all forms of their cultural heritage are protected and that full Inuit control and governance are achieved lie in the broader political context and are addressed under more recent human rights provisions, including the *Declaration of the Rights of Indigenous Peoples*, which has yet to be fully implemented.

Cultural Heritage, Traditional Knowledge and Intellectual Property[1]

Daphne Zografos Johnsson and Hai-Yuean Tualima

Introduction

The notion of cultural or natural heritage has evolved considerably to include 'traditional knowledge'. The term traditional knowledge, or its abbreviation 'TK', is sometimes used to describe the entire field of traditional knowledge (TK) and traditional cultural expressions (TCEs). There are presently no agreed definitions of TK and TCEs, but TK can be described to refer to a living body of knowledge that is developed, sustained and passed on from generation to generation within a community, often forming part of its cultural and spiritual identity. It encompasses knowledge, know-how, skills, innovations and practices that are passed between generations, in a traditional context, and that form part of the traditional lifestyle of indigenous and local communities who act as their guardian or custodian. TK can be, for example, agricultural, environmental or medicinal knowledge, or knowledge associated with genetic resources. TCEs can be described as the forms in which traditional culture is expressed. They can be, for example, dances, songs, handicrafts, designs, ceremonies, tales, or many other artistic or cultural expressions.[2]

---

1 *This article does not necessarily represent the views of the World Intellectual Property Organization (WIPO) or any of its Member States. It is not a substitute for legal advice. Its purpose is limited to providing basic information and draws from WIPO pre-existing publications and in particular from 'Intellectual Property and Genetic Resources, Traditional Knowledge and Traditional Cultural Expressions. An Overview'. All WIPO publications for further reading and more in-depth analysis and study are available from WIPO at : www.wipo.int/tk and, particularly, www.wipo.int/tk/en/resources.*

WIPO is one of the specialized agencies of the United Nations and the leading intergovernmental organization dedicated to the promotion and use of IP. WIPO seeks to develop a balanced and effective international IP system that rewards creativity, stimulates innovation and contributes to the economic, social and cultural development of all countries, while safeguarding the public interest.

2 A WIPO Glossary of Key Terms proposes definitions and descriptions of the terms used most frequently in the field. It is available at http://www.wipo.int/tk/en/resources/glossary.html.

Xanthaki, Valkonen et al. (eds.), *Indigenous Peoples' Cultural Heritage: Rights, Debates and Challenges.*

Intellectual property (IP) refers to creations of the mind such as inventions; literary and artistic works; designs; and symbols, names and images used in commerce. IP is protected in law by, for example, patents, copyright and trademarks, which enable people to earn recognition or financial benefit from what they invent or create. Under the conventional IP system, TK and TCEs are generally regarded as being in the public domain and, therefore, not eligible for IP protection. TK and TCEs, from the perspective of people outside the communities (or 'third parties'), constitute a rich, affordable, and in many cases, easily accessible source of inspiration and innovation, if not a template for reproduction or superficial adaptation.

In recent years, indigenous peoples and local communities as well as governments, mainly in developing countries, have demanded IP protection for traditional forms of creativity and innovation, thereby rejecting a public domain status of TK and TCEs.They argue the issue of the public domain opens them up to misappropriation and unwanted use, harms their cultural identity and deprives them of the benefits that they could otherwise draw from their use.[3] Those stakeholders ask for a more balanced IP system that would meet their interests and concerns as holders and custodians of a rich and diverse cultural heritage that should be protected as part of their identity and as a potential source of income.

Indigenous peoples and local communities have unique needs and expectations in relation to IP, given their complex social, historical, political and cultural dimensions and vulnerabilities. They face challenges unlike any other that IP law has yet presented, as the protection of TK and TCEs intersect every category of IP and often involve other legal issues, as well as ethical and cultural sensitivities, reaching well beyond IP.

Importantly, human rights form a crucial part of the context for protection of TK, TCEs and GRs, insofar as the needs and interests of their holders are concerned. In 2007, the United Nations General Assembly adopted the Unit-

3 The debate about appropriate protection centers on whether, and how, changes should be made to the existing boundary between the public domain and the scope of IP protection. The term 'public domain' refers to elements of IP that are ineligible for private ownership and the contents of which any member of the public is legally entitled to use. Elements of IP that are in the public domain should not be confused with those that are 'publicly available', for example, content on the Internet may be publicly available but not in the public domain from an IP perspective. A WIPO document, *Note on the Meanings of the Term 'Public Domain' in the Intellectual Property System with Special Reference to the Protection of Traditional Knowledge and Traditional Cultural Expression/Expressions of Folklore* (document WIPO/GRTKF/IC/17/INF/8) provides a detailed analysis of the application of this concept to the protection of TK and TCEs.

ed Nations Declaration on the Rights of Indigenous Peoples. The Declaration recognizes that 'indigenous peoples and individuals are free and equal to all other peoples and individuals and have the right to be free from any kind of discrimination, in the exercise of their rights, in particular that based on their indigenous origin or identity' (Article 2). Article 31 provides that indigenous peoples 'have the right to maintain, control, protect and develop their Intellectual Property over such cultural heritage, traditional knowledge and traditional cultural expressions.' The Declaration is frequently referred to in the work of the World Intellectual Property Organization (WIPO).

In 1998, WIPO launched an ambitious work programme on those issues, starting with world-wide fact-finding missions in 1998 and 1999[4], regional consultations, workshops and roundtables concerning TK, TCEs and genetic resources, to ascertain the needs and expectations of indigenous peoples and local communities as well as government representatives and representatives of industry and civil society around the world. In 2000, WIPO members established and Intergovernmental Committee on Intellectual Property and Genetic Resources, Traditional Knowledge and Folklore (IGC), where exchanges of experiences and building-up of expertise around the issues culminated, in 2009, with the launch of text-based negotiations to develop an international legal instrument or instruments that would ensure the balanced and effective protection of TK, TCEs and genetic resources.[5]

What Does 'Protection' Mean in an IP Context?

'Protection', in the IP context, refers to the use of IP laws, values and principles to prevent unauthorized or inappropriate uses, by third parties, of TK and TCEs. The objective of IP protection is to make sure that the intellectual innovation and creativity embodied in TK or TCEs are not wrongly used.

IP protection can take two forms – positive and defensive protection. Positive protection could enable traditional holders, if they so wish, to acquire and exercise property rights over their TK and TCEs, prevent culturally offensive and demeaning uses by third parties, authorize uses by third parties under mutually agreed terms, and/or financially benefit from their commercial exploi-

4 The report is available at http://www.wipo.int/edocs/pubdocs/en/tk/768/wipo_pub_768.pdf.

5 See Background Brief 2: *The WIPO Intergovernmental Committee on Intellectual Property and Genetic Resources, Traditional Knowledge and Folklore* available at http://www.wipo.int/export/sites/www/tk/en/resources/pdf/tk_brief2.pdf.

tation, for example, through the granting of licenses and earning of fees and royalties or through building up their own handicraft enterprises. Defensive protection, on the other hand, does not grant property rights over the subject matter of TK and TCEs, but aims to stop such rights from being acquired or maintained by third parties. Defensive strategies include the use of documented TK to preclude or oppose patent rights on claimed inventions that make direct use of TK.

Protection in the IP sense is different from 'preservation' and 'safeguarding', which involve the identification, documentation, transmission, revitalization and promotion of cultural heritage. The objective in that case is to ensure that TK and TCEs do not disappear and are maintained and promoted.

'Protection', 'preservation' and 'safeguarding' are not mutually exclusive. Although their objectives are different, implementing them together may be mutually supportive, for example, through documentation and the compilation of inventories. However, these different forms of protection may also conflict. Preservation efforts that document TK and TCEs, particularly in electronic (digitized) form, can make them more accessible and vulnerable to uses that are against the wishes of their holders, thereby undermining the effort to protect them in an IP sense. It is therefore advisable to have policies in place for the strategic management of IP during the recording, digitization and dissemination of TK and TCEs.

Options for the IP Protection of TK and TCEs

The legal options for the IP protection of TK and TCEs that are currently available or discussed, aside from the non-IP options,[6] are large and diverse, both in terms of the scope they would cover and the objectives they would serve. Some countries and communities have already elected some of those options, while others are still considering them.[7] It should also be emphasized that the new IP-related protection does not intend to replace, or interfere with, the customary laws, protocols and practices that define how communities develop,

6 Non-IP legislative and policy measures can include, for example, trade practices, consumer protection and labeling laws, the use of contracts, customary and indigenous laws and protocols, cultural heritage preservation, civil liability and common law remedies such as unjust enrichment, rights of privacy, blasphemy, as well as criminal law.

7 See Background Brief 3: *Developing a National Strategy on Intellectual Property and Traditional Knowledge, Traditional Cultural Expressions and Genetic Resources*, available at http://www.wipo.int/export/sites/www/tk/en/resources/pdf/tk_brief3.pdf.

hold, transmit and use TK and TCEs within their own traditional context.[8] Additionally, it does not mean that conventional IP systems would be forced upon TK and TCEs but rather that values and principles embedded in IP law (such as that creations of the human mind should be protected against misappropriation) could be adapted and redeployed for new subject matter and for new beneficiaries.

When considering those options, it is first necessary to examine the available legal and policy options under conventional IP systems. Existing IP rights can indeed be useful for the protection of TK and TCEs; for example, rights granted by trademarks and geographical indications, as well as the protection afforded by unfair competition laws, can be very helpful in protecting reputations associated with TK and TCEs and related goods and services. If there are gaps in existing national legislation, it may be possible to fill them by adapting the existing IP framework or protecting TK and TCEs through *sui generis* IP systems. These options will be examined in the following paragraphs.

Protecting TK and TCEs with Existing IP Rights

Existing IP laws have been successfully used to protect against some forms of misuse and misappropriation of TK and TCEs, including through the laws of patents, copyright, trademarks, geographical indications and trade secrets.[9]

Existing IP to Protect TCEs

TCEs can sometimes be protected by existing systems, such as copyright and related rights, geographical indications, trademarks and certification and collective marks.

Contemporary original adaptations of TCEs, made by members of the communities or by third parties, may be copyrightable. Copyright protects the products of creativity against certain uses such as reproduction, adaptation, public performance, broadcasting and other forms of communication to the public. Performances of TCEs may come under international related rights protection, such as that provided under the WIPO Performances and Phonograms Treaty, 1996, and the WIPO Beijing Treaty on Audiovisual Performances (2012), on an equal footing with the rights that would be granted to any other performer.

8 See Background Brief 7: *Customary Law and Traditional Knowledge*, available at http://www.wipo.int/export/sites/www/tk/en/resources/pdf/tk_brief7.pdf.

9 WIPO provides information, practical assistance and technical advice to enable traditional holders to make more effective use of existing IP systems, if they so wish to.

Article 15.4 of the Berne Convention for the Protection of Literary and Artistic Works (1886) provides a mechanism for the international protection of unpublished and anonymous works, including TCEs. Copyright can also provide protection against insulting, derogatory, offensive, demeaning or degrading use of a work, an issue that is often a concern in relation to TCEs, which embody spiritual qualities and the very cultural identity of a community.

IP laws that aim at the protection of established reputation, distinctiveness or goodwill, including trademarks, collective or certification marks, geographical indications, as well as unfair competition may offer direct or indirect protection of TCEs, in particular handicrafts, artworks or traditional products intended for commercial exploitation by communities.[10]

Traditional signs and symbols could be directly protected as registered trademarks. Registering and using a trademark can increase consumer recognition of authentic TCEs and add to their commercial value. Registration gives the trademark owner the exclusive right to prevent others from using an identical or confusingly similar mark on identical or similar goods or services. Trademark law also provides protection against the registration of offensive and deceptive marks by others, for example, if someone applies for a trademark that falsely implies that a good or service has an indigenous origin, where such origin would be a significant factor for the purchaser, and this is not actually the case, the trademark must be objected.

Collective and certification marks can be used to inform the public of certain characteristics of the products or services marketed under such marks. Registering and using a collective or certification mark can help indigenous communities to distinguish their TCEs from others, and promote them and the artists who made them nationally and internationally. It can help improve their economic position and ensure that they get fair and equitable returns. Collective and certification marks can also raise public awareness and provide reassurance to consumers as to the authenticity of the goods they are buying. While certification marks or authenticity labels cannot prevent the sale of imitations, they can discourage them by distinguishing the genuine TCEs.

A geographical indication is a sign that can be used on goods with a specific geographical origin and possessing qualities, reputation or characteristics that are essentially attributable to that place of origin. These products are often the result of traditional processes and knowledge, carried forward by a commu-

---

10 See Background Brief 5: Intellectual Property and Traditional Handicrafts, available at http://www.wipo.int/export/sites/www/tk/en/resources/pdf/tk_brief5.pdf and International Trade Center UNCTAD/WTO and WIPO, *Marketing Crafts and Visual Arts: The Role of Intellectual Property: A Practical Guide* (ITC/WIPO: Geneva, 2003).

nity from generation to generation in a given region. TCEs, such as handicrafts made using natural resources, with qualities derived from their geographical origin, may qualify for registration as geographical indications. Geographical indications do not directly protect the actual knowledge or know-how associated with the TCEs. Instead, knowledge often remains in the public domain under conventional IP systems, and is open to misappropriation by third parties. However, they can contribute to their indirect protection in several ways. They can protect TCEs against misleading and deceptive trading practices, protect the reputation or goodwill accumulated over time, and safeguard a niche market. In addition, they can prevent others from using a protected geographical indication on goods that do not come from the defined area or do not possess the requisite quality or characteristics.

Finally, unfair competition law can be used to restrain dishonest practices in the marketplace, and can be a useful means of combating false and misleading claims as to authenticity or origin – for example, where a cheaply made souvenir item carries a label falsely indicating that it is 'authentic', 'indigenous made', or originates from a particular community, measures can be taken by those producing the authentic products to prevent those claims.

Existing IP to Protect TK

Existing IP laws have been successfully used to protect TK against some forms of misuse and misappropriation, including the laws of patents, trademarks, geographical indications, industrial design, unfair competition and trade secrets or confidential information.

Innovations that are based on TK and have been developed in a traditional context are, in principle, patentable, just in the same way as innovations that come out of modern laboratories, providing that the patent applicants fulfill the required patentability criteria of novelty, inventiveness and industrial applicability. Besides, existing patent laws requires from patent applicants that they disclose, to some extent, the TK that has been used in, or relates to, their claimed inventions. Such provision grants defensive protection to TK to the extent that technical measure be taken in order to give it any effect in practice. Implementation measures have been adopted internationally to expand and make more widely accessible the content of the documentation that is available on TK as prior art,[11] and improve the search tools available to patent examiners in this regard, including the International Patent Classification System.

The law of confidentiality and trade secrets may also be used to protect non-disclosed TK, including secret and sacred TK. Courts may grant remedies for

11 For example, the Traditional Knowledge Digital Library that has been compiled by India.

breach of confidence when customary laws of secrecy are violated by a third party user who would reveal secrets that were supplied in confidence to him or her.

Adaptation of Existing IP and *Sui Generis* Systems

Debates within and outside WIPO have underlined the limitations of existing IP laws in meeting all the needs and expectations of TK and TCEs holders.[12] TK and TCEs are rooted in the traditions of their holders and not static, but the result of a living and collective creative process, they do not easily fit within the scope of protection that is currently provided by IP rights. For example, while trademark law can provide defensive protection against offensive and deceptive uses of indigenous names, signs and symbols where third parties apply to register such signs as trademarks, it will not prevent the offensive use of such signs where the user does not seek to register a trademark. Moreover, trademark law will not prevent the registration of indigenous names, signs and symbols by third parties where the signs are not considered offensive or deceptive; similarly, while copyright protection may be available for tangible, contemporary TCEs, pre-existing TCEs, and mere imitations and recreations thereof, are unlikely to meet the originality and identifiable author requirements and remain, for copyright purposes, in the public domain. Additionally, TK and TCEs are often held collectively by communities, rather than by individual owners, and collective ownership is often alien to most current IP systems.

Certain adaptations or modifications to IP law may be needed to better accommodate the interests of TK and TCEs holders, and some legal initiatives of that kind have been undertaken both internationally and by particular countries.[13] For example many countries and some regional organizations have opted for directly protecting TCEs by adapting their copyright law, either by referring to TCEs as a form of copyright work, or by including provisions spe-

---

12 For more details, see the two 'gap analysis' prepared by the WIPO Secretariat that appreciate to which extent the existing conventional IP system ensure protection of TCEs and TK respectively. http://www.wipo.int/edocs/mdocs/tk/en/wipo_grtkf_ic_13/wipo_grtkf_ic_13_4_b_rev.pdf and http://www.wipo.int/edocs/mdocs/tk/en/wipo_grtkf_ic_13/wipo_grtkf_ic_13_5_b_rev.pdf.

13 The online WIPO Database of Traditional Knowledge, Traditional Cultural Expressions and Genetic Resources Laws gathers national and regional laws, treaties and regulations on the protection of TK, TCEs and genetic resources. It is freely accessible at http://www.wipo.int/tk/en/databases/tklaws/.

cifically designed for TCEs within their copyright legislations. But it should be reminded that such provisions are not enforceable beyond the boundaries of those countries or regions. Other examples of adaptations, in the field of trademark law, include a the United States of America's Database of Official Insignia of Native American Tribes, which prevents third parties from registering these insignia as trademarks, and the adaptation of New Zealand's trademark law to take into account cultural offensiveness, especially to Maori, in the trademark registration process. At the international level, the principal tool for locating technical information for patent purposes, the International Patent Classification (IPC), has been expanded to take better account of TK subject matter, in particular concerning medicinal products based on plant extracts. This increases the likelihood that patent examiners locate already published TK that is relevant to claimed inventions in patent applications, without adversely affecting the legal status of TK from the point of view of TK holders.

However, in some cases, adapting existing IP rights may not be considered sufficient to cater for the holistic and unique character of TK and TCEs. A decision may then be taken to protect TK and TCEs through *sui generis* systems. *Sui generis* systems are specialized measures or laws aimed exclusively at addressing the characteristics of specific subject matter, such as TK and TCEs. Some countries and regions have opted for such option and have developed their own specific systems for protecting their TK and TCEs.

When considering a *sui generis* system for the protection of TK and TCEs, key questions include defining the objectives of protection and identifying the subject matter to be protected. It is also important to clarify what the TK and TCEs are to be protected against, and what forms of behavior should be considered unacceptable or illegal. Other issues to consider include the formalities to be required (such as registration), the sanctions and penalties that should apply, the exceptions and limitations attached to the rights (for example, the use of TCEs in archives, libraries or museums for non-commercial cultural heritage purposes), the duration of protection, the application in time of legal protection (retroactive or prospective), the enforcement of rights and dispute resolution mechanisms, and the protection of foreign beneficiaries.

The on-going negotiations in the IGC regarding the development of an international legal instrument (or instruments) of protection could possibly lead to the adoption of such as *sui generis* system or systems at the international level.[14] The IGC is considering the key questions highlighted above, but the answers to those questions, and others, remain subject to debate, as the WIPO

14 The two relevant draft texts that have been developed so far as work-in-progress on TK and TCEs, respectively, are available at http://www.wipo.int/edocs/mdocs/tk/en/wipo_

Member States still disagree on basic principles, objectives and substantive provisions. The status of the instrument(s) to be adopted remains open as well, the options ranging from a legally binding treaty to a declaration.

Indigenous Peoples and Local Communities' Participation in the IGC

Since the inception of the IGC, the focus has been on an inclusive approach to promote the direct involvement and meaningful engagement of all stakeholders, especially indigenous peoples and local communities. WIPO's work is founded on extensive consultation with representatives of indigenous peoples and local communities and other NGOs, which are permanent observers to WIPO or specifically accredited to the IGC.[15]

Indigenous peoples and local communities are able to participate and express their views in the IGC decision-making process, in accordance with the 2007 UN Declaration on the Rights of Indigenous Peoples. During IGC sessions, they may intervene on any issue on the agenda and make drafting proposals, which are incorporated in the text under discussion if supported by at least one Member State. Representatives of indigenous peoples and local communities are also included in drafting groups and informal consultations. In 2005, the WIPO General Assembly established a WIPO Voluntary fund to facilitate the participation of accredited indigenous peoples and local communities. Through this mechanism more than 80 representatives of indigenous peoples and local communities from around the world have been funded to participate in IGC sessions.

Each IGC session is preceded by panel presentations chaired by and composed of representatives of indigenous peoples and local communities, whose participation is funded by WIPO. These presentations are an invaluable source of information on the experiences, concerns and aspirations of indigenous peoples and local communities regarding the protection, promotion and preservation of GRs, TK and TCEs.

Other practical measures to enhance the participation of indigenous peoples and local communities in the IGC have included briefings, consultative processes and logistical support. Practical Workshops for Indigenous Peoples and Local Communities on IP and GRs, TK and TCEs are also organized by

grtkf_ic_28/wipo_grtkf_ic_28_5.pdf and http://www.wipo.int/edocs/mdocs/tk/en/wipo_grtkf_ic_28/wipo_grtkf_ic_28_6.pdf.

15 Information on participation: http://www.wipo.int/tk/en/igc/participation.html.

WIPO, which impart knowledge of the main principles of the IP system, and explain, amongst other things, the rationale, objectives and methodology of the negotiations that are taking place in the IGC.[16]

Finally, since 2009, WIPO has offered the opportunity for an Indigenous Fellow to work, within the WIPO Secretariat, on issues relevant to IPLCs, including the IGC. The WIPO Indigenous Fellowship builds on a series of initiatives to ensure that indigenous peoples are actively involved in the work of WIPO on issues that matter to them and recognizes the strong expertise that exists within indigenous communities.[17]

Conclusion

By providing a specialized forum for the structured exchange of information and views within WIPO, the IGC process has succeeded in building up a robust international understanding of the issues. Its discussions have taken place with the firm and, since 2009, explicit objective of reaching agreement on an international legal instrument (or instruments) that will ensure the balanced and effective protection of TK, TCEs and genetic resources. The exploratory 'forum' has evolved into a true negotiating body, framed by clear and tight schedules and sound working methods.

Recognizing traditional forms of creativity and innovation as protectable IP would be an historic shift in international law, enabling indigenous peoples and local communities as well as governments to have a say over the use of their TK and TCEs by third parties. However, the issues are complex and there is no 'one-size-fits-all' solution likely to suit all the needs of holders in all countries. Diversity is the very essence of TK and TCEs, precisely because they are so closely intertwined with the cultural identity of many diverse communities, and convergence requires flexibility and time in fashioning an international instrument.

---

16 Information on the Practical Workshops: http://www.wipo.int/tk/en/indigenous/workshop.html.

17 Information on the WIPO Indigenous Fellowship Program: http://www.wipo.int/tk/en/indigenous/fellowship/.

Wider Use of Traditional Sámi Dress in Finland: Discrimination against the Sámi?

Piia Nuorgam

1 Introduction

1.1 *Wider Use of Sámi Dress and its Effects on Sámi Culture*

In 2014, Tanja Poutiainen, a successful Finnish Alpine skier, finished her long career in slalom racing at an event in Austria. After Poutiainen's final race, she donned an outfit that had been bought from a Finnish company called Pilailupuoti (lit. "joke shop") which was very similar to the Sámi *gákti*, the traditional clothing of the Sámi people. This obvious, yet extremely poor, copy of the Sámi *gákti* is marketed by Pilailupuoti for fancy balls and similar occasions as "Pohjolanasu" (lit. costume of the North) at its shops around Finland and on its website.[1] Pilailupuoti even places this costume in the same category as other clothing designed to imitate the "Spaniards, Roma and other foreigners". The Sámi criticised Poutiainen for choosing what was obviously non-authentic Sámi clothing and an offensive imitation of the *gákti* and the criticism was noted in the media.[2]

That same year the Sámi association *Mii* in Rovaniemi[3] received a request from a central European couple, through a Finnish friend of theirs. The couple was planning to wed at a local reindeer farm in Rovaniemi during the winter and planned a small wedding celebration with their closest family. For this event they requested the Sámi association to provide them with 14 children between the ages of 5 and 7 to line the aisle in traditional dress, ostensibly to act as some sort of aesthetic accoutrements to their nuptial. This request included detailed instructions on how the children should stand and graciously offered to pay a small fee for the children's services.

These two cases are far from unique. Sámi culture and dress have been exploited outside of the Sámi for commercial purposes in Finland for decades, as

---

1 'Costume of North', Pilailupuoti-shop <http://www.pilailupuoti.com/tuote/pohjolan-asu/> accessed 20 December 2015.

2 <http://yle.fi/uutiset/tanja_poutiaisen_pukuvalintaa_kritisoidaan_voimakkaasti/7140720>, accessed 15 December 2015.

3 Rovaniemi is the administrative capital of Finland's northernmost province, Lapland, and is located near the Arctic Circle.

Xanthaki, Valkonen et al. (eds.), *Indigenous Peoples' Cultural Heritage: Rights, Debates and Challenges.*

a product or as component of services. This is especially the case in Lapland, the northern part of the country.[4] Frequently, the Sámi people and culture are represented outside of the Sámi community in old-fashioned ways, which maintain stereotypes and prejudices. For example, they are romanticized, described as shamans or drunkards, as living in primitive villages, or as Santa's helpers. This caricature is apparent in the 2015 tourism promotion video '100 Days of Polar Night Magic', made by the state-funded company 'Visit Finland'.[5] In '100 Days of Polar Night Magic' the Sámi are presented as dirty shamans chanting, dancing and singing in their *lavvu*, a traditional tent.

Sámi culture and dress are exploited by non-Sámi entities in all kinds of products and services; indeed, one of the most popular souvenirs in Lapland in 2014 was a doll in mock Sámi dress.[6] This unwanted and unendorsed use of Sámi traditional dress by outsiders is having significant negative impacts on Sámi culture, both culturally and economically. The economic effects are clear – the Sámi do not benefit from the sale of the products and services that use Sámi dress in unwanted and unauthorised ways.[7] Perhaps of greater concern, however, are the cultural impacts that follow such exploitation. The Sámi say that this unwanted use of their traditional dress by outsiders offends the Sámi and is having a negative impact on Sámi culture. Sámi Committees, researchers, and organisations have consistently highlighted the negative effects these stereotypes have on the Sámi's identity and self-image, both collectively and

4 Indigenous Sámi people inhabit area called Sápmi, which encompasses areas of northern Finland, Norway Sweden and the Kola Peninsula of Russia.

5 '100 days of Polar Magic' <http://www.visitfinland.fi/news/100-days-of-polar-night-magic-mainos/>, accessed 15 December 2015. <http://yle.fi/uutiset/likaiset_lappalaiset_seko_myy_maailmalla__visit_finlandin_mainosvideo_suututtaa/8312073> accessed 15 December 2015. After the stir, Visit Finland decided to change the video.

6 'The Most Popular Souvenirs' (*Travel Rovaniemi, Spring 2015. 23st Annual Volume*) 14. Estimated income from tourism in Lapland is about 630 million euros per year. See 'Lapin matkailustrategia 2015-2018' Lapin Liitto, Sarja A; 43:2015) <http://www.lappi.fi/lapinliitto/c/document_library/get_file?folderId=2265071&name=DLFE-25498.pdf>, accessed 20 December 2015.

7 Sámi traditional dress is also an important part of the Sámi handicraft tradition, known as duodji. Legal protection could support duodji as a traditional Sámi livelihood, at least indirectly. Duodji means 'handicraft', 'work', 'accomplishment' or 'creation'. With reference to handicraft it is understood as meaning a concrete creation. Duodji involves extensive know-how in acquiring materials, knowing the characteristics of materials, working methods, how to use the finished product and the cultural meanings associated with the product. See P. Sammallahti, *Suoma-Sámi sátnegirji* (Girjegiisá 2014), and G. Guttorm, 'Duodji – Sami handicrafts – who owns the knowledge and the work' in J.T. Solbakk (ed.), *Traditional Knowledge and Copyright* (Samikopiija Karasjok 2007) 65-66.

individually.[8] Many of them – and Sámi youth themselves – have been especially worried about the effects that the distorted, humiliating, and false stereotypical image given and maintained by the Pilailupuoti and tourism industry in general has on young Sámi people in their formative years.[9] The Sámi, like all human beings, desire that their dignity be respected and protected, and do not want to see their cultural identity degraded, ignored, or used as a cartoonish prop.

1.2 *Discussion on the Need for Protection of the Sámi Dress*

The Sámi have discussed the need to protect the *gákti* against misuse by outsiders since the 1930s; and attempts have been made to educate the tourism industry in Rovaniemi about the meaning the *gákti* has to the Sámi and the effects caused by extensive outside exploitation, but to little avail.[10] One attempt to secure some sort of protection for Sámi products occurred in the 1980s when the Sámi agreed on the establishment of a certification trademark, Sámi Duodji, but this has not met the expectations set for it.[11] The trademark, which main goal is to promote sales of handicrafts, is usually ill suited to protect heritage that has more cultural than commercial significance. Traditional Sámi dress

---

8 M. Aikio and P. Aikio 'Saamelaiskulttuuri ja matkailu' in R. Huopainen (ed.), *Selviytyjät, Näyttely pohjoisen ihmisen sitkeydestä*. (Lapin maakuntamuseon julkaisuja 7, Jyväskylä, 1993) 95-96. Aikios' explain the reactions of Sámi to the wider use of Sámi Dress and Sámi Culture in tourism. See also Saamelaiskomitean mietintö 1976: 46, 81.

9 Sámi youth have organized demonstrations against the misuse of Sámi dress twice, in 1995 and 2008, and have organized a seminar to discuss the issue in 2011. See for example 'Sámekultuvrra ávkkástallama livččii vejolaš bissehit' 18 October 2011. <http://yle.fi/uutiset/samekultuvrra_avkkastallama_livccii_vejolas_bissehit/6626533>, accessed 16 February 2016. Interview with I-M. Helander, Chairperson, Suoma Sámi Nuorat (Inari, 20 August 2016). See also Rovaniemi Declaration at the 19th Saami Conference, 2008, para. 14.

10 Interview with emeritus professor (Sámi culture and language) P. Sammallahti, 20 August 2016. In the very beginning, waiters in hotels were using the Sámi dress as work outfit. 1990's Sámi association in Rovaniemi had a massive campaign to inform the tourism industry on Sámi views.

11 First discussion on the need for trademark was in 1950's, but it did not lead to establishment of it. See V.P. Lehtola: 'Saamelaisten parlamentti, Suomen saamelaisvaltuuskunta 1973-1995 ja Saamelaiskäräjät 1996-2003' (Saamelaiskäräjät 2005) 54. The Sámi Duodji-trademark was established by the Nordic Saami Council <http://www.Sámicouncil.net/en/?deptid=3329&cHash=8028f9b35a8940cdb048d74866379b29>, but has been poorly managed over the years by it. In 2015-2016, the Council set a Sámi Duodji trademark revitalization project to assess the functioning of the trademark and went through a round of negotiations with handicraft organisations in four countries to study the current needs. The author led the project.

embodies the core values and codes of Sámi culture and is an important part of the people's culture, cultural heritage, and traditional knowledge. Often the use of indigenous peoples' cultures by non-indigenous people has been discussed under the concept of cultural appropriation, which has been defined as "taking… from a culture that is not your own – of intellectual property, cultural expression or artefacts, history and ways of knowledge".[12] Cultural appropriation typically occurs where there is a power imbalance and has been linked to racism and the experiences of historical and continuing dispossession that indigenous peoples are facing or have had to face.[13] Even though cultural appropriation might be a vague concept, it combines the different aspects of the phenomena and looks at the issues in broad perspective. From a human rights perspective, the Sámi's right to their traditional dress can be seen in terms of at least three different notions of rights, depending on the aim of the protection sought. It can be approached as an (intellectual) property right, a cultural right, and a right to equality and non-discrimination.[14]

The Sámi have often claimed that they have no means to protect their traditional dress.[15] During the stir surrounding the Visit Finland marketing video, Tiina Sanila-Aikio, president of the Saami Parliament in Finland, asserted that the tourism industry's consistent refusal to listen to the Sámi and its active attempts at ignoring Sámi concerns constitutes structural racism.[16] With reference to her statement, the present chapter looks at the wider use of traditional Sámi dress by outsiders, as well as the demands and arguments calling for the protection of the dress and dignity of the Sámi people as an issue of equality. Particular emphasis is placed on Sámi children and youth and the

---

12 B. Ziff and V. Rao Pratima (eds.) 'Introduction to Cultural appropriation: A Framework for Analysis', in *Borrowed Power: Essays on Cultural Appropriation*, (Rutgers University Press 1997) 2.

13 Angela R. Rileya and Kristen A. Carpenter, 'Owning Red: A Theory of Indian (Cultural) Appropriation', 94 *Tex. L. Rev.* 859. 2016, 1-2; and R. Tsosie, 'Reclaiming Native Stories: An Essay on Cultural Appropriation and Cultural Rights', 34 *Arizona State Law Journal* 299, 2002, 311.

14 Mattias Åhren has dealt extensively with the issue in his PhD thesis of 2010. See M. Åhren, *The Saami Traditional Dress and Beauty Pageants: Indigenous Peoples' Rights of Ownership and Self-determination over Their Cultures*, Universitetet i Tromsø, Juridisk fakultet, 2010.

15 For example 'Dárpmehuvve go oidne sirkusis turistagávttiid, sirkus dadjá daid albma gáktin' 13 June 2013. <http://yle.fi/uutiset/darpmehuvve_go_oidne_sirkusis_turistagavttiid_sirkus_dadja_daid_albma_gaktin/6687397>, accessed 10 January 2016.

16 '"Likaiset lappalaiset, sekö myy maailmalla?" – Visit Finlandin mainosvideo suututtaa', 17 September 2015 <http://yle.fi/uutiset/likaiset_lappalaiset_seko_myy_maailmalla__visit_finlandin_mainosvideo_suututtaa/8312073> accessed 10 January 2016.

impact which the issue might have on them. The chapter focuses on the following questions: What kind of meaning does the traditional dress have for the Sámi? Does self-government give the Sámi a possibility to have a say in the use of the dress? Does the Finnish Act on Non-Discrimination offer protection to Sámi through its protection of the dignity of persons against harassment? Pilailupuoti's action will be assessed more carefully in light of the concept of harassment. Pilailupuoti has been chosen as an example because its Pohjolanasu product has constantly invoked feeling of ill will and raised questions on the morality and equity of its actions.[17] The chapter proceeds as follows: section two first discusses traditional Sámi dress, its significance and the related customs. Section three looks at the Sámi views and actions and legal status of the Sámi in Finland and its relevance to these considerations. Section four provides a view on the issue by looking at the legal framework of equality. The last section puts forward and discusses the author's conclusions.

2 Sámi Dress and Related Customs as Part of the Sámi Cultural Heritage

2.1 *Sámi Dress – as Part of Sámi Identity*

Sámi dress and its accessories have changed from being of value to everyday life and survival to being a way to show and strengthen the Sámi identity, especially for young Sámi.[18] The people's traditional dress is unique and very distinguishable from the Finnish, Norwegian, or Swedish national costumes. In the Finnish Sámi region there are five main designs seen in Sámi dress and its accessories. Variations between the designs lie in the cut and in decorations, as well as in the cultural signs that the outfits convey. The regional boundaries are still strong and the accessories are specific to the dress of each region.[19] Traditional dress is worn mostly on particularly important occasions, such as

17 Another example is from 2015 when a Finnish representative to a beauty pageant called Miss World decided to present herself in Pilailupuoti's costume. 'Suomen Miss Maailma – kilpailija edustaa pilailupuodin lapinpuvussa' 1 November 2015 <http://yle.fi/uutiset/suomen_miss_maailma_-kilpailija_edustaa_pilailupuodin_lapinpuvussa/8493787>, accessed 10 January 2016.

18 S.R. Somby: 'Beaivenieidda duodji. Duodjeárbevieru kultuvrralaš mearkkašumit ja enkulturašuvdna golmma sohkabuolvva áigge Gáregasnjargga ja Kárášjoga guovllus 1900-logus.' (Pro gradu – dutkamuš. Giellagas Instituhtta, Oulu Universitehtta 2003) 56, 115. See also T. Lehtola 'Saamelainen perintö' (Kustannus-Puntsi. Jyväskylä 2001) 121 and Rovaniemi Declaration at the 19th Saami Conference, 2008, para. 20.

19 See n 18, T. Lehtola 128.

weddings, funerals, and celebrations,[20] and is part of Sámi cultural communication: the colours, shapes and decorations of an outfit link a Sámi person to both the community she or he comes from and the Sámi people in general. The traditional dress a person wears indicates membership in a certain family, village, region, and generation.[21] In addition it can indicate e.g. marital status and occupation. Sámi dress is used in the Sámi community to strengthen social bonds and local identity. These cultural functions have been described in various ways by Sámi researchers.[22] Saara Tervaniemi has used the concept of cultural symbol to describe things that are important to the Sámi. These symbols define, build and delineate the community; essentially, they help Sámi feel the existence of the Sámi community.[23] The traditional dress is a key element not only in the collective identity of the people but also in the individual identities of Sámi persons; it tells in subtle ways a story behind the person through the cultural signs within it. Altogether, there are more than 30 designs in the traditional dress worn throughout Sápmi.[24] These designs vary in different areas, but have many common elements and similarities that they are recognised as Sámi dress. This dress is thus something that is common to all Sámi throughout Sápmi, regardless of the state in which a particular Sámi person lives and what she/he does for a living; it unites the Sámi people across borders.

There appear to be certain rules governing how Sámi dress and its accessories are related to regions and local Sámi communities and families: that is, people from a certain area wear the particular dress of that area. This is not the whole picture, however, as there also seems to be a common understanding throughout Finland and Sápmi on who is entitled to wear traditional Sámi outfits, even though this varies depending on the region. When 64 members of the Sámi handicrafters association in Finland were asked who, in their opin-

20 However, it has recently seen a revival in everyday use by many Sámi, and can be seen being worn by Sámi people on any given day in towns and cities throughout Sápmi.

21 J. Lehtola et al., *Sámi Duodji, Saamenkäsityö, Sámi Handicraft* (Sámi Museum – Saamelaismuseosäätiön julkaisuja no. 7, Inari 2006) 38. See also V.P. Lehtola; 'Saamelaiset, historia, yhteiskunta ja taide' (Kustannus-Puntsi, 1997) 11.

22 See e.g. V. Hirvonen, *Saamenmaan ääniä. Saamelaisen naisen tie kirjailijaksi* (Suomalaisen kirjallisuuden seura, 1999), 184: *Duodji* is "a part of ethnic identity, a skill through which an individual experiences belonging to a community and sharing common values with the other members of the community". See also n 18, S.R. Somby, 2003, 86, 114. "Duodji and the skills it involves are the building-blocks of personal, social and ethnic cultural identity."

23 S. Tervaniemi, 'Symbolista sodankäyntiä saamelaisuudesta' *AGON, N:ot 37-38*, 23 May 2013, 14.

24 P. Nuorgam, '*Mánnávuođa muittut*' (Bumbá-lágádus 2016) 42-51. Some designs correspond to Sámi regions that a span across national borders.

ion, has the right to wear the traditional gákti, 75 per cent answered, "a Sámi or person who has a connection to Sámi society";[25] 20.3 per cent responded, "only Sámi can wear the dress"; and 4.7 per cent said, "anyone, as long as they wear it appropriately". No one answered "whoever wants to". Since almost all people answered that either Sámi persons or persons who have a connection to Sámi society may wear the dress, Sámi tradition seems to indicate that the right to wear the Sámi dress is bound to the Sámi origin of the wearer, with an exception to this main rule for people having a connection to Sámi society. People were also asked in an open-answer question, "What is your opinion based on?". More than twenty people said that it was taken from their family, relatives, community or just simply traditions. Almost twenty people explained either how to wear the dress or what the exceptions are. Two exceptions were mentioned when non-Sámi were allowed to wear Sámi dress: marriage to a Sámi or when honouring a person in recognition of something that he/she has done for the community, albeit that it was expected that the person also shows respect for the Sámi people and traditions.

2.2 *Customs Related to Sámi Dress – Customary Norms?*

Researcher Elina Helander-Renvall has studied Sámi customary norms on land use in certain areas of northern Norway. She defines customary norms as traditions and concepts of justice,[26] describing "Sami customary rules [as] dynamic, adjusting over time, flexible, based on common understanding and social acceptance, well-known locally, and practiced in specific situations and contexts, 'traditions' from the past, transferred to new generations according to contemporary needs".[27] It is striking how similar the customary norms she describes are to (social) norms and customs on the use of traditional dress mentioned above. The Sámi have clear legal conceptions regarding who can wear Sámi dress and how; these vary in different areas, just as the conceptions of land use do. The results of the questionnaire to handicrafters conducted by the Sámi Council's Sámi Duodji trademark revitalization project confirm that

25 The survey was part of Sámi Duodji-trademark revitalization project and was completed between November 2015 and January 2016. Most of the questions were single response questions. See n 11.

26 E. Renvall-Helander, 'Saamelainen tapaoikeus', in P. Magga and E. Ojanlatva (eds.), *Ealli biras* = Elävä ympäristö: saamelainen kulttuuriympäristöohjelma (Saami Museum – Saamelaismuseosäätiön julkaisujano. 9, Inari 2013) 132.

27 E. Renvall-Helander, 'On Customary Law Among the Saami People' in N. Bankes and T. Koivurova (eds.), *The Proposed Nordic Saami Convention, National and International Dimensions of Indigenous Property Rights.* (Hart 2013) 290.

the rules concerning the use of Sámi dress have taken on their present forms over a long period time and that they are traditions, "agreed on" communally. The rights related to Sámi dress are thus essentially collective in nature. In addition, even though the dress is a product of handicraft, it is not possible to identify a single craftsperson as the creator of the designs. Helander-Renvall posits with regard to land use that customary norms within the community are perhaps not even perceived as being rules in the same manner as written laws are. They are more like a code of conduct for the social environment of the Sámi community; one notices the nature of the rules when some conflict requires that the rules be articulated or when research is done on them.[28] The same can be applied to a conflict surrounding Sámi dress that centres on demeaning use by outsiders. The problem is that the Sámi legal perceptions and customs have not gained recognition and acknowledgment in Finnish jurisprudence. In fact, it is essentially accepted under the current Finnish intellectual property regime that anyone may use the Sámi dress commercially: it is not regarded as meeting the requirements for protection under intellectual property law, or falls within some exception to IP protection, which means that it can be freely used by anyone. This is clearly against the Sámi custom and legal perception on the Sámi dress.

Case law and research on Sámi law has shown that Sámi customs can constitute customary law and can act as one of the sources of law alongside national and international law.[29] Knowing and acknowledging these norms is essential if there is clear determination to solve the conflicts and redress the harms caused by the wider use of Sámi traditional dress.[30] Do the Sámi then have a right and a mandate to have a say in when and how traditional dress is worn, and can they exercise that right?

3 Collective Right to Have a Say on the Wider Use of Sámi Dress?

3.1 *Sámi Views on Cultural Heritage, the Sámi Dress and its Wider Use*

But what are the Sámi's demands regarding Sámi dress and Sámi cultural heritage in general? The nature of the protection sought in the demands has varied. On the one hand, there have been calls for ownership; on the other hand, there

28 See n 26.

29 See generally on Sámi customs and their interpretation as customary law E.V. Svensson, 'Sami Legal Scholarship: The Making of a Knowledge Field', in C. Allard and S.F. Skogvang, *Indigenous Rights in Scandinavia, Autonomous Sami Law*, (Ashgate, 2015) 223-225.

30 See also n 13, A.R., Rileya and K.A. Carpenter, 2016, 4.

have been calls for at least negative protection. In their declaration regarding cultural heritage 2008, the Saami Council specifically stated that the Sámi have the right to their own material and intellectual cultural heritage and required the tourism industry to stop misappropriation of the Sámi traditional dress.[31] At the same time Saami Parliamentary Council (SPR)[32] declared that the 'Sámi people have the right to maintain, control, protect and develop their cultural heritage, traditional knowledge and traditional cultural expressions and their intellectual property rights'.[33] In the same vein they stated that Sámi symbols cannot be used without the consent of Sámi and only for purposes acceptable to the Sámi. In 2011 SPR expressed that their view on cultural heritage is in line with Declaration on the Rights of Indigenous Peoples, and repeated what they had declared in 2008 on 'Sámi's right to maintain, control, protect and develop their cultural heritage' and stated that the 'States have both [a] duty to respect Sámi's right to determine over their traditional knowledge and traditional cultural expression and to guarantee this right...'[34] In 2011 SPR also made a point that where businesses in Norway, Sweden, Finland and Russia express and use Sámi culture they must do so in accordance with ethically acceptable principles and demanded that states make an action plan for this together with the Sámi. As an example for implementation SPR mentioned ethical rules and quality certification mechanism.[35]

Representatives of the Saami Parliaments have been part of the expert group negotiating the Draft Nordic Saami Convention, which contains a dedi-

---

31 The Sámi have posited many times, they have not placed anything in the public domain. They have called for sui generis protection for Sámi folklore. See Saami Council statements at WIPO's IGC 4/2002 and Saami Council Statement 1 IGC 5/2003. The Saami Council has in the Rovaniemi Declaration at the 19th Saami Conference called for the right for the Sámi to own their material and intellectual cultural heritage and the possibility to control and develop it. In the same breath, it has been declared that the intention is not to establish an absolute exclusive right to Sámi culture but rather the Sámi gladly share parts of their culture. Among other things, the Declaration demands that decisions on requests coming from other than Sámi persons to exploit the elements of Sámi culture should be directed to Sámi institutions. The actions of the Finnish state and the private sector, which may affect the Sámi culture, may only be carried out on the condition that the impacts of the actions on the culture are assessed in advance. See Rovaniemi Declaration at the 19th Saami Conference, 2008, sections 13-15, 22, pp. 6-8. The Saami Council has also discussed the issue in its Conferences in 1980 and 1986.

32 Saami Parliamentary Council is a cooperation body of the Saami Parliaments in Finland, Sweden and Norway.

33 Declaration of the Saami Parliamentary Council 2008 Rovaniemi, 2.

34 Declaration of the Saami Parliamentary Council 2011 Kirkenes, para. 6.

35 See n 52, para. 22.

cated article on the protection of cultural expressions that would also cover Sámi dress. Article 31 of the Draft Convention provides: "the states shall make efforts to ensure that the Sámi people gain influence over such activities and a reasonable share of the financial revenues. The Sámi culture shall be protected against the use of cultural expressions that in a misleading manner give the impression of having a Sámi origin".[36] In 2008, the Saami Parliamentary Council and the Saami Council formed a joint committee to discuss the Sámi symbols, such as the flag and the dress, but the committee has not been very active, nor have they produced any statements on the issue.

Most of the wider use of cultural expressions occurs in Finland and it is therefore interesting to see how the Saami Parliament in Finland[37] has dealt with the issue. It seems to have quite rarely addressed the demeaning use of Sámi dress over the last two decades. There might be several reasons for this including primarily the limited budget and its having to focus on land rights, language, and education as well. Still, in view of the attention that Sámi society has drawn to the issue and the recurring instances of misappropriation, it would seem – at least to judge by the statements and guidelines on the issue – that the Saami Parliament has given little political attention to the matter until recently.

Though the Sámi dress has economic value, its cultural meaning and value cannot be understated and over time has been viewed as more substantial. The issue of dress and handicraft might to some extent have a gender-related dimension as well, since statistics show that a majority of the people doing handicraft are women.[38] Moreover, the overwhelming majority of craftspersons who work with soft materials – and hence sewing garments and dresses – are women. In this connection, one could examine the gender balance in the Saami Parliament, which was established in 1972 as the Sámi Delegation and took its current form in 1996. From the very beginning, the Delegation had very

---

36 Unofficial version of the 'Draft Nordic Saami Convention 2007'. <www.galdu.no/getfile.php/3131394.2388.../3_2007_samekonvensjon_eng.pdf>, accessed 30 August 2016.

37 Where reference to Saami Parliament is made in this chapter, the author is referring to the Saami Parliament of Finland, unless stated otherwise.

38 This was confirmed in statistics compiled from a survey made by the Saami Council Sámi Duodji-trademark revitalization project. See n 11. 74.1% (157 persons of 212) who answered the survey where women. Closer analysis of the data showed that in Finland around 90% of those who are making handicrafts from soft materials are women. On the other hand the issue is more complex; handicraft as an issue has been on the political agenda on Sámi and their discussions for decades, but it seems that the politicians have not been able to solve the demands for protection and on demand to support the sales of Sámi handicraft and the support for it as a livelihood.

few women among its 20 members. The proportion of women has gradually increased over time, but it is only in the last three Parliaments – since 2008 – that almost half of the members have been women. Hence, the gender balance of the Parliament can be a factor in the slow progress of views and Parliamentary positions on Sámi Dress.

As mentioned in the introduction, wider use of traditional dress has been an issue since the 1930s. Through the actions taken and the political documents on record, one can see that the Sámi have consistently wanted to protect the dress. Yet, there have been other voices, arguing for wider use of the dress. For example, in 1970s when the Sámi Delegation discussed the use of the dress at a secondary school in Rovaniemi on a festive occasion, some of the members looked upon the idea favourably and thought it would publicize Sámi culture.[39] At the end of the day, the main reason for the limited political attention might be the collective nature of the customs related to Sámi dress: no single person owns it; on the contrary, it belongs to all Sámi and, as noted, there are over 30 different outfits in four countries, all with local traditions of their own, making the issue a complex one. It seems that it has been difficult to determine who has legitimacy as the proper rights holder to act on the issue and at the same time has the responsibility to do so.

Even though political attention to the issue of dress has been limited over time, it has increased over the last decade and especially recently. In 2007 the Saami Parliament stated that the tourism industry should act in a culturally sustainable manner, meaning that Sámi culture should be portrayed with respect and the information given on it should be accurate.[40] In its statement to the Minority Ombudsman in 2010 (at present the Non-Discrimination Ombudsman), the Saami Parliament explained the importance of the Dress in Sámi culture and stated that the use of Sámi dress should be governed or guided through regulations and guidelines that adhere to Finland's obligations under international law.[41] In 2016 the Saami Parliament released a guide on how to present the Sámi and Sámi dress in pictures for the purposes of the tourism industry. The guide says that the Sámi and the Sámi dress should be presented truthfully and in cooperation with Sámi themselves.[42] Even though the dress has not been a topical matter until lately, the Saami Parliament has worked

39 See n 11, V.P. Lehtola, 81.

40 Saamelaiskäräjien lausunto Lapin matkailustrategialuonnoksesta 13.6.2007, s. 2-3. Since then it has repeated these views in many documents.

41 Saamelaiskäräjien lausunto Vähemmistövaltuutetulle 2010, 10-12.

42 <http://www.houseoflapland.fi/wp-content/uploads/2016/11/Saamelaisten_kuvaohjeistus.pdf>, accessed 17 October 2016.

towards the recognition of traditional knowledge in legislation and, as a result, Finland has now passed an Act on the Nagoya Protocol, which will affect the benefit sharing in use of traditional knowledge related genetic resources of the Sámi; however, since it's scope is limited, this will have questionable effect on the issue of dress.[43] The Saami Parliament has also participated in the meetings of WIPO's Intergovernmental Committee on Genetic Resources, Folklore and Traditional Knowledge and according to its action plan for 2016-2019 plans to do so also in future to make sure that traditional knowledge endures for future generations.[44] All in all the political interest in these issues has started to increase in Finnish political discourse.

3.2 *Fundamental Right to One's Language and Culture*

The Finnish Constitution has two separate but related sections concerning the Sámi, namely section 17.3 and subsection 4 of section 121. Subsection 4 of section 121 will be discussed further in chapter 3.3. The first one, section 17.3 provides that "[t]he Sámi, as an indigenous people… have the right to maintain and develop their own language and culture". According to the preparatory works of the Constitution, the aim of the section was to secure the survival of linguistic and national minorities and their cultures. The materials also state that the content and status of the Sámi's fundamental right to maintain and develop their culture is recognised in and follows from international law and the relevant international conventions.[45] Finland has ratified all relevant human rights conventions, with the exception of the International Labour Organization's Convention Concerning Indigenous and Tribal Peoples in Independent Countries (ILO 169), which is now being considered by the Finnish Parliament.

Even though this section on the Sámi in the Constitution talks about a collective right, it secures the linguistic and cultural rights of Sámi individuals as well. This follows from the fact that the model used in setting out the fundamental right to culture in Finland's Constitution was Article 27 of the UN International Covenant on Civil and Political Rights (ICCPR), which states: "In those States in which ethnic, religious or linguistic minorities exist, persons belonging to such minorities shall not be denied the right, in community with the other members of their group, to enjoy their own culture, to profess and

43 Finnish government Bill, HE 126/2015 vp. The Nagoya Protocol on Access to Genetic Resources and the Fair and Equitable Sharing of Benefits Arising from their Utilization (ABS) to the Convention on Biological Diversity is a supplementary agreement to the Convention on Biological Diversity.

44 Saami Parliament Action Plan 2016-2019, 15 April 2016, 14.

45 Finnish government Bill, HE 309/1993 vp, 65.

practice their own religion, or to use their own language." The Convention on the Rights of the Child (CRC) uses the same language (Art. 30) with specific application to indigenous children.[46] The case law of the Human Rights Committee (HRC) has confirmed that indigenous peoples have the right to have their distinct cultural identity protected.[47] The HRC has also called several times for positive measures to implement the right and to protect peoples against the acts of other persons within the state party.[48]

The Committee responsible for the Convention on the Rights of the Child (CRC) has issued a number of general comments expressing a position on the status of indigenous children in different areas, with one comment explicitly referring to indigenous children and their rights under the Convention. On many occasions the Committee has emphasised the need to respect the collective cultural values and identity of the child and to respect culture, languages and traditions in general.[49] In line with HRC, CRC has required states to take positive measures through legislative, judicial, or administrative authorities both against its action but also against acts of other persons that might lead to denial or violation of the right.[50] The Committee has stressed that the needs of indigenous children are unique and should be specifically addressed. In light of the Committee's views, it would be critical that Sámi children and youth have a secure environment in which to build their Sámi identity; this would be an environment without stereotypes of the Sámi as being underdeveloped, without their being romanticized, and without false characteristics being imputed to them. Some television programmes have portrayed the Sámi in this way and the tourism industry and shops like Pilailupuoti continue to reinforce the stereotypes created.[51] As one of the most visible parts of the identify of Sámi children and youth the Sámi dress holds great meaning and value, and deserves adequate protection.

---

46 Finland has ratified the Convention in 1991 (59/1991). So far there is only one case judged by the Committee and it concerned a violation of other articles of the Convention.

47 For instance in *Sandra Lovelace v. Canada*. Communication No. R6/24, U.N.Doc. Supp. No. 40 (A/36/40/) at 166 (1981), para. 13.1, 16, 17.

48 General Comment No. 23: The rights of minorities (Art. 27): 08/04/94. CCPR/C/21/Rev.1/ Add.5 6.1.

49 CRC/C/GC/11. 12 February 2009. General Comment No. 11 (2009). Indigenous children and their rights under the Convention, para. 18.

50 See n 49, para. 17.

51 Television programs Hymyhuulet and Pulttibois had two Sámi characters, whom were presented being alcoholics', hay in the hair, and black teeth with the dress copies on. The program were aired first time 1980's and 1990's and have been aired many times after that. <https://fi.wikipedia.org/wiki/Pulttibois>, accessed 30 August 2016.

The mental health of Sámi youth is also an area with unique challenges. According to the research of Omma et al. in Sweden, young Sámi have more suicidal ideation/death wishes/life weariness compared to the majority of the Swedes, problems exacerbated by harsh circumstances and experiences of bad treatment relating to their ethnicity. It is stated that the "[s]uicidal behaviour is not necessarily primarily an expression of a wish to die, but part of an internal existential dialogue contributing to building a human identity". The research also states that "the majority of young Sami share the experience of being forced to defend the Sami culture and the Sami way of living".[52] There has not been any research in Finland on the mental health of Sámi youth separately but the situation in Sweden is quite similar in many ways and there is a reason to believe that mental health is an issue within the Sámi youth of Finland as well. Finland's country report to CERD Committee raised a similar issue – Sámi youth in Finland were tired of justifying being a Sámi.[53] In addition, the suicide figures of the Sámi in Finland indicate mental health problems are an issue among the young Sámi in Finland too.[54] The Swedish studies on mental health also reinforce the connection between the realisation of the rights of indigenous peoples and mental health solutions. With better realisation, and security in ones culture, better mental health follows.

Sámi have for a long time also highlighted how little the majority population knows about the Sámi and how important it would be to include education on the Sámi in the national school curriculum. So far the calls for raising the awareness of the Sámi have not led anywhere even though e.g. The European Commission against Racism and Intolerance (ECRI) has recommended that the Finnish authorities take measures to teach the Sámi culture in schools.[55] In light of this situation – the Sámi's constant need to justify their existence – it seems unconscionable that the Sámi should also be consistently offended and

52 L. Omma, M. Sandlund, L. Jacobsson: 'Suicidal expressions in young Swedish Sami, a cross-sectional study.' *Int J Circumpolar Health.* 2013;72. doi: 10.3402/ijch.v72i0.19862. Epub 2013 Jan 171, 8.

53 CERD Committee monitors the implementation of International Convention on the Elimination of All Forms of Racial Discrimination. CERD/C/FIN/23. Committee on the Elimination of Racial Discrimination. Consideration of reports submitted by States parties under article 9 of the Convention. Twenty-third periodic reports of States parties due in 2015. 23 December 2015, para. 41.

54 L. Soininen 'The Health of the Finnish Sami in Light of Mortality and Cancer Pattern'. <https://helda.helsinki.fi/bitstream/handle/10138/154662/THEHEALTHO_korjattu.pdf?sequence=3>, accessed 30 August 2016.

55 ECRI Report on Finland (fourth monitoring cycle), adopted on 21 March 2013, published on 9 July 2013, para. 106.

humiliated by the ongoing rebuilding and maintaining of stereotypes by the tourism industry and other private actors.

3.3 *Saami Parliament – Self-Government Body*

The above has thus concluded that Sámi have cultural rights and introduced certain instruments for the implementation of those rights. Subsection 4 of section 121 of the Finnish Constitution establishes the legal foundation for the Saami Parliament, a body responsible for the self-government that aims to implement the people's cultural and linguistic rights. According to subsection 4 of section 121 of the Constitution, "In their native region, the Sámi have linguistic and cultural self-government, as provided by an Act." The Act on the Saami Parliament states that "the Sámi as an indigenous people shall be ensured cultural autonomy within their homeland in matters concerning their language and culture."[56] The aim of the law has been to ensure that Sámi can, as extensively as possible, control their economic, social and cultural development and participate in the planning of their development on the national and international level.[57] Within the Sámi homeland, the Saami Parliament may make proposals and issue statements to state authorities. Furthermore, section 9 of the Act affirms that authorities are to negotiate with the Sámi Parliament regarding "all far-reaching and important measures that directly or indirectly may affect the Sámi's status as an indigenous people," including matters relating to the management, use, leasing, and assignment of state lands, among other issues. The problems associated with section 9 arise from it being read in conjunction with the previous sections, thus limiting its application only to actions with affect the Sámi homeland, although a majority of Sámi live outside this region. Another problem is that the government does not have an agreement with the Saami Parliament that establishes how and under what circumstances consultations should be arranged. Hence, it can be questioned whether the Saami Parliament can genuinely participate in and influence decisions that affect the Sámi people, their culture, and their indigenous status. The statutory mandate of the Sámi Parliament is limited, and its input is restricted further.[58] Ultimately, under the current practice the Sámi only have a

---

56 Laki saamelaiskäräjistä (17.7.1995/974), section 1.

57 Finnish government Bill, HE 248/1994 vp., 14.

58 The lack of procedure on section 9 of the Act was noted and the degree of participation was noted by the Special Rapporteur on the Rights of Indigenous Peoples in 2010, when Rapporteur paid an official country visit to Sápmi in 2010. Report of the Special Rapporteur on the rights of indigenous peoples on the situation of the Sami people in the Sápmi region of Norway, Sweden and Finland. A/HRC/18/35/Add.2, 38.40.

right to be consulted in issues that fall within the Saami Parliament's mandate and where a matter is officially recognised as a "Sámi matter". This, however, can also act as an effective tool if the Saami Parliament calls for negotiations and most importantly the officials are in fact willing to listen and take into account the Sámi view on the issue.

3.4 *Legal Protection for Sámi Dress?*

Apart from the Act on the Saami Parliament, there are a few Acts dealing exclusively with Sámi matters and approximately 100 Acts, decrees, or regulations that mention the Sámi. Most refer to the Act on the Saami Parliament or language, however none of these instruments protects Sámi dress specifically. Even though dress is one of the key expressions of the culture, it has no specific legal protection, nor are there any special measures to ensure that the Sámi can have a collective say in how Sámi dress can or cannot be used by outsiders. By contrast, as mentioned previously, intellectual property law appears to allow anyone to use Sámi dress commercially.[59]

However, the importance of the dress and handicraft has been acknowledge many times. The Finnish Parliament voted in the spring of 2015 on an amendment to the Act on the Saami Parliament, but the amendment was rejected. In the suggested amendment, it was proposed that Sámi culture be defined in an open and non-exhaustive way.[60] Sámi culture would include the Sámi language, the Sámi cultural heritage, cultural expressions, art, traditional knowledge, traditional livelihoods, and the contemporary forms of practicing these, as well as other ways and forms in which the Sámi can practice their culture as an indigenous people. According to the explanatory part of the bill containing the amendment, these are the essential elements of the Sámi culture; Sámi handicraft was also explicitly mentioned.[61] Also salient in this regard is the draft Nordic Saami Convention article 31 which mentions "traditional cultural expressions" and the preparatory materials which cite Sámi handicraft and wearing traditional Sámi dress as examples of these.[62]

Significantly, Finland has ratified the UNESCO Convention on the Protection and Promotion of the Diversity of Cultural Expressions, which states that cultural expressions "are those expressions that result from the creativity of

59 See n 14, 137-138, 140-142.

60 Finnish Government Bill, HE 167/2017 vp, 48.

61 See n 45, 30-31.

62 Draft Nordic Saami Convention, 2007. The draft is currently under negations.

individuals, groups and societies, and that have cultural content".[63] It has also ratified the UNESCO Convention for the Safeguarding of the Intangible Cultural Heritage 2003, which defines in article 2, paragraph 1 intangible cultural heritage as "the practices, representations, expressions, knowledge, skills… that communities, groups and, in some cases, individuals recognize as part of their cultural heritage". According to paragraph 2 of the article, "intangible cultural heritage… is manifested, inter alia, in… (e) traditional craftsmanship".[64] In the implementation of the Convention, traditional Sámi handicraft has been listed as falling within the scope of the instrument.[65] Overall, the value and importance of Sámi handicraft and dress as part of Sámi culture has been acknowledged many times on the preparatory works on laws and draft conventions, but this has not in practice led to legal protection. By ratifying the UNESCO conventions Finland has however committed itself to, among other things, safeguarding the intangible cultural heritage in general and ensuring respect for, and raising awareness about, it.

Even though the mandate of the Saami Parliament does not give it a collective mandate on the Sámi dress and and other legal instruments do not specifically protect the Sami dress, there are other legal avenues available to protect the dignity of the Sámi from the most offensive instances of misappropriation. One legal approach, which has been raised by the Non-Discrimination Ombudsman herself, is that the demeaning use of Sámi dress may be viewed as harassment, which is a form of discrimination.[66] Let us thus turn to the relevant legislative provisions on equality and non-discrimination.

63 Laki kulttuuri-ilmaisujen moninaisuuden suojelemista ja edistämistä koskevan yleissopimuksen lainsäädännön alaan kuuluvien määräysten voimaansaattamisesta (600/2006).

64 Valtioneuvoston asetus aineettoman kulttuuriperinnön suojelemisesta tehdyn yleissopimuksen voimaansaattamisesta (47/2013).

65 Wikilist <https://wiki.aineetonkulttuuriperinto.fi/wiki/Saamelainen_k%C3%A4sity%C3%B6perinne> accessed 1 August 2016.

66 Non-Discrimination Ombudsman Kirsi Pimiä, "Oikeus omaan kieleen ja kulttuuriin – yhdenvertaisuuslain mahdollisuudet" (Sámi Youth Conference, 17 November 2015, Helsinki). <http://www.syrjinta.fi/web/fi/toiminta/-/asset_publisher/dFjOo5GQyvQO/content/yhdenvertaisuusvaltuutettu-kirsi-pimian-puhe-saamelaisnuorten-konferenssissa-17-11-2015?inheritRedirect=false&redirect=http%3A%2F%2Fwww.syrjinta.fi%2Fweb%2Ffi%2Ftoiminta%3Fp_p_id%3D101_INSTANCE_dFjOo5GQyvQO%26p_p_lifecycle%3D0%26p_p_state%3Dnormal%26p_p_mode%3Dview%26p_p_col_id%3Dcolumn-2%26p_p_col_pos%3D2%26p_p_col_count%3D3>, accessed 20 May 2016. She said that combating cases of harassment can be sometimes difficult, since it is explained or defended to be humour or comedy.

4 Pilailupuoti – Harassment?

4.1 *Right to Non-discrimination*

The right not to be discriminated against is guaranteed in various human rights instruments. Finland has accepted or ratified all of the central ones or is a party to them as a member of the UN, the Council of Europe, and the European Union.[67] Treaty bodies interpreting the provisions on equality have emphasized in their general comments or recommendations that indigenous peoples are free and equal in dignity and rights, and free from any discrimination, and that states have positive obligations to take measures to prevent discrimination.[68] The CRC Committee has also called upon the states actively identify the existing and potential areas of discrimination and hence gaps and barriers to the enjoyment of the rights of indigenous children. CRC call for the states to identify the children whose right may demand special measures. Hence, CRC Committee requires states to recognize the special needs of indigenous children in order to eliminate conditions that cause discrimination, and to take special measures to respond to or accommodate those needs, such as changes in legislation, administration and allocation of resources. This is to ensure that indigenous children enjoy their rights on an equal level with non-indigenous children.[69]

Finland has guaranteed both the right to equality and prohibited discrimination in section 6, subsections 1 and 2 of its Constitution: "Everyone is equal before the law. No one shall, without an acceptable reason, be treated differently from other persons on the ground of sex, age, origin, language, religion, conviction, opinion, health, disability or other reason that concerns his or her person." According to the preparatory works of the Constitution, the provisions include both the traditional requirement of formal equality as well as the idea of equality in fact. The section has been described as being a prevailing principle of justice. The Finnish Non-Discrimination Act (2002, amended 2014), which gives more substance to the constitutional right mentioned, is ap-

---

67 Universal Declaration on Human Rights, Art. 7, CCPR 26, International Covenant on Economic, Social and Cultural Rights, Art. 2.2. ICERD, European Convention on the Protection of Human Rights and Fundamental Freedoms, Art. 14.

68 See e.g. HRC GC NO 31: Nature of the General Legal Obligation Imposed on States Parties to the Covenant:26.05.2004 CCPR/C/21/Rev1/Add13 8. and CESC GC NO 20, Non-discrimination in economic, social and cultural rights (Art. 2, para. 2, of the International Covenant on Economic, Social and Cultural Rights), E/C.12/GC/20, 2 July 2009, 9.

69 See n 49, para. 24, 25, 26.

plied to both public and private activities.[70] One of the main goals of the law is to promote de facto non-discrimination and actions that aim to improve situations for those that are disadvantaged.[71] The Act prohibits discrimination on the basis of origin, language, belief or other personal characteristics. It extends this prohibition to direct and indirect discrimination, harassment, and denial of reasonable accommodation as well as a instructions or orders to discriminate which also constitute discrimination.[72]

4.2 *Harassment*

Section 14 of the Non-Discrimination Act reads: "The deliberate or de facto infringement of the dignity of a person is harassment, if the infringing behaviour relates to a reason referred to in section 8(1) [prohibited grounds e.g. origin, language] and as a result of the reason, a degrading or humiliating, intimidating, hostile or offensive environment towards the person is created by the behaviour".[73] The former Act (from the year 2002) also mentioned a group's dignity but this was removed when the Act was revised in 2014. Even though the current provision refers only to a person, the preparatory works indicate that it was also meant to apply to activities, which are directed to a certain group as well, whereby it also protects a group's dignity.[74] Dignity relates here to the inherent dignity and to the equal and inalienable rights of all members of the human family and to everyone's right to enjoy equally all the rights and freedoms. It is mentioned that the dignity of a person can be infringed by acting in a way that demonstrates a fundamental lack of respect to a person on a prohibited ground or based on a prohibited ground, or that questions a person's right to be treated equally. Further, any act that is to be deemed harassment would normally need to be an action that is continual, evident, or public.[75] An example for present purposes would be a situation where an entrepreneur makes publicly available in his or her shop (or on the Internet) material portraying an ethnic group in a degrading or humiliating way. Whether an act constitutes

---

70 (1325/2014) Section 2.(2) This Act does not, however, apply to activities pertaining to private or family life or the practising of religion.

71 Finnish Government Bill, HE 19/2014 vp., 54.

72 Chapter 3, Prohibition of discrimination and victimisation, Section 8 Prohibition of discrimination (1) (2).

73 Council Directive 2000/43/EC of 29 June 2000 implementing the principle of equal treatment between persons irrespective of racial or ethnic origin (Racial Equality Directive) obligated Finland to enact national legislation prohibiting harassment.

74 See 71, 78.

75 T. Ojanen, M. Scheinin, 'Yhdenvertaisuus ja Syrjinnän kielto', in P. Hallberg et al. (eds.), *Perusoikeudet*, (toinen uudistettu painos WSOY Pro 2011) 246.

harassment is assessed according to objective criteria; subjective views are not decisive.[76] In addition, creating the environment mentioned in the section is required. For example, joking in way that humiliates an entire population can offend a person, even though this was not the intention.[77] Thus, when looking at the content and the scope of the law, norms on harassment could protect the dignity of the Sámi and hence Sámi dress from demeaning use.

There is very little legal praxis in Finland on what constitutes harassment. Only one case has been considered in the Supreme Administrative Court (SAC). In the case A and B et al., it was alleged that the state-owned Finnish broadcasting company (Yle) had discriminated against the Roma as an ethnic group by broadcasting a TV show and a series that in the opinion of the Roma infringed their dignity and portrayed them in a very prejudicial manner. [78] The SAC upheld decisions made by the lower courts that the action did not constitute harassment. The fact that the Roma themselves were involved in making the programme and that it actually promoted discussion in general on the situation of the Roma were used as the main arguments. In addition, the Court emphasized that the programme was lightly humorous. The Court determined that the evidence did not establish that the programme had factually caused serious harmful effects. The right not to be discriminated against was weighed against freedom of expression. The Court had thus set a high threshold for findings of harassment.

With this in mind one can ask, how should the actions of Pilailupuoti be assessed? Can they be seen as constituting harassment? Even though the SAC did not seem to put much weight on a person's or group's own view on offensiveness, let us look at the response from the Sámi to Pilailupuoti. In the questionnaire about the Sámi Duodji certification trademark, 63 people were asked what they thought about the use of the dress in the Pilailupuoti case. It was a multiple-response question with a possibility to choose several options. Thirty-five people (55.6 per cent) answered either "it offends me" or "it humiliates or degrades the Sámi", which means that over half of the people were offended personally or in the name of the Sámi people. Forty-four people chose either "it increases or exacerbates prejudice against the Sámi" or, "it humiliates or degrades the Sámi"; 34 per cent felt that it reinforces prejudices; 28 per cent responded that "it can affect in a negative way Sámi's self-image or identity". Altogether 51 persons chose one of the negative options offered. Only two

76 See 71, 78.

77 See n 71.

78 KHO:2011:22, 9.3.2011/588, <http://www.finlex.fi/fi/oikeus/kho/vuosikirjat/2011/201100588>, accessed 20 January 2016.

chose "It does not offend me" and seven "it has no effect on the Sámi". In addition, 25 chose an 'and/or' option where they could write an open answer. For the most part, the open answers indicated disappointment that the Sámi as a people and Sámi culture or knowledge of handicraft were made fun of or demeaned in that way. Respondents also mentioned the deceptiveness regarding the origin of the product, the economic exploitation of Sámi culture, or other negative elements.[79] The responses on the questionnaire coincide rather well with earlier Sámi views and statements on the use of the dress by outsiders.

Offensiveness or humiliation, the first part of the requirement for harassment, would thus be met if Sámi were asked. Clearly offensiveness or humiliation (cultural value, meaning, and consequences) can only truly be assessed by the people in question. However, both the preparatory works of the Non-Discrimination Act and the related case law seem to confirm that harassment is to be assessed on the basis of 'objective criteria', namely, the judgment of the majority of people about the nature of the action taken.[80] It means that denigration has to be obvious to the majority of people as well. Since the Sámi are a minority in Finland, and as mentioned one about whom the majority often knows very little, it seems that merely selling a copy of the dress is unlikely to meet the objective criterion for infringement. However, if case was brought to Non-Discrimination tribunal and administrative courts, they would also have to take into account the human rights of the Sámi as indigenous people and assess the need for protection of the Sámi identity from subjective opinion and actions by the majority Finns.

As for the second part of the requirement, proving a creation of such *environment,* the SAC has also set the bar high. In many of the cases in the European context, the harassment at issue either has occurred at work or has been sexual, incidents whose sphere of influence can easily be recognized.[81] Can the Sámi really even have a chance to prove that the environment created by Pilailupuoti fulfils the requirement, since the sphere of influence is not as clear-cut as in some other types of harassment? If the environment were only the store, it might be easier, but since it is the Internet, the sphere of influence is practically the whole of Finland. In the Roma case that came before the SAC, there was a great deal of evidence presented by the Roma people on the prejudice

79 See n 11.

80 Finnish government Bill, HE 19/2014 vp, 78.

81 Employment Tribunal, 24 October 2012, *Beyene v. JDA International Ltd,* Case No. 2703297/11., Employment Tribunal, 5 November 2012, *Henry v. Ashtead Plant Hire Co Ltd,* Case No. 3202933/1. In both of these cases an employee had used an insulting phrase about a colleague in front of other people.

they faced since the TV programme and still the Court did not find that Yle had created the atmosphere mentioned in the requirement. Moreover, the definition of harassment in the EU Racial Discrimination Directive, which was the model for the norm on harassment, has been criticized as being unclear and far from perfect. As Makkonen notes the effect of the "prohibition of harassment remains not just uncertain but also limited".[82]

The relevance of the prohibition on harassment seems unclear in the Pilailupuoti case, but it seems that in certain cases where the offensiveness is clear to the majority and the sphere of influence is defined, it can protect the dignity of Sámi and be used when trying to hinder the most offensive misappropriation of the Sámi dress and culture. An example would be where a person pretends to be a Sámi by wearing Sámi dress and does so in a demeaning way on a single occasion; for example at a party. In other words, prohibition against harassment protects the dignity of a person as a Sámi, not the dress itself, even though the dress is a manifestation of Sámi identity. Hence, under the contemporary interpretation, it seems the Sámi dress as a component of Sámi identity is protected only indirectly.

5 Conclusions

Thus far, Sámi demands for the protection of the Sámi dress as a distinctive and vital expression of culture seem to have gone unheeded – at least judging from the inertia of the Finnish state. This is unexpected in light of the Sámi's legal status as an indigenous people in the Finnish Constitution. The state of affairs is perhaps even more surprising given that the principles and terms governing the interpretation of the Sámi's fundamental rights follow from international law on indigenous peoples, which has seen considerable progress during the last few decades. Hence, although there is formal protection in the Constitution, it has not been implemented in practise. The collective right to decide on what is important in Sámi culture and have it protected is in practise a right to be consulted. Nor does the Sámi dress enjoy any specific legal protection at this time.

For the above-mentioned reasons, it seems that Sanila-Aikio's statement regarding structural racism in the tourism industry against the Sámi is partly accurate. This is particularly worrisome if it means that both private and state actors ignore the need to provide special protection for traditional Sámi dress

82 T. Makkonen, *Equal in Law, Unequal in Fact, Racial and Ethnic Discrimination and the Legal Response Thereto in Europe*, (Brill-Nijhoff 2012) 242.

as part of the people's cultural identity. It is quite clear that the Finnish Government has not taken the issue seriously. At the same time, one might ask whether the Sámi Parliament and other Sámi actors have used all the political and legal means at their disposal to effectively articulate the need to protect the dignity of the Sámi and of Sámi dress directly. The Non-Discrimination Act can, in certain cases, protect Sámi's dignity and the dress. It can also be anticipated that scope of the norm on harassment is actually wider than what the legal praxis indicates when the norm is read together with fundamental rights pertaining Sámi and human rights, which obligate the protection of Sámi's cultural rights and accommodation of the needs of Sámi children and youth. In this respect the Non-Discrimination Ombudsman may have a greater role to play by raising awareness, and using her mandate to take the cases to Finnish Non-Discrimination and Equality Tribunal.

More research is certainly needed on the benefits and shortcomings of other avenues for the protection of Sámi dress and other culturally significant element. Namely the laws and mechanisms for consumer protection and the laws and self-regulatory mechanisms in the private sector, one example being the Council of Ethics in Advertising. As mentioned, the tourism industry and the Sámi have also seen positive developments lately. One important actor in the industry – the House of Lapland – took an important initiative and requested guidelines on Sámi dress, which the Saami Parliament provided to an extent. It remains to be seen what kind influence this will have on the industry and private actors. Yet, this positive development shows that the Saami Parliament and other Sámi organizations could benefit from intensifying their cooperation with the different actors in the tourism industry. Close cooperation with the self-regulatory mechanisms of commercial actors and with actors promoting consumer protection in order to provide the industry with guidelines that are more comprehensive on human rights might be a step in the right direction for the protection of Sámi dress. An additional option would be for the Saami Parliament to use its mandate to propose to the Finnish Parliament that it pass an Act on the protection of Sámi symbols similar to the Act that exists on protection of the Finnish Flag. This Act makes public mutilation of the flag or its disrespectful use punishable by law (section 8) and prohibits forms of the flag that distort the prescribed colors and dimensions.

Reasons for demanding protection of traditional Sami dress are both cultural and economic. Traditional dress has an economic value to Sámi handcrafters and, in a wider context, promotes the economic development of the Sámi community as a whole. Generally speaking, demands that the cultural heritage of the Sámi be protected should be addressed, for they reflect a desire to protect the distinctive nature of Sámi culture, the Sámi community, Sámi identity, and the Sámi way of life. The fact that anyone can exploit Sámi dress and culture commercially as he or she chooses undermines this distinctiveness and blurs the differences between the Sámi and other people. Over time this could increase the risk that the Sámi will be assimilated into the majority population in a manner contrary to the spirit of international treaties, declarations, and the Finnish Constitution. Hence, protection of traditional Sámi dress should be seen as protection of the Sámi cultural identity and, ultimately, their human dignity – one of the essential underlying values of human rights. This is particularly salient given that young people have stated repeatedly how they feel and how worried they are about their Sámi identity and place within society as Sámi. We should listen to them and act – for the benefit of all concerned.

The Cultural Heritage of South Africa's Khoisan

Willa Boezak

It takes a village to raise a child.

When the elephants fight, it's the grass that suffers.
African proverbs

Introduction

The Khoisan's /'kɔɪsɑːn/ approach to culture is a holistic one. Over thousands of years they have cultivated an integrated life-style, undergirded by socio-religious values. In a sense it is therefore artificial to discuss separate cultural issues as if they are silos in the life of this indigenous nation. However, the erosion of their cultural heritage occurred systematically during protracted colonial and neo-colonial eras which allows for a focused approach. Some cultural strands survived the colonial onslaught while others became extinct. In modern times efforts have been made and still are being made, to restore, preserve and promote their heritage.

The following five areas will be dealt with here: land, identity, leadership structures, languages and religion. These are all inter-related. Other relevant issues, such as their indigenous knowledge system and legislation protecting their intellectual property, are too complex to be included here. In this chapter we will look at the current state of these 5 foci, their historical context and the possibilities to preserve them for future generations.

Mother Earth

Colin Bundy points out that it was archaeologists who first exposed falsehoods like the myth of the 'empty lands'.[1] The *terra nullius* idea, of course, was used as moral justification for the colonial invasion. The very first people who bore the onslaught of colonial oppression in South Africa were coastal Khoisan communities. It was the Portuguese, craving to 'discover' the world outside of Europe,

1 Colin Bundy, *The Rise and Fall of the South African Peasantry* (James Currey Publications 1988), 8-10.

Xanthaki, Valkonen et al. (eds.), *Indigenous Peoples' Cultural Heritage: Rights, Debates and Challenges.*
 ISBN 978-90-04-34218-7. PP. 253-272

who reached the Cape in 1488. Having survived tempestuous seas, they called it *Cabo Tormentuoso* (Cape of Storms). H.C. Bredekamp sketches the ambiguous nature of Bartholomeus Diaz's achievement: It '[M]arked the beginning of a new era of exploration and trade, but for the indigenous Khoikhoi and San it was the beginning of a process of colonial subjugation'.[2] It was also marked by Diaz's murder of a Khoikhoi herder on the beach of Mossel Bay.[3]

Two decades of intermittent, reasonably peaceful trading contacts turned ugly when, in 1510, Portuguese Viceroy Francisco de Almeida tried to manipulate the barter by kidnapping some Khoikhoi children near Table Bay. A skirmish ensued culminating in the killing of De Almeida and about sixty of his soldiers. Rationalizing their part in the unfortunate incident, the Europeans began to scandalize the Khoisan's nature and lifestyle. */Hui-!keib* /'hu:i: kaɪb/ ("The Cape", with clicks) was then avoided for a hundred years by passing seafarers, while views such as 'Those people are uncivilized, godless and bloodthirsty' abounded. 'They are cruel and kill strangers', Thomas Stevens remarked in 1579. That demonization reached its peak with: 'They are cannibals'.[4]

The first land dispossession under Dutch colonial rule occurred in 1657 when the first farms were granted to so-called 'free burghers' (Dutch citizens), without the permission of the local chief. That land-theft resulted in a war orchestrated by Doman, a young Goringhaiqua /gərɪŋ'haɪkwɑ:/ warrior (1659-60). Further encroachment on Khoisan land led to another war of resistance from 1673-77 by the Cochoqua /'kətʃəʊkwa:/ (guttural tʃ). But something that puzzled the Europeans was the Khoisan's ancient custom that during war they would rather strike at the enemies' property, than taking their lives.[5] Ironically it was this ingrained, humane view that made it easier for foreigners to subjugate the aboriginal inhabitants ruthlessly. One of the more extended wars of resistance later was waged in the Eastern Cape under the leadership of Captain Klaas Stuurman (1799-1803).

Another downside of these land wars was that the Europeans then applied Roman Dutch law, which meant that land won through wars became the ter-

2 H.C. Bredekamp, 'From Fragile Independence to Permanent Subservience' in T. Cameron and S. Spies (eds), *An Illustrated History of South Africa* (Southern Book Publishers 1986), 102.

3 E. Boonzaier et al. *The Cape Herders – A History of the Khoikhoi of Southern Africa* (David Philip 1996), 52-56.

4 W. Boezak, *Struggle of an Ancient Faith – the Khoisan of South Africa* (Bidvest Data 2016), 40.

5 V.C. Malherbe, 'The Khoi Captains in the Third Frontier War' in S. Newton and V.C. Malherbe, *The Khoikhoi Rebellion in the Eastern Cape: 1799-1803* (UCT Centre for African Studies 1984), 97-98.

ritories of the conqueror. It became a pattern: the two successive colonial regimes, namely the Dutch (1652-1800) and the English (1800-1910), would repeatedly use violence and oppressive legislation to dispossess the indigenous people. Because both hunter-gathering and pastoralism were intimately linked to land, these age-old economies were virtually destroyed.[6]

Different worldviews regarding land caused huge conflicts. While the Khoisan regarded land as a gift from *Tsui//Goab* / 'zu:ɩ'gwa:b/ (one name for the Supreme Being) and not something that could be privately owned by anyone, it was simply another commodity for the colonists. A *khoeseb* /'kɔɪseb/ (chief) could not privately own the tribe's territory, and only administered it on behalf of his people – as usufruct. So, signing a treaty with white trek-farmers or the colonial government did not mean the right to ownership. Land is Mother Earth. These different approaches frequently led to misunderstandings, wars, and loss of land. 'Western historians in the 1800s unashamedly… justified the right of certain nations to conquer, rule and actively transform those "others" whom they branded as inferior to themselves'.[7]

Certain cultural rites of passage tied a tribe to a specific territory. With the birth of a child, its umbilical cord was buried in the family kraal, and his or her funeral was undertaken near that spot. Ongoing rituals at ancestral graves further strengthened the spiritual attachment to specific territories. Moreover, Khoisan Africans had acquired a green cosmology that was geared toward the enhancement of harmony between all living beings. They had lived in close proximity to nature – with the Creator as Giver of rain, health and abundance. The colonial invasion had severed that sacred link. It was therefore much more than loss of territories and subsistence. Devastating smallpox epidemics broke out in 1713 at the Cape added to the depletion of Khoisan people. It lingered on for years and many more died when some fled to the rural areas, unknowingly taking the virus with them.[8] As can be seen on the chart, Khoisan communities had lived all across the land. (See map).[9]

6 Bredekamp, 'The Origin of the Southern African Khoisan Communities', in T. Cameron (n 2), 30.

7 Boonzaier, 57.

8 Ibid, 85.

9 H.C. Bredekamp and O. van den Berg (eds), *A New History Atlas for South Africa* (Edward Arnold Publishers 1986).

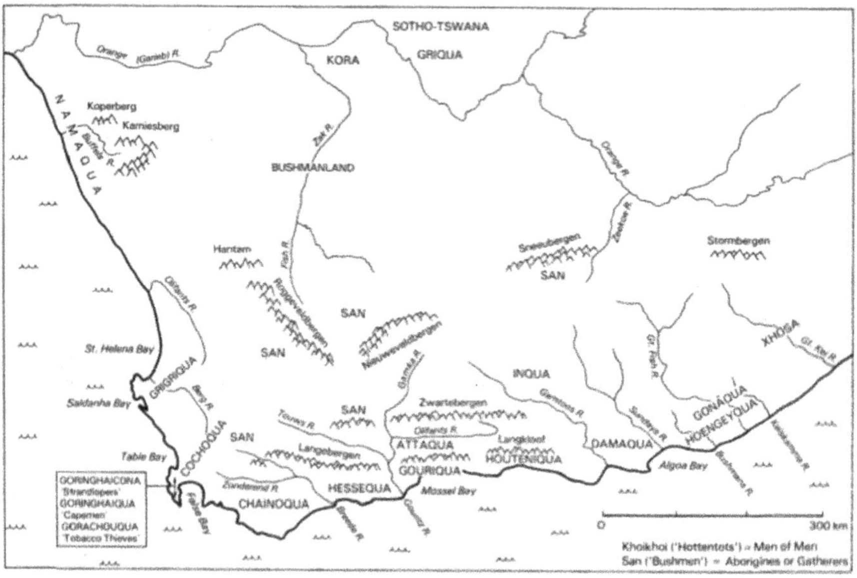

MAP 1 *Two major Khoikhoi groupings in the 17th an 18th centuries*

In the meantime the Bushmen/San were hunted down during the 1700s on a scale that constituted genocide. Colonial land-grabbing led to violent clashes first with the Obiqua /'Ʊbıkwa:/ San of the Boland and continued for the next 100 years. So, for instance, the entire Bushmen population of Sneeuberg (Snow Mountain) was wiped out by so-called commandos under the auspices of the Dutch East India Company. The sad thing is that colonists and trek-farmers increasingly forced their Hottentot/Khoikhoi servants to fill the ranks of those commandos. What is even worse is that the white Dutch Reformed Church still had a long debate in 1913: 'Is the Bushman an animal or a human being?'[10]

While we cannot assume that relations between the Khoikhoi herders and Bushmen/San hunters in the pre-colonial era were always harmonious, there was at least a relatively stable situation of co-existence based on mutually acknowledged territories. The continuing, violent land-dispossession left the herders with much less grazing land and the hunters with virtually no hunting grounds. This led to unnecessary friction and even bloodshed between indigenous factions who had built an age-old mutual understanding regarding territories. In short, the different attitudes between the indigenous people and colonists toward land were culturally grounded in different perceptions formed by African communalism and European individualism. The latter

10 Boezak, *Struggle of an Ancient Faith*, 145.

eroded African communal values. It created and intensified cultural and racial animosities in a land where a premium had been put on the common southern African derivation.

In the aftermath of the South African (or Anglo-Boer) War of 1899-1902, which was waged essentially over the region's rich natural resources such as diamonds and gold, the whites negotiated a settlement among themselves – which included the Natives Land Act of 1913.

> Together with later legislation the Act confirmed the right of the white conquering minority to ownership of some 87% of the land on which were developed highly productive commercial farms, and confined the ownership rights of the indigenous black majority to the remaining 13%, which became overgrazed, eroded and impoverished. That remained the situation until 1994.[11]

That effectively meant that South Africa was then regarded as a white country with a relatively small portion allocated to Blacks. Khoisan Africans, however, were totally left out of the equation. Following the unbanning of the African National Congress (among other organizations) and the release of Nelson Mandela in 1990, the *Convention for a Democratic South Africa* began. At these CODESA talks by all stakeholders, a path was carved out for a new South Africa. Khoisan leaders were not invited to the round table and even though the Paramount Chief of the Griqua /'grıkwa:/ National Conference made his wish known to be part of the talks, his request was turned down. The Restitution of Land Rights Act of 1994 focused on redressing land dispossession after 1913. Because the Khoisan had been dispossessed long before that cut-off date, it meant a denial of their right to reclaim their heritage. The legislative context of all land reform policies in South Africa is its Constitution.[12] Since its promulgation leaders from the aboriginal nation have protested and made appeals to have it amended.

Ancestral land was then restored to some communities. For instance, in 1972 the Apartheid regime had forcefully removed the ǂKhomani /'kɵmɑnı/ San from a park in the Northern Cape. With the assistance of WIMSA (Workgroup of Indigenous Minorities in Southern Africa) and SASI (South African San Institute), they lodged a claim with the new government and six farms outside

11 M. Engelbrecht, 'Racially motivated land dispossession in Gordonia', unpublished paper (Kimberley 4 April 2013), 1.

12 Act 108 of 1996, especially sections 25, 26, 27 and 36.

the park were handed over in 1999 and another 25 000 hectares in 2002.[13] In similar vein a dispossessed farm of the Griqua National Conference, Ratelgat /'rɑ:təlgɑt/ (guttural g), was given back to them in 1999 – without any costs.

During the past three years special national land summits were organized by the Department of Rural Development and Land Reform. A National Khoisan Reference Group was established to assist the government formulating a policy framework that focuses on restitution, reform, and redistribution. Although the 1913 cut-off date still stands, land claims by Khoisan communities would henceforth be regarded as *exceptions*. Also included is the possibility to have their sacred spaces and cultural places, such as graves, be declared as historical landmarks and heritage sites. The map included in this chapter clearly shows that the Khoisan had inhabited the entire South African surface. Today, however, they are citizens of a modern-day Republic under the jurisdiction of the Constitution. Realpolitik, therefore, dictates that – as responsible South Africans who respect the Constitution – the following factors should be seriously considered.

- Realism: It must be remembered that history, although it may be unfair and cruel, cannot be changed or ignored. Even though there is sufficient historical and scientific evidence to show that they are southern Africa's aboriginal people, they cannot wish away the fact that colonialism happened. The clock cannot be turned thousands of years back when their ancestors were the only human beings in this region.
- Reasonableness: Reliable maps along with rock art sites also affirm where the different tribes had lived. However, reasonableness means that they cannot reconstruct a land or provinces in which only Khoisan people exist or rule. When they claim land they will have to be reasonable. E.g. it will not be reasonable for the Griqua to reclaim the whole Griqualand West and East, although solid documentation is available that they had ruled there in the 18th and 19th centuries.
- Responsibility: Today the issue is not simply a matter of 'giving back the land'. It is a complex socio-political and macro-economic issue that has to do with national matters like food security.[14]

---

13 N. Crawhall and R. Chennels, *The* ǂKhomani *San: From Footnotes to Footprints – the History of the their Land Claim,* booklet (Trans Orange Press, undated), 3.

14 W. Boezak, 'A Historical View of the Khoisan', at a meeting of the South African Department of Rural Development and Land Reform (unpublished paper, Johannesburg March 2015).

Coupled with this is the correct interpretation of ILO Convention 169. Its preamble recognizes the aspiration of indigenous peoples to exercise control over their own institutions, way of life, economic development and to maintain and develop their own identities, languages and religion within the framework of the states in which they live.[15] That the South African state has not as yet ratified ILO 169 is indicative of its reluctance to grant the Khoisan their rightful place within the country's cultural landscape. Perhaps it is fear of the implications of self-determination. However, the Khoisan have never indicated that their right to self-determination would lead to land-grabbing or a 'state within a state'.

Another vexed question is how *colonial churches* can practice restorative justice, such as the white Dutch Reformed Church that now possesses large tracts of land, which belonged to the Khoisan's ancestors. The same question arises with respect to *missionary churches*, like the Moravians, who also have huge pieces of ill-gained land. Land reform, restitution, and redistribution will not be complete without taking this into account.

In conclusion: the very first thing the Khoisan had been dispossessed of by colonialists was land. Wars of resistance proved futile, exacerbated by ongoing foreign diseases. The Khoisan regard land as Mother Earth, the God-given space where they have practised their culture for millennia. It is inextricably linked to their heritage in all its forms and without it the aboriginal people will not be able to reclaim their rightful place and dignity. However, as citizens honouring the country's Constitution, their land reform plans should be realistic, reasonable, and responsible. The South African government, on the other hand, needs to ratify ILO Convention 169, granting the Khoisan's right to self-determination.

First Indigenous Nation

African-American philosopher, Cornel West, has coined the phrase: 'the normative gaze'. Via pseudo-sciences like phrenology and physiognomy the foundation for the Eurocentric principle of negative comparison had been laid in the sixteenth century.[16] Kieskamp says that a 'Chain of Life' was designed: God at the top, then human beings, and animals. On various lists of humans the

---

15 International Labour Organisation Convention (No 169) concerning Indigenous and Tribal Peoples in independent countries, 1989.

16 C. West, *Prophesy Deliverance! An Afro-American Revolutionary Christianity* (Beacon Press 1982), 57.

Khoisan were put on the lowest rung of human existence, nearer to apes and without a soul. The Eurocentric principle meant that when compared to Europeans, the Khoisan seemed to have missed every standard that indicated the existence of what was regarded as civilization: a king, jurisdiction, laws, script, arts, agriculture, money, marriage and religion.

These prejudices were augmented by fear of the unknown especially after hearing stories of shipwrecked people meeting hostile savages – accompanied by illustrations and ethnological descriptions. Jan van Riebeeck, mandated by the Dutch East India Company to establish a refreshment post at the Cape in 1652, did not, therefore, arrive with an objective mind. He was indeed already filled with the ideas of white supremacy.[17]

Moreover, Christian ideologues misappropriated the Biblical story of Noah who had cursed his son, Ham: that his descendants – supposedly Africans – would be 'the lowest of slaves to his brothers'. Together these ideas provided the moral justification for the vicious enslavement of those with a dark skin – a colour theologically associated with Satan and sin, morally with evil and aesthetically with ugliness. No wonder then that over time advancing colonists had murdered numerous 'soulless Bushmen' without a qualm.[18] But who are the Khoisan really and what is the nature of their cultural identity?

Recent linguistic and biological tests have proven beyond a doubt that the first modern human beings (*homo sapiens*) evolved on the African continent – the cradle of humanity.

Oldest DNA

In a newspaper article Elsabé Brits quotes Drs Peter Foster and Matsumura of the University of Cambridge who stated that the Khoikhoin and Bushmen/San, all originally being hunter-gatherers, stem from the same genetic stock. On the basis of extensive tests it was found that the Khoisan people of southern Africa possess 'the oldest DNA', i.e. human genes, on earth.[19] Renowned South African geneticist Himla Soodyall agrees with her peers and she is doing ongoing tests in Khoisan communities today. Archaeological evidence points in the same direction. Philip Tobias states that remains of modern human civilization at Klasies /ˈklɑːsɪs/ River Mouth Cave, more than 100,000 years old, led to the con-

17 J. Kieskamp, in A. Bank (ed), *The Khoisan Identities and Cultural Heritage*, IHR, Univ. of the Western Cape infoSOURCE (Cape Town 1998), 163-70.

18 W. Boezak, *Struggle of an Ancient Faith*, 40-42.

19 E. Brits, 'Oudste DNS – Khoisan' in *Die Burger*, 18 March 2006.

clusion that the ancestors of the Khoisan of South Africa are part of the same, large division of Sub-Saharan peoples. Archaeologists Hilary and Jeanette Deacon emphasize: 'Biological tests... strengthen the view that the Khoikhoin and San shared the same ancient southern African genetic heritage'.[20]

Khoikhoin means 'genuine people' (singular: a people person) and *Sa* means 'to gather', while the plural (with –n) means 'gatherers' (of *veldkos* /'feltkɔs/ i.e. wild edible plants). The names *Hottentotten* (Hottentots) and *Bosjesmannen* (Bushmen) were given to them by the Dutch – both neutral, descriptive designations at the time. Since then 'Hottentots' has been reduced to an insult: '*hotnots*', a term rightly regarded today as hate-speech.

Alan Barnard's ethnographic approach indicates a nomadic movement *within* southern Africa: 'At least some of the ancestors of the Khoi Bushmen migrated from or through what is now Zimbabwe or eastern Botswana... After the Khoi Bushmen divergence, the ancestors of the Khoikhoi moved slowly southwards'.[21] (See map).

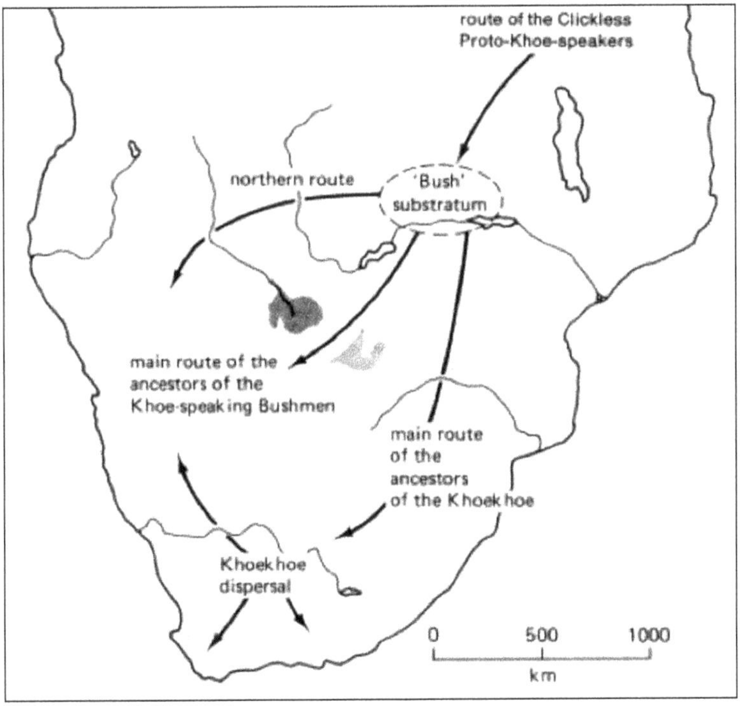

MAP 2 *Nomadic movement within southern Africa*

20 H. and J. Deacon (eds), *Human Beginnings in South Africa* (David Philip 1999), 171.

21 A. Barnard, *Hunters and Herders of Southern Africa: A Comparative Ethnography of the Khoisan Peoples* (Cambridge University Press 1992), 34-35.

However, when the German anthropologist Leonard Schultze coined the amalgam *Koïsan* in 1928, he did it on the basis of their common southern African derivation. The two names indicate a division that came about 2 000 years ago when herding had been introduced as an optional, economic lifestyle. The amalgam 'Khoisan' indicates an actual process of intermingling, intermarriage, acculturation and assimilation which occurred over centuries. Some historians have reasoned for many years that the Khoisan were originally from East Africa Contrary to these migrationist views historian Yvette Abrahams boldly states:

> There is simply no evidence to make a systematic distinction between who hunted and gathered for a living, and people who also herded cattle, sheep and goats. We all hunted and gathered, even if we kept livestock. We all shared a set of values, arts and culture. There is absolutely no evidence that our people came from anywhere else. Cows did, not people, after all, we had bartered and traded for centuries.[22]

Hilary and Jeanette Deacon, conclude: 'We can confidently state that the ancestors of the Khoikhoin and the San were an indigenous population that originated and diversified within southern Africa'.[23] Isaac Schapera concurs that the Khoikhoin and the Bushmen/San share the same origin by highlighting the similarities of their belief systems.[24]

This scientific evidence accumulatively plays a crucial role when the Khoisan claim they are in fact South Africa's aboriginal people. Despite this the South African government thus far has not shown any political will to grant the status of 'first nation' to them. The right to self-identification thus has been met with historical distortion and official denialism. After the abolishment of slavery in 1834-38, the free slaves and the Khoisan were all lumped together as the new working classes and jointly called 'people of colour'. Since 1948 the *Apartheid* regime continued to reclassify the majority of Khoisan people as 'Cape Coloured' and used their Group Areas Act of 1950 to forcefully remove them from their remaining ancestral land.[25]

Professor Rodolfo Stavenhagen, UN Special Rapporteur on the Fundamental Freedoms of Indigenous Peoples, visited South Africa in 2005. He took note of the fact that the Khoisan's identity was forcefully changed under the old

---

22 Y. Abrahams, 'Bill makes all groups indigenous' in *Eland* (4-17 April 2013), 14.

23 Deacon and Deacon, *Human Beginnings in South Africa*, 129, 171.

24 I. Schapera, *The Khoisan Peoples: Bushmen and Hottentots* (Routledge & Keegan Paul 1965), 360-76.

25 SA Race Classification Act of 1950.

race classification laws, and recommended that 'actions should be undertaken towards the removal of all legitimate claimants to indigenous identity of the stigma to having been classified as "Coloured"'.[26] To be sure, the individual rights of all South Africans, including the Khoisan's, are guaranteed in the Constitution.[27] But what about their collective rights?

Since the advent of South Africa's new, democratic dispensation in 1994, the Khoisan people have incessantly yet unsuccessfully tried to convince the government of their status as the country's first indigenous nation. That fact does not imply a dominant position in the wider society. They also do not accept the assumption that because all Africans are indigenous, no grouping can claim to be South Africa's aboriginal people. The ILO's controversial resolution pertaining to self-determination should not be seen as a threat.

> The peoples concerned shall have the right to decide their own priorities for the process of development as it affects their lives, beliefs, institutions and spiritual wellbeing and the lands they occupy or otherwise use, and to exercise control, to the extent possible, over their own economic, social and cultural development.[28]

Rather, with the right to self-definition and self-identification as its pillars, self-determination has essentially to do with steering their own cultural destiny. Article 11 (1) of the UN Declaration on the Rights of Indigenous Peoples states:

> Indigenous peoples have the right to practise and revitalize their cultural traditions and customs. This includes the right to maintain, protect and develop the past, present and future manifestations of their cultures, such as archaeological and historical sites, artefacts, designs, ceremonies, technologies and visual and performing arts and literature.

The Khoisan accept the argument that in South Africa, as in other African countries, all Africans are indigenous because they are 'non-dominant', original inhabitants – hence culturally different from white colonists. However, they are not simply Africans in the broader, generic sense of the word, but specifically the autochthonous population of southern Africa. This internal differentiation is significant – an issue that should be urgently dealt with by the country's De-

26 R. Stavenhagen, *Report of the UN Special Rapporteur on Indigenous Peoples' Mission to South Africa*, 2005.

27 Act 108 of 1996, Articles 30, 31.

28 ILO 169, Article 7 (1).

partment of Justice.[29] Yet, in an official brochure the symbolism of the national coat of arms is explained as follows: 'Contained within the shield are some of the earliest representations of humanity in the world. Those depicted were the very first inhabitants of the land, namely the Khoisan people'.[30]

In conclusion: Overwhelming scientific evidence has proven the Khoisan's special identity as South Africa's first indigenous nation. It links them inextricably to their cultural heritage. The government's continuing denialism and refusal to grant them their inherited status, constitutes a serious violation of human rights.

Participation in the Protection of Their Cultural Heritage

Besides land loss during the colonial eras, the Khoisan's ancient leadership structures had been destroyed. Loss of control over their cultural heritage not only meant loss of face, but in fact constituted ethnocide. In light of this history of systematic dispossession, the question remains: If cultural heritage is essentially inheritance, what is left to promote, preserve, and develop? It is here that the unique story of the Griqua comes to the fore. Of all five major groupings it is the only one that has consistently managed to keep their identity and culture intact in an organized fashion.[31]

To be sure, cultural remnants had been kept alive in and by all communities, whether it was the Khoi reel dance on isolated farms or the Nama-language spoken by elders. The ≠Khomani-San deserves special mention though. Having had to endure unspeakable hardship, a strong leader, !Gam /Gaub Regopstaan Kruiper /'gam gaɵb regɔpstɑːn krəɵpər/ began to ensure their future during the last century. He eventually found refuge in the 1980s for his clan on a tourism farm.[32] Further momentum among Khoisan groups was gained in the late 1990s – a revival that was assisted by academics, notably historian H.C. Bredekamp and archaeologist Janette Deacon. But it was the Griqua who, with

29 P.L. Waldman, *The Griqua Conundrum: Political and socio-cultural Identity in the Northern Cape, South Africa*, PhD Thesis, Univ of the Witwatersrand, Johannesburg (2001), fn 8.

30 South African Dept of Arts & Culture's booklet, *The National Identity Passport* (underlined, undated), 6.

31 A. Morris, 'The Griqua and the Khoikhoi' in *Kronos*, Journal of Cape History (No 24, Nov 1997) 112. 'The 1980 census figures indicate that the category "Griqua" includes nearly 100 000 people'.

32 N. Crawhall and R. Chennels, *The #Khomani-San: From Footnotes to Footprints* (Trans Orange Publishers undated), 2.

unbroken leadership structures, were able to survive and adapt throughout the colonial and post-colonial *Apartheid* /a'partheɪd/ eras in an organized form.

Literally thousands of pages have been written on their extraordinary history.[33] In a nutshell: Around 1750 a free slave, named Adam Kok, had gathered the rest of the dispossessed *≠Karixuriqua* /karɪ'gɵrikwa:/ (Griqua) on the West Coast along with people of mixed descent, married a Khoisan woman and had built a strong following through his sons. Under their and other Griqua leaders' guidance two huge territories were demarcated (Griqualand West and Griqualand East) but later annexed by the British Colonial government. The chieftaincy was eventually taken over during the late 1800s by Andrew le Fleur I, who then established the Griqua National Conference in 1904. Today their culture is preserved via various structures including an independent church. A recent study by the University of the Free State has shown: 'The Griqua are evidently aware of their very specific cultural traditions and rituals'.[34]

As mentioned earlier, when the Griqua National Conference (GNC) was refused participation at the CODESA, they made submissions in 1995 at the UN's Working Group on Indigenous Populations. The outcome was that the late President Mandela started direct talks with them, which eventually led to the establishment of the National Khoisan Council in 1999 – an official forum mandated to negotiate with government regarding constitutional accommodation. The same year researchers were commissioned to draw up a Status Quo report concerning the Khoisan's historical leadership structures. Five major groupings were identified: Bushmen/San, Cape Khoi, Griqua, Korana, and Nama. In 2001 about 600 delegates of these self-identifying groups in terms of the United Nations characteristics, gathered for the first time in a town called Oudtshoorn. The theme of the consultative conference was: *≠gui !nâgusib guisib !nâ* /'gɵɩ 'nagɵsɪb 'gɵɩsɪb 'na/ (with clicks) – Diversity in Unity.[35] It was indicative of their acknowledgement that although there were cultural differences, they wanted to revitalize their traditions and customs as a united people.

Khoisan Africans felt left behind when already in 2003 Parliament passed the Traditional Leadership and Governance Framework Act No. 41 (for Black South

33 The most comprehensive academic work: Michael Besten, *Transformation and Reconstruction of Khoe-San Identities: AAS le Fleur I, Griqua Identities and Post-Apartheid Khoe-San Revivalism (1894-2004)*, unpublished PhD thesis, Leiden University, 2005.

34 University of the Free State, *A Socio-economic & Cultural Study of the Griqua People of South Africa* (Centre for Development Support 2010), 14.

35 National Khoisan Consultative Conference (Institute for Historical Research, University of the Western Cape, archived document (Bellville 2001).

Africans). The Constitution's Chapter 12 has been implemented which provides for the recognition of traditional leadership, according to customary law. Since then a new legislative framework has been issued to accommodate the Khoisan alongside recognized traditional leaders. The latest version is the National Traditional and Khoisan Leadership Bill, expected to be promulgated by Parliament in 2016. The SA government's willingness to let them participate in existing structures beside traditional communities, is a step in the right direction.

Those communities and their leaders that would be recognized, will serve with already recognized traditional leaders in national, provincial, and local Houses. Moreover, recognized Khoisan councils will receive support to preserve, promote and develop their cultural heritage. In a real sense that will mean opportunities for all cultural groupings in terms of state funding.

However, while it is expected that certain standards should be maintained, applicants will be subjected to some unreasonable criteria that do not take their historical fragmentation into consideration. For instance, a community must have 'a history of self-identification by members of the community concerned, as belonging to a unique community distinct from all other communities' and 'a proven history of coherent existence from a particular point in time up to the present'.[36] These stipulations ignore harsh historical realities, such as the removal of whole communities under *apartheid* via the Group Areas Act. What is therefore needed, human rights lawyer Lesle Jansen argues, is an approach that will restore the human dignity of the Khoisan with restorative justice. Such an approach will fully take the cultural vulnerability of Khoisan Africans into consideration, allowing them sufficient time to rebuild their heritage.

> A restorative approach is necessary to address the root causes of Khoi-San vulnerability; the classification of being labelled Coloured, denoting them being neither European nor Black made them to be politically invisible. A history of self-identification may be difficult to prove. Groups may no longer occupy a specific area and may have been forced to stop observing certain Khoi-San customary laws and practices.[37]

At a recent seminar on cultural heritage organized by the Expert Mechanism of the Rights of Indigenous Peoples (EMRIP) Juha Karhu posed a challenging question: 'When states do accommodate indigenous peoples constitutionally,

---

36 The National Traditional and Khoi-San Leadership Bill 2015, Ch 2, Part 1, Articles 5 (1) (a) and (v).

37 Lesle Jansen, Power Point Presentation, *Report back on York University/Natural Justice Report,* Natural Justice, Cape Town (2014), Slide 10.

are they then empowered or domesticated?'[38] Thus, would official recognition of some Khoisan leaders and their communities come at too high a price? Will they be empowered or domesticated? After closer scrutiny it seems that Khoisan and traditional leaders will not be of equal rank. The Act will also exclude any recognition as first indigenous nation.

In conclusion: Since the inception of the official National Khoisan Council in 1999 strides have been made regarding legislation that would constitutionally accommodate the Khoisan. The relevant Act to recognize Khoisan leaders and their communities is expected to be promulgated by the SA Parliament in 2016. Recognition will enable the Khoisan to promote, preserve and develop their cultural heritage with state funding and to make use of the state's infrastructure. However, while willing to participate in the protection of their cultural heritage at this level, certain criteria will unfairly exclude most communities because of historical factors beyond their control.

Languages

Before the dawn of South Africa's democracy in 1994 only two languages enjoyed official status, namely Afrikaans /ɑfrɪ'kɑ:ns/ (stemming from the Dutch colonial era, 1657-ca. 1800) and English (from the British colonial era, 1800-1910). South Africa is a complex, multi-cultural, multi-linguistic society but its Constitution ensures that: 'Everyone has the right to receive education in the official language or languages of their choice in public institutions...'[39] Implementation, however, proved to be so challenging that new legislation has been deemed necessary: 'All learners have the constitutional right to be educated in their mother-tongue'.[40]

Not a single aboriginal Khoisan language is included in the list of 11 official languages. And yet, to be fair, in Chapter One of the Constitution it is stated that a special language board would also 'promote the Khoi, Nama and San languages', which it does.[41] This vehicle is called the Pan South African Language Board (PanSALB). An additional council for the advancement of Khoisan languages has been established because most of those had become extinct, e.g. the

38 UN EMRIP Seminar on the Promotion and Protection of the Rights of Indigenous Peoples with Respect to their Cultural Heritage, University of Lapland, Rovaniemi, Finland, 26-27 Feb 2015. My paraphrase.

39 Act 108 of 1996, Sect 29/2.

40 South African Official Languages Act 12 of 2012.

41 Sect 6/5.

Griqua's Xiri /'gɪrɪ/ (guttural g), the Bushmen's /Xam /'ɑm/ (with click) and Korana. The only Khoisan language that is still being spoken, written and taught in some schools, is Namagowab /'nɑmɑgʉə'vɑb/. The Bushman language, N/u /'nʉ/ (with click), is slowly but surely being rekindled and preserved.[42]

Historians Richard Elphick and V.C. Malherbe observe that the Nama Khoi-language is closely related to a specific group of (Bushman/San) 'hunter languages'.[43] However, linguist Nigel Crawhall cautions that within the Khoisan language stock there are three radically different language families, namely, Khoe, Ju /'dʒʉ/ and !Ui-Taa /'ʉɪtɑ:/ (with click).[44] At a practical level this means that frequently members from different groups could not even understand one another. The fact of diversity, however, does not negate the fundamental and original unity of the Khoisan.

Here is a peculiar fact that has been brought to light: Afrikaans is actually part of the Khoisan's cultural heritage. Although historians, such as Robert Ross, have alluded to that connection in the 1980s, it was only recently endorsed by thorough research commissioned by the *Afrikaanse Taalraad* /'tɑ:lrɑ:d/ (Afrikaans Language Board).[45] The foundation for Afrikaans had already been laid in the late 1500s when the Khoisan coastal communities had tried to communicate with passing European seafarers on their way to the East. It developed rapidly when the Dutch established their fort at the Cape and imported slaves from Angola, Indonesia, Malaysia, etc.

Diversity and the geographical dispersal of the rural slave population inhibited a unifying culture. Some slaves used a form of creolized Portuguese, but most slaves, masters and Khoisan conversed in an evolving form of Dutch, which contributed to the development of Afrikaans. At first this new language was ridiculed as a 'Hottentot' and a 'kitchen', slave language. In 1875 a white Afrikaner movement, the *Genootskap van Regte Afrikaners* /gə'nʉətskɑp 'fɑn 'regtə ɑfrɪ'kɑ:nərs/ (guttural g's – Society of Real Afrikaners) started to gather all the various strains and standardized them. This society never acknowledged the coastal Khoisan's creativeness, and annexed it wholly as part of their culture. Because Afrikaans was the Apartheid regime's preferred language, it gained the negative connotation of being the 'language of the oppressor'.

42 PanSALB CD, *The n/u Language Project* (Lingo Software 2006).

43 R. Elphick and V. Malherbe, 'The Khoisan to c 1770' in R. Elphick and H Giliomee (eds), *The Shaping of South Africa: 1652-1820* (Longman Penguin 1989) 4-7.

44 N. Crawhall, 'Languages, genetics and archaeology' in H. Soodyall (ed), *The Prehistory of South Africa* (Jonathan Ball Publishers 2006) 109-24.

45 R. Ross, *Cape of Torments* (Routledge & Kegan Paul 1983), 2; C. van Rensburg, *So kry ons Afrikaans* (Lapa Uitgewers 2012), 13-28.

In conclusion: The different aboriginal languages of the Khoisan have become extinct, except for the Khoikhoi's Namagowab and the Bushmen's N/u. The former is being taught with state funding at schools in those parts of the country where Nama people reside. The latter is being preserved in less formal ways, but a CD was released by PanSALB. Lastly, Afrikaans, despite its connotation, is part of the Khoisan's cultural heritage – its official status a proud beacon.

In the meantime it is interesting to note that rock art (petroglyphic) is actually their earliest form of sacred texts.

Ancient Religion

Rock art sites are clear indicators that the Khoisan had lived everywhere in South Africa – undeniably an integral part of the Khoisan's cultural heritage. Correct interpretations of these texts reveal ancient religious customs in which the healing of the sick and rainmaking rituals by shamans played a crucial role.[46] It is heartening that today there are still shamans among the ǂKhomani San of the Kalahari practising these ancient rituals.

The Khoisan's ancient religion needs redress. Irrespective of the fact that rock art sites were out of their reach, the damage done by Christian missionaries since the 18th century is incalculable. For them the aboriginal inhabitants were godless heathen – spiritually empty vessels in whom the true religion had to be instilled. By then the Khoisan had been rendered landless and virtually powerless. In those circumstances mission-stations became safe havens, securing a fixed address instead of them being harassed as vagrants or turned into slaves on the white trek-farmers' farms.

The plusses were that the missionaries taught them to read and write and the advantages of agriculture. Liberal missionaries, such as Dr Johannes van der Kemp and Dr John Philip, fought for the Khoisan's human rights. New laws were made to improve their lot. Ordinance 50 of 1828 did away with the humiliating carrying of passes and granted land rights. Yet even they remained in the Christian Western Civilization mold. Baptism meant loss of identity and survival on mission-stations meant forgoing their own cultural practices, traditions, customary laws and indigenous faith. W.M. Freund poignantly remarks: 'Christianization went hand in hand with the destruction of the older Khoikhoi culture'.[47]

46 S. Ouzman, 'The Magical Arts of a Raider Nation' in *South African Archaeological Society* (Goodwin Series, vol 9, Dec 2009) 101-12; Boezak, *Struggle of an Ancient Faith*, 49-58.

47 W.M. Freund, 'The Cape under the transitional governments, 1795-1814' in Elphick and Giliomee (n. 5) 342.

Today the vast majority of Khoisan people are Christians, but two major groups tried to retain some elements of their original faith by establishing own churches, namely, the Nama Qua Church and the Griqua Independent Church (GIC). In the former they read from a Namagowab bible and the older folk still pray in that language. After services they would easily dance the traditional Nama-step. Hundreds of GIC-members gather every year on 31 December, singing and praying till the early hours of the New Year, while a sheep is slaughtered. This is a link to an ancient, religious Khoikhoi custom, called the *ǂguri-ab* /'gʉrɪ-ab/ (with click) – an annual thanksgiving ceremony.[48]

As stated earlier, in 2001 the first National Khoisan Consultative Conference (NKCC) was held. I was asked to present a paper on 'Khoisan Faith', in which I explained the holistic approach with religion and culture inextricably woven. Their lifestyle was filled with values pertaining to the heavenly realm, Mother Earth, fellow human beings and every living entity. The challenge is how the ancient faith could be revitalized, and three options were posed to the conferees. They voted for the third option.

1) Had the time arrived for them to establish their own separate Christian Church where all the tenets and elements of their ancient belief system can be incorporated?
2) The Nama Qua Church and Griqua Independent Church already exist: Should they instead take up this challenge?
3) Mainline churches' Khoisan-members should challenge their clergy to include Khoisan symbolism in existing liturgies and sacraments – i.e. incorporation or inculturation.[49]

The Khoi ritual of breaking and sharing an *askoek* /'ɑskʉk/ (ash loaf) with everyone present, even strangers, serves as an example of the African value of incorporation. The ritual is based on an attitude of life: *khoi-/namxa-sîb* /'kɔɪ namga sɪb/ (*with* guttural g) – neighbourly love. A missionary working in the northern region of South Africa during the 19th century conceded that it was precisely this communal trait which was exploited by foreigners, who really were immoral land robbers.[50] Exclusivity has never been a facet of African philosophy. Gabriel Setiloane argues that the colonists had misused the ancient African tradition of sharing and kindness. He states that:

48 Scapera, 376; Cf W Hoernlé, *The Social Organisation of the Nama – and other Essays* (Witwatersrand University Press 1985), 32-34, 55.

49 W. Boezak, 'Khoisan Faith', NKCC (n 34), 10.

50 G. Meyer, *Die Gemeente te Steinkopf* (Pro Ecclesia 1927) 23, 45.

> Africa fell a prey to the wiles and greed of the European interloper coming in all disguises – a wandering shipwrecked traveller, explorer, teacher, missionary... However, the resolution: 'This land belongs to us' (*lomhlaba ongowethu* ɵlɔm'ɵl*a*:b*a* *ɔŋg*ɵwetɵ/), does not necessarily foreclose or shut out any other consideration borne out of the generosity of hearts begotten and nurtured in *Botho-Ubuntu-Ubuntungushi* /'bɔ:tɔ ɵ'bɵntɵ ɵ'bɵntɵ'gɵʃ*ι*/ (the value of incorporation).[51]

Currently I try to educate the broader South African public regarding the aboriginal faith and culture of the Khoisan with a series called *The Umbilical Cord Lectures.* Khoisan communities themselves, such as the Outeniqua of George, hold Full Moon prayer sessions augmented by reel dancing and story-telling. At the same time the South African Human Rights Commission is conducting hearings chaired by Commissioner Danny Titus, assessing their concerns.[52] Although the outcome is not known yet, a submission was made regarding firstly, the possibility that the Khoisan's faith be included in school curriculums (Comparison Religion) and secondly, the South African Council of Churches to review their church history and catechism books.

In conclusion: Although the majority of Khoisan people today are devout Christians, many seem to long for earlier times when they could still freely practise their ancient religion. Successive eras, especially the advent of missionary Christendom, effectively destroyed that. Various avenues are being sought today to revitalize at least some aspects. The two independent Christian-Khoisan churches have also managed to retain some ancient rituals.

The National Khoisan Heritage Route

South Africa has a range of state and private institutions geared toward the preservation of culture – governed by relevant legislation. Besides a Department for Arts and Culture (with Freedom Park and the National Heritage Council under its auspices), the Commission for the Promotion and Protection of the Rights of Cultural, Religious and Linguistic Communities has been

---

51 G. Setiloane, 'Land in the Negotiations Chamber' in *Journal of Black Theology in South Africa* (vol. 5 no. 2, 1991) 37; Cf W. Boezak, *God's Wrathful Children: Political Oppression & Christian Ethics* (Wm Eerdmans 1995) 228-29.

52 The SAHRC is a so-called Ch 9 institution, its functions described in the Constitution. It has the powers 'to take steps to secure appropriate redress where human rights have been violated (Article 184, 2b).

established in 2003 (CRLC) – a constitutional body.[53] Legislation such as the National Environmental Management Act (NEMA), the National Heritage Resources Act (NHRA) and the Intellectual Property Amendment Act collectively strengthen the reserve of communities to revitalize their cultural heritage.[54]

A promising sign of a joint venture between the Khoisan and the South African government which will link the numerous aboriginal sacred spaces and historical landmarks, is the planned National Khoisan Heritage Route (NKSHR).[55] This idea originated with the Khoisan themselves when about 200 delegates met in 2002 at the McGregor Museum, Kimberley. It did not take root because of lack of state funding. It is therefore ironic that, ten years later, the government relaunched it as their 'Draft Final Report'. However, the relevant department does work together with representatives of the National Khoisan Council.

L. van Rensburg defines culturally significant places quite broadly as '[A]ssociated with living heritage, includes monuments, historical settlements, landscapes and natural features of cultural significance, archaeological and paleontological sites, graves and burial grounds, movable objects recovered from soil and water.'[56]

Despite the obvious pitfalls pertaining to cultural or heritage tourism, the NKSHR provides a possible platform for the Khoisan to showcase their unique inheritance. It clearly meets the UN's standard:

> States shall provide redress through effective mechanisms, which may include restitution, developed in conjunction with indigenous peoples, with respect to their cultural, intellectual, religious and spiritual property taken without their free, prior and informed consent or in violation of their laws, traditions and customs.[57]

53 Act 108 of 1996, Article 185.

54 Act 107 of 1998; Act 25 of 1999; Act 28 of 2013.

55 South African Dept of Arts & Culture, *The National Khoisan Route* (Draft Final Report 2012).

56 L. van Rensburg and L. Kotze, 'Legislative protection of cultural heritage resources: A South African perspective'. Paper presented at the 8th Annual Qualitative Methods Conference: *Something for Nothing,* May-Sept 2002.

57 UNDRIP, Article 11 (2).

Indigenous Peoples' Right to Own Legal Orders and Governance Systems in The International Human Rights Regime

Anne-Maria Magga

1 Introduction

In the colonization processes all over the world, indigenous peoples' own governance systems and legal orders were formally replaced by legal regimes and institutions of the settler societies.[1] By the same token, colonialism has led to a demise or at least gradual erosion of indigenous peoples' own systems for self-determination and autonomous governance. Despite the historical and ongoing settler colonialism, many indigenous peoples have managed to retain *de facto* their own legal orders and institutions of autonomous governance, which are grounded on their own customs, traditions and values, even if they are not necessarily recognized *de jure*.[2] In recent decades, indigenous peoples' legal orders and laws have started also to gain stronger recognition and protection under international law.

In this chapter, I will examine how the international human rights regime has acknowledged and interpreted indigenous peoples' rights to their own legal orders, governance systems and customary laws with special focus on indigenous lands and livelihoods as an integral part of their cultural heritage. By examining the reindeer husbandry as part of Sámi culture, I highlight the importance of indigenous peoples' own institutions in the successful governance of their cultural heritage. I am thus interested in how international instruments have affirmed indigenous peoples' right to govern their lands and consequently, cultural heritage in accordance with their own laws. In this chapter, the concept of cultural heritage is thus understood widely as encompassing both tangible and intangible aspects. As noted by James Anaya, 'autonomous governance for indigenous communities is considered instrumental to their capacities to control the development of their distinctive cultures, *including their use of lands and resources*.'[3] Indigenous peoples' legal orders encompass essentially also the set of rules that regulate the land tenure systems, and set

1 J. Anaya, *Indigenous Peoples in International Law* (2nd ed. OUP 2004).
2 Ibid. 152-153.
3 Ibid. 152.

Xanthaki, Valkonen et al. (eds.), *Indigenous Peoples' Cultural Heritage: Rights, Debates and Challenges.*
 ISBN 978-90-04-34218-7. PP. 273-293

up dispute resolution mechanisms.[4] Jeremy Webber even contends that the indigenous peoples' land rights necessarily presuppose the continuation of indigenous legal orders and indigenous institutions.[5] By this he means that 'rights are intrinsically bound up with the legal order they have been defined and according to which they have been interpreted, adjusted and developed'.[6] By extension, this tends to apply also to indigenous cultural heritage rights as I will demonstrate in the course of this chapter.

In this sense, indigenous peoples' own legal orders and customary laws can thus be considered an integral part of their successful self-determination and self-governance over, for instance, their lands and cultural heritage. Customary laws refer to both ongoing practices and perceptions about the legal validity of such practices.[7] Many indigenous and non-indigenous scholars have, however, avoided using the concept of *customary law* and preferred instead to use the terms *indigenous law* or *indigenous legal orders,* which do not cement law as something traditional and static as suggested by the prefix *customary*.[8] John Borrows has resisted the use of *customary law* by referring to the fact that indigenous peoples' law consists also of natural, sacred, deliberate and written law.[9] Keeping this critique in mind, I refer to *customary laws* when analyzed instruments use that wording.

In legal literature, however, the place of indigenous custom in legal hierarchy or conflicts of laws is far from clear.[10] Those questions remain outside the scope of this chapter. It aims instead to demonstrate the problems that arise when customary law systems are ignored altogether in the governance of indigenous cultural heritage, such as that of reindeer husbandry. In the words of Brendan Tobin, however, 'Indigenous peoples' right to self-determination would mean little if it did not allow them the freedom to govern their affairs in accordance with their own laws, customs and traditions'.[11] Nevertheless, self-

4 Ibid. 152.

5 J. Webber, 'The Public-Law Dimensions of Indigenous Property Rights', in T. Koivurova and N. Bankes (eds.) *The Proposed Nordic Sámi Convention. National and International Dimensions of Indigenous Property Rights* (Hart Publishing 2014) 80.

6 Ibid. 83.

7 E. Helander, *Samiska rättsuppfattningar* (Lapland University Press 2004) 9-10.

8 J. Borrows, *Canada's Indigenous Constitution* (University of Toronto Press 2011); V. Napoleon, 'Thinking about Indigenous Legal Orders', in R. Provost and C. Sheppard (eds.) *The Dialogues on Human Rights and Legal Pluralism* (Springer 2013) 229.

9 J. Borrows (nr 10) 23.

10 B. Tobin, *Indigenous Peoples, Customary Law and Human Rights – Why Living Law Matters* (Routledge 2014).

11 Ibid. 52.

determination as such falls outside the scope of the chapter. While there is a great deal of research on indigenous peoples' right to self-determination,[12] indigenous peoples' right to their own legal orders in management of their cultural heritage has gained surprisingly little attention by international lawyers thus far. This is quite surprising given the centrality of own legal orders and laws for indigenous peoples' self-determination.

In analyzing the protection of indigenous peoples' legal orders in instruments and case-law, I am focusing on how they become articulated in connection with rights to lands. This may seem an odd way to approach cultural heritage at first glance, but there are several reasons for this choice. First, cultural heritage as such has not gained that much attention in analyzed instruments. This is obviously linked with my second point, that is, indigenous peoples' understanding of cultural heritage can differ remarkably from that of western cultures. Mattias Åhrén has differentiated the notion of land in properterial terms and in cultural rights terms.[13] In the former sense, the land is considered as a material commodity subject to lease and purchase, and falling under the protection of private property. For indigenous peoples land is as much a cultural right as it is a material right, laying the foundation for indigenous peoples' cultural heritage, identity and traditional livelihoods. This notion has also been the backdrop for the Inter-American Court of Human Rights landmark cases as will be demonstrated later. And third, it is important to note that traditional institutions can be also considered an integral part of cultural heritage as they maintain cohesion in indigenous communities and transfer traditional teachings and knowledge from generation to generation. Therefore, I approach cultural heritage as encompassing both indigenous lands and livelihoods. However, I do not contend that indigenous rights should be framed in cultural terms only. As Patrick Macklem argues, limiting indigenous difference only to a set of cultural rights delimits equally important aspects of indigenous difference that merits constitutional protection: sovereignty, land and territo-

12 See e.g. J. Anaya (nr 2); M. Scheinin and P. Aikio, *Operationalizing The Right of Indigenous Peoples to Self-Determination* (Åbo Akademi 2004); M. Scheinin, J. B. Henriksen and M. Åhrén, 'Saami People's Self-Determination', in *Gáldu Čála. The Journal of Indigenous Peoples Rights* (2007) 3; M. Åhrén, *The Saami Dress and Beauty Pageants. Indigenous peoples' right to self-determination* (University of Tromsø 2010); A. Xanthaki, *Indigenous Rights and United Nations Standards. Self-determination, Culture and Land* (Cambridge University Press 2007).

13 M. Åhrén (nr 14) 122.

rial rights, and treaty rights.[14] My chapter thus offers only partial insight into the complex issue.

In the first part, I will analyze how the United Nations Declaration on the Rights of Indigenous Peoples (UNDRIP) and ILO Convention No. 169 affirm indigenous peoples' right to their own legal orders. Regardless of its non-binding nature, the Declaration has had serious implications for the development of customary international law as well as the jurisprudence of human rights monitoring bodies during recent years.[15] The emphasis in the analysis is on the interconnections between indigenous peoples' legal orders and land rights because the land has been seen as a prerequisite for implementing a set of other rights, including cultural heritage rights as we will see in my case study. In the second part, I will analyze how the Inter-American Court of Human Rights has interpreted and applied indigenous peoples' customary laws and the concept of cultural heritage when deciding indigenous peoples' land claims. After the analysis of relevant international instruments and jurisprudence, I will demonstrate how the denial of indigenous peoples' right to govern their cultural heritage in their own legal orders is in violation of rights identified in the previous section by investigating the case of Sámi reindeer husbandry in Finland and analyzing how non-recognition of the traditional Sámi governance system called *siida* violates the aforementioned rights. The case illuminates the problems that arises when indigenous peoples are denied the right to govern their cultural heritage, reindeer husbandry, in their own institutions according to their own customs and laws. Finally, I will argue that the imposition of foreign governance systems and laws ultimately undermines Sámi reindeer herders' self-determination. The aim of the chapter is to illustrate how indigenous peoples' traditional governance systems are an integral part of securing a set of other rights, including rights to cultural heritage and lands.

---

14 P. Macklem, *Indigenous Difference and the Constitution of Canada* (University of Toronto Press 2001) 75.

15 T. Koivurova, 'Jurisprudence of the European Court of Human Rights Regarding Indigenous Peoples: Retrospect and Prospects', in *International Journal of Minority and Group Rights* 18 (2011) 1; M. Åhrén 'The Provisions on Lands, Territories and Natural Resources in the UN Declaration on the Rights of Indienous Peoples. Introduction', in C. Charters and R. Stavenhagen (eds.) *Making the Declaration Work: the United Nations Declaration on the Rights of Indigenous Peoples* (Copenhagen 2009) 212-213; Special Rapporteur on the Rights of Indigenous Peoples 2013. *Rights of Indigenous Peoples*. UN/Doc. A/68/317, para. 64.

2 Indigenous Peoples' Right to Own Legal Orders, Governance Systems, and Customary Laws under International Law

In analyzing indigenous peoples' right to their own legal orders, governance systems, and customary laws, James Anaya's distinction between constitutive and ongoing aspects of self-determination is helpful in understanding the role of indigenous institutions in the protection of their lands and cultural heritage.[16] The former refers to the constituent moments such as establishment of institutions. So, when establishing or modifying institutions they should be done in a way that is acceptable to indigenous peoples: 'Constitutive self-determination [...] requires that such institutions and arrangements in no case be imposed upon indigenous peoples.'[17] The latter refers to the ongoing aspects of the implementation of self-determination: 'The underlying objective of the self-government norm, is that of allowing indigenous peoples to achieve meaningful self-determination through political institutions and consultative arrangements that reflect their specific cultural patterns and that permit them to be genuinely associated with all decisions affecting them on an ongoing basis'.[18]

Indigenous peoples' own laws and governance systems thus become crucial in both aspects of self-determination. On one hand, they can be classified as a substantive right of their own as UNDRIP does. On the other hand, they provide procedural safeguards in consultations and juridical proceedings as is evident in ILO Convention 169. Meaningful self-determination is to be achieved through political institutions that reflect indigenous peoples' own values, customs and traditions, as emphasized by James Anaya:

> Independently of the extent to which indigenous peoples have retained de facto or de jure autonomous institutions from previous eras, they generally are entitled to develop autonomous governance appropriate to their circumstances on grounds instrumental to securing ongoing self-determination.[19]

---

16 J. Anaya, 'Self-Determination as a Collective Human Right under Contemporary International Law', in M. Scheinin and P. Aikio (eds.) *Operationalizing the Right of Indigenous Peoples to Self-Determination* (Åbo Akademi 2000) 3.

17 J. Anaya (nr 2) 156.

18 Ibid. 156.

19 Ibid. 152.

2.1 *ILO Convention No 169: Customary Laws as Procedural Rights*

International Labor Organization's Convention 169 concerning Indigenous and Tribal Peoples in Independent Countries was opened for ratification in 1989. It revised the earlier ILO Convention 107 (1957), which reflected rather assimilationist and integrationist tenets towards indigenous peoples.[20] In contrast to its predecessor, ILO Convention 169 respects the distinct cultures and ways of life of indigenous peoples and aims for revitalization of indigenous cultures by setting standards especially for the procedural rights.[21] It does so, however, without reference to the right to cultural heritage as such[22] and having an emphasis on land rights.

ILO Convention 169 upholds the substantive right of indigenous peoples to retain their own customs and institutions.[23] A number of articles embody respect towards customary laws and indigenous peoples' traditional institutions. The Convention provides that in applying national laws and regulations to the indigenous and tribal peoples, due regard shall be given to their customs or customary laws.[24] Given its obligatory status as a binding treaty, the states are principally obliged to take into account these peoples' customs and customary law systems when both developing and implementing national legislation. This pertains obviously to land rights, too, as the Convention requires, that states recognize, respect and identify indigenous peoples' land rights.[25]

Article 14 lays down requirements for the states to recognize the rights of ownership and possession of the indigenous peoples over the lands, which they have traditionally occupied.[26] Respect towards indigenous peoples' customs related to land ownership is apparent in Article 17. The article demands that the governments shall respect indigenous peoples' inheritance systems related to property and lands.[27] Also procedures established by indigenous peoples for the transmission of land rights among their members shall be respected.[28] This implies that the Convention recognizes that indigenous peoples have developed their own property and inheritance institutions that are distinct from European ones.

20 Ibid. 58.

21 J. Anaya, *International Human Rights and Indigenous Peoples* (Aspen publishing 2009) 138;

22 M. Scheinin et al. (nr 14) 59.

23 International Labour Organisation, Convention No. 169 concerning Indigenous and Tribal Peoples in Independent Countries, 05 September 1991, (ILO Convention 169), art. 8.1.

24 Ibid. art. 8.1.

25 Ibid. art. 14, 15 and 17.

26 Ibid. art. 14.1.

27 Ibid. art. 17.1.

28 Ibid. art. 17.1.

As noted earlier, Article 8 states that governments shall respect indigenous peoples' customs when applying national laws. Furthermore, Article 14 provides that governments shall identify those lands traditionally occupied by indigenous peoples and establish adequate procedures within the national legal system to resolve land claims by the peoples concerned. When Article 8 is read together with Article 14, it seems evident that these land demarcations and land claims shall be decided in accordance with the customs, laws and land tenure systems of indigenous peoples.

Article 15 deals with management of natural resources and provides that indigenous peoples' rights to natural resources situated on the lands they have traditionally occupied shall be safeguarded. It also requires that indigenous peoples' participation in the management and conservation of natural resources be safeguarded. This provision, however, does not provide full ownership over natural resources. However, even in cases where the State retains the ownership of natural resources, the Convention requires that states shall establish and maintain consultation procedures in order to assess the effects of the planned activity for their traditional lands.[29] As for conducting consultations, it is required that when applying the provisions of the Convention, the states consult the peoples through appropriate procedures and that they take place in particular through indigenous peoples' representative institutions.[30] Given the variety of indigenous peoples' social organizations and institutions, this can be construed to encompass both the formal institutions as well as indigenous peoples' traditional institutions such as the village and tribal councils, or for instance Sámi *siidas*. The obligations do not seem to depend on the form of organization or the recognition of the state in that sense.

The question that emerges in connection with the abovementioned obligations is the ranking of customary laws in the system of legal sources. Article 8 asserts indigenous peoples' right to uphold their customs and institutions as far as "these are not incompatible with fundamental rights defined by the national legal system and with internationally recognized human rights".[31] The article seems to refer to the traditional laws that allow inhuman or degrading treatment, justify oppression or violence against children or women, and other kinds of actions that amount to pain or suffering of animals and peoples.[32] The Convention remains silent about other situations, such as land use conflicts, and instead provides that governments shall establish procedures to resolve

29 Ibid. art. 15.2.

30 Ibid. art. 6.1 (a).

31 Ibid. art. 8.2.

32 J. Anaya (nr 2) 139.

conflicts which may arise from integration of indigenous customs and state law.[33]

In Norway, where ILO 169 has been ratified, the conflicts between Sámi customary law and Norwegian law highlight the challenges related to the use of indigenous law as a source of law.[34] After the ratification of ILO 169, the convention was incorporated into the Finnmark Act and Reindeer Husbandry Act and accordingly, the obligation to respect Sámi customs has had consequences for the application of law by courts and administrative bodies in Norway.[35] The ratification of ILO 169 has given Sámi law a formal status in Norwegian law and "customary law should be considered both in the legislative process and in the application of the law."[36] This has been evident in the Supreme Court case of *Selbu*, in which the Court ruled that reindeer herders had acquired pastoral rights to the land on the basis of customary use, and in the *Svartskog* case, in which the Court ruled that local people had acquired property title.[37] Apart from those cases, the hierarchy between Sámi customary law and other legal sources in Norwegian courts when contradictions arise has not been solved.[38]

2.2 *UNDRIP: Operationalizing Self-Determination through Indigenous Peoples' Own Institutions*

As opposed to the ILO Convention 169, the emphasis of the Declaration is on the right to self-determination, but it also contains provisions dealing with a wide spectrum of issues relevant for indigenous peoples. Due to its more recent origin, UNDRIP has more focus on indigenous peoples' right to own institutions and legal orders when compared to ILO Convention 169. In doing so, the Declaration purports to realize one of its main objects, that is, indigenous peoples' right to self-determination. Instead of using the term *customary law* as such, the Declaration refers to indigenous peoples' "customs, laws, traditions and land tenure systems".[39] As in ILO Convention 169, the right to customary laws or judicial systems is not absolute. Indigenous peoples have the right to maintain their customs in accordance with international human rights stand-

33 ILO Convention 169, art. 8.2.

34 Ø. Ravna,The Legal Protection of the Rights and Culture of Indigenous Sámi People in Norway', in *Journal of Siberian Federal University* 11 (2013) 6, 1587.

35 Ø. Ravna, 'Sámi Legal Culture – and its place in Norwegian law', in J. Ø. Sunde and K. E. Skodvin (eds.) *Rendezvous of European Legal Cultures* (Fakbokforlaget 2010) 149.

36 Ø. Ravna (nr 38) 1586.

37 Ibid. 1582.

38 Ibid. 1588.

39 United Nations Declaration on the Rights of Indigenous Peoples (UNDRIP) A/RES/61/295, arts. 26, 27 and 34; cf. B. Tobin (nr 12) 53.

ards.[40] The practices and customs that are incompatible with international human rights standards are apparently beyond the scope of the protection. What these standards are, remains unspecified, yet it seems apparent that at least customs and traditions that discriminate against women or amount to inhuman treatment cannot be justified in any case.

The Declaration recognizes the right of indigenous peoples to preserve their legal institutions. Article 5 states that "Indigenous peoples have the right to maintain and strengthen their distinct political, legal, economic, social and cultural institutions" without being excluded from the decision-making on the state level. [41] When read together with Article 4 concerning the right to self-governance, it is quite evident that it is indigenous peoples' own institutions that should implement and execute the self-governance in the first place. Regardless of their right to their own institutions, indigenous peoples should also retain their right to participate in the political life of the State in matters pertaining to them.

Article 34 of the Declaration lays down indigenous peoples' right to "promote, develop and maintain their institutional structures and their distinctive customs, spirituality, traditions, procedures, practices and, and in case where they exist, juridical systems or customs".[42] Without reference to customary laws as such, Article 34 obviously protects indigenous legal customs and traditions. The protection of cultural heritage is laid out in Article 32, which states that indigenous peoples have the right to protect their cultural heritage. When read together with Article 34, this protection should be implemented obviously in accordance with indigenous customs and traditions.

The customary laws and land rights become closely intertwined in the Article 26, which states that "Indigenous peoples have the right to own, use, develop and control the lands, territories and resources that they possess *by reason of traditional ownership or other traditional occupation or use*, as well as those which they have otherwise acquired".[43] The article clearly states that customs, traditions and land tenure systems must be foundations for resolving indigenous peoples' land rights. The article requires that states shall give legal recognition and protection to indigenous peoples' lands, territories and resources.[44] Recognition and protection of land rights shall be conducted with

40 UNDRIP, article 34.

41 Ibid. art. 5.

42 Ibid. art. 34.

43 Ibid. art. 26.2.

44 Ibid. art. 26.3.

"due respect to the customs, traditions and land tenure systems of the indigenous peoples concerned".[45]

Article 27 goes on to oblige states to establish and implement "a fair, independent, impartial, open and transparent process to recognize and adjudicate indigenous peoples land rights and rights to territories and resources, including those which were traditionally owned or otherwise occupied or used".[46] Again, in adjudicating land rights and rights to territories and resources in such processes, due recognition to indigenous peoples' laws, traditions, customs and land tenure systems' should be given. Koivurova interprets that these processes should be separate from regular domestic court proceedings.[47] In any case, processes should be carried out in conjunction with the indigenous peoples concerned and indigenous peoples shall have the right to participate in these processes.[48] The provision, however, does not provide that land claims should be resolved solely on the basis of customary laws, but they have clearly a central role to play.

The Declaration also requires that states consult with indigenous peoples through their own representative institutions concerning any project affecting their lands and territories and other resources.[49] Indigenous peoples have also "the right to access to and prompt decision through just and fair procedures for the resolution of conflicts and disputes with States or *other parties*, as well as to effective remedies for all infringements of their individual and collective rights".[50] Collective rights include self-evidently collective land rights, too. Such decisions shall give due consideration to the customs, traditions, rules and legal systems of the indigenous peoples concerned as well as to international human rights.[51] Interestingly, these articles expand the duty to respect indigenous law onto the third parties, too. This indicates that disputes and conflicts with private sectors and extractive industries need to be settled in accordance with indigenous peoples' customs, rules and legal systems in addition to international human rights. The declaration clearly affirms that in the conflicts over the lands and resources with extractive industries, indigenous peoples' legal orders cannot be ignored.

---

45 Ibid. art. 26.3.

46 Ibid. art. 27.

47 T. Koivurova (nr 17) 22.

48 UNDRIP, art. 27.

49 Ibid. art. 32.2.

50 Ibid. art. 40.

51 Ibid. art. 40.

2.3 *Inter-American Court of Human Rights: Indigenous Laws as an Origin of Indigenous Peoples' Land Rights*

The Inter-American Human Rights system has recognized and used indigenous peoples' customary laws as a source of law in its jurisprudence related to land rights. The following analysis focuses on the role and significance of customary laws in the decisions concerning land rights. As James Anaya notes, "inasmuch as property is a human rights, the fundamental norm of nondiscrimination requires recognition of the forms of property that arise from the traditional or customary law tenure of indigenous peoples, in addition to the property regimes created by the dominant society".[52] The fact that we cannot avoid dealing with indigenous peoples' own legal orders when deciding land rights, and *vice versa*, has been a leading principle for the Inter-American Court of Human Rights.

The Inter-American Human Rights system, consisting of the Inter-American Commission on Human Rights and the Inter-American Court of Human Rights,[53] is known for its progressive case-law as regards indigenous peoples and its innovative implementation of international human rights instruments relevant for indigenous peoples. Both organs have repeatedly emphasized a need to take into account the unique cultural and historical context and juridical systems of indigenous peoples.[54] The court cases demonstrate that for indigenous peoples the lands are as much a cultural right as they are a material right, laying the foundations for indigenous peoples' cultural heritage, identity and livelihoods. This notion has also been the backdrop for the argumentation of the Inter-American Court of Human Rights, for instance, in the landmark case of *The Mayagna (Sumo) Awas Tingni Community v. Nicaragua*:[55]

52 J. Anaya (nr 2) 142.

53 The Commission and the Court are two independent organs which monitor the compliance of American Convention on Human Rights: the Commission examines individual petitions and submits them further to the Court. See Organization of American States 2010. Petition and case system. Available at www.oas.org/en/iachr/docs/pdf/HowTo.pdf [last accessed 19 August 2015].

54 Inter-American Commission on Human Rights. *Indigenous and tribal people's rights over their ancestral lands and natural resources: Norms and Jurisprudence of the Inter-American Human Rights System* (Inter-American Commission on Human Rights, OAS 2010) OAE/Ser.L/V/II. Doc 56/09, Available at: www.oas.org/en/iachr/indigenous/docs/pdf/ancestrallands.pdf [last accessed in 20 June 2015].

55 I/A Court H. R. *Case of the Mayagna (Sumo) Awas Tingni Community v. Nicaragua*. Reparations and Costs, Judgement of Janurary 31, 2001. Series Case No. 79.

> For indigenous communities, relations to the land are not merely a matter of possession and production but a material and spiritual element which they must fully enjoy, even to preserve their cultural legacy and transmit it to future generations.[56]

That interpretation has rendered many indigenous land claims successful in the Inter-American Court of Human Rights. The Court has applied the provisions on the right to property and culture in an innovative manner to indigenous peoples' land claims. This is evident especially in its landmark decisions in the cases of *Mayagna (Sumo) Awas Tingni Community v. Nicaragua*, *Xakmok Kasek v. Paraguay*, *Saramaka*, and *Sawhoyamaxa*, which I will analyze next.

In the *Awas Tingni* case, the Commission filed a petition against Nicaragua for violating the rights of the *Mayagna* community to property. The Commission argued that despite the lack of official title, the Community had communal property right to lands and natural resources based on traditional land use and occupation of ancestral territory. Those patterns of use and occupation generate customary law property systems. The Commission held unanimously, that indigenous customary law norms and practices create property rights, which must be protected and treated as property rights.[57]

The Court applied a so-called evolutionary interpretation of the international instruments and argued that the international human rights system has autonomous meaning irrespective of the domestic laws and national court's interpretation.[58] In order to treat different forms of property without discrimination, the Court identified that some specifications are required on the concept of property. Accordingly, it interpreted the concept of property in a manner that it also protects the rights of indigenous peoples to communal property: "Indigenous peoples have a communal form of collective property of the land, in the sense that the ownership of the land is not centered on an individual".[59] The Court thus used the community's own customary laws as the basis when deciding that the *Awas Tingni* community had a communal property right to the lands. It iterated, that "As a result of customary practices, possession of the land should suffice for indigenous communities lacking real title to property to obtain official recognition of that property".[60]

56 Ibid. para. 149.
57 Ibid. para. 140.
58 Ibid. para. 146.
59 Ibid. para. 149.
60 Ibid. para. 151.

The Court came to the decision, that states cannot discriminate different forms of property that arise from different property regimes and customary law systems. As one of the legal advisors in the case James Anaya concludes, the Court was the first international tribunal to rule out that "the international human right of property embraces the communal property regimes of Indigenous peoples as defined by their own customs and traditions".[61] It was thus asserted that property rights stem from Indigenous peoples' customary use of lands and that traditional ownership and customary laws are grounds for obtaining official recognition of their ownership.

In a similar vein in *Saramaka v. Suriname*[62] and *Xakmok Kasék v. Paraguay*, the origin of indigenous peoples' land rights was seen to stem from ancestral use and occupancy and not from any act of the state. In *Xakmok Kásek*,[63] the Commission presented a case to the Court in which it alleged that Paraguay had failed to guarantee the right of the indigenous community to ancestral property and as a consequence, prevented the community from practicing traditional economic activities and having access to their ancestral lands. The Court ordered Paraguay to ensure the community members' right to ownership of their traditional lands and, consequently, to the use and enjoyment of those lands. As a reparation, the Court ordered Paraguay to return the traditional lands to the community. In its ruling, the Court relied on its previous findings in the *Awas Tingni* case, according to which "the traditional possession by the indigenous peoples of their lands has the same effects as a title of full ownership granted by the State".[64] In conclusion, the Court recognized, that the community had entitlement to the lands they were dispossessed of, even if they lacked the official title to them or even if the lands were privately owned.

In *Sawhoyamaxa v. Paraguay*,[65] the question was whether a continuation of land rights exists where indigenous peoples have unwillingly left their traditional lands or lost possession thereof. By applying, *inter alia*, Article 13 of ILO 169, the Court held that indigenous communities' close relationship with their traditional lands is not only a question of means of survival but also the

61 J. Anaya (nr 2) 146-147.

62 *Saramaka* v. *Suriname* 2007 Inter-American Court of Human Rights. Series C No. 172 (No. 28, 2007).

63 I/A Court H.R. Case of the *Xákmok Kásek Indigenous Community of the Enxet-Lengua Peoples and its Members v. Paraguay*. Judgment of August 24, 2010. Case no. 12,420.

64 Ibid. para. 109.

65 I/A Court H. R. *Case of Sawhoyamaxa Indigenous Community v. Paraguay.* Merits, Reparations and Costs. Judgement of March 29, 2006, Series C No. 146.

basis of their worldview and cultural identity, and therefore, the relationship with lands must be secured under right to property.[66] The Court reiterated that an indigenous notion of ownership and possession of land does not necessarily conform to the classic concept of property, but deserves equal protection under right to property.[67] According to the Court, demanding and imposing western ways of using and having property on indigenous systems "would render protection under Article 21 of the Convention illusory for millions of persons."[68] This would be discriminatory for peoples who have different understanding of property.

The court invoked its previous rulings in the cases of *Moiwana Community*[69] and *Yakye Axa*,[70] and drew conclusions that even in the cases where the community has unwillingly left its land, indigenous peoples maintain property rights to their lands and are entitled to restitution. The Court thus analyzed whether the enforcement of restitution of lands has a time restriction. It came to the conclusion that as long as indigenous peoples maintain their relationship with traditional lands, the right to restitution remains.[71] Since the community depended on traditional livelihoods and considered the lands as their own, the restitution right had not lapsed. Finding a violation of property rights, the Court ordered Paraguay to restore the traditional lands of the *Sawhoyamaxa* community.

In conclusion, the *Sawhoyamaxa* case affirmed that there is a continuation of land rights where indigenous peoples have unwillingly left their traditional lands or lost possession thereof. According to the Court, despite the fact that an indigenous community lacks a legal title and the lands have been lawfully transferred to third parties in good faith, indigenous peoples do have a right to restitution.[72] The most far-reaching finding in the case was that neither the loss of material possession nor prohibitions on access to traditional territories by the formal owners are obstacles to the continuous territorial rights and right to restitution of indigenous communities.[73] This entails that in addition to the

66 Ibid. para. 121.

67 Ibid. para. 120.

68 Ibid. para. 120.

69 Case of *Moiwana Community v. Suriname*. Judgement of June 15, 2005, Series C No. 124, para. 134.

70 Case of *Yakye Axa v. Paraguay*, Judgement of June 17, 2007. Series C No. 125.

71 *Sawhoyamaxa Indigenous Community v. Paraguay*, para. 121.

72 Ibid. para. 138.

73 *Inter-American Commission on Human Rights* (nr 58) para. 127; This is in contrast to, for instance, the Australian Supreme Court case of *Mabo v. Australia*, in which the break in

origin, also the extinction of such rights have to have respect for indigenous customs – whether they are officially recognized or not.

What has been remarkable in the Court's decisions is its willingness to see interconnections between indigenous peoples' lands and cultural heritage. The Court has reiterated in numerous cases that: "For indigenous communities, their relationship with the land is not merely a matter of possession and production, but rather a material and spiritual element that they must enjoy fully, even in order to preserve their cultural legacy and transmit it to future generations."[74] In its report *Indigenous and Tribal Peoples' Rights over their Ancestral Lands and Natural Resources*, the Inter-American Commission explains that in the Inter-American system, the right to territorial property is viewed as a fundamental basis for culture, economic survival and enjoyment of other fundamental human rights for indigenous peoples.[75] This is well-reflected in the cases of *Xakmok Kasek* and *Sawhoyamaxa*, in which the Court paid particular attention to the close relationship of indigenous peoples to their traditional lands and natural resources recognizing them as the fundamental basis for their culture.[76] Hence, according to the Court's interpretation, indigenous peoples' special relationship with their traditional lands falls under the right to property as interpreted in the light of provisions of ILO Convention 169 and UNDRIP.[77]

3 The Case of Sámi Reindeer Husbandry and the Siida System in Finland

As other indigenous peoples, the Sámi in Norway, Sweden and Finland have retained their traditional governance system called the *siida* system in reindeer husbandry. It is highlighted by the Sámi themselves that reindeer husbandry is a manifestation and integral part of Sámi cultural heritage and it keeps Sámi languages and traditional knowledge alive and communities robust. *Siida* is a flexible family and kinship-based social and land use unit that has its own

continuity for whatever purpose was taken to extinguish native title, see B. Tobin (nr 12) 111-112.

74 I/A Court H.R. *Case of the Mayagna (Sumo) Awas Tingni Community v. Nicaragua*. Reparations and Costs, Judgement of Janurary 31, 2001. Series Case No. 79. para. 149.

75 *Inter-American Commission on Human Rights* 2010, 1-2.

76 I/A Court H.R. *Case of the Xákmok Kásek Indigenous Community of the Enxet-Lengua Peoples and its Members v. Paraguay*. Judgement of August 24, 2010. Case no. 12,420, para. 85.

77 *Inter-American Commission on Human Rights* 2010, 3.

rules for the distribution of the lands, waters and resources.[78] *Siidas* have been basic units of Sámi society since time immemorial, and during the Swedish rule, so-called Lapp villages were officially used as taxation units.[79] During that era, Finnish and Swedish authorities recognized Sámi people's ownership to their traditional lands until the abolition of the Taxed Lapp Land system during the 19th Century.[80]

Whereas *siidas* or Lapp villages were incorporated at least partially in the official management of reindeer husbandry in Norway and Sweden, the introduction of a central management of reindeer husbandry in Finland started to gradually erode the autonomy of the *siida* system from the end of the 1800s. In 1898, all the reindeer owners were obliged to establish co-operatives in the areas where they had not done so.[81] The co-operative system was founded on an agricultural reindeer husbandry model practiced by Finnish settlers in southern Lapland, where they had established co-operatives already during 1700–1800.[82] In the Sámi reindeer herding area, the first co-operatives were established as late as 1898 as a result of the senate's order, while *siidas* continued their existence in parallel with co-operatives.

In reindeer husbandry legislation, *siidas* were replaced by the co-operatives: the first Reindeer Husbandry Act (1932) and none of the subsequent acts include any references to the *siida* system whatsoever.[83] The preparatory works for the current Reindeer Husbandry Act instead explicitly state that the Reindeer Husbandry Act extends the co-operative model also to the Sámi area, where reindeer husbandry is organized around a *siida* model.[84] The govern-

78 M. N. Sara, 'Siida and Traditional Sámi Reindeer Herding Knowledge', in *The Northern Review* 30 (2009) 157.

79 K. Korpijaakko, *Saamelaisten oikeusasemasta Ruotsi-Suomessa. Oikeushistoriallinen tutkimus Länsi-Pohjan Lapin maankäyttöoloista ja -oikeuksista ennen 1700-luvun puoliväliä.* [The legal status of the Sámi in Sweden-Finland. Legal historical study on land use conditions and rights in Lapland before the mid-18th Century] (Lakimieskustannus 1989); M. Åhrén, 'Indigenous Peoples' Culture, Customs and Traditions and Customary Law – The Saami People's Perspective', in *Arizona Journal of International and Comparative Law* 21 (2004) 67-74.

80 K. Korpijaakko (nr 83); M. Åhrén (nr 83) 89.

81 Keisarillisen senaatin kuulutus 28.5.1898.

82 J. Kortesalmi, *Poronhoidon synty ja kehitys Suomessa* [The birth and development of reindeer husbandry in Finland] (SKS 2007), 364.

83 Finnish Reindeer Husbandry Act (RHA) 239/1932; 444/1948 and 848/1990. Outside the reindeer husbandry, the Skolt Sámi Act is founded on *siida* meetings (sij'dd sååbbar), in contrast to the Sámi Parliament Act (974/1995) where the *siida* system goes unrecognized.

84 PeVL 3/1990 vp, 3.

mental bill, however, falsely states that due to the similarities between Sámi and Finnish reindeer husbandry, there is no need to separate reindeer husbandry administratively or legally.[85] As a consequence, the current Reindeer Husbandry Act (848/1990) contains no mention of Sámi reindeer husbandry, nor recognition of the *siida* system. However, the Sámi organizations and Sámi parliament have constantly highlighted the differences between Sámi and Finnish reindeer husbandry.

Despite the imposition of a state-centric co-operative system in the Sámi reindeer herding area, the *siida* system has remained in many places the functioning governance system, which governs and organizes land use within the territory of a co-operative. As demonstrated in the previous section, indigenous peoples have both a substantive right to maintain, develop and preserve their traditional institutions as well as to have their customs respected in formal negotiations and consultations with the states and third parties. I will demonstrate next how the lack of recognition of the *siida* violates many international standards in the following ways: the *siida* lacks a legal status and protection in the legislation; its customary land use system, borders or codes for membership are not formally registered anywhere; and there is no obligation to negotiate directly with *siida*s.

Due to the lack of legal status, it is hard for *siida*s to bring suit against the State or third parties in the cases of encroachments upon *siida* lands or violations of its borders. This is problematic in the Sámi homeland area, where the usufruct and ownership rights on the so-called state lands have not been solved to date in spite of numerous attempts.[86] In the Sámi customary law system, however, *siida*s continue to be considered as the land rights holders.

In a couple of Supreme Administrative Court cases related to Sámi reindeer husbandry, the definition of *siida* has been central. In the *Nellim* case, in which Inari Sámi reindeer herders sued the co-operative for implementing forced slaughter, the defendants questioned the existence of the *Nellim siida* altogether since there exist no official records about existing *siida*s and their members.[87] In the *Käsivarsi* case, the question of whether one person could count as a *siida* and therefore be entitled equally to construct a fence was essential.[88] In both cases, the facts that *siida*s are not acknowledged as rights holders in law and they are not officially registered anywhere, pose difficulties for individuals before the courts.

---

85 HE 244/1989, 4.

86 K. Korpijaakko (nr 83).

87 Finnish Supreme Administrative Court KHO:2011:13, 11.2.2011/318.

88 Finnish Supreme Administrative Court KHO:2012:126, 27.12.2012/3665.

As asserted in ILO 169 and UNDRIP, indigenous peoples have the right to maintain their own distinct legal institutions and customs.[89] These entail self-evidently customary land use practices. Within many co-operatives, *siida*s have maintained their land use systems, which have existed in some places for centuries. However, the Reindeer Husbandry Act obscures the existence of such a system. It merely states that 'The task of a reindeer herding co-operative is to ensure that the reindeer of the cooperative's shareholders are looked after in the territory of the reindeer herding co-operative'.[90] When it comes to the rights of the individual reindeer owner, the act remains silent about Sámi ownership rights to *siida* lands and stipulates only that "Reindeer owners residing in the reindeer herding area have a right to have their reindeer looked after in the territory of the reindeer herding co-operative".[91] By ignoring the *siida* system, the legislation also denies those underlying rules for division of lands and membership in *siida*s. Due to the fact that *siida* land use systems, borders and members are not registered anywhere, it is hard for reindeer herders to have recourse to legal remedies for protecting their land from encroachments or the exclusive right to reindeer husbandry in the co-operatives. This poses serious threats for reindeer husbandry as indigenous cultural heritage since it is basically open to any citizen of the European Union.

In the light of the analyzed instruments and case-law, indigenous peoples' land rights must be decided on the basis of their own customs and legal orders. Pursuant to Article 14 of ILO 169 and Article 27 of UNDRIP, states should establish processes "giving due recognition to indigenous peoples' laws, traditions, customs and land tenure systems" in order to adjudicate and recognize indigenous peoples' rights to lands which they have traditionally used or occupied. In Finland, there have been no such procedures where *siida* borders or land rights would have been determined. They have never been examined by the courts either.

International standards also provide, that negotiations over natural resources and lands should be run with indigenous peoples' representative institutions paying due respect to their customs and traditions. Pursuant to, for instance, Finnish Mining Act (621/2011), the co-operative concerned must be heard before applying for mining permission.[92] Also, the authorities have to find out in cooperation with co-operatives the impacts of the proposed mining project on reindeer husbandry. A hearing procedure also applies to the Sámi

89 ILO Convention 169, art. 8; DRIP, art. 5 and 34.

90 RHA 848/1990, 7 §.

91 Ibid. 9 §.

92 Finnish Mining Act 621/2011, 38 §.

parliament when the projects have "far-reaching consequences for Sámi as an indigenous people".[93] In a similar vein, the Reindeer Husbandry Act 3 § lays down a consulting obligation for state authorities to consult with the representatives of the reindeer herding co-operative when the plans concerning the "State land" will have a substantial effect on the reindeer herding.[94] The acts do not oblige authorities to consult directly with *siida*s or respect Sámi customs and traditions in consultations. This can be problematic if the board or head of the co-operative gives permission to some activities without having consent from a *siida* whose lands are affected. From the viewpoint of Sámi reindeer herders, distinguishing impacts on Sámi culture, on the one hand, and on reindeer herding, on the other, seems artificial since reindeer husbandry and Sámi culture are inseparable.

4 Conclusions

In this chapter, I have encompassed both indigenous livelihoods and lands under the rubric of cultural heritage and shown through the case of reindeer husbandry, how the rights to lands are a prerequisite for the implementation of the right to cultural heritage: without lands, there is no reindeer husbandry. Instead of viewing cultural heritage narrowly as tangible or intangible "property", the analysis shows that also domestic law should start to acknowledge interconnections between indigenous peoples' governance systems, lands and cultural heritage and move focus from a narrow view of cultural heritage and protection of individual cultural objects or artefacts to the real implementation of indigenous peoples' self-governance through their own institutions. This interpretation has rendered many cases successful in the Inter-American Human Rights System. Culture for indigenous peoples should be comprehended as comprising of complex relationships with lands and animals rather than material objects or cultural products in the western sense of the term.

Both UNDRIP and ILO169 also affirm that indigenous peoples' have the right to preserve their distinct governance systems and legal orders and states must respect indigenous peoples' own laws and customs when implementing national laws or negotiating, for instance, over the use of natural resources. From international instruments and jurisprudence it follows, that foundations of land and territorial rights must derive from indigenous peoples' own legal orders. These rights are integral in order to protect their lands and natural re-

93 Ibid. 38 §.

94 RHA 848/1990, 53 §.

sources from encroachments and thus preserve indigenous peoples' cultural heritage.[95]

The Inter-American Court of Human Rights has interlinked the concepts of property and cultural heritage in an evolutionary manner to indigenous peoples' land rights cases. In conclusion, the Court has recognized the continued relevance of autonomous indigenous legal orders. In the cases of *Awas Tingni, Saramaka* and *Sawhoyamaxa* the Court held that the customary use of lands is a foundation for obtaining official recognition of property and that indigenous land titles must stem from indigenous law, and not from the state law. The jurisprudence of the Court stands in stark opposition to that of the European Court of Human Rights, which has interpreted the rights to property in a narrow sense and failed to accord protection for collective rights of indigenous peoples.[96] Due to rapidly evolving customary international law, however, the decisions of the Inter-American Court set an important precedent for other human rights bodies including the ECHR.

My analysis of the case of the *siida* system in reindeer husbandry in Finland shows, that non-recognition of indigenous governance systems and legal orders violates ultimately the Sámi rights to their lands and cultural heritage. The colonial process where *siidas* were gradually replaced by the co-operatives as administrative units, obscures the fact that *siidas* have *de facto* continued to exist as autonomous legal orders parallel to the co-operative system. The main problem with the reindeer husbandry legislation is that it does not recognize Sámi governance systems, leaving them without any legal status and protection, which is problematic when conflicts and disputes arise over *siida* lands, borders and membership. The current reindeer husbandry legislation stands thus in stark contrast with Sámi traditions and customs leaving the reindeer husbandry, which is an integral part of Sámi culture, without protection. As Jeremy Webber argues, initial recognition of indigenous rights to land must draw on indigenous law.[97] By extension, protection and management of indigenous cultural heritage must derive from Indigenous peoples' own institutions. Against this notion and analyzed insruments, it can be interpreted that the imposition of state institutions and laws on indigenous peoples aims to nullify the continuation of those rights and hereby perpetuate the dispossession of indigenous peoples from their lands and livelihoods that set the basis for their cultural heritage.

95 *Inter-American Commission on Human Rights* (nr 58) para. 101.

96 T. Koivurova (nr 17) 34-36.

97 J. Webber (nr 6) 79.

Finnish reindeer husbandry legislation is thus in violation of international human rights standards and customary international law that all clearly affirm that indigenous peoples have the right to maintain, preserve and develop their own traditional institutions and legal orders, and govern their lands in accordance with their own customs and laws. In spite of the facts that UNDRIP is not a legally binding convention and Finland has not ratified the ILO Convention 169, many of their provisions have already been crystallized into customary international law.[98] In order to comply with international standards, Finland should acknowledge *siida* as a rights holder in the Reindeer Husbandry Act. In Norway, the *siida* system was brought into the Reindeer Husbandry Act in 2007.[99] Following the example of Norway, the next step would entail determining and registering the *siida* borders, members and rules of land use.[100] Third, the government should establish procedures for adjudication of *siida* lands in order to provide reindeer herders with an opportunity to claim the official title to the lands they have traditionally occupied if they wish so. Constitutional and administrative courts may not be competent to decide such issues, so there is a need to establish separate juridical institutions with experts on indigenous law and reindeer husbandry.

As exemplified by the chapter, indigenous peoples' governance systems already have complex rules and procedures in place for governing their lands, livelihoods and cultural heritage. Denial of the right to practice self-governance within indigenous peoples' own governance systems according to their own laws undermines their status as self-determining *peoples*.

98 J. Anaya (nr 2) 147–148; B Tobin (nr 12) 54; M. Åhrén (nr 14).

99 M. N. Sara, 'Land Usage and Siida Autonomy.' *Arctic Review on Law and Politics* 3 (2011) 138.

100 Ibid. 138.

Under the Umbrella: The Remedial Penumbra of Self-Determination, Retroactivity and the Restitution of Cultural Property to Indigenous Peoples

Shea Elizabeth Esterling

Introduction

The year 2014 saw the closure of the Second International Decade of the World's Indigenous Peoples.[1] The jewel in its crown that had eluded the initial International Decade of World's Indigenous Peoples[2] was the passage of the 2007 U.N. Declaration on the Rights of Indigenous Peoples [UNDRIP or the Declaration].[3] Much praise, and rightly so, has been lavished upon the UNDRIP. Commendation has centered on its progressive standards in relation to autonomy, the control and restitution of land, free prior and informed consent [FPIC] and self-determination. In particular, much of this praise and subsequent interest have focused on the UNDRIP's progress in relation to the latter. Yet, scant attention has been paid to the remedial role of self-determination in relation to the restitution of cultural property to Indigenous Peoples despite its potential profound significance as a tool for achieving the restitution of cultural property.

Accordingly, the following chapter seeks to rectify this lacuna by exploring the relationship between self-determination and cultural property and its restitution. Ultimately it demonstrates that aside from some concerns, self-determination has great potential to aid in the continuing efforts to secure the restitution of the traditional cultural property of Indigenous Peoples. The

1 U.N.G.A., *Resolution adopted by the General Assembly on 20 December 2004: Second International Decade of the World's Indigenous People*, U.N. Doc. G.A. Res. A/RES/59/174 (24 February 2005).

2 *See* U.N.G.A., International Decade of World's Indigenous Peoples, U.N. Doc. A/48/163 (21 December 1993). *See also* International Working Group for Indigenous Affairs, *First International Decade of World's Indigenous Peoples, at* http://www.iwgia.org/human-rights/un-mechanisms-and-processes/2nd-un-decade-on-indigenous-peoples/1st-un-decade-on-indigenous-peoples (15 January 2015).

3 United Nations Declaration of the Rights of Indigenous Peoples, GA Res. 61/295, UN GAOR, 61st Sess., 107th plen mtg, U.N. Doc. A/Res/61/295 (13 September 2007) [hereinafter UNDRIP].

Xanthaki, Valkonen et al. (eds.), *Indigenous Peoples' Cultural Heritage: Rights, Debates and Challenges.*
 ISBN 978-90-04-34218-7. PP. 294-326.

chapter proceeds as follows. First, it lays the foundations for such an inquiry by detailing core concepts such as self-determination, cultural property, the repatriation debate and non-retroactivity. With the foundation laid, the paper then examines how the concepts of self-determination and cultural property traditionally have been linked through the cultural aspect of the penumbra of self-determination and looks briefly at the logic of these links. The chapter eventually dispels potential theoretical concerns by revealing a different facet of self-determination which links the concepts of self-determination and cultural property as well as restitution and yet has received little attention. Next, the chapter explores the significance of this facet of self-determination: its remedial aspect paves the way for the retroactivity of the law. This inquiry then offers an analysis of alternative approaches to achieve the retroactivity crucial to the restitution of cultural property to Indigenous Peoples, but also highlights their shortcomings. Yet not all is gloom and doom; this chapter concludes with a brief exploration of general and *sui generis* rights that in combination hold much promise for the future.

1 Self-Determination, Cultural Property, the Repatriation Debate and Non-Retroactivity

A. *Self- Determination: From Political Concept to International Human Right*

In 1918, U.S. President Woodrow Wilson declared that 'peoples may not be dominated and governed only by their consent. "Self-determination" is not a mere phrase. It is an imperative principle of action, which statesmen will henceforth ignore at their peril.'[4] Evolving from this political concept, self-determination slowly gathered recognition as a right in international law within the limited context of decolonization and the equality of states as a right to political power accompanying statehood. However, more recently it has come to be recognized as a right within International Human Rights Law [IHRL].

The shift to a specific human right was manifested by its appearance in the twin articles of the International Covenant on Civil and Political Rights [ICCPR] and the International Covenant on Economic, Social and Cultural Rights [ICESCR] which both provide that '[a]ll peoples have the right to self-determination. By virtue of that right they freely determine their political status and

4 W. Wilson, War Aims of Germany and Austria (1918) reprinted in M. Dixon et al. (eds.), *Cases & Materials on International Law* (5th edn., OUP 2011) 220. Ultimately, it served as the foundation for the 1919 Treaty of Versailles.

freely pursue their economic, social and cultural development.'[5] Self-determination traditionally has been divided into two aspects: external and internal self-determination. As regards the former, it was developed within the context of decolonization and is exercised mainly through either secession or independence. As regards internal self-determination, it has been developed within IHRL and finds its clearest expression in General Recommendation 21 issued by the Convention on the Elimination of Racial Discrimination [CERD][6] which offers that the focus is on participation in the democratic process, autonomy and self-government within the state.[7] It is this modality of self-determination that was initially and cautiously offered to Indigenous Peoples under IHRL.[8] In turn, inclusion as a human right did not result in an automatic expansion of the concept of self-determination from peoples living under colonialism to all peoples including Indigenous Peoples. Only after a lengthy, intense and contentious debate which predominately occurred within the drafting process of the UNDRIP concerning who are the beneficiaries of this right, has a general consensus been reached that an equal right of self-determination is applicable to Indigenous Peoples in IHRL.

Indeed, not to give an equal right of self-determination to Indigenous Peoples would be both discriminatory and violate the principle of equality in contradiction to the entire ethos of IHRL in general and Articles 1 and 2 of the UNDRIP in particular concerning the full enjoyment of rights and the free and equal enjoyment of rights.[9] In turn, presenting a monumental and praiseworthy development in the struggle for the rights of Indigenous Peoples, the

---

5 International Covenant on Civil and Political Rights, G.A. Res. 2200A (XXI), 21 U.N. GAOR Supp. (No. 16) at 52, U.N. Doc. A/6316 (1966), 999 U.N.T.S. 171, *entered into force* Mar. 23, 1976 at Art. 1(3)[hereinafter ICCPR]; International Covenant on Economic, Social and Cultural Rights, G.A. Res. 2200 (XXI), U.N. GAOR, 21st Sess., Supp. No. 16, U.N. Doc. A/6316 (1966), 993 U.N.T.S. 3, at Arts. 1,3,6, 15 *entered into force* January 3, 1976 at Art. 1(3)[hereinafter ICESCR](emphasis added).

6 Committee on the Elimination of Racial Discrimination, General Recommendation 21, The right to self-determination, U.N. Doc. A/51/18, annex VIII at 125 (1996) at para. 10; *See also Reference Re Secession of Quebec* [1998] 2 SCR 217, Canadian Supreme Court at para. 126.

7 *See* A. Xanthaki, *Indigenous Rights and United Nations Standards: Self-Determination, Culture, and Land* (CUP 2007)160-66 (detailing democracy, autonomy and participation relevant to fulfilling an internal right to self-determination).

8 *See* W. Barney Pityana, Situation of Indigenous Peoples in Africa, DOC/OS(XXVI)/130 at para. 11 *reprinted in* P. Thornberry, *Indigenous Peoples* (Manchester University Press 2002) 257.

9 UNDRIP (n3) Arts. 1 and 2.

right to self-determination has been unequivocally recognized as applicable to Indigenous Peoples through its inclusion in the Declaration at Article 3. Mirroring much of the language of the right to self-determination offered in the aforementioned twin articles of the ICCPR and the ICESCR, Article 3 of the UNDRIP provides: 'Indigenous Peoples have the right of self-determination. By virtue of that right they freely determine their political status and freely pursue their economic, social and cultural development.'[10]

B *Cultural Property*

Aside from self-determination, the UNDRIP also addresses the issue of the restitution of cultural property. Specifically, Article 11(1) states:

> Indigenous peoples have the right to practise and revitalize their cultural traditions and customs. This includes the right to maintain, protect and develop the past, present and future manifestations of their cultures, such as archaeological and historical sites, artefacts, designs, ceremonies, technologies and visual and performing arts and literature.

In order to fulfill this right to practice and revitalize their cultural traditions and customs, Article 11(2) subsequently imposes the procedural obligation that:

> States shall provide redress through effective mechanisms, which may include restitution, developed in conjunction with indigenous peoples, with respect to their cultural, intellectual, religious and spiritual property taken without their free, prior and informed consent or in violation of their laws, traditions and customs.

In the legal context, the term cultural property first appeared in the 1954 Hague Convention for the Protection of Cultural Property in the Event of Armed Conflict[11] followed in 1970 by the Convention on the Means of Prohibiting and

10 Ibid. Art. 3.

11 *See* I. M. Goldrich, Comment, 'Balancing the Need for Repatriation of Illegally Removed Cultural Property with the Interests of Bona Fide Purchasers: Applying the UNIDROIT Convention to the Case of the Gold Phiale' 23 Fordham International Law Journal 118, 133 (1999)(noting that this was the first time the term had appeared in international law). *See also,* M. Frigo, 'Cultural property v. Cultural Heritage; A "battle of concepts" in International Law' 86 IRRC 367 (June 2004) [citation omitted]; L. Prott and P. J. O'Keefe, '"Cultural Heritage" or "Cultural Property"?' 1 International Journal of Cultural Property 307, 318 (1992); R. O' Keefe, 'The Meaning of "Cultural Property" Under the 1954 Hague

Preventing the Illicit Import, Export and Transfer of Ownership of Cultural Property (UNESCO Convention) and most recently in 1995 in the International Institute for the Unification of Private Law (UNIDROIT) Convention on Stolen or Illegally Exported Cultural Objects (UNIDROIT Convention). Article 1 of the UNESCO Convention and Article 2 of the UNIDROIT Convention which collectively make up the present international framework for the protection of cultural property, offer that it is property that is important for 'archaeology, prehistory, history, literature, art or science....'[12] However, the real substance of both these definitions lies in the identical list that both provide[13] which outline the broad contours of this concept including that it is both religious and secular in nature as well as animate and immovable but more commonly inanimate and movable. Finally, implicit in this list is that cultural property only includes tangible items which is often underscored; yet it is the tangible nature of cultural property as objects that can be touched, seen and preserved and so 'have the likelihood of becoming symbols with different layers of meaning to many different groups'[14] that makes them capable of restitution and hence at the center of the repatriation debate.

C *The Repatriation Debate*

> [R]epatriation is perhaps the most intractable and contentious part of the bitter art wars.[15]
>
> *Daniel Shapiro*

It is cultural property that lies at the center of the repatriation debate. Broadly speaking, repatriation can refer to any return of cultural property. For instance,

---

Convention' XLVI Netherlands International Law Review 26 (1999); J. Blake, 'On Defining the Cultural Heritage' 49 International and Comparative Law Quarterly 61 (2000).

12 International Institute for the Unification of Private Law, Final Act of the Diplomatic Conference for the Adoption of the Draft UNIDROIT Convention on the International Return of Stolen or Illegally Exported Cultural Objects, *done* June 24, 1995, 34 I.L.M. 1326 [hereinafter UNIDROIT Convention] at Art. 2; UNESCO, Convention on the Means of Prohibiting and Preventing the Illicit Import, Export and Transfer of Ownership of Cultural Property, *adopted* Nov. 14, 1970, 823 U.N.T.S. 232 [hereinafter UNESCO Convention] at Art. 1 [emphasis added].

13 UNIDORIT Convention, (n12) Annex; UNESCO Convention (n12) Art. 1.

14 J. Watkins, 'Cultural Nationalists, Internationalists and "Intra-nationalists": Who's Right and Whose Rights?' 12 International Journal of Cultural Property 78, 81 (2005).

15 D. Shapiro, 'Repatriation: A Modest Proposal' 31 New York University Journal of International Law & Policy 95 (1998).

it can refer to the return of cultural property to a state after its illegal export while it can also refer to the return or more accurately the restitution of cultural property to its owner after theft. In turn, simply stated at its core the repatriation debate concerns whether or not the cultural property of states and Indigenous Peoples that has been removed should be returned upon their requests by the current possessors[16] of such property.

In relation to the repatriation of cultural property, the rationale for its repatriation is three-fold: the restoration of the sacred link between people, land and cultural heritage, the amelioration or reversal of internationally wrongful acts, including discrimination and genocide and repatriation as 'an essential components of a people's ability to maintain, revitalise and develop their collective cultural identity.'[17]

The historical theft, illicit trafficking or any other form of historical removal of cultural property has generated modern indigenous claims for repatriation. These requests characteristically are made many years after the initial removal of such property with many suggesting that the initial removal occurred under dubious conditions at best as part and parcel of the circumstances and incidents of colonialism. To add insult to injury, these requests are further typified by the fact that the international framework for the protection of cultural property in which this debate is contained lacks any clear legal obligation to return such property. Ultimately, this stems from the fact that the current framework for the protection of such property relegates the issue of repatriation especially as regards Indigenous Peoples but more significantly limits it through the principle of non-retroactivity.

---

16 The term possessor rather than owner is deliberate here as many states and Indigenous Peoples that desire repatriation do not see the would-be defendants as the legal owners of the property in any respect as they often claim a wrong was at the heart of their acquisition of the property. In turn, at the core of the dispute is both the possession of cultural property and the concept of ownership. The preferred word is possessor in the sense that the UNIDORIT Convention uses this word; to include any person against whom a claim for restitution of an object should be brought.

17 A.F. Vrdoljak, *International Law, Museums and the Return of Cultural Objects* (Cambridge University Press 2006) 299-30 as paraphrased by and *reprinted in* K. Kuprecht, 'Human Rights Aspects of Indigenous Cultural Property Repatriation' Working Paper No. 2009/34, NCCR Trade Regulation, Swiss National Centre of Competence in Research, (2009) 15, *at* http://www.google.co.uk/url?sa=t&rct=j&q=&esrc=s&source=web&cd=1&ved=0CCQQFjAA&url=http%3A%2F%2Fphase1.nccrtrade.org%2Fimages%2Fstories%2Fpublications%2FIP7%2FWorking%2520Paper%2520Kuprecht%252023062009.pdf&ei=fGz4VPHICe2t7AbFvICwDw&usg=AFQjCNGjphJMl2XBTqLeKrgSBzqPsAFTvw&bvm=bv.87519884,d.ZGU.

D Non-Retroactivity

> Sorry about that. It's something that happened in history.[18]
>
> *Tony Blair*

Necessary for a stable and predictable legal system, non-retroactivity is the idea that '[u]nless a different intention appears from the treaty or is otherwise established, its provisions do not bind a party in relation to any act or fact which took place or any situation which ceased to exist before the date of the entry into force of the treaty with respect to that party.'[19] As the UNESCO and UNIDROIT Conventions came into effect in 1972 and 1998 respectively, this not only leaves the most famous requests by successor states for the restitution of their cultural property without a claim under these treaties,[20] this fundamental norm of international treaty law also has the effect of preventing the claims for the restitution of cultural property to Indigenous Peoples removed as part and parcel of colonialism; long before the UNESCO and UNIDROIT Conventions came into effect.

Despite the Mataaua Declaration which calls on the international community to recognize a cultural property regime that has retroactive coverage,[21] it

18 Former Prime Minister Tony Blair made this statement during a visit to China in 2003 when asked by Chinese supporters of the repatriation of their cultural property to justify the British Museum's continued possession of approximately 23,000 relics from the Middle Kingdom looted from the Summer Palace in Beijing during a brief invasion by Anglo-French armies in 1860. Not surprisingly, this statement enraged the Chinese supporters. O. August, 'China Relics Row Echoes Battle for Elgin Marbles' Times (London), Sept. 20, 2003, A13 available at http://www.timesonline.co.uk/tol/news/uk/article1161019.ece (accessed Apr. 9, 2008).

19 U.N., Vienna Convention on the Law of Treaties, *adopted* May 23, 1969, 1115 U.N.T.S. 331; 8 I.L.M. 679, *entered into force* January 27, 1980.

20 Most notably it leaves frustrated the requests by the successor states of Greece for the return of the Elgin Marbles housed in the British Museum and of Egypt for the return of the Bust of Nefertiti from the Egyptian Museum in Berlin. For an excellent account of the repatriation issue surrounding these pieces see respectively: J.H. Merryman, 'Thinking About the Elgin Marbles' 83 Michigan Law Review 1881 (1984-85); K.G. Siehr, 'The Beautiful One Has Come – To Return' in J. Merryman (ed.), *Imperialism, Art and Restitution* (Cambridge University Press 2006) 114; S.K. Urice, 'The Beautiful One Has Come- To Stay' in J. Merryman (ed)., *Imperialism, Art and Restitution* (Cambridge University Press 2006) 135.

21 The Mataatua Declaration on Cultural and Intellectual Property Rights of Indigenous Peoples, Preamble, June 1993 at para. 2.5. *available at* http:/www.wipo.int/tk/en/databases/creative_heritage/indigenous/link0002.html.

is 'well documented that neither UNESCO 1970 nor UNIDROIT 1995 was ever intended to unlock the imperial trophy cases'.[22] Both conventions make this clear though their explicit non-retroactivity. The former explicitly embodies this idea in Article 7 which lays out its key limited repatriation obligations that state parties undertake as evidenced through the language of '*after entry into force* of this Convention.'[23] Although Article 15 of the 1970 UNESCO Convention does allow states parties to negotiate their own terms regarding the repatriation of cultural property that was acquired before the Convention took effect, many states have not exercised this option. This non-retroactivity is most aptly demonstrated in *R. v. Heller*.[24]

Under the auspices of legislation implementing the 1970 UNESCO Convention known as the Cultural Property Export and Import Act, in *R. v. Heller* Canada prosecuted Issaka Zango and Ben Heller. These dealers from New York imported a Nok terracotta sculpture into Canada without the appropriate export certificate from Nigeria, and so at the request of Nigeria, they were prosecuted in Canada. Zango and Heller were arrested in Calgary in 1981 with the terracotta piece that Zango purchased in 1979 which was to be sold to Mobil Oil of Canada Ltd. for USD 650,000. They were charged with illegal export under §37 of the Cultural Property Export and Import Act. Nigeria claimed the sculpture as a piece of cultural property which had been illegal exported. However, the sculpture had been part of a private collection in Paris from the 1950s until the 1970s when Zango, an innocent purchaser, acquired the item. Although at the time of the import both the requesting State of Nigeria and Canada were parties to the Convention, thus making both the Convention and so the Act applicable, counsel for the accused argued there was no evidence regarding when the object had been illegally exported from Nigeria. In reaching his decision, the judge reasoned that the Act needed to be interpreted in a manner consistent with the UNESCO Convention. In doing so, he relied on Article 7(a) of the UNESCO Convention to conclude that the Act can only apply to property 'illegal exported after entry into force' of the Convention in the states

22 J. Shuart, Note, 'Is All "Pharaoh" in Love and War? The British Museum's Title to the Rosetta Stone and the Sphinx's Beard' 52 Kansas Law Review 667, 717 (2004) *citing* Memorandum from Lyndel V. Prott, Director, International Standards Unit, Division of Cultural Heritage, UNESCO, to the Parliament Select Committee on Culture, Media and Sport, *available at* http://www.parliament.thestationaryoffice.co.uk/pa/cm199900/cmselect/cmcumeds/371/371ap51.htm (last visited Feb 23, 2004).

23 UNESCO Convention (n12) Art. 7 [emphasis added].

24 *R. v. Heller* [1983] 27 Alberta Law Reports (2d) 346.

concerned.[25] As the prosecution failed to introduce evidence that the object had been exported from Nigeria after June 1978 when Canada became party to the Convention and Canada and Nigeria have not exercised the option under Article 15 concerning property acquired before the UNESCO Convention took effect, the accused was acquitted.

The UNIDROIT Convention does not remedy this situation[26] as it also explicitly includes a clause on non-retroactivity. Article 10 states that the UNIDROIT Convention: '[s]hall apply on in respect of a cultural object that is stolen *after this Convention enters into force* in respect of the State where the claim is brought... [and] shall apply only in respect of a cultural object that is illegally exported *after this Convention enters into force* for the requesting State as well as the State where the request is brought.'[27] It does note in its preamble that this convention 'in no way confers any approval or legitimacy upon illegal transactions whatever kind which may have taken place before the entry into force of this Convention'.[28] Yet, such an admonition is of little use without the force of the law.

With such an obstacle, where has this left property at the center of the repatriation debate? In effect, 'because formal mechanisms for resolving property rights in cultural objects – particularly those expropriated during periods of colonial rule or military occupation – are limited, repatriation claims tend to rely more on political fervor, moral arguments and emotional appeals rather than on substantive law.'[29] After all, '[h]eritage is both intensely personal and intensely political... as heritage is hotly contested because we each have our own views on what represents heritage, and what is worth conserving.'[30] Consequently, without any meaningful legal claim available via the international framework for the protection of cultural property as a result of its explicit non-retroactivity coupled with a desire to rely on more than simply political fervor

---

25 R.K. Patterson, 'Case Notes: Bolivian Textiles in Canada' 2 International Journal of Cultural Property 359, 361 (1993)[citations omitted].

26 Prott notes that '[f]rom the first meeting of the Study Group [for the UNIDROIT Convention] it was clear that, although there was a substantial amount of agreement among experts and States alike that something should be done to limit illicit traffic for the future, a draft which tried to deal with past issues would have little hope of success.' L.V. Prott, *Commentary on The UNIDROIT Convention on Stolen and Illegal Exported Cultural Objects* (Institute of Art and Law 1997) 78.

27 UNIDROIT Convention, (n 12) Arts. 10(1)-(2) [emphasis added].

28 UNIDROIT Convention, (n 12) Preamble.

29 J. Shuart, (n 22) 673.

30 J. Watkins, (n14) 88 *citing* Graeme Aplin, *Heritage Identification, Conservation, and* Managements 358 (2002).

and emotional appeal, Indigenous Peoples have turned elsewhere to secure the restitution of their traditional cultural property; namely Article 11 of the UNDRIP.

2 Linking Self-Determination and Cultural Property: The Cultural Penumbra of Self-Determination and the Dangers of a Maximizing Approach

A *The Cultural Penumbra of Self-Determination*

The UNDRIP provides for the separate regulation of cultural property independent of self-determination. However, Indigenous Peoples and their advocates have consistently linked cultural property and self-determination; in general through the links between self-determination and culture and in particular through the links between self-determination and cultural property. Indeed, a key tenant of Cultural Indigenism, a new approach that advocates for indigenous values and perspectives in cultural property issues,[31] focuses on links with self-determination.[32]

Self-determination and cultural property have been linked repeatedly by a variety of sources under IHRL. Broadly speaking, self-determination has been linked to all human rights with the Human Rights Committee [HRC][33] noting in General Comment 12 that it is 'apart and before all of the other rights' [34] in the ICCPR. Cassesse noted that self-determination is a 'manifestation of the totality of rights embodied in the Covenant [ICCPR].'[35] More specifically, international instruments link self-determination with the concept of culture. The aforementioned CERD General Recommendation 21 which details inter-

31 Cultural Indigenism is a new approach that has emerged within the discourse of the international framework for the protection of cultural property that has produced a surge of literature which advocates for indigenous values and perspectives in relation to cultural property. Kuprecht identifies as prominent among these the writings of Elazar Barkan, Ana Filipa Vrdoljak, Catherine Bell and Robert K. Patterson who both constitute and define this approach which has a 'better understanding of indigenous cultures... [and] a newly defined respect for their diversity...' ibid. 8-9.

32 Ibid. 18.

33 The HRC is the body charged with interpreting the rights included in the ICCPR when complaints are brought to it under the Optional Protocol.

34 Human Rights Committee, General Comment 12, Compilation of General Comments and General Recommendations Adopted by Human Rights Treaty Bodies, U.N. Doc. HRI/GEN/1/Rev.1 at 12 (1994) [herein after General Comment 12], at para. 1.

35 A. Cassesse, *Self-Determination of Peoples* (Cambridge University Press 1995) 35.

nal self-determination notes that it is 'the rights of all peoples to pursue freely their economic, social and *cultural development* without interference.'[36] Moreover, the abovementioned twin articles on self-determination [Article 1(3)] of the ICCPR and ICESCR as well as Article 3 in the Declaration also make the connection between self-determination and culture explicitly clear in referring to the fact that peoples and in the case of the later specifically Indigenous Peoples have the right to freely determine their *cultural development*.

Consequently, it is unsurprising that cultural rights have been linked to self-determination under IHRL through various decisions and instruments. Although the HRC did not find a violation of Article 27, in *Diergaardt et al. v Namibia* it noted that 'the provisions of Article 1 [the right to self-determination] may be relevant in the interpretation of other rights protected by the Covenant, in particular article []... 27 [the right to enjoy one's culture].'[37] Following suit, in *Mahuika*[38] the HRC stressed once again the non-justiciability of self-determination but again offered that 'the provisions of Article 1 may be relevant in the interpretation of other rights protected by the Covenant, in particular Article 27.'[39] Moreover, it is arguable that internal self-determination is also closely linked with Article 27 of the Universal Declaration on Human Rights [UDHR][40] and Article 15 of the ICESCR[41] as both have at their core the concept of participation.

---

36 CERD, *General Recommendation 21*, (n6) para. 4 [emphasis added].

37 *J.G.A. Diergaardt (late Captain of the Rehoboth Baster Community) et al. v. Namibia*, Communication No. 760/1997, U.N. Doc. CCPR/C/69/D/760/1997 (2000) at para. 10.3. *See also Mahuika v New Zealand*, Communication No 547/1993, Human Rights Committee, U.N. Doc. CCPR/C/70/D/547/1993 (27 October 2000) at para. 9.2 [hereinafter *Mahuika*].

38 *Mahuika*, (n 37).

39 Ibid. para. 9.2. Xanthaki notes that this link could be even further implicit recognition that Indigenous Peoples are beneficiaries of the right to self-determination. Xanthaki, (n 7) 134.

40 UDHR Article 27 reads: '(1) Everyone has the right freely to participate in the cultural life of the community, to enjoy the arts and to share in scientific advancement and its benefits. (2) Everyone has the right to the protection of the moral and material interests resulting from any scientific, literary or artistic production of which he is the author.' Universal Declaration of Human Rights, G.A. Res. 217A (III) U.N. GAOR, 3d Sess., U.N. Doc. A/810 (1948), at Art. 27.

41 ICESCR Article 15(1) provides: 'The States Parties to the present Covenant recognize the right of everyone: (a) To take part in cultural life; (b) To enjoy the benefits of scientific progress and its applications; (c) To benefit from the protection of the moral and material interests resulting from any scientific, literary or artistic production of which he is the author.' ICESCR (n 5) Art. 15(1).

The links between self-determination and culture have been especially encouraged in relation to Indigenous Peoples and their cultural property. Thornberry notes, '[m]uch of the indigenous understanding and claiming on the issue [of cultural heritage] consists in spelling out the further implications of self-determination, indigenous peoples frequently link heritage to this fundamental concept.'[42] Even prior to the Declaration, Indigenous Peoples themselves stressed the link between cultural property and self-determination noting that in exercising the right they must be 'recognized as the exclusive owners of their cultural and intellectual property.'[43] Within the context of the Declaration, Indigenous Peoples continued to stress this link noting that '[t]he Special Rapporteur on the protection of the cultural heritage of indigenous people had placed her study within the overall framework of self-determination and the working group should do the same.'[44] Specifically, in her *Study on the protection of the cultural and intellectual property of indigenous peoples*[45] Special Rapporteur Daes noted that:

> The protection of cultural and intellectual property is connected fundamentally with the realization of the territorial rights and self-determination of indigenous peoples. Traditional knowledge of values, autonomy or self-government, social organization, managing ecosystems, maintaining harmony among peoples and respecting the land is embedded in the arts, songs, poetry and literature which must be learned and renewed by each succeeding generation of indigenous children. These rich and varied expressions of the specific identity of each indigenous people provide the required information for maintaining, developing and, if necessary, restoring indigenous societies in all of their aspects.[46]

---

42 Thornberry (n 8) 392.

43 The Mataatua Declaration (n 21).

44 Mr. José Urrutia, Report of the working group established in accordance with Commission on Human Rights resolution 1995/32, U. N. Doc. E/CN.4/1997/102 (1997) at para. 89.

45 The Sub-Commission on Prevention of Discrimination and Protection of Minorities endorsed a study regarding the protection of the cultural and intellectual property of Indigenous Peoples by Special Rapporteur Mrs. Erica-Irene Daes. *See* Erica-Irene Daes, *Study on the protection of the cultural and intellectual property of indigenous peoples, by Erica-Irene Daes, Special Rapporteur of the Sub-Commission on Prevention of Discrimination and Protection of Minorities and Chairperson of the Working Group on Indigenous Populations*, U.N. Doc. E/CN.4/Sub.2/1993/28(1993).

46 Ibid. para. 4.

Unsurprisingly, she concluded that the further erosion of their heritage will be destructive of their self-determination and development.[47] Daes emphasized this link throughout her studies on the cultural property of Indigenous Peoples noting in the document following up the aforementioned study that 'to be effective, the protection of indigenous peoples' heritage should be based broadly on the principle of self-determination, which includes the right and the duty of indigenous peoples to develop their own cultures and knowledge systems.'[48] In her final report, Daes maintained this link adding only 'to develop their own [indigenous] cultures and knowledge systems, and *forms of social organization.*'[49]

Ultimately, the logic of this link between self-determination and cultural property has been summarized as follows:

> Cultural property/heritage and cultural rights both aim – at least to some extent – at protecting human identity. Cultural identity in its individual dimensions of human identity is an aspect of human dignity. Thus, the protection of cultural property or heritage can be seen as protecting a human right. Cultural identity in its collective dimension may contribute to constituting a group and hence be one factor giving rise to the right to self-determination.[50]

In essence, cultural rights and cultural property are a pre-requisite to self-determination. Yet it also has been suggested that self-determination is a pre-requisite to cultural rights.[51] The International Law Association noted in its 2010 report that "[t]he recognition of the rights of indigenous peoples to determine their own identity and maintain and develop their cultures is deeply rooted

47 Ibid. para. 162.

48 Erica-Irene Daes, *Preliminary Report of the Special Rapporteur, Mrs. Erica-Irene Daes, submitted in conformity with Sub-Commission resolution 1993/44 and decision 1994/105 of the Commission on Human Rights*, U.N. Doc. E/CN.4/Sub.3/1994/31 (1994) at para. 2.

49 Erica-Irene Daes, *Protection of the Heritage of Indigenous People: Final Report of the Special Rapporteur*, [Annex "Principles and Guidelines for the Protection of the Heritage of Indigenous People" paras. 21 and 22], U.N. Doc. E/CN.4/Sub.2/1995/26(1995) at para. 2.

50 K. Ziegler, 'Cultural Heritage and Human Rights' Working Paper No 26/2007, University of Oxford Faculty of Law Legal Studies Research Paper Series (2007), *at* http://ssrn.com/abstract=1002620.

51 A. Cristescu, *Special Study in the Right to Self-determination- Historical and Current Development on the Basis of United Nations Instruments,* U.N. Doc (E/CN.4/Sub.2/404/Rev.1) (1981) at para. 641.

in self-determination"[52] Regardless, both approaches conceptualize this link as one with its roots in the cultural aspect of self-determination. Ultimately, linking the right of self-determination with cultural property in such a fashion follows a maximizing approach to self-determination.

B *The Dangers of a Maximizing Approach to Self-Determination*

There are two principal approaches to self-determination in terms of its scope: a minimalist and a maximalist approach.[53] A minimalist approach advocates that self-determination be viewed only as independence and has been favored by many states. Xanthaki argues that an examination of international documents regarding self-determination indicates that this is too restrictive of an understanding.[54] On the other hand, a maximalist approach to self-determination views it as a broad umbrella right encompassing economic and/or cultural aspects.[55] In turn, as an umbrella right, self-determination casts a shadow or penumbra which encompasses other aspects and their conceptual components; the penumbra of self-determination.[56] Xanthaki notes that this understanding as an umbrella right is entrenched in claims:

> … for democracy and political rights; distinct political and judicial systems; territorial integrity; political independence and non-intervention; or concerning the name of a country and border adjustments; religious freedom; and educational provisions. In its distorted form, nationalism, fundamentalism, racism and even ethnic cleansing have all been justifies in the name of self-determination.[57]

---

52 International Law Association, *Rights of Indigenous Peoples*, The Hague Conference (2010) 16.

53 *See generally* Xanthaki, (n 7)146-55.

54 Ibid. 146.

55 Ibid. 152.

56 The expression the 'penumbra of self-determination' reflects that in use in U.S. Constitutional law of a 'penumbra of rights' which refers to a group of implied rights derived from those explicitly laid out in the Constitution. The U.S. Supreme Court offers: 'specific guarantees in the Bill of Rights have penumbras, formed by emanations from those guarantees that help give them life and substance.' *Griswold v. Connecticut*, 381 U.S. 479, 384 (1965). Here, I develop this term to reflect the idea that in deploying self-determination as an umbrella right it casts shadows or a penumbra that has the potential to incorporate other aspects such as cultural, economic, social and remedial aspects which in essence function as its implied powers.

57 Xanthaki, (n 7)152 [citation omitted].

In turn, many indigenous advocates follow a maximalist approach and it appears to be supported by the language of the twin article of 1(3) located in the ICCPR and the ICESCR which understand self-determination as a people's pursuit of their 'economic, cultural and social development.'[58]

Although the maximalist approach does have its benefits, including viewing self-determination as an evolving concept which can respond to current international needs, there are serious issues with such an approach.[59] First, to use self-determination as an umbrella right risks distorting its meaning and scope and so serves as a poor and irresponsible legislative method.[60] To make self-determination all things to all peoples risks that it will be nothing to no one. In turn, this downside focuses on the risks that a maximalist approach to self-determination has for the right itself. However, of greater significance is the concern that is generated by linking self-determination to other claims. Xanthaki describes this as a poor tactic:

> [c]laims that are justified by loose links with established rights, and even more so with a right as controversial as self-determination, are not convincing. Very often, other human rights can serve as a legitimate basis for these claims, but the use of self-determination obscures this.[61]

In fact, Xanthaki specifically highlights this danger in relation to the cultural aspect of the right to self-determination as an area of particular risk:

> [a]dding a cultural aspect to the right of self-determination fails to provide a solid basis for culture-related claims and adds nothing to the human rights cannon; on the contrary, it practically disempowers a series of cultural rights by drawing attention away from them and hinders their further interpretation and evolution.[62]

For instance, in relation to Article 11 of the UNDRIP regarding cultural property:

> If the right [...] contained in Article 11... simply elaborate[s] upon the application of Article 27 of the ICCPR to indigenous peoples, then the revi-

58 Ibid. 152-3.

59 Ibid. 153.

60 Ibid. 153 [citation omitted].

61 Ibid. 154 [citation omitted].

62 Ibid. 154.

> sion [of Article 11][63] makes a significant difference. Restitution is no longer an intrinsic element of the right to enjoy culture;[64] nor is it required as part of the cessation of an ongoing wrongful act. Instead, restitution becomes a possible remedy for the violation of this right.[65]

However, what is novel under discussion here is that the link between cultural property and self-determination does not raise these concerns, as surprisingly, it is not rooted in the cultural aspect of the penumbra of self-determination. Rather, this link approaches claims for restitution of cultural property as part of the remedial nature of both self-determination and cultural restitution. Indeed, both self-determination on the one hand and cultural property in relation to the issue of its restitution on the other have remedial features that are ripe for analysis.

3 Under the Umbrella: The Remedial Penumbra of Self-Determination

The less explored penumbra of self-determination, this remedial aspect, has been articulated by Anaya. Specifically, he details two different aspects of self-determination: substantive and remedial.[66] As regards the former, Anaya provides that it consists of two normative strains: constitutive self-determination

63 Originally Article 11 was not penned as it now stands. Draft Article 12 which preceded it offered: 'Indigenous peoples have the right to practice and revitalize their cultural traditions and customs. This includes the right to maintain, protect and develop the past, present and future manifestations of their cultures, such as archaeological and historical sites, artifacts, designs, ceremonies, technologies and visual and performing arts and literature, as well as *the right to the restitution of cultural*, intellectual, religious and spiritual *property* taken without their free and informed consent or in violation of their laws, traditions and customs.' 1994/45 Draft United Nations Declaration on the Rights of Indigenous Peoples, U.N. Doc. E/CN.4/Sub2/1994/56 (1994) [emphasis added].

64 Article 27 is part of the norm of cultural integrity. As such, in theory remedial measures are intrinsic to this cultural right in broader IHRL although this has not played out in practice. *See Mr. Jarle Jonassen v. Norway, Communication No. 942/2000*, U.N. Doc. CCPR/C/76/D/881/1999 (2002) (casting doubt on the ability of Article 27 to remedy historical injustices against Indigenous Peoples; denying restitution to Indigenous Peoples in relation to their historical lands).

65 A. F. Vrdoljack, 'Reparations for Cultural Loss' in F. Lenzerini (ed), *Reparations for Indigenous Peoples: International and Comparative Perspectives* (Oxford 2008) 214.

66 J. S. Anaya, *Indigenous Peoples in International Law* (2nd edn, Oxford University Press 2004) 104.

and on-going self-determination. Constitutive self-determination 'requires that the governing institutional order be substantially the creation of processes guided by the will of the people, or peoples, governed.'[67] In turn, constitutive self-determination does not specify the outcome of such processes but stipulates that where they occur 'participation and consent such that the end-result in the political order can be said to reflect the collective will of the people, or peoples concerned.'[68] The on-going aspect of substantive self-determination 'requires that the governing institutional order, independently of the processes leading to its creation or alteration, be one under which people may live and develop freely on a continuous basis.'[69] In turn, this requires that both individuals and groups can make meaningful decisions regarding all aspects of their lives.[70] Collectively then, substantive self-determination fuelled opposition to and the demise of colonization.

On the other hand, remedial self-determination deals with situations that stray from the substantive elements of self-determination to provide for prescriptions; hence in the context of colonization the remedial aspect was decolonization.[71] Specifically, remedial self-determination

> … is identified as a universe of human rights precepts concerned broadly with peoples, including indigenous peoples, and grounded in the idea that all are equally entitled to control their own destinies. Self-determination gives rise to remedies that tear at the legacies of empire, discrimination, suppression of democratic participation, and cultural suffocation.[72]

Anaya is not alone in recognizing and emphasizing a remedial aspect to self-determination. Special Rapporteur Daes understands self-determination in a remedial fashion by focusing on its ability to serve as a mechanism for belated state-building 'through which indigenous peoples are able to join with all the other peoples that make-up the state on mutually agreed and just terms, after

67 Ibid. 105.

68 Ibid.

69 Ibid.

70 Ibid. 106.

71 Ibid. 107.

72 Ibid. 98. He supports such a view by suggesting that self-determination is a framework complemented by other human rights norms that work together to comprise a government institutional order. Specifically, he argues that self-determination stands on the two pillars of the norms of non-discrimination and cultural integrity; norms by their nature which require special measures. ibid. 99.

many years of isolation and exclusion.'[73] Further, Xanthaki understands Benedict Kingsbury's relational approach to self-determination – which focuses on a constructive relationship between the state and Indigenous Peoples – as remedial noting that it is triggered by a disruption in the relationship between these two groups.[74]

On Anaya's understanding of remedial self-determination, it is easy to discern how linking this aspect of self-determination with cultural property requires the restitution of the latter. Indeed a few have identified the relationship between self-determination and the restitution of cultural property. Rebecca Clements[75] argues that the restitution of cultural property is the first step towards self-determination. Her work builds on the work of Berman.[76] He argues that the 'self' in self-determination has both a subjective and objective understanding. The subjective understanding is 'constituted primarily by the aspirations and efforts of a people to achieve self-determination' and results in the political concept of nationality, while the objective self is defined in terms of group characteristics.[77] Berman considers the latter undesirable, as it creates the possibility that outsiders can impose identity on the group. However, Clements notes that the subjective and the objective will overlap in stable communities as people both identify themselves by both their group belonging in the same way that they identify the other. At the root of this identity is tradition which changes over time as culture is constantly in a process of renewal and reaffirmation; therefore the first step towards self-determination is the restitution of cultural property.[78] Yet, as aforementioned it also has been

73 Special Rapporteur Eric-Irene Daes, *Explanatory Note Concerning the Draft Declaration on the Rights of Indigenous Peoples* U.N. Doc. E/CN.4/Sub.2/1993/26/Add.1 (1993).

74 Xanthaki, (n 7) 150. *See also* B. Kingsbury, 'Reconstructing Self-Determination: A Relational Approach' in P. Aikio and M. Scheinin (eds.), *Operationalizing Self-Determination* (Åbo Akademi University 2000) 24.

75 R. Clements, 'Misconceptions of Culture: Native Peoples and Cultural Property under Canadian Law' 49 University of Toronto Faculty Law Review 4, 24 (1991).

76 N. Berman, 'Sovereignty in Abeyance: Self-Determination and International Law' 7 Wisconsin International Law Journal 51, 52 (1988).

77 Clements (n 75) 4.

78 Ibid. *See also* ibid. (n 50) (discussing how cultural property helps to fulfill self-determination through the conceptual link of cultural identity which in its "collective dimension may contribute to constituting a group and hence be one factor giving rise to the right of self-determination.") ibid. Therefore, the restitution of cultural property plays a central role in this process of identity and so group formation for self-determination. This does not suggest that Indigenous Peoples do not have the right of self-determination without the restitution of their cultural property; rather the point is that they enjoy the right to

suggested that self-determination is a pre-requisite to cultural rights.[79] It also has been proposed that self-determination is a pre-requisite more specifically for the restitution of cultural property. Vrdoljak suggests that '[t]he continuing denial or limitation on the exercise of the right to self-determination is clearly manifest in respect of enjoyment and development of culture.'[80] As a corollary then, the full right to the enjoyment of cultural property requires self-determination. In turn, Vrdoljak continues and identifies the right to self-determination as one of three bases for claims of cultural loss.[81] Indeed, she explores that in fact many national initiatives for the restitution of human remains are based on the enjoyment of human rights and the right to self-determination.[82]

Yet regardless of this causality dilemma, cultural property and its restitution have been linked to self-determination and it is to the importance of this link that this chapter now turns.

4 Paving the Way for Retroactivity?: The Importance of the Remedial Penumbra of Self-Determination and Cultural Property

Undoubtedly, self-determination has been linked with the cultural property of Indigenous Peoples.[83] However, what is novel here is the link between self-determination and the restitution of cultural property rooted in the remedial nature of both concepts[84] and which potentially presents a significant development in securing the restitution of the traditional cultural property of Indigenous Peoples. In turn, limited attention has been paid to the significance of remedial self-determination in relation to the restitution of cultural property to Indigenous Peoples. Specifically, linking remedial self-determination with restitution has the potential to pave the way for the application of the principle of retroactivity as it alters the doctrine of inter-temporal law; an alteration

self-determination more fully where they are in possession of the past and present manifestations of their cultural property which form their group identity. As Steinbeck notes: "[h]ow can we live without our lives? How will we know it's us without our past?" J. Steinbeck, The Grapes of Wrath 114 (1976) *reprinted in* J. H. Merryman, 'The Public Interest in Cultural Property' in J. H. Merryman *Thinking About the Elgin Marbles: Critical Essays on Cultural Property, Art and Law* (Cambridge University Press 2000) 94.

79 A. Cristescu, (n51) para. 641.

80 Vrdoljack (n 65) 198.

81 Ibid. 203.

82 Vrdoljack (n 65) 217.

83 *See* ibid. Section II.

84 *See* ibid. Section III.

which is crucial to the restitution of cultural property given the non-retroactive nature of the repatriation debate.

A Overcoming Non-Retroactivity and Inter-Temporality

As aforementioned, the repatriation debate is characterized by its non-retroactivity and is the main limitation regarding the restitution of cultural property to Indigenous Peoples under the current international legal framework for the protection of cultural property.[85] Its contextualization in the Declaration does not automatically overcome this limitation.[86] As Allen observes, the Declaration is prospective on a literal reading of the text and not retroactive.[87] Further, human rights law is not by its nature retroactive. For instance, the HRC is precluded *ratione temporis* from adjudicating cases if the facts complained of date to a period prior to that on which the Optional Protocol of the ICCPR entered into force with respect to the state party concerned. Ultimately, linking self-determination in its remedial aspect with the restitution of cultural property can pave the way for retroactivity, as it alters the doctrine of inter-temporal law.

This principle of non-retroactivity is rooted in international law in the well-established principle of inter-temporality.[88] As Judge Huber of the Permanent Court of Arbitration noted in the 1928 *Island of Palmas Case*, 'a juridical fact must be appreciated in the light of the law contemporary with it, and not of the law in force at the time when a dispute in regard to it arises or falls to be settled.'[89] The International Court of Justice more recently confirmed this principle in the *Right of Passage over Indian Territory*, noting that 'the validity of a treaty concluded as long ago as the last quarter of the eighteenth century, in the conditions then prevailing... should not be judged upon the basis of practices and procedure which have since developed only gradually.'[90] In turn,

85 *See* ibid. Section I(D).

86 A priori, the Declaration as a soft law instrument is not enforceable rendering the issue of non-retroactivity moot. However, this does not detract from the merit of this line of inquiry and conclusion given the potential for the Declaration to crystallize on its own into customary international law or to serve as the basis for a future treaty.

87 S. Allen, 'The UN Declaration on the Rights of Indigenous Peoples and the Limits of the International Legal Project' in S. Allen and A. Xanthaki (eds.), *Reflections on the UN Declaration on the Rights of Indigenous Peoples* (Hart 2011) 240 (highlighting this in relation to the restitution of land under Article 28 but with equal applicability to Article 11).

88 *See generally* T.O. Elias, 'The Doctrine of Intertemporal Law' 74 American Journal of International Law 285 (1980). *See generally also* F. Lenzerini (ed.), *Reparations for Indigenous Peoples: International and Comparative Perspectives* (Oxford University Press 2008).

89 U.S. v Neth., 2 R.I.A.A. 829, 845 (Permanent Court of Arbitration 1928).

90 Port. v. India, 1960 I.C.J. 6, 37 (Apr. 12).

non-retroactivity requires events to be judged in light of law contemporaneous with the claim.

Therefore, success depends on both the act complained of and when the act complained of took place to establish its legality or illegality. As Merryman notes in relation to the Elgin or Parthenon Marbles, a case with analogies with Indigenous Peoples' claims for the restitution of their cultural property:

> [i]n international law, however, as in domestic law, the rule is that the legal effects of a transaction depend on the law in force at the time. The justice, as well as the practical necessity of such a principle is obvious. It is both fair and practically advantageous that people be able to rely on the existing law to determine the legality of their actions. The most obvious applications of this principle occur in our own constitutional prohibition against ex post facto laws and in our legal system's bias against retroactive legislation. Thus if the removal of the marbles was proper under the then applicable international law, as it seems to have been, then the British are legally entitled to keep them.[91]

Indeed, the time and the historical circumstances surrounding the removal of the bulk of Indigenous Peoples' cultural property often deemed such removal legitimate. Frequently, these wrongs emerged as a result of early adventures in anthropology and/or archaeology when these disciplines first explored cultural property 'outside of the civilized world'[92] and then embarked upon an unprecedented campaign of collection and removal often as a result of mixed motives which ranged from the mercenary 'fortune and glory kid, fortune and glory'[93] to the paternalistic and even the outright egregious. This was especially true in the case of the collection of human remains at the hands of archaeologists, anthropologists and government officials often working in conjunction in the name of pseudo-scientific research to confirm the intellectual, racial and overall inferiority of Indigenous Peoples and their culture as a means to justify their subjugation if not elimination. Commonly referred to as Cultural Darwinism,[94] ultimately these wrongs were part of the broader historical pattern of colonialism and nation-building that required either the assimilation or destruction of indigenous culture which was supported and deemed legiti-

91 Merryman (n 20) 1900.

92 M. Lindsay, 'The Recovery of Cultural Artifacts: The Legacy of our Archaeological Heritage' 22 Case Western Reserve Journal of International Law 165, 167 (1990).

93 Indiana Jones and The Temple of Doom (Paramount Pictures 1984).

94 Kuprecht (n 17) 12.

mate by the government, public policy and contemporaneous law and subsequently enforced by the courts.[95]

Therefore as aforementioned, linking self-determination in its remedial aspect with the restitution of cultural property is particularly vital to the efforts of Indigenous Peoples to secure such restitution, as it paves the way for retroactive application by altering the doctrine of inter-temporal law which characterizes the repatriation debate.

> The modern international law of self-determination, however, forges exceptions to or alters the doctrine [] of … intertemporal law. Pursuant to the principle of self-determination the international community has deemed illegitimate historical patterns giving rise to colonial rule and has promoted corresponding remedial measures… notwithstanding the law contemporaneous with the historical colonial patterns. Decolonization demonstrates that constitutional process may be judged retroactively in light of self-determination values – notwithstanding… contemporaneous legal doctrine – where such processes remain relevant to the legitimacy of governmental authority or otherwise manifest themselves in contemporary inequities.[96]

B *The Dangers of Remedial Self-Determination?*

However, as with the maximizing approach to self-determination, there are issues with the remedial approach to self-determination that may not deem it a fit tool to secure the restitution of cultural property to Indigenous Peoples. Specifically, remedial self-determination which comes in the form of secession or independence is not a rule of international law outside of decolonization. Some scholars have suggested that aside from colonization, external self-determination can be exercised in the face of gross violations of human rights where peoples are so severely persecuted or mistreated that it is necessary to preserve their existence. Thornberry is a leading proponent of such a position which he has gleaned from *Katangese Peoples' Congress v Zaire*, though he notes it is by no means completely clear.[97] In addition, numerous other scholars support this view of remedial secession.[98] In turn, the external variant of

95 *See generally Johnson v. M'Intosh*, 21 U.S. 543, 589 (1823).

96 Anaya, (n 66) 107.

97 Thornberry (n 8) 257. Thornberry also relies on the Declaration on Principles of International Law to support this theorem concerning the relationship between misgovernment and self-determination. Ibid. 95.

98 *See* Xanthaki, (n 7) 141-3 (detailing scholars that support this view).

self-determination starts to look more like a remedy; a remedy which began as a measure to rectify colonization and now has been extended to gross violations of human rights. However, as Xanthaki notes, this approach necessarily raises the issue of the interpretation: who decides what suffices as grounds for remedial secession and what constitutes a gross violation of human rights?[99] Moreover, Xanthaki also points out that it is by no means guaranteed that this relationship between self-determination and remedial secession for gross violations of human rights exists under international law.[100]

To a certain extent, this calls into question the strength of the argument here for using the remedial aspect of self-determination to secure the restitution of cultural property. First, this situation of the restitution of cultural property is outside of the established context of colonization for remedial self-determination. Second, arguably the matter of securing the restitution of cultural property to Indigenous Peoples is also beyond the less well-established context of remedial self-determination as a remedy for *gross* violations of human rights.[101] However, two counterpoints should be noted. First, the human rights violation under discussion here of the removal of cultural property as part and parcel of the incidents of colonialism very closely approximates the situation of colonialism where remedial external self-determination has been deemed acceptable as a rule of IHRL. Second, the remedy here in the context of this violation of human rights [the removal of cultural property] is not that of secession or independence under the more controversial aspect of external self-determination but a remedy that would fall under internal self-determination:[102] the restitution of cultural property in the form of the owner-

99 Ibid. 143-5. Ultimately, she argues that the interpretation must be on an ad hoc basis and the interpreter must be the international community in the form of the U.N. General Assembly. Ibid.

100 Ibid.

101 Although, it does remain difficult to see how the wholesale removal of cultural property – often forcibly – from Indigenous Peoples during colonialism is not a gross violation of human rights. This is a direct example of the issue of interpretation raised by Xanthaki. *See* Xanthaki, (n 99) and accompanying text. However, this removal is a violation of human rights. Yet regardless, the issue remains that use of remedial self-determination for gross violations of human rights is not an established principle of international law.

102 Note, Anaya proposes this dichotomy between constitutive and remedial self-determination as an alternative to the internal/external divide prevalent in IHRL. *See* ibid. Section I(A)(discussing internal and external modalities of self-determination). He rejects this traditional dichotomy on the grounds that it is premised on an untenable position: a world comprised of a limited number of 'peoples' in mutually exclusive communities – i.e. states. Anaya (n 66) 105. Alternatively, he proposes this dichotomy as it recognizes

ship, possession and control of such property. In turn, this similarity regarding colonialism and this difference regarding internal self-determination militates against the criticisms leveled at the concept of remedial self-determination as a mechanism to secure the restitution of cultural property to Indigenous Peoples. Nonetheless, it is necessary to ask: are there any alternative avenues even better equipped to secure retroactivity than the remedial facet of the penumbra of self-determination?

5 Alternative Avenues? International Humanitarian Law and Continuing Violations

It is arguable that retroactivity could be achieved without resorting to any of the aspects of self-determination via importing precedent developed in International Humanitarian Law (IHL) and/or the concept in IHRL of continuing violations. However, each of these alternatives face serious issues.

A *International Humanitarian Law*

The precedent from IHL stems from the aftermath of the Second World War. It concerns the Allied program of restitution for cultural property confiscated by the Nazis in Germany since 1933 in the Declaration of the Allied Nations against Dispossession Committed in Territories under enemy Occupation or Control (London Declaration) of 1943,[103] which has been described as 'an act of humanitarian intervention by the international community in the domestic activities of a state'.[104] It was so far reaching that it was suggested that this program represented new principles of international law.[105] In this regime, there are a number of significant features that could prove helpful for indigenous ef-

the reality that of today's world that there are multiple human associations 'including but not exclusively those organized around the state, [and so] it is distorting to attempt to organize self-determination precepts into discrete internal versus external spheres defined by reference to presumptively mutually exclusive peoples.' Ibid. In turn, presumably for Anaya such a statement/criticism that there is no guarantee of a relationship between external self-determination and remedial session for human rights violations does not resonate with his notion of self-determination.

103 5 January 1943, 8 *Dep't St. Bull.* (1943) 21. *See generally* A. F. Vrdoljak, 'Genocide and Restitution: Ensuring Each Group's Contribution to Humanity' 22 European Journal of International Law 17, 25-28 (2011)(discussing the London Declaration generally).

104 Vrdoljak (n 103) 25 [citation omitted].

105 Ibid. 27 [citation omitted].

forts to achieve the restitution of cultural property in general and in particular to overcome the hurdle of inter-temporal law.

In general, it could help flesh out the details and provide clarity to any restitution of cultural property that occurs under Article 11 which is left open on its face. Under this IHL regime, restitution applied to transactions 'even when they purported to be voluntary in effect.'[106] In essence, a presumption was made in favor of the claimant that any transaction during the period of National Socialism constituted a confiscation, if the individual from whom the property was confiscated was a member of a group subject to persecution because of race, religion, nationality, ideology or political opposition to National Socialism, or because of any threats or duress, by government act or abuse of such act, and as the result of measures taken by the Nazi regime and its affiliates.[107] The possessor carried the burden of proof that the cultural property had been acquired through a 'normal transaction' and proof of payment was not sufficient to overcome this burden.[108] When assessing claims for restitution, due recognition was to be given to the difficulties faced by claimants especially in relation to the production of evidence through the loss of documents, death or unavailability of the witnesses or their residence abroad.[109] Finally, there was no time limit attached to this restitution scheme.[110] Many of the transactions under colonialism regarding the transfer of cultural property from Indigenous Peoples also generate significant evidentiary problems because of the time that has passed and also their nature as colonial suggests dubious transfers. These presumptions in IHL in favor of claimants would work to the benefit of Indigenous Peoples in relation to the restitution of their cultural property if applied to IHRL to flesh out the details of Article 11 and/or any future treaty right.

Beyond this, this IHL model of restitution may also be helpful in overcoming the hurdle of inter-temporal law without resort to the remedial aspect of self-determination. By its very nature this IHL regime was both retroactive[111]

106 *Dep't St. Bull.* (n 103) 65.

107 Vrdoljak, (n 103) 26 [citation omitted].

108 Ibid. 26 [citations omitted].

109 Ibid. 26-7 [citations omitted].

110 Ibid. 27 [citations omitted].

111 This is not the only example of a retroactive application of the law in IHL in relation to the restitution of cultural property. UN Security Council Resolution 1483 which was passed in response to the invasion of Iraq in 2003 required member states to return cultural property illegally removed from Iraq not only from 2003 onwards but since 6 August 1990, the date of the first invasion of Iraq. *See* Security Council Resolution 1483, P7, U.N. Doc. S/RES/1483 (22 May 2003).

and applied to transfers regardless of the apparent legality of the transaction at the time. Specifically, in creating this restitution scheme Allied governments recognized that the confiscation of property was part and parcel of the program of persecution of groups and incorporated into domestic law as a mean of legitimization. Therefore, regardless of the *lex loci*, it was not permissible 'to plead that an act was not wrongful or *contra bonos mores* because it conformed with a prevailing ideology concerning discrimination against individuals' belonging to particular groups.'[112]

Hence, these principles of this post-Second World War scheme for the restitution of cultural property could prove significant for Indigenous Peoples claims under Article 11 of the Declaration. In general, the IHL principles could help flesh out details and provide clarity to any restitution that occurs under Article 11 which is left open by its language. In particular, these principles could also prove important in overcoming the hurdle of non-retroactivity and the related issue of inter-temporal law faced by Indigenous Peoples in their quest for restitution under IHRL without resort to any link with remedial self-determination.[113] However, the issue with this approach lies in the fact that these principles, however helpful, are precedents that exist within the context of IHL rather than IHRL and that the removal of indigenous cultural property under discussion herein has not usually occurred in the situation of armed conflict.

B *Continuing Violations*

The concept of the doctrine of continuing violations in IHRL serves as an exception to the rule of non-retroactivity by allowing the admission of claims otherwise inadmissible *ratione temporis*. This doctrine also could potentially overcome the hurdle of inter-temporal law without resort to the remedial penumbra of self-determination. Arguably the doctrine of continuing violations has its roots in an evolutionary approach to inter-temporality. In the aforementioned *Island of Palmas Case*, Judge Huber of the Permanent Court of Arbitration noted that 'a juridical fact must be appreciated in the light of the law contemporary with it, and not of the law in force at the time when a dispute in regard to it arises or falls to be settled.'[114] Yet, he continued to note that sovereignty over the Palmas Islands was at the time based upon the rule of discovery but that the maintenance of sovereignty depended on how the law

112 Vrdoljak (n 103) 26 [citations omitted].

113 *See* ibid. Section I(D) and Section IV.(A) discussing the issue of non-retroactivity and the related issue of inter-temporality as the main problem for Indigenous Peoples in securing the restitution of cultural property).

114 U.S. v Neth. (n 89) 845.

and fact evolved. In essence, he took an evolutionary approach to the rule of inter-temporality allowing in this particular case for the original title to divest based on legal developments.[115]

Despite some suggestion that this "extension" of the rule of inter-temporality has not been followed,[116] this evolutionary approach was also taken in subsequent cases such as *Advisory Opinion on Namibia.*[117] Further, the Institute de Droit International adopted a resolution in 1975 which provides that the legality or the illegality of an historical act must be judged according to the law in force at the time but that the continuing effects of these events can be judged by more recent standards.[118] In turn, continuing violations operate in a situation where the alleged violation of a right took place before the relevant treaty entered into force. Continuing violations allow for consideration of the alleged violation where it has or continues to have effects after the treaty enters into force thereby overcoming its non-retroactivity.

Indeed, Indigenous Peoples and their advocates have highlighted the need for the concept of continuing violations in light of the non-retroactivity of IHRL and have made use of it to their benefit. In *The Case of the Moiwana Vs. Suriname Community*,[119] the concept of continuing violations had to be utilized as Suriname did not recognize the jurisdiction of the Inter-American Court of Human Rights [IACtHR] until November 1987 and the alleged incident under consideration took place in November 1986. At issue was a military operation carried out by the State in the village of the Moiwana where thirty-nine unarmed members of the community were killed. The IACtHR held that it did not have jurisdiction *ratione temporis* to examine the events of this armed attack in November 1986 but that it did possess jurisdiction through the concept of continuing violations to examine just that; the effects which continued to exist in the community of the Moiwana and of course events which occurred after Suriname recognized jurisdiction.[120] Specifically, the

115 *See* Dinah Shelton, 'The Present Value of Past Wrongs' in F. Lenzerini (ed.), *Reparations for Indigenous Peoples: International and Comparative Perspectives* (Oxford University Press 2008) 62.

116 *See* Anthony D'Amato, International Law, 'Intertemporal Problems' in *Encyclopedia of Public International Law* 1236 (1992).

117 *Legal Consequence for the States of the Continued Presence of South Africa in Namibia (South West Africa), notwithstanding Security Council Resolution 276 (1970), Advisory Opinion,* (1971) ICJ Rep. 16 *reprinted in* Shelton (n 115) 63.

118 Shelton, (n 115) 63.

119 *Caso de la Comunidad Moiwana v. Suriname*. Execepciones Preliminares, Fondo, Reparaciones y Costas. Judgment of June 15, 2005.

120 Ibid. para. 39.

court found that the forced displacement of the community from their lands was a continuing violation as they could not return and in turn linked this internal displacement with violations of the American Convention on Human Rights [ACHR] including the right to personal integrity, the right to private property, freedom of movement and residence, the right to a fair trial and the right to judicial protection.[121] Therefore, the concept of continuing violations was the key to finding state liability. Further, within the specific context of the restitution of the cultural property and human remains, Indigenous Peoples have highlighted the need for the concept of continuing violations in light of the non-retroactivity of human rights law. Prior to the adoption of the Human Tissue Act 2004 in the UK, which is legislation that is explicitly retroactive that allows for [but does not compel] the restitution of human remains to Indigenous Peoples,[122] it was recognized by indigenous advocates that under existing human rights law such as the Human Rights Act that the date of acquisition of human remains was a highly unlikely route to follow since museums would have had such remains in their collection for many years. In turn, Kevin Chamberlain and the Working Group on Human Remains argued that the retention of human remains at a museum is an offense which continued to violate the community's right every day that the remains are kept from their rightful resting place. In essence, the retention of human remains presents a continuing violation and so time would begin to run when a request for return is made and refused thereby overcoming the issue of non-retroactivity.[123]

However, the concept of continuing violations does not provide a secure method to overcome non-retroactivity. In particular, continuing violations would be on shaky grounds in securing retroactivity in relation to cases of restitution rooted in cultural renewal. Yet, even beyond situations regarding renewal, continuing violations remain a tenuous tool as the jurisprudence of the HRC in relation to continuing violations demonstrates that it is unclear. In *J.L. v Australia*,[124] the complainant was a solicitor who refused to pay the annual fee required by the Law Institute of Victoria on the grounds that he

121 Mauricio Iván Del Toro Huerta, 'The Contributions of the Jurisprudence of the Inter-American Court of Human Rights to the Configuration of Collective Property Rights of Indigenous People's' 10 at http://www.law.yale.edu/documents/pdf/sela/Del_Toro.pdf.

122 Section 47 allows a select group of nine museums to de-accession human remains from their collections provided that they are less than 1,000 years old when the legislation comes into force. However, it does not require this return. *See* Human Tissue Act 2004, c. 30 Part 3 Miscellaneous Section 47.

123 K. Chamberlain, *We Need to Lay Our Ancestors to Rest – The Repatriation of Indigenous Human Remains and the Human Rights Act*, at 337.

124 *J.L. v. Australia*, Communication No. 491/1992, U.N. Doc. CCPR/C/45/D/491/1992 (1994).

considered recent fee increases invalid. Yet, he continued to practice law without a certificate denied to him by the Institute on the grounds of this refusal of payment. Further, at the request of the Institute the Supreme Court of Victoria fined him, struck him of the roll of barristers and solicitors and ordered that he be imprisoned for contempt of court. The complainant alleged a violation of Article 14 proceedings before an independent and impartial tribunal; though the alleged violations took place before entry into force of the Optional Protocol for Australia in 1991 he argued that they had continuing effects. The HRC agreed and noted that although the denial of an impartial and fair hearing took place before 1991 'the effects of the decision taken by the Supreme Court continue until the present time. Accordingly, complaints about violations of the author's rights allegedly ensuing from these decisions are not in principle excluded.'[125]

By contrast, in *Kurowski v Poland*[126] the HRC found that the complaint was inadmissible *ratione temporis.* Here, the complainant alleged a violation of Article 25 of the ICCPR which offers the right to have access on terms of equality to public services in the country of the individual. Specifically, the complainant was dismissed from his public service position allegedly on the grounds of political persecution as a result of his affiliation with the Polish United Workers' Party and leftist views but as the dismissal took place in 1990 before entry into force of the Optional Protocol for Poland in 1991, the HRC found it inadmissible. As the ICCPR Commentary notes, it is difficult to discern the distinction between these two cases where in the former striking off the roll of solicitors was considered admissible as a continuing violation and in the later dismissal as a public servant was not considered as such; at best it is suggested that striking off continues to deny an individual access to their livelihood whereas dismissal from a public service job does not preclude an individual from seeking another public service job.[127]

However, if this is splitting hairs, then in the following cases the difference on which side of the line the decisions fall in relation to continuing violations is almost imperceptible. In contrast to *Kurowski*, in *Aduayom et al v Tongo*,[128] the complaint was considered admissible despite the factual similarity. Here,

125 Ibid. para. 4.2.

126 *Mr. Eugeniusz Kurowski v. Poland,* Communication No. 872/1999, U.N. Doc. CCPR/C/77/D/872/1999 (2003).

127 S. Joseph et al., *The International Covenant on Civil and Political Rights: Cases, Materials, and Commentary* (2nd ed. Oxford University Pres 2005) 62.

128 *Aduayom et al. v. Togo*, Communications Nos. 422/1990, 423/1990 and 424/1990, U.N. Doc. CCPR/C/51/D/422/1990, 423/1990 and 424/1990 (1996).

the complainants like *Kurowski* also alleged that their dismissal from civil service was the result of political persecution and again, the alleged violation took place before the entry into force of the Optional Protocol respectively 1985 and 1988. Yet the HRC, unlike *Kurowski*, found the case admissible noting that

> ... the alleged violations had continuing effect after the entry into force of the Optional Protocol for Togo, in that the authors were denied reinstatement in their posts until... 1991... and that no payment of salary arrears or other forms of compensation had been affected. The Committee considered that these continuing effects could be seen as an affirmation of the previous violations allegedly committed by the State party. It therefore concluded that it was not precluded *ratione temporis* from examining the communications...

As the ICCPR Commentary notes, it is extremely difficult to locate a distinction between these two cases which deems the former inadmissible and the later admissible; it is offered that a possible difference could lie in that the alleged political persecution in the later was more clear but the perceived merits of a complaint are not the grounds on which it is deemed inadmissible *ratione temporis*.[129]

In sum, after *Kurowski* the line between continuing and non-continuing violations is ambiguous at best. With the murky waters of continuing violations, the stretch into IHL and at least questions surrounding the promise of the concept of remedial self-determination, where does this leave Indigenous Peoples in their quest for the restitution of their traditional cultural property?

Some Conclusions: General vs. Specific Rights Regarding the Restitution of Cultural Property to Indigenous Peoples

Indigenous Peoples stress that the restitution of cultural property is integral to the maintenance, development and renewal of their culture and identities as they emerge from the shadows of imperialism and colonialism. Indeed, past centuries saw the removal of much of their cultural property as part and parcel of the process of marginalization and assimilation that they suffered at the hands of the dominate state. In turn, '[i]n the context of indigenous claims for reparations, restitution is the most unsettling for states because it often involves a direct confrontation with colonial and assimilation policies

129 S. Joseph et al. (n 127) 63.

and practices.'[130] Yet Indigenous Peoples view restitution as vital to building, maintaining and developing their culture, overcoming these injustices and even their survival in the 21st century. Dodson, an indigenous activist notes: '[a]s indigenous peoples, we are acutely aware that our survival as peoples depends on the vitality of our culture. The deepest wound that colonization has inflicted has come from a process of stripping us of our distinct identities and cultures.'[131] The link between cultural property and restitution and self-determination becomes more evident because the restitution of cultural property is a victory, even if partial, over assimilationist policies as it can lead to cultural development and renewal.

Claims for the restitution of cultural property are not simply cultural claims but are also remedial claims aimed at rectifying the disastrous impacts of colonization. This chapter argued that both cultural claims and remedial claims exist in the multi-faceted penumbra of self-determination; respectively the cultural and remedial aspects of self-determination. While the linkages between self-determination and cultural property rooted in the cultural aspect of self-determination have been explored, less attention has been paid to the remedial aspect of self-determination. Yet this remedial aspect of self-determination provides a conceptual link to cultural property and its restitution and is of profound significance as a tool in relation to the restitution of cultural property. This chapter has sought to rectify this lacuna by exploring the relationship between self-determination and cultural property and its restitution at the intersection of their remedial aspects. It demonstrated that aside from some limited concerns with the conceptualization of self-determination as remedial, this facet of self-determination is crucial to the continuing efforts to secure the restitution of cultural property to Indigenous Peoples by overcoming the non-retroactivity at the heart of the repatriation debate. Finally, in light of the limited concerns with remedial self-determination this chapter has explored alternative avenues to secure retroactivity ultimately concluding that these alternatives pale in comparison with the remedial aspect of self-determination.

---

130 Vrdoljak (n 65) 213.

131 M. Dodson, *Cultural Rights and Educational Responsibilities,* The Frank Archibald Memorial Lecture, University of New England, 5 September 1994 *cited in* Moira Simpson, 'Museums and restorative justice: heritage, repatriation and cultural education' 61 Museum International 121, 123 (2009). Simpson details evidence that suggests that cultural renewal has a positive effect on the survival of Indigenous Peoples who have endured colonial and post-colonial trauma.

Yet one obvious objection remains: what if the UNDRIP has already overcome non-retroactivity. In contrast to Allen,[132] Vrdoljak starts from the position that the UNDRIP by its nature is retroactive.[133] Indeed, this is a viable approach given that the Declaration is part of a specific category of rights, i.e. *sui generis* rights for Indigenous Peoples.[134] *Sui generis* rights are not rights derived from a positive legal system but rather in the case of Indigenous Peoples 'arise *sui generis* from the historical condition of indigenous peoples as distinctive societies with the aspiration to survive as such.'[135] Differing from broader IHRL which is non-retroactive, its *sui generis* nature opens up the possibility that it is not bound by the same principles given the focus of *sui generis* rights not on the positive legal system but on social consequences.

However, this objection is not fatal to the significance of this inquiry into the remedial penumbra of self-determination as a means to secure the restitution of cultural property by breaking the bonds of non-retroactivity. As Gilbert notes in what is essentially part of the general versus specific rights debate:

> ... the choice might not be of one versus another. Rather, an adequate level of protection for indigenous peoples might be based on both paths. On the one hand, general human rights norms of non-discrimination and equality are flexible enough to include some protection for indigenous peoples, but on the other hand, such flexibility relies on a parallel development of a specific regime of protection... Hence, the development of jurisprudence from the UN human rights treaty bodies... on the rights of indigenous peoples does not preclude the development of a specific regime. Quite the opposite; these developments indicate that 'the evolution of the times' supports the emergence of a specific focus on the protection of indigenous peoples.[136]

In turn this opens up the further possibility that when considered in tandem, despite their varying degree of issues, remedial self-determination, precedent

---

132 Allen (n 87) 40.

133 Vrdoljak, (n 65) 214.

134 Interestingly, Indigenous Peoples deny the *sui generis* nature of the Declaration. However, this seems borne more from clever political advocacy and strategy rather than reality. *See generally* Allen, (n 87).

135 H. Berman, 'Are Indigenous Populations Entitled to International Juridical Personality?' 79 American Society of International Law Proc. (1989)193 *reprinted in* J. Gilbert, 'Indigenous Rights in the Making: The United Nations Declaration on the Rights of indigenous Peoples' International Journal on Minority and Groups Rights 14 (2007)207, 210.

136 Gilbert (n 135)211.

from IHL and continuing violations present a bulk of evidence suggesting the nascent development of retroactivity for the restitution of cultural property to Indigenous Peoples in broader IHRL that indeed complements any retroactivity in the *sui generis* scheme of the soft law Declaration.

Reparations for Wrongs against Indigenous Peoples' Cultural Heritage

Federico Lenzerini

1 Introduction: The Significance of Cultural Heritage for Indigenous Peoples

"Heritage is everything that defines our distinct identities as peoples. It is bestowed on us by our ancestors and endowed to us by nature. It includes our socio-political, cultural and economic systems and institutions; our worldview, belief systems, ethics and moral values; our customary laws and norms [...] It includes traditional knowledge, which is the creative production of human thought and craftsmanship, language, cultural expressions which are created, acquired and inspired, such as songs, dances, stories, ceremonies, symbols and designs, poetry, artworks; scientific, agricultural, technical and ecological knowledge and the skills required to implement this knowledge and technologies. Heritage includes human genetic material and ancestral human remains. It includes what we inherited from nature such as the natural features in our territories and landscapes, biodiversity which consists of plants and animals, cultigens, micro-organisms and the various ecosystems which we have nurtured and sustained. It includes our sacred cites, sites of historical significance, burial sites. It also includes all documentation of us on film, photographs, videotapes and audiotapes, scientific and ethnographic research reports, books and papers. Our heritage cannot be separated into component parts. It should be regarded as a single integrated, interdependent whole. We do not award different values to different aspects of our heritage [...] We do not differentiate levels of protection to the different aspects of our heritage. All aspects are equal and require equal respect, safeguarding and protection. In the same vein, we do not see protection of our rights to our cultures as separate from territorial rights and our right of self-determination".[1]

As epitomized by the quote above, the concept of indigenous cultural heritage is a very complex one. It goes much beyond the idea of cultural heritage prevailing in the Western world and adopted by most pertinent international legal instruments. Its existence and characterization are determined by the ho-

1 Mililani Trask, Leader of the Indigenous World Association. Taken from <www.galdu.org/web/index.php?odas=3366&giella1=eng> accessed 21 July 2015.

Xanthaki, Valkonen et al. (eds.), *Indigenous Peoples' Cultural Heritage: Rights, Debates and Challenges.*
 ISBN 978-90-04-34218-7. PP. 327-346

listic and spiritual vision of life of indigenous peoples themselves. Its components cannot be separated from each other, because it would be tantamount to separating the components of a living body and pretending that such a body would live and work properly. In the majority of cases its significance and value cannot be measured on the basis of objective criteria – like, e.g., economic, artistic, or architectural worth – but rather on the basis of its ethnological meaning, i.e. how significant and valuable a given element of cultural heritage is *perceived* to be by its holders and bearers. An indigenous community finds its reason for existence in its own cultural heritage, through establishing with it a process of symbiosis, which reaches the point of leading the community to coincide with its own heritage itself.

In attempting to provide a definition of indigenous cultural heritage, one might refer to the one offered by the UNESCO *Mexico City Declaration on Cultural Policies* of 1982, according to which the cultural heritage of a people "includes the works of its artists, architects, musicians, writers and scientists and also the work of anonymous artists, expressions of the people's spirituality, and the body of values which give meaning to life. It includes both tangible and intangible works through which the creativity of that people finds expression: languages, rites, beliefs, historic places and monuments, literature, works of art, archives and libraries".[2] This definition is, however, too narrow. Indeed, for indigenous peoples cultural heritage includes not only the tangible and intangible products created by the community and/or its members, but also the natural "background" in which they are located – i.e. land and natural resources – as well as the animate and inanimate components of the human person, including genetic materials and mortal remains. In addition, as previously mentioned, indigenous peoples' cultural heritage represents a complex reality in the context of which all elements – including tangible properties and intangible heritage – are holistically intertwined as essential elements of the cultural identity of indigenous communities themselves, being therefore inseparable from each other. This is a common feature of all elements of indigenous existence, including human rights as well as all animate and inanimate beings existing in the world.

The purpose of the present contribution is to explain the decisive role of reparation in the event of wrongs suffered by indigenous peoples relating to their cultural heritage, as well as to ascertain the present status of international law in the field, in light of the pertinent rules and relevant practice. Also, attention will be devoted to the critical factors which in some cases can make

---

2 See <http://portal.unesco.org/culture/en/files/12762/11295421661mexico_en.pdf/mexico_en.pdf> accessed 6 September 2015, 23.

it hard to translate existing rules into concrete practice, and to the steps which should be taken to increase the effective realization of the right of indigenous peoples to reparation for cultural-heritage-related wrongs.

2 The Role of Reparations and the Status of the Right to Redress in International Law, with Special Regard to Indigenous Peoples

Reparation represents the necessary therapy for the "pathological phase" of human rights.

In a sense, enjoyment of human rights is like living life. Sometimes human beings are lucky enough to live their lives without serious impediments and without experiencing any significant threat to their health until they get very old. In many cases, however, during the course of their life individuals have to experience serious diseases or other dangers threatening their life and, when this happens, they need to have access to all possible remedies which are likely to solve the problem. When no such remedy is available, the resulting loss – i.e. the life of the person – is irreplaceable. Similar considerations may be developed with respect to human rights. At present, legal rules proclaiming human rights exist virtually everywhere in the world, and it is possible to assume that human beings are automatically protected by virtue of those rules. It may be possible that, during the whole course of her life, a person will not experience any violation of her legally recognized rights. Conversely, in most cases people are not so lucky. When a breach of human rights takes place, one of the fundamental cornerstones of human societies is infringed – as the very foundations of human co-existence and its social basis are offended – and some action to remedy such breach is therefore indispensable. In this respect, the necessary ultimate treatment to remedy human rights breaches is indeed reparation. It follows that human rights cannot be *effective* if appropriate reparation is not ensured in the event of a violation. Such an essential role of reparation in the dynamics of human rights is symbolized by the words of the Inter-American Court of Human Rights (IACtHR), according to which the obligation to repair human rights breaches represents "a customary norm that constitutes one of the basic principles of contemporary international law on State responsibility".[3]

Once the significance of reparation in the general context of human rights is properly understood, further considerations are needed to appropriately comprehend its particular importance when indigenous peoples are concerned. In

3 See *Case of the Plan de Sánchez Massacre v. Guatemala*, Reparations, Series C No. 116, Judgment of 19 November 2004, 52.

fact, the effects of violations of human rights may be drastically different, depending on their overall impact on the life of the victim(s). Needless to say that the more such an impact is significant, the more reparation is indispensable. With respect to indigenous peoples, in many cases the wrongs they are forced to suffer as a result of the violation of their rights reach the point of disrupting the whole life of the community, sometimes even having an intergenerational dimension. This is due to the previously noted holistic and spiritual vision of life characterizing most such communities, in the context of which all human rights have a communal dimension and are interdependent. Consequently, most wrongs do not affect one right only, or the rights of certain members of the community only, but reverberate on the whole existence and stability of the community itself. To illustrate the point, let us assume that a violation of indigenous peoples' land rights is committed: such violation also implies the impossibility for the community concerned to properly enjoy its right to self-determination and autonomy as well as its cultural rights, because all such rights find their own *raison-d'être* and concrete realization on the ancestral territories traditionally occupied by the community. Similarly, the killing of members of the community usually affects not only the families of the victims, but also the community as a whole. Similar considerations apply to violations affecting the cultural heritage of indigenous peoples, understood in accordance with the broad understanding described above.

Concrete examples of the inter-link just explained are, once again, offered by the practice of the IACtHR. One of its judgments, in particular, offers a formidable description of the complexity as well as of the collective characterization of reparation for wrongs suffered by indigenous peoples. The case concerned a massacre perpetrated in 1986 by the army of Suriname in the ancestral territories of the Moiwana community, when their village was also razed to the ground and many survivors of the massacre were forced to flee. Among the various aspects of the case considered by the Court, the fact that the victims did not have any access to judicial guarantees and judicial protection attains particular significance for our purposes. In this respect, the IACtHR went beyond its previous jurisprudence,[4] according to which, in general terms, "a longstanding absence of effective remedies is typically considered by the Court as a source of suffering and anguish for victims and their family members".[5] In fact, the Court stressed that, in light of the specific cultural views and beliefs of

4 See *Case of the Serrano-Cruz Sisters v. El Salvador*, Merits, Reparations and Costs, Series C No. 120, Judgment of 1 March 2005, 113-115.

5 See *Case of Moiwana Community v. Suriname*, Preliminary Objections, Merits, Reparations and Costs, Series C No. 124, Judgment of 15 June 2005, 94.

the community concerned, "the ongoing impunity [had caused] a particularly severe impact upon the Moiwana villagers, as a N'djuka people [...] [because] justice and collective responsibility are central precepts within traditional N'djuka society".[6] As a consequence, in determining reparation for the moral damages suffered by the members of the Moiwana community, the IACtHR took into account "their inability, despite persistent efforts, to obtain justice for the attack on their village, particularly in light of the N'djuka emphasis upon punishing offenses in a proper manner [...]. Such long-standing impunity [...] humiliates and infuriates the community members, as much as it fills them with dread that offended spirits will seek revenge upon them".[7] Furthermore, the Court also considered the "deep anguish and despair" suffered by the members of the community surviving the massacre, as they were impeded to honour and bury their loved ones in accordance with the fundamental norms of their own culture. Indeed, since the community had been prevented from performing its various death rituals according to its culture, "the community members fear "spiritually-caused illnesses," which they believe can affect the entire natural lineage and, if reconciliation is not achieved, will persist through generations".[8] Last but not least, the IACtHR included among the moral damages to be repaired the forced displacement of the Moiwana community members from the community's traditional land, which had "devastated them emotionally, spiritually, culturally, and economically", on account of the "vital spiritual, cultural and material importance" of their relationship with their ancestral territory.[9]

The latter point was very significantly reiterated in a later judgment, in which the Court, in determining reparation for non-pecuniary damage suffered by an indigenous community relocated from its ancestral lands, declared that it was going to "assess the special meaning that land has for indigenous peoples [...] This means that any denial of the enjoyment or exercise of property rights harms values that are very significant to the members of those peoples, who run the risk of losing or suffering irreparable harm to their life and identity and to the cultural heritage to be passed on to future generations".[10] In this respect, the Court did not miss the opportunity to emphasize the inherent collective nature of the ancestral relationship between indigenous com-

---

6 Ibid. 95.

7 Ibid. 195 a).

8 Ibid. 195 b).

9 Ibid. 195 c).

10 See *Case of the Xákmok Kásek Indigenous Community v. Paraguay*, Merits, Reparations and Costs, Series C No. 214, Judgment of 24 August 2010, 321.

munities and their traditional lands. In fact, "the sorrow that [the individuals concerned] and the other members of the Community feel owing to the failure to restore their traditional lands, the gradual loss of their culture [...] give rise to suffering that necessarily violate the mental and moral integrity of all the members of the Community".[11]

Following the same line of reasoning, in an earlier case concerning the massacre of members of the Maya community in Guatemala, the Court found that the death of the women and elders had "produced a cultural vacuum, [as] [t]he orphans did not receive the traditional education handed down from their ancestors".[12] This was connected to the fact that "[t]raditions, rites and customs have an essential place in [the] community life [of Mayan people]. Their spirituality is reflected in the close relationship between the living and the dead, and is expressed, based on burial rites, as a form of permanent contact and solidarity with their ancestors. The transmission of culture and knowledge is one of the roles assigned to the elders and the women".[13] Consequently, the IACtHR concluded that reparation granted "to the members of the community as a whole" was essential.[14]

It follows that – in general terms – when programmes of reparations are established in favour of indigenous peoples, it is to be ensured that the collective dimension of the vision of life of the peoples concerned, which in its turn translates into a communal perception of the wrongs suffered by their members, is taken as the main parameter to be used for structuring the forms and modalities of the specific measures of redress to be allocated. Hence, "the individual reparations to be awarded must be supplemented by communal measures; said reparations [are to be] be granted to the community as a whole".[15]

What has just been described is only part of the picture. As previously stressed, in order to ensure effectiveness of human rights, reparation must be *appropriate*, meaning that it must be concretely suitable to fully restore the wrongs suffered by the victim according to his/her own perspective. In other words, a reparatory process would be void if and to the extent that it would not produce the effect of leading the victim to *feel* fully restored. It is evident that such an outcome may only be fulfilled through taking into proper consideration the social and cultural specificity of the victim, as well as his/her specific

---

11 Ibid. 244.

12 See *Case of the Plan de Sánchez Massacre v. Guatemala*, Reparations, Series C No. 116, Judgment of 19 November 2004, 49(12).

13 Ibid. 85.

14 Ibid. 86.

15 See *Case of Moiwana Community v. Suriname* (n 5) 194.

needs existing in the context of the situation determined by the wrong done. In concrete terms, this translates into a requirement of tailoring the specific forms of reparation to be established on the basis of the said needs. "Reparations consist in those measures necessary to make the effects of the committed violations disappear. The nature and amount of the reparations depend on the harm caused at both the material and moral levels".[16]

In principle, "[t]he reparation of harm caused by a violation of an international obligation requires, whenever possible, full restitution (*restitutio in integrum*), which consists in restoring the situation that existed before the violation occurred. When this is not possible [...] [it is necessary] to order the adoption of a series of measures that, in addition to guaranteeing respect for the rights violated, will ensure that the damage resulting from the infractions is repaired, by way, *inter alia*, of payment of an indemnity as compensation for the harm caused".[17] Depending on the circumstances characterizing any specific situation, certain forms of redress, which in a given case are fully appropriate to repair the wrong suffered by the victim concerned, may not be enough, or even be inappropriate, when a different victim, bearing different needs, is concerned. Again, this is particularly true as far as indigenous peoples are concerned. Indeed, as previously noted, violations of the rights of those peoples usually produce collective implications going much beyond the suffering caused to their individual members. At the same time, the wrongs suffered by indigenous peoples, as perceived by them both individually and collectively, do not limit their impact to the material side of their life, but usually pierce the deeper dimension of their spiritual existence, therefore assuming an intergenerational connotation. It follows that a reparatory process aimed at redressing a wrong suffered by an indigenous community must address *all* such elements and put in practice all necessary measures to provide appropriate redress for them all. For indigenous peoples, reparation not only redresses a specific wrong, but in many cases allows the community to recover its whole existence and the harmony of the life of the community for the centuries to come. This implies, among other things, that the form of reparation prevailing within the Western context – i.e. monetary compensation – is usually not adequate, or at least not sufficient, to ensure effective redress for the pain suffered by indigenous communities.

Once again, formidable practical examples of the argument just put forward may be found in the context of the practice of the IACtHR. For instance, in establishing reparations in the case of the Moiwana community in Suriname

---

16 See, inter alia, ibid. 171.

17 Ibid. 170.

explained above, the Court did not limit itself to establishing monetary compensation for both pecuniary and non-pecuniary damage, but added a significant amount of other reparatory measures which were considered necessary for properly restoring the damage suffered by the community concerned according to its own perspective. Those measures included the obligation by the respondent government to investigate and punish the responsible parties in the instant case;[18] to "employ all technical and scientific means possible [...] to recover promptly the remains of the Moiwana community members killed during the 1986 attack [...] [and to] deliver them as soon as possible thereafter to the surviving community members so that the deceased may be honored according to the rituals of N'djuka culture";[19] to "adopt such legislative, administrative and other measures as are necessary to ensure the property rights of the members of the Moiwana community in relation to the traditional territories from which they were expelled, and provide for their use and enjoyment of those territories [...] includ[ing] the creation of an effective mechanism for the delimitation, demarcation and titling of said traditional territories";[20] to establish a developmental fund "directed to health, housing and educational programs for the Moiwana community members";[21] to organize a public ceremony to recognize "its international responsibility for the facts of the instant case and issue an apology to the Moiwana community members";[22] to establish a monument – having a design and location to be decided upon in consultation with the victims' representatives – serving as a reminder to the whole nation of what happened in the Moiwana Village and preventing that it may be repeated in the future.[23]

The considerations developed in the present section involve to a notable degree indigenous peoples' cultural heritage. It is sufficient to think, among the examples just provided, of the following: the mortal remains of the dead members of the Moiwana community in Suriname; the traditions, rites and customs of Mayan people in Guatemala; the traditional lands – including natural resources located therein – of all indigenous communities, which are part of their own cultural heritage on account of the spiritual and (more generally) cultural significance attributed to them by those communities.

18 Ibid. 207.
19 Ibid. 208.
20 Ibid. 209.
21 Ibid. 214.
22 Ibid. 216.
23 Ibid. 218.

The right of indigenous peoples to reparation for the wrongs suffered is today recognized by a number of provisions included in the international legal instruments concerning those peoples, particularly the 2007 *United Nations Declaration on the Rights of Indigenous Peoples* (UNDRIP).[24] Indeed, nine of the forty-six articles of the latter – i.e. articles 8(2), 10, 11(2), 12(2), 20(2), 28, 29(3), 32(3) and 40 – include provisions relating to the matter of reparation.[25] The cultural aspect represents the rationale and the cornerstone with respect to most of them. Some of them are even devoted to the right to reparation for loss of cultural heritage. In particular, Article 11(2) UNDRIP establishes that "States shall provide redress through effective mechanisms, which may include restitution, developed in conjunction with indigenous peoples, with respect to their cultural, intellectual, religious and spiritual property taken without their free, prior and informed consent or in violation of their laws, traditions and customs". More specifically, Article 12(2) deals with ceremonial objects and human remains, with respect to which States "shall seek to enable the access and/or repatriation [...] through fair, transparent and effective mechanisms developed in conjunction with indigenous peoples concerned".

The provisions concerning reparation for violations of indigenous peoples' land rights are also especially pertinent to the present investigation, for the reasons explained above. Among them, Article 28 is of particular significance, stating that "Indigenous peoples have the right to redress, by means that can include restitution or, when this is not possible, just, fair and equitable compensation, for the lands, territories and resources which they have traditionally owned or otherwise occupied or used, and which have been confiscated, taken, occupied, used or damaged without their free, prior and informed consent". The same article continues by establishing that "[u]nless otherwise freely agreed upon by the peoples concerned, compensation shall take the form of lands, territories and resources equal in quality, size and legal status or of mon-

24 UN GA Res. 61/295, 13 September 2007.

25 For a more comprehensive assessment of the right of indigenous peoples to reparation under the UNDRIP see F Lenzerini, "Reparations, Restitution and Redress", in M Weller and J Hohmann (eds.), *The UN Declaration on the Rights of Indigenous Peoples. A Commentary* (Oxford University Press 2017), forthcoming. See also, more in general, F Lenzerini (ed.), *Reparations for Indigenous Peoples. International and Comparative Perspectives* (Oxford University Press 2008); among the contributions included in this volume see, with particular respect to cultural heritage, A Vrdoljak, "Reparation for Cultural Loss", 197ff; of the same author see also *International Law, Museums and the Return of Cultural Objects* (Cambridge University Press 2008) 228ff. On the specific subject of the present chapter see K Kuprecht, *Indigenous Peoples' Cultural Property Claims. Repatriation and Beyond* (Springer 2014).

etary compensation or other appropriate redress". The use of the term "appropriate" shows that, whatever kind of reparation is selected, it must be adequate to effectively restore the damage suffered by the community concerned.

The UNDRIP is not the only existing international legal instrument recognizing the right of indigenous peoples to reparation for breaches of their land rights. The same rule is, in fact, established by the 1989 ILO *Convention concerning Indigenous and Tribal Peoples in Independent Countries*.[26] In particular, Article 15(2) states that indigenous peoples shall receive fair compensation for any damages, which they may sustain as a result of programmes for the exploration or exploitation of natural resources located in their traditional lands. Also, Article 16 establishes that, in the event of relocation of indigenous communities from their ancestral lands with respect to which return is not feasible, those communities are entitled to reparation which, when possible, should take the form of "lands of quality and legal status at least equal to that of the lands previously occupied by them, suitable to provide for their present needs and future development".

In general terms, as authoritatively affirmed by the International Law Association (ILA)'s Resolution No. 5/2012,

> States must comply with their obligations – under customary and applicable conventional international law – to recognise and fulfil the rights of indigenous peoples to reparation and redress for wrongs they have suffered, including right relating to lands taken or damaged without their free, prior and informed consent. Effective mechanisms for redress – established in conjunction with the peoples concerned – must be available and accessible in favour of indigenous peoples. Reparation must be adequate and effective, and, according to the perspective of the indigenous communities concerned, actually capable of repairing the wrongs they have suffered.[27]

This statement confirms that, beyond treaty law, the right of indigenous peoples to reparation for the wrongs suffered has today crystallized into a principle of customary international law. This conclusion is also evident from the perspective of legal logic; in fact, once it has been established that reparation is an essential element for guaranteeing the effectiveness of human rights, the provisions of customary international law which protect such rights (including

26 See <www.ilo.org/dyn/normlex/en/f?p=NORMLEXPUB:12100:0::NO::P12100_ILO_CODE:C169> accessed 6 September 2015.

27 See <www.ila-hq.org/en/committees/index.cfm/cid/1024> accessed 6 September 2015.

those protecting the fundamental rights of indigenous peoples) must necessarily embrace the right of access to reparation that is adequate to restore the wrong suffered.

3 International Practice of Reparation for Wrongs Perpetrated against Indigenous Peoples' Cultural Heritage: Successful Cases and Critical Factors

In the event of loss by indigenous peoples of their cultural heritage, international law – as noted in the previous section – prescribes that the peoples concerned should be ensured adequate and effective reparation for the wrongs suffered due to the said loss. In principle, as previously emphasized, the specific form to be taken by a reparation for it to be *adequate* and *effective* is to be established on a case-by-case basis. This said, with respect to the case in point we may assume that the most – if not the only – satisfactory form of reparation that is practicable in order to *effectively* restore the wrongs suffered by an indigenous community for being deprived of its cultural heritage is represented, when feasible, by *restitutio in integrum*. At the same time, it is to be considered that, for indigenous peoples, loss of cultural heritage may occur in very heterogeneous ways, which include not only deprivation of tangible objects, but also taking of lands and/or natural resources, prevention of the possibility of practising and living in accordance with their cultural traditions, including religious rituals, hunting and fishing, traditional medicine, etc. Indeed, any aspect of the life of indigenous peoples has a cultural connotation. In other words, consistent with the concept of indigenous peoples' cultural heritage as described in the quote at the beginning of this chapter,[28] every wrong suffered by indigenous peoples involves damage of such heritage. It follows that any process of reparation in favour of indigenous peoples entails some measure of redress for loss of cultural heritage. In each different situation, reparation should assume different forms depending on the specificity of the case, ranging from the return of movable heritage to the community concerned, to the reintegration of indigenous peoples' spiritual relationship with their ancestral territories and the resources located therein, or to the reconstruction of the connection between present and past generations.[29] Having this in mind,

28 See text corresponding to n 1 above.

29 A very interesting case is represented by a collection of photographs of Aboriginal Australians held by the Berndt Museum of Anthropology located in Perth, Australia, with respect to which the need was emphasized that the members of the "Stolen Generation"

in the present section particular attention will be devoted to reparation for wrongs consisting in deprivation of tangible movable cultural heritage of indigenous peoples, a topic which epitomizes the recent evolution of international law towards recognizing the right of such peoples to obtain redress for loss or damage of their cultural heritage.

The existence of the right of indigenous peoples to restitution of their cultural property is supported – in addition to the general legal framework described in the previous section – by instruments of international law specifically devoted to movable cultural heritage. For example, the 1995 *UNIDROIT Convention on Stolen or Illegally Exported Cultural Objects*[30] establishes, at Article 5(3)(d), that, in the context of the return of illegally exported cultural objects, the court or other competent authority of the State party to which return of a cultural object has been requested must order that such a return is ensured, if it is established that the removal of the object concerned has significantly impaired "the traditional or ritual use of the object by a tribal or indigenous community". Similarly, the *Principles & Guidelines for the Protection of the Heritage of Indigenous People*, also adopted in 1995,[31] request governments and international organizations to "assist indigenous peoples and communities in recovering control and possession of their moveable cultural property and other heritage".[32] In addition, they stress that human remains and associated funeral objects "must be returned to their descendants and territories in a culturally appropriate manner, as determined by the indigenous peoples concerned",[33] while moveable cultural property "should be returned

– victims of the infamous policy carried out by the Australian government in the XXth Century resulting in the removal of children of Aboriginals and Torre Strait Islanders from their families – were allowed to have access to the photographs. Indeed, the latter might help in assisting them "to cope better with their profound sense of loss and disorientation", as those images might allow them "to reconnect to their families, even if it is only in the form of a photograph […] Not only is it important for the older generations to identify their family history, but it is also crucial that this information be passed to the younger generations, which is imperative for reclaiming and forming identity". See JE Stanton, "Snapshots on the Dreaming: Photographs of the past and present", in LV Prott (ed.), *Witnesses to History – Documents and Writings on the Return of Cultural Objects* (UNESCO 2009), 242, 248-249.

30 See <www.unidroit.org/instruments/cultural-property/1995-convention> accessed 19 September 2015.

31 See UN Doc. E/CN.4/Sub.2/1995/26, 21 June 1995, available at <http://ankn.uaf.edu/IKS/protect.html> accessed 19 September 2015.

32 See Principle 19.

33 See Principle 21.

wherever possible to its traditional owners, particularly if shown to be of significant cultural, religious or historical value to them".[34]

In sum, international law provides a sound legal basis for the reparation campaigns developed in the last few decades at various levels, by indigenous peoples and their supporters, in order to recover their lost cultural property and obtain compensation for the cultural loss suffered as a result of wrongs perpetrated against their cultural heritage.

One of the most renowned of the said campaigns has been the one aimed at obtaining the return to New Zealand of the Māori *Mokomokai* – mummified heads of Māori people of high lineage, decorated by traditional tattooing – either to be returned to their relatives or, when the latter are unknown, to the Museum of New Zealand Te Papa Tongarewa, in Wellington. In 2007, ruling on the decision of the museum of natural history of its town to return one of those heads to New Zealand, a French tribunal emphasized that such a return would have represented an unjustified damage to French national heritage.[35] The rationale of the decision of the French tribunal was reinforced by the fact that, once returned to their relatives, the *Mokomokai* were to be buried according to the Māori tradition; hence, the whole of humanity (including future generations) would be deprived forever of the possibility of enjoying such pieces of cultural heritage. This argument, however, even coupled with the one according to which the *Mokomokai* concerned had to be considered as part of French cultural heritage, was eventually not enough to overcome the awareness of the fundamental importance of returning to the Māori community an essential piece of their own cultural and spiritual heritage. Therefore, the decision of the Tribunal was *de facto* reversed by the French National Assembly, which on 4 May 2010 passed a bill ordering French museums to return to New Zealand all Māori mummified heads still in their possession.[36] The new law was given proper operation in the following years. For example, twenty *Mokomokai* were returned from France to their respective tribes in New Zealand, to be given a proper burial, in January 2012.[37] The behaviour of the French government

34 See Principle 22.

35 The decision was released by the Administrative Tribunal of Rouen in October 2007; see "France stops Maori mummy's return", BBC News, 25 October 2007, <http://news.bbc.co.uk/2/hi/europe/7061724.stm> accessed 11 September 2015.

36 See *Loi no 2010-501 du 18 mai 2010 visant à autoriser la restitution par la France des têtes maories à la Nouvelle-Zélande et relative à la gestion des collections*, <http://legifrance.gouv.fr/affichTexte.do?cidTexte=JORFTEXT000022227321> accessed 11 September 2015.

37 See "France returns 20 mummified Maori heads to New Zealand", BBC News, 24 January 2012, <www.bbc.com/news/world-asia-16695330> accessed 11 September 2015.

was part of a wider practice developed by a number of countries – including Australia, the United States, the United Kingdom and other European States – pursuant to which hundreds of *Mokomokai* held in museums and private collections around the world were returned to New Zealand.[38]

Human remains represent the category of indigenous peoples' cultural heritage with respect to which reparation has been practised more frequently in recent times. For example, in Argentina, in 1994, the remains of the Mapuche Chief Inakayal, previously kept in the La Plata museum since his death in 1888, were returned to his homeland, Patagonia, where they were buried by indigenous descendants.[39] Also, in June 2005, all known human remains belonging to ancestors of the Haida Nation (an indigenous nation of the Pacific North-West coast of North America) located in North America were repatriated and reburied,[40] while some problems were experienced when trying to recover the Haida remains held by European institutions.[41] In fact, "many European institutions remain apprehensive about the process [of repatriation], to some extent because there is a sense of pride and national identity tied up in housing these collections".[42] However, for example, in 2010 the remains previously held at the Pitt Rivers Museum, at the University of Oxford, were returned to the Haida Nation and subsequently reburied in the community's traditional territory.[43]

In 2003, a *Joint Statement* was released by the prime ministers of the United Kingdom and Australia. In that document they agreed to "increase efforts to repatriate human remains to Australian indigenous communities" and recognized "the special connection that indigenous peoples have with ancestral remains". Furthermore, they endorsed "the repatriation of indigenous human remains wherever possible and appropriate from both public and private col-

38 For a more comprehensive assessment of the case of the Māori *Mokomokai* see F Lenzerini, "The Tension between Communities' Cultural Rights and Global Interests: The Case of the Māori *Mokomokai*", in S Borelli and F Lenzerini (eds.), *Cultural Heritage, Cultural Rights, Cultural Diversity: New Developments in International Law* (Brill-Nijhoff, 2012), 157ff.

39 See ML Endere, "The Return of Inakayal to Patagonia", in Prott (n 29) 283ff.

40 See Skidegate Repatriation & Cultural Committee, "End of Mourning Ceremony", <www.repatriation.ca/Pages/End%20of%20Mourning.html> accessed 15 September 2015; see also M Simpson, "The Repatriation of Haida Ancestors", in Prott (n 29) 260ff.

41 See L Bourgon, "Grave Injustice. The Haida Nation's quest to repatriate the stolen bodies of its ancestors", *The Walrus*, April 2013, <http://thewalrus.ca/grave-injustice/> accessed 15 September 2015.

42 Ibid.

43 Ibid.

lections". Last but not least, they praised the British institutions that had already negotiated agreements with indigenous communities for the release of remains, particularly the Edinburgh University, which had "completed repatriation requests of a large collection of remains".[44]

One further example of return of human remains to indigenous peoples occurred in May 2007, when the Natural History Museum in London returned 17 Aboriginal mortal remains to Tasmania, Australia, on the condition that some of them, instead of being buried, would be preserved in Tasmania under the joint control of the Museum and the Tasmanian Aboriginal Centre.[45]

More generally with respect to the return of cultural property to indigenous communities, in the United States the *Native American Graves Protection and Repatriation Act* (*NAGPRA*)[46] was passed in 1990; since then, according to the most recently updated statistics available at the time of this writing, the following Native American human remains and cultural items have been repatriated: 50,518 individuals' human remains; 1,185,948 associated funerary objects; 219,956 unassociated funerary objects; 4,914 sacred objects; 8,118 objects of cultural patrimony; 1,624 objects that are both sacred and patrimonial.[47] One of the most famous cases of successful application of the NAGPRA is represented by the repatriation of the *Ahayu:da* – twin gods of war – to the Zuni community. The process of repatriation, although starting in the late 1970s, well before the NAGPRA, notably increased after its entry into force, leading to the outcome of allowing repatriation of virtually all known *Ahayu:da* existing in North America.[48]

---

44 *Joint Statement by Prime Minister Blair (United Kingdom) and Prime Minister Howard (Australia) on the Repatriation of Human Remains*, 2003, in Prott (n 29) 268-269.

45 See AL Bandle, A Chechi, M André Renold, "Case 17 Tasmanian Human Remains – Tasmanian Aboriginal Centre and Natural History Museum London", Platform ArThemis, Art Law Centre, University of Geneva, March 2012, <https://plone.unige.ch/art-adr/cases-affaires/17-tasmanian-human-remains-2013-tasmanian-aboriginal-centre-and-natural-history-museum-london/case-note-17-tasmanian-human-remains> accessed 20 September 2015.

46 Pub. L. 101-601, 25 U.S.C. 3001 et seq., 104 Stat. 3048.

47 See National Park Service, U.S. Department of the Interior, "National NAGPRA Frequently Asked Questions", <http://www.nps.gov/nagpra/FAQ/INDEX.HTM> accessed 20 September 2015; the available statistics were updated at 30 September 2014.

48 On the case of the *Ahayu:da* see, *inter alia*, WL Merrill, EJ Ladd, TJ Ferguson, "The Return of the *Ahayu:da*. Lessons for Repatriation from Zuni Pueblo and the Smithsonian Institution", (1993) 34 *Current Anthropology* 523ff.; VV AA, "The Return of the *Ahayu:da* to Zuni Pueblo", in Prott (n 29) 255ff.; TJ Ferguson, 'Repatriation of *Ahayu:da*: 20 Years Later', (2010) 33 *Museum Anthropology* 194-195.

Another very famous case of return of stolen cultural property to indigenous peoples is the one concerning the sacred Sioux *ghost dance shirts*. Those shirts were taken from the dead bodies of some of the Sioux massacred by the U.S. Army in Wounded Knee on 29 December 1890 and subsequently displayed at the National Museum of Natural History, at the Smithsonian Institution. The Institution had a total of twenty-nine objects taken from the bodies of the Sioux killed in Wounded Knee, including the shirts. All of them were returned to the descendants of the victims in 1988.[49] Ten years later, in 1998, the Glasgow City Council's Arts and Culture Committee decided to return another of those shirts, which was previously held by the Kelvingrove Museum, in Glasgow, to the Wounded Knee Survivors' Association for display in Wounded Knee in a museum built to commemorate the massacre.[50]

The examples provided so far refer to successful cases. However, as it may be easily imagined, other cases exist in which indigenous peoples encounter huge problems in obtaining return of the cultural heritage of which they have been deprived. Indeed, in some cases their efforts have proved unsuccessful, while other cases are still pending even after decades of struggle. For example, in the previously mentioned case of the return of the *Ahayu:da* to the Zuni people, while it was characterized by huge success in the United States – mainly thanks to the NAGPRA – so far it has been much less successful with respect to the *Ahayu:da* claimed from European museums and other institutions, including the Musée du Quai Branly in Paris or the Ethnological Museum in Berlin.[51] European institutions fear that repatriation of those cultural objects would establish an unwelcome precedent that might encourage other people to claim other pieces included in their collections. Worse yet, in April 2013 a French judge even found that selling *Katsina "friends"* (which are among the most sacred ritual objects of the Hopi Native American community) at an auction in Paris was fully legitimate, as "the claim that Hopi cultural patrimony is exclusively their property has no legal basis according to French law".[52] Other cases have recently occurred in which indigenous peoples' sacred objects have been

49 See R Thornton, "Repatriation as Healing the Trauma of History", in Prott (n 29) 239.

50 See M Simpson, "Posing a Challenge for the Future", in Prott (n 29) 240-241.

51 See R Donadio, "Zuni Ask Europe to Return Sacred Art", *The New York Times*, 8 April 2014, <www.nytimes.com/2014/04/09/arts/design/zuni-petition-european-museums-to-return-sacred-objects.html?_r=1> accessed 20 September 2015.

52 See CR Ganteaume, "Respecting Non-Western Sacred Objects: An A:shiwi Ahayu:da (Zuni war god), the Museum of the American Indian–Heye Foundation, and the Museum of Modern Art", *The National Museum of the American Indian*, 15 April 2013, <http://blog.nmai.si.edu/main/2013/04/respecting-non-western-sacred-objects.html> accessed 20 September 2015.

sold at auctions; for instance, after the case of the *Katsina "friends"* just referred to, Native American tribes have failed to stop the sale of their own ceremonial objects in France at least another three times.[53]

The lack of success of the attempts to return certain indigenous cultural objects must not be taken as evidence contradicting the conclusion drawn in section 2 of this chapter, i.e. that, in addition to treaty law, the right of indigenous peoples to reparation for the wrongs suffered – including for the loss of their own cultural heritage – has today crystallized into a principle of customary international law. On the contrary, this conclusion remains fully valid even in the presence of concrete cases with a final outcome which *prima facie* seems to challenge it. Indeed, it usually happens with respect to virtually any rule of international law that the distance between the recognition of a given obligation "on paper" and its full concrete implementation in the life of people may remain quite lengthy. In other words, violations or derogations happen every day throughout the world with respect to any existing legal rule. As emphasized by the International Court of Justice in the *Nicaragua* case, "[i]t is not to be expected that in the practice of States the application of [a rule of international law] should have been perfect, in the sense that States should have refrained, with complete consistency, from [behaviours inconsistent with it] [...] The Court does not consider that, for a rule to be established as customary, the corresponding practice must be in absolute rigorous conformity with the rule".[54] More specifically with respect to the human rights field, it is self-evident that many States in the world have an awful human rights record – in spite of the many existing international obligations by which they are unquestionably bound – and even governments with a better reputation often try to circumvent their obligations through using very sophisticated legal arguments, including the need of balancing conflicting rights. With respect to movable cultural heritage of which indigenous peoples have been deprived, its return to the community that created and originally kept it is sometimes hindered for a number of reasons. Among the critical factors which in some cases make such return difficult to achieve in practice, the fact that the heritage in point may be considered as part of the cultural heritage of the country concerned emerges, as well as the consideration that its return to the said community might factually deprive the rest of the world of the opportunity of enjoying

53 See "Native Americans fail to halt artefact auction in France", *The Guardian*, 10 June 2015, <www.theguardian.com/world/2015/jun/10/native-americans-artefact-auction-france> accessed 20 September 2015.

54 See *Case concerning Military and Paramilitary Activities in and against Nicaragua* (*Nicaragua v. United States*), Merits, Judgment of 27 June 1986, (1986) *ICJ Reports* 186.

such heritage, or the existence of conflicting property claims by private owners. Not to mention other "less commendable" considerations, e.g. the abovementioned willingness (common to many European museums) to prevent a Pandora's box from opening, scattering innumerable claims of restitution of cultural property from all over the world. In any event, when such complex situations occur, they are not always treated in the proper way, i.e. according to the content and rationale of applicable international law. However, the case of the Māori *Mokomokai* described above indicates the way to be followed when dealing with cultural heritage of importance for indigenous peoples, even when other interests are at stake, notwithstanding the fact that also the latter are commendable. Indeed, in the *Mokomokai* case, the French government had no hesitation in passing a law establishing that those cultural objects had to be returned to their traditional owners, even at the price of impoverishing French cultural heritage and of depriving the whole world from having access to them, the fate of which was to be buried. In fact, when cultural property is of special spiritual significance for indigenous peoples – as is the case with the *Mokomokai* – its return to the community to which the property concerned culturally belongs is an essential prerequisite for ensuring preservation of its cultural identity and integrity, as well as for guaranteeing proper enjoyment of fundamental human rights by its members.[55]

It is true that the practice concerning return to indigenous peoples of the cultural property of which they have been deprived is still not absolutely uniform. However, such practice, considered as a whole, denotes a progressively growing awareness by the international community that the actual realization of indigenous peoples' internationally recognized human rights cannot prescind from proper reparation for the wrongs suffered by those peoples in relation to their cultural heritage.

4 Conclusion: The Way Forward

In the previous sections we have ascertained that international law fully recognizes the right of indigenous peoples to "maintain, control, protect and develop their cultural heritage, traditional knowledge and traditional cultural expressions",[56] and consistently prescribes their related right to reparation for wrongs suffered for being deprived of their cultural heritage and, more in general, for the rupture of their spiritual relationship with the latter. We have

55 See, more comprehensively on this point, Lenzerini (n 38) 165ff, particularly 173ff.

56 See Article 31 UNDRIP.

also seen that such reparation may take different forms, which depend on the specific element of indigenous peoples' cultural heritage that is affected, as well as on the characteristics of the violation suffered. With respect to deprivation of movable cultural property in particular, the most appropriate form of reparation is definitely represented by return of such property to the community concerned. Finally, we have noted that in certain instances it may be quite complex to translate the rights just mentioned into concrete practice, due to a number of factors. Among those factors, a key one is that in many cases non-indigenous subjects – either individuals or private or public institutions – may hold rights over cultural property of indigenous origin which are legally protected, usually taking the form of private property rights. Also, when a cultural property produced by, or originally belonging to, indigenous peoples has remained in a given country for a long time, it may be considered as part of its national cultural heritage, which the country concerned has a legally protected interest to keep. Not to mention extra-legal arguments, particularly the fear by museums and other institutions that, if they agree to return certain items to indigenous peoples, they would encourage other persons or entities to claim restitution of other pieces included in their collections. It is therefore evident that indigenous peoples' claims for recovering their own cultural property are sometimes unsuccessful *not* because their right to obtain return of such property is not protected by international law, but because different legally-protected and other interests exist over the property concerned, making it quite hard for the right claimed by indigenous peoples to prevail over the other interests at stake.

Generally speaking, one may not reasonably object to the consideration that, when different legally-protected rights are involved which are incompatible with each other, the decision concerning which one should prevail is to be taken on a case-by-case basis, after establishing a balance among the different interests at stake. However, with respect to the case under discussion, particular weight is to be attributed to the fundamental significance of cultural heritage for indigenous peoples. Indeed, for those peoples the importance of such heritage usually goes much beyond the one determined by a mere property right, having a deep spiritual significance to the point of playing an essential role for ensuring the preservation of indigenous communities' cultural identity and, *a fortiori*, for their very cultural and physical survival. Reparation for wrongs against indigenous peoples' cultural heritage is consequently essential for ensuring respect of the basic and fundamental human rights of indigenous peoples, which in principle certainly take the lead over a "simple" right to property held by private persons or institutions having the heritage concerned in their possession (although the latter right is also protected by law).

It emerges from the foregoing that it is essential that the necessary steps are taken for further improving the effectiveness of reparatory processes concerning cultural-heritage-related wrongs suffered by indigenous peoples. These steps should follow two parallel and related avenues. The first consists in increasing the amount of legal instruments and rules, at both international and domestic levels, prescribing the obligation to return cultural heritage of indigenous peoples to their original and legitimate owners, irrespective of the existence of any other property right over such heritage.[57] At the same time, ratification should be promoted of the instruments already existing proclaiming or implicitly presupposing the said obligation, like the 1995 UNIDROIT Convention, which at the moment of this writing has been ratified by 37 States only.[58] The second avenue to pursue addresses the need to raise awareness – among competent bodies and institutions, as well as within the civil society as a whole – about the fundamental significance of cultural heritage for indigenous peoples, a significance which goes much beyond a mere perception of "property" and attains attributes of deep spirituality, playing a decisive role in shaping and preserving the identity of the communities concerned. With such awareness in mind, it will be plainly and automatically recognized that return to indigenous peoples of their own cultural heritage represents – in addition to a well-established legal obligation – an ethically due gesture, greatly facilitating its actual realization in practice.

57 Examples of existing domestic legislation of the kind advocated in the text are represented by the NAGPRA (see n 46 and corresponding text) and French Loi nº 2010-501 du 18 mai 2010 (n 36).

58 See <www.unidroit.org/status-cp> accessed 22 September 2015.

Contributors

Dr Mattias Åhren
is Professor at the Faculty of law, University of Tromsø – The Arctic University of Norway.

Dr Willa Boezak
is the Advisor to Paramount Chief Alan le Fleur, the Griqua National Conference's Council of Chiefs; an Advisor to the National Khoisa Council of South Africa and the Chairperson of the Western Cape Cultural Commission.

Stefan Disko
is an independent heritage consultant and Advisor on World Heritage to the International Work Group for Indigenous Affairs (IWGIA).

Dr Shea Esterling
is Lecturer in Law in the School of Law at the University of Canterbury, Chistchurch, New Zealand.

Violet Ford
is an Inuit lawyer, originally from Nunatsiavut, Canada and the former vice president of the Inuit Circumpolar Council.

Dr Jérémie Gilbert
is Professor of Human Rights Law at the University of Roehampton, United Kingdom.

Dr Carina Green
holds a PhD in Cultural Anthropology and is currently working at the Swedish Biodiversity Centre at the Swedish University for Agricultural Sciences. She works also as a lecturer at the Uppsala University.

Dr Leena Heinämäki (LL.D)
is Senior Researcher at the Northern Institute for Environmental and Minority Law, Arctic Centre, University of Lapland.

Dr Elina Helander-Renvall
is Senior Scientist at the Arctic Centre, University of Lapland

Dr Thora Herrmann
is Associate Professor at the Geography Department at the Université de Montréal.

Dr Veli-Pekka Lehtola
is Professor of Sámi culture at the Giellagas Institute for Sámi studies at the University of Oulu, Finland.

Dr Federico Lenzerini
is Professor of international law and human rights at the Department of Law of the University of Siena, Italy.

Anne-Maria Magga
is a PhD candidate in the Faculty of Social Sciences at the University of Lapland.

Inkeri Markkula
is a Researcher at the Arctic Centre, University of Lapland.

Piia Nuogram
is a PhD candidate in the Faculty of Law at the University of Lapland.

Dr Øyvind Ravna
is Professor at the Faculty of law, University of Tromsø – The Arctic, University of Norway and adjunct professor at the Faculty of Law, University of Lapland, Finland.

Hai-Yuean Tualima
is a WIPO Indigenous Fellow at the World Intellectual Property Organisation.

Dr Jarno Valkonen
is Professor of sociology at the University of Lapland.

Dr Sanna Valkonen
is Associate Professor of Sámi research at the University of Lapland (Postdoctoral researcher of the Academy of Finland (-8/2017).

Dr Alexandra Xanthaki
is Professor of Law at Brunel University London, United Kingdom.

Dr Daphne Zografos Johnsson
is Legal Officer in the Traditional Knowledge Division of the World Intellectual Property Organization (WIPO).

Index

www.ingramcontent.com/pod-product-compliance
Lightning Source LLC
LaVergne TN
LVHW020633300926
849161LV00004B/682